Researching tourist satisfaction

The analysis and interpretation of statistical data can be daunting, but it is a vital part of any successful research project. This text offers a clear, concise guide to the concepts and practice of research design, providing both a thorough grounding in techniques and a discussion of the key issues raised by such methods in relation to the attitudes, behaviour and levels of satisfaction of tourists.

It covers the nature of research itself, the design of a research project, qualitative and quantitative research, questionnaire design and implementation, different types of data and their coding, correlations, multiple regression analysis, and the coding and significance of data. It makes extensive reference to software packages, in particular SPSS, NCSS and MINITAB.

After working through this text, the reader will feel confident in the application and interpretation of data and will have gained a sound understanding of the nature of tourist satisfaction. It is directed to second and third year undergraduates, postgraduates and all those carrying out research projects in tourism.

Chris Ryan is a Senior Lecturer at Massey University, New Zealand. He has written and researched widely in tourism and is author of *Recreational Tourism: A social science perspective.*

Researching tourist satisfaction

Issues, concepts, problems

Chris Ryan

London and New York

First published 1995
by Routledge
11 New Fetter Lane, London EC4P 4EE

Simultaneously published in the USA and Canada
by Routledge
29 West 35th Street, New York, NY 10001

© 1995 Chris Ryan

Typeset in Scantext September by Solidus (Bristol) Limited
Printed and bound in Great Britain by
Biddles Ltd, Guildford and King's Lynn

British Library Cataloguing in Publication Data

A catalogue record for this book is available from the British Library

ISBN 0–415–10157–3 (hbk)
ISBN 0–415–10158–1 (pbk)

Library of Congress Cataloging in Publication Data
Ryan, Chris, 1945–
    Researching tourist satisfaction : issues, concepts, problems /
Chris Ryan.
        p.   cm.
    ISBN 0–415–10157–3 (hbk) ISBN 0–415–10158–1 (pbk)
    1. Tourist trade—Research.   I. Title.
G155.A1R93   1995
338.4'791'072—dc20   94–7224
                                                         CIP

Contents

Figures

Tables

Acknowledgements

The following acknowledgements are made in appreciation of the permission given to use materials:

SPSS Inc., 444 North Michigan Avenue, Chicago, Illinois 60611–3962, USA, sales telephone 800 543 2185, for permission to replicate instructions, output and quotations from Norusis. SPSS is a registered trademark of SPSS Inc.

Minitab Inc., 3081 Enterprise Drive, State College, PA 16801–3008, USA, sales telephone 814 238 3280, for permission to replicate instructions and output. MINITAB is a registered trademark of Minitab Inc.

Dr Jerry L. Hintze, NCSS, 865 East 400 North, Kaysville, Utah, 84037, sales telephone 801 546 0445, for permission to replicate instructions. NCSS is a registered trademark of Dr Jerry L. Hintze.

PWS-Kent Publishing Company, 20 Park Plaza, Boston, Massachusetts 02116, USA, for the diagram from Davis, D. and Cosenza, R., *Business Research for Decision Making*, 2nd edition, 1988.

Routledge, 11 New Fetter Lane, London EC4P 4EE, UK, for permission to replicate sections from Ryan, C., *Recreational Tourism, a social science perspective*, 1991, and MacCannell, D., *Empty Meeting Grounds*, 1992.

Wadsworth Publishing Co., Belmont, California 94002, USA, for permission to quote from Babbie, E.R., *The Practice of Social Research*, 1983, and use of the cartoon based on the Rube Goldberg system.

Ryan, C., 'Leisure and tourism, the application of leisure concepts to tourist behaviour – a proposed model' in *Tourism – the state of the art*, Seaton, A., 1994, reprinted by permission of John Wiley and Sons, Ltd, 22 Eastcastle Street, London W1N 7PA, UK.

Tony Seaton, The Scottish Hotel School, University of Strathclyde, Curren Building, 94 Cathedral Street, Glasgow G4 0LG, UK, for material used from draft copy of *Tourism – the state of the art*, Seaton, A., 1994, reprinted by permission of John Wiley and Sons, Ltd.

In addition, quotations are utilised from various journals referenced in accordance with usual practice. However, the author would wish to thank the authors, and their publishers, for the use of the materials. If any unknowing use has been made of copyright material could the owners please contact the author via the publishers.

Introduction

The genesis of any book can be diverse. This is the case here. For about three years in succession, my wife, Anca, and I spent Easter holidays at Portmeirion, the Italianate village in North Wales. It might be said to lack 'authenticity'. Indeed, some of its statues are two dimensional, and some of its apparently two-storey cottages consist of a single floor. From another view, however, it possessed the authenticity of the vision of its founder and architect. Situated on a small promontory jutting into an estuary, surrounded by woodland, it possessed an air of tranquillity, with each corner a testament to the care of its founder. I would find it very peaceful simply to sit and watch the birds wheel around the campanile. During the hours between ten o'clock and five o'clock the village would fill up with day visitors. Sometimes I would sit on my balcony overlooking the village to enjoy the sun and quietly read the paper. I would at times view the tourists, and catch odd snippets of conversation relating to a view, a flower or a piece of architecture. This gave me some pleasure. Equally, I became part of their scenery – a figure on a balcony – another figure properly posed in place; an 'inhabitant'. We were tourists viewing tourists, enjoying (on the whole) each other's 'proper' presence.

Some time later I spent some successive periods at Porto Heli, Greece, as the guest of Brian Amstutz and Linda Reynolds of Saronic Sailing. Again I noted how groups of like-minded tourists came to share an experience of sailing and windsurfing, and noted how they reacted and came together as groups. Again, a major component of the tourist experience was a relaxation in a 'dream' inhabited by other 'dreamers'. A small village still, although obviously bearing the signs of a tourist destination, Porto Heli exercised a lazy charm of tavernas, of little rush, and, for each group of tourists, a fortnight of good company.

A third influence was that of supervising student projects and theses at the Nottingham Business School. The students were undertaking work either for final year degree projects, or theses relating to the MA in Tourism, or the MBA. In many cases their work related to attitudinal surveys. Students would spend several hours composing questionnaires, interviewing, inputting data into computers and writing up their results, but unless they took care to take advice, in some instances one felt that they simply missed opportunities. Why? It is difficult to be precise, but let me simply generalise. In some cases it was a fear of statistics. It was not always hard to see why this occurred. Some students on the MA in Tourism were graduates in non-quantitative disciplines, and might not have done any maths of any kind since the age of sixteen. In other cases it was a reluctance to believe that their own experience had any form of validity. Possibly they thought that to have due weight a thesis should have questionnaires and tables, even if they felt unsure about the ways in which such data should or could be handled. Consequently, the subjective, that essence of the tourist feeling I had found in some of my previous holidays, and which they too had shared in their own ways, was not always present in their thinking when deciding what to pursue for their thesis topic, or how to design their research.

A number of problems were thus posed through my experiences with students. When could the subjective be a pertinent part of data? How could statistics be used? And how did this relate to the tourist experience? Can such experiences be duly summed, and the average taken? And what of the many paradoxes involved in tourism itself and the research process? To take but one obvious point, the most quantitative of studies is often derived from respondents' perceptions of questions – the apparently 'objective' process of statistical inference is based upon processes of subjectivity, varying perceptions of importance of the task in hand, or possibly simply an altruistic motive where the respondent seeks to help a student.

At one stage in my teaching, one of my students, Jane Lutz, who is now a lecturer at the Centre for Urban and Regional Studies, Birmingham University, said to me something along the lines of, 'what we want, Chris, is some guide to the issues'. This is a perpetual student plea, and Jane would be the first to acknowledge that there is no single answer, and certainly, no single book. This book emerged from the handouts and notes given to students and I hope it will be of assistance to other students and other teaching staff. It doesn't cover everything; it assumes that students are on courses with teaching staff to support their research efforts. It also assumes that students on such courses have some familiarity with conventions relating to the use of computers; that, for example, inputting a line of data requires the use of the 'return' or 'enter' key at the end of the line. Certainly I know from talking to colleagues at other universities in the UK, Canada, the USA and New Zealand that many postgraduate courses in tourism now include a research methods unit of one form or another, and that generally students do have access to suites of computers; so such assumptions are not, I feel, unwarranted. Unfortunately, until quite recently books in this field have either been general statistics books or texts on research methods, without specific reference to tourism research. In my teaching experience, students do find it easier to relate to research examples when they arise from the field in which they are working.

This posed another problem. A book on tourism research *per se* would cover many topics, from economic forecasting to anthropological studies – for such is the diversity of academic disciplines upon which tourism draws. Rightly or wrongly I have resorted to a specific theme, that of tourist satisfaction. This raised a number of interesting questions, and certainly seemed to be in an area appropriate to many student projects. It also supported another of my observations – that many operators of tourist attractions could monitor better the reactions of their own visitors; and I hope that this book will also help them.

I owe thanks to many people over quite a long period of time. To Alan Owen, who taught me statistics at Croydon Technical College – I was not one of his best students, but he did succeed in making me unafraid of figures. Rather disrespectfully, we students called him the 'Welsh Wizard' because of his enthusiasm and ability to scratch formulae across the blackboard at the drop of a hat – but something must have rubbed off. To Eric Hall, of Nottingham University, I owe insights gained into personality theory and motivation. To my 'buddy' Brian Wheeller, of Birmingham University, I owe friendship, many insights, and his recognition of the frailty of human effort has had an effect. To Professor Farouk Saleh at the University of Saskatchewan I owe much for giving me many research opportunities. To Jane Lutz, Dave Montgomery, Dave Bampton and all their fellow students I owe feelings of impotency as I have tried to find another way to explain some item or other relating to research, and equally, thanks for allowing me to share their own discoveries. To Professors Peter Franklin and Myra Shackley of the Nottingham Business School – I must acknowledge their support as colleagues and friends. To Professor Francis Terry – thanks for the research monies! Additionally, I must also thank Dr Ian Glendon of the Aston Business School for some of his comments on part of the script. Finally, I must also say thank you to Francesca Weaver at Routledge, who had faith in me, and for her professional guidance. I hope that this book will be of some help to students undertaking research into tourist attitudes, perceptions and causes of satisfaction. It is an interesting, fascinating subject.

Chapter 1

Research values

INTRODUCTION

This chapter is divided into two broad sections. It considers the normative values inherent in research, and does so from the perspective of what are categorised as implicit and explicit values. The former include what may be termed a 'world view' as to the nature of research, and the text briefly outlines the nature of the current debate between the empirical tradition, and what might, for want of a better term, be viewed as a deconstructionist approach. The explicit values discussed relate to the more general ethics of enquiry, namely those requiring rigour and honesty, which should penetrate each aspect of research from design through to the reporting of results.

This discussion will lead to Chapter 2, which considers the research proposal, research design, the differences between deductive and inductive methods of research, and other issues relating to the planning of research.

WHY UNDERTAKE RESEARCH?

'Research is too abstract? It is not practical.' This criticism has been made, and no doubt will continue to be made. There are many possible responses to this contention. First, it can be pointed out that there are many different types and levels of response, and that in many senses it is possible that the critic is often engaged in research when talking to customers. Closer examination of the criticism often indicates that what is being criticised is poorly designed or implemented research, badly communicated research, poorly directed research, or simply research that is unsure of its purpose. Sometimes research is criticised as being unintelligible, and there is little doubt that that will remain the case from the perspective of research not being easily comprehended by many at one time. But situations change, and what was innovative and largely incomprehensible for one generation might become the tool of management for some future generation. In the field of tourism one such development is the slow acceptance of Geographical Information Systems. Two decades ago this was a field of study for the few. Spatial theories were studied in abstract, databases were for those with access to large-frame computers, and the thought of a marriage between the two was imagined by only a few. Today the 'take-off' point for the use of such systems has indeed been reached. The Automobile Association is a major source of database information; the systems are being adapted by local authorities; bodies involved with national parks and heritage site operators analyse topography and catchment areas. Thus the stage is set for these systems to become more widely adopted by a larger number of tourist operators. The abstract thought of the past is set to become commonplace in the immediate future.

Good research is an indispensable aid to understanding phenomenon in order to act more effectively. It is inherently practical as it seeks to explain the relationship between apparently connected activities, and the nature of that relationship. How do tourists respond to an attraction? Do they like it? What do they like about it? How do they interact with it? Can the interaction be increased in order to make it more satisfactory? How do tourists feel about levels of crowding? Does this inhibit satisfaction, or enhance it? Is there a relationship between the level of enjoyment, the time of day or season the visitor comes, the number of other people present, the nature of the interpretation given – all these and many other questions can provide the sources of research into tourism.

If research has practical implications either in the present, short-, medium- or long-term future, there is also a responsibility to ensure that it is well designed and pertinent to a carefully defined problem. Research therefore needs to possess many attributes if it is to succeed in its avowed aim of aiding understanding to permit effective action. These attributes are present whether the researcher is seeking to:

report, or
describe, or
predict, or
explain, or
control, or
any combination of these activities.

To be effective research in tourism requires:

careful observation;
thorough and painstaking care by the researcher;
possession of significant technical skills;
good communicative skills;
openness and continuing curiosity;
logical reasoning and imagination or lateral thinking;
ability to perceive both the detail and the whole;
ability to build models of relationships, and to discard them if necessary;
integrity – faithfully to report assumptions, findings, interpretations and the reasons for them.

Yet the process is not without tedium, disappointments and frustrations, as well as being a source of fascination and excitement, even where driven by prosaic needs of simple customer monitoring. The process has also some inherent problems, and these can now be discussed.

SOURCES OF ERROR IN RESEARCH

The normal process of humans explaining why things occur is one that is subject to many sources of potential error. The process of planning a research design and undertaking that research is in itself a necessary self-discipline to guard against those sources of everyday error, but in doing so pitfalls still await the unwary researcher. Babbie (1979:10–13) has categorised these potential sources of mistakes, convoluted thinking and the protection of self interest as the nine errors of personal human enquiry, which are:

1 *Inaccurate observation.* Often we look without actually seeing. Asked to recall the exact sequence of circumstances after an event poses problems of accuracy. Yet researchers need to ensure that they know what was happening before they seek to explain why it happened – and hence the need for careful observation.

2 *Over-generalisation.* Seeking to explain why something has happened creates a danger of generalising from the first few similar occurrences that are encountered. The fact that the first three tourists interviewed might report similar reactions to an attraction does not mean that this view is representative. Therefore, there is a need to ensure that the size and nature of any sample is adequate to ensure a representative reporting of attitude or behaviour.

3 *Selective observation.* Once a pattern of behaviour and motivation is identified, there is a danger of seeking to explain all actions by reference to that generalisation. For example, tourists may be blamed by older members of the host community for inducing behaviour changes among the young, and so tourist actions such as entering a bar or disco might be interpreted as reinforcing a process of leading the young 'astray'.

4 *Deduced information.* Having created generalisations that give rise to selective observation, it becomes difficult to cope with behaviour that does not fit the preconceived model. It is tempting to view such behaviour as aberrant, and, should it not fit the normal category, to ignore it. For example, the tourist who tells off a young person for exhibiting an unapproved behaviour might be categorised by an older resident as some-one visiting a relative, and hence 'not really a tourist'.

5 *Illogical reasoning.* It is only too common to say that something is the exception that proves the rule. But does this idea make sense? How can a contradictory item prove the thing it rejects? Why should the fact that it has rained two days in succession mean that the third day of our holiday will be warm and sunny? There is, prima facie, little reason why this should be.

6 *Ego involvement in understanding.* Inasmuch as the researcher spends time, intellectual and often physical effort in the collection and collation of data,

there can occur a defensive proprietary sense about the theory being constructed. Contrary evidence might be seen as an unwelcome intrusion, evoking a series of defensive mechanisms such as ignoring the evidence, throwing doubt on the source of the challenge, or even, *in extremis*, manipulating the 'awkward' evidence to present a more favourable outcome.

7 *Premature closure of enquiry.* If it is thought that a process is known and understood, it may be explored no further. The problem for the researcher is one of knowing when sufficient research has been undertaken. There is a danger that ceasing exploration might simply reduce the evidence of the contradictory, thereby reducing the validity of what is known.

8 *Mystification of residuals.* If a model is constructed and tested, and found to explain some but not all the phenomena under examination, there is a temptation to state that the unexplained is 'too complex'; that it is the result of random events. But it might be far from random – all it might mean is that the researcher has not identified other causal variables.

9 *To err is human.* The above tendencies, when combined with the world view that a researcher possesses – a view derived from tradition, authority and 'received wisdom', can cause errors to arise. But even as researchers seek to challenge or confirm the conventions of their discipline, further sources of error can become important.

Research requires a close examination of, and making explicit, the assumptions and norms that percolate the topic being considered, and (it must also be noted), the actual research methods employed. It is a process of continuous questioning and testing of ideas, concepts and views in a structured attempt to reach a better understanding of the subject being studied.

THE IMPLICIT NORMS IN RESEARCH

While this book is orientated towards relatively small-scale research of the type undertaken by students, small attraction operators, and limited market research projects, it is necessary to consider the wider research context to ensure that researchers are aware of their assumptions. There is a tendency to see research as being 'objective'; as defining clear relationships between determining and determined variables. Indeed, much of the latter part of this book is written upon that assumption when discussing the statistical techniques that might be used in analysing tourist attitudes.

However, there are limits to such an empirical perspective. Such limitations must be recognised by researchers if they are to be aware of the nature and implications of the parameters within which they operate. All too often the implicit values are left undisturbed in the mind of the researcher.

It is a cliché to argue that our thinking is conditioned by the generally accepted norms and societal views of our own time. To simplify the argument considerably, before Columbus sailed to the Americas in 1492 the view was held that the world was literally bordered by danger – one could fall off its edge. The 'objective' view of the perils of exploration was real – the journey would encounter not only storms, fluctuating winds and all the problems associated with sailing a few miles from the coast, but, having survived the monsters of the deep, there would also come a time when the explorers would inevitably be drawn into unimaginable disaster as they were swept from the world in a deluge of water. Today this view is held only by a minority. From the fifteenth century a new world view began to dominate thinking, and with that view a perspective developed which encouraged exploration, changed patterns of thought, and, through the upheaval of the Reformation, a scientific approach.

The model of the world view that has dominated until recently has tended to be a mechanistic view of cause and effect. The identification of a determining variable means that creating a change in that factor leads to subsequent changes in defined outcomes. There is, at a simple level, a view of the scientific method as being essentially linear. For example, disease might be treated by identifying and attacking a virus so as to complete a cure. But just as such a view has come to be challenged, not only from the holistic view of alternative medicine, but also by 'conventional' medical researchers, so similar challenges have been occurring across the whole of social and scientific research.

What, it might be wondered, has this to do with research into tourist attitudes and behaviours? This debate, and the concept of a changing world view that is beginning to question the concept of a linear objectivity, and to replace it with a model of chaotic reality, where the subjective is also data, is affecting research in tourism. The parallel nature of the debate within tourism studies can be seen by reference to various definitions of research, scientific method and tourism, and the subsequent implications for research. For example, Davis and Cosenza (1988) quote Kerlinger (1986:10) in defining scientific research as being:

> systematic, controlled, empirical, and critical investigation of hypothetical propositions about the presumed relations among phenomena.

This, they argue, poses difficulties for researching business, in that business decisions are taken within a context of information that is often descriptive in nature. Companies need to assess the nature of their competition, the type of advertising campaigns that may be taking place, the nature of consumers, and the factors that affect success in the market place. Hence it is difficult to quantify the nature of presumed relationships between phenomena. They therefore advance a definition of business research as being:

> systematic, controlled, empirical, and critical investigation of phenomena of interest to managerial decision makers (Davis and Consenza 1988:8).

Such a definition can certainly be applied to tourism research. Is it not often stated that tourism is, or is about to become, the world's largest industry? Certainly tourism can be defined as an economic and business activity. Ryan (1991b:5) suggests one such approach whereby tourism is defined as being:

> a study of the demand for and supply of accommodation and supportive

services for those staying away from home, and the resultant patterns of expenditure, income creation and employment.

This definition creates at least two approaches to tourism research. The first is akin to the scientific process advanced by Kerlinger, and as adopted in economics. Research might seek to investigate the hypothetical relationships between causal and determined variables. For example, econometric modelling might be undertaken linking the number of trips or expenditure of tourists to factors such as the level of wages, rates of inflation between host and tourist generating countries, transport costs and other 'measurable' determinants. However, it would be difficult to conduct experimentation in the sense that is understood by research in the traditional physical sciences.

The second perspective is to view tourism as being a subset of business problems. Hence it is possible to view tourism research as requiring descriptive data of the nature described by Cosenza and Davis, namely information about the structure of the hospitality industry, the flows of travellers, the levels of advertising expenditure, and the content of that advertising. But it can be objected that this definition of tourism is but a partial view, and that tourism is essentially concerned with the motivations and experiences of those travelling. From this perspective it becomes an 'experiential' phenomena. Przeclawski (1993:11) points out that tourism is not simply an economic process, but also a psychological, social and cultural happening. Tourism is concerned with the feelings and experiences gained from social settings, and from seeking, or finding oneself alone, in new surroundings, often of great beauty, which bestow cathartic experiences. It is not for nothing that holidays are looked forward to and remembered for long periods of time. Vacations are often one of the highest recurring expenditures in a family budget and hence, on this account alone, must be considered to bring significant personal value to the participant. Equally, tourism is a psychological process for the members of the tourist receiving communities; and tourism is a change agent in cultural processes. Through demonstration affects, and acculturation, tourism is one of the means by which change generally flows from the technologically advanced societies to the less developed. Different authors have sought to capture this process in different definitions of tourism, and one such definition is:

> the means by which people seek psychological benefits that arise from experiencing new places, and new situations that are of a temporary duration, whilst free from the constraints of work, or normal patterns of daily life at home (Ryan 1991b:6).

Yet even this is inadequate, in that it serves as a definition from the viewpoint of the tourist, but leaves aside the nature of the impact upon the host business and residential communities, both of which might have very different perspectives upon the nature of tourist activity that is taking place around them. In a sense, therefore, definitions either tend to the specific to reflect a particular concern, namely the economic or psychological as in the above examples, or they tend to the extremely wide, such as that of McIntosh and Goeldner (1986), namely:

> tourism may be defined as the sum of the phenomena and relationships arising from the interaction of tourists, business suppliers, host governments and host communities in the process of attracting tourists and other visitors.

Already these definitions of tourism indicate the nature of the challenge to the tourism researcher. On the one hand the problem may be posed in such global terms as to defeat research, which by its nature and often by reason of its funding is focused on the highly specific, or, on the other hand, when such research is focused, it omits the context of much of the phenomenon under study. It also indicates that, from the psychological perspective, in order to understand the tourist the researcher has to deal with complex sets of motivations and needs, and the nature of the interaction between tourist, hosts and place that generates processes of change, satisfaction, self evaluation or otherwise as the case might be. This all seems very much removed from the processes of scientific research as initially defined. The process, from this perspective, seems to be not so much empirical as subjective, not so much the development of generalised rules, but rather the reiteration of personal experiences that may or may not have validity for others, or indeed may have varying validity for the same individual under another set of circumstances.

Yet this is recognised in the physical sciences and in contemporary tourism research. It has been noted by a number of authors that many tourists engage in play, both formally in terms of actually playing a game or a sport, and informally in the sense of playing out a role different to that which is the norm of their everyday life. Additionally, as noted by MacCannell (1976), tourists in many well known tourist locations purchase not the 'backroom' or everyday reality of the place, but the signposts that have come to mark the significance of fame. In short, as Urry (1991:85) notes, what is consumed is not simply the reality, but the representations and symbols of the reality, while equally there is an emergence of the 'aestheticisation of consumption' (Urry 1991:14). Tourism is thus immersed in a universe of signs, where the tourist fulfils the dream, purchases the image of the brochure, plays out the tourist or explorer role at whim; and, if tourism is an accumulation of experience that adds to a feeling of self, overlaps with other areas of work and leisure. Lutz and Ryan note this in the field of business tourism when they state:

> The provision of specific services for businesswomen is an authentic service, and a symbol of a recognition of need – both are consumed, but the process does not stop at that point. The experience of consumption creates changed expectation, and an acknowledgement that the service is a symbol. As in other forms of human behaviour the female executive thus indulges in role playing and role distancing. The business woman recognises that the provision of 'feminine services' fulfils many functions. It is a token of recognition, it is a

promise of service, yet, beyond the provision of some peripheral convenience it may have little intrinsic value other than its existence as a symbol of intangible service. But the symbol is consumed, and the symbol provider may be asked to act upon the promise inherent in the symbol (Lutz and Ryan 1993:356).

Tourism can be perceived as the example *par excellence* of the products of the post-industrial society. It is a conspicuous consumption of symbols, a searching for different experience based upon fantasy. In Disneyland, for example, tourists 'play' at being explorers in nineteenth-century darkest Africa on a river trip where, suspending their sense of disbelief, photographs are taken of model hippos, while a 'guide' takes the passengers past anitromic models of 1950s Hollywood B-movie head-hunting natives.

Post-industrial societies move away from mass production and consumption of products and services to something that is increasingly 'individualised'. The process inherent in such societies is characterised by four features; privatisation, individuation, commercialisation and pacification (Rojek 1993). There is an inherent paradox present. On the one hand, concern about the quality of service emphasises the needs of the individual. But these concerns lead to mechanistic processes of coding, routinisation, and synchronisation on the part of commercial operators. This paradox is to the fore in niche market tourism products offering holistic experiences where the tourist buys a package through the agent or in response to careful targeting based on postcode selection or purchased mailing lists of magazine subscribers. In short, individuality is reduced to computer codes in order to make possible the recognition of that individuality.

The concept of tourism as a complex, individualistic matrix of experiences implies a process of chaos, role playing, deliberate ludic involvement on the part of the tourist, with a consequent complexity in assessing impacts. Note also that in the post-industrialised societies of the west the activities of the tourist industry take place within a context where the modularisation of leisure and other experiences (e.g. by the use of video, personalised cassette players and eventually virtual reality) is common, where such activities are supplied by increasingly professional commercial undertakings and where the user adopts an increasingly passive pattern of consumption. Indeed, the promise of virtual reality is travel and sensation without leaving the armchair. While these processes have the by-product that undertaking research in tourism becomes increasingly complex as researchers seek to understand the contemporary nature of tourism in a more dynamic society, it should be noted that this is not a problem unique to tourism. Within the field of the physical sciences it is becoming the mainstream view that the nineteenth-century view of science as being linear where small changes in initial conditions lead to small (or at least bounded) changes in resultants is inadequate. In fact, what science has been finding upon re-examination is that uncertainty tends to be the rule rather than the exception. This is what has been termed chaos theory or sometimes complex dynamics in non-linear systems.

These non-linear systems appear to give random results on a local level, but on a global level, order begins to reappear out of the chaos. Systems may be random and unpredictable, but apparently they may be bounded by things called 'attractors', which essentially define the domain in which the function can be random. Some of the 'attractors' with which Mandelbrot (1989) experimented in the field of mathematics can be plotted on computers to make fractals, quite complex pictures creating a sense of repetitive order out of initial random events.

Therefore, to return to the initial definitions: at one level tourism would seem to defy empirical research in the sense that the notion of such objective assessment of relationships between cause and effect is inadequate when considering the nature of tourism as an experience of place and events, and as an interaction between tourist and host. Tourists have their own experiences, unique to themselves, and hence research from this view can only be subjective, a list of individual case studies which might serve to help others derive their own meaning. On the other hand, such confusion, such chaos is the norm, but each individual happening when added to other happenings could form a valid group, and each group when added to other clusters could make a greater totality, which when viewed from afar makes a pattern. In this sense conventional research processes might have a validity in creating a model of what is occurring. However, the order of the group does not imply a model for the individual, for individuals continue their own idiosyncratic game playing.

Therefore, it can be argued that much of what is subsequently described in this book involves the construction of a model, where the complexities of reality are distilled into an abstraction of a few key variables. For example, behaviour might be defined along dimensions of four or five factors that result from a factor analysis of responses to a larger number of questions. But in interpreting the results the researcher should be aware of the nature of the 'objectivity' implicit in those results. The methodology itself is based upon a mechanistic model. The respondents indulged in a certain role at the time of response; would they so respond in a different place, or in the same place at a different time? If tourists switch between roles, would the same factors or patterns actually emerge? The constructionist view of the world is that an underlying consistency is present, at least over the appropriate time span that is of interest to the researcher. From the viewpoint of the deconstructionist that cannot be assumed, and indeed the importance of the perceived consistency would be called into question in terms of how important are the derived factors in being an explanation of an individual's actual experience at that time and place. From a traditional market research stance, the latter problem would be approached from a different research perspective, namely that of 'qualitative' research as distinct from 'quantitative' research. Yet, as will be noted in subsequent pages, this is not without its problems.

Thus research poses many questions for the researcher, and they are questions concerning values as well as techniques; indeed, the two are not divorced. It is an underlying premise of this book that the researcher into tourism is fortunate from many perspectives. To any researcher with an interest in people, the very nature of tourism is a never ending source of fascination. Humans on holiday are engaged in so many behaviour patterns that the range tends to exceed the number portrayed in 'everyday' life, while the problems of research design in attempting to cope with, describe, and illuminate these behaviours are such that the researcher will inevitably be drawn into a rich and fascinating literature and experience of social science research. Questions of authenticity, reality, pretence, role play, escape and wish fulfilment are so entangled with the topic of tourism that, even from the business perspective of understanding the needs of the client, no researcher can escape a consideration of the issues outlined above.

STATISTICS AND SYMBOLS

In the world of individual and unique experience that is the data of the researcher concerned with tourist attitudes and behaviours, where do the manipulation of means, standard deviations and the other paraphernalia produced by statistical packages sit? Is it an exercise of futility in that the essence of the tourist experience is never going to be grasped by the researcher who uses such methods? Tourism can be regarded as the example *par excellence* of a post-modernist world where basic wants are satisfied, and status is derived from the possession of symbols. So important is the possession of the 'right' training shoes, that it has been reported that 'street-wise' kids have mugged others to obtain them. Is the difference between a middle-class executive seeking status from possessing an experience of, say, climbing to Everest base camp, and the young mugger one of degree, but not of kind?

If tourism is about not only the cathartic, and the authentic, but also about the possession of symbols, or the translation of experience into symbols, so too, the statistician possesses symbols of understanding, for that is the nature of statistics. The experience of the place is the foundation of the souvenir (that symbol of place) and the statistic (the symbol of at least a type of knowledge). Both souvenir and statistic say something about the people who travel. Both are statements of not only the *fact* of travel, but the *purpose* of travel. Indeed, as will be noted in later chapters, there is much in statistics that is concerned about the explanation of events. Both symbols and statistical models are parsimonious in their 'explanations' of the reality of experience. Both seek to encapsulate the complex within the parameters of the few, 'important' aspects of place or experience.

The parallels exist, but the analysis cannot be pursued too far. Statistics exist within strict boundaries that limit application. The patterns discovered are often not ones of causality, but correlation and covariance. Symbols are unbounded; they change. While every number is a symbol, not every symbol is a number. MacCannell has noted that:

> The social sciences occupy the gap between statistical and symbolic significance. The condition of their existence is to struggle endlessly with the

question of the possibility of a convergence of the symbolic and statistical orders on more than a superficial level (1992:92).

Therefore, if there appears to be a split between the qualitative and the quantitative, this division is not simply one of two approaches that may be used in a pragmatic manner by a researcher as a means of obtaining complementary results. Both involve a manipulation of symbols to understand a phenomenon which in itself is rich in symbolism. Yet, beneath the functions ascribed by the researcher to the playing on the beach, the lying in the sun, the bartering for the rugs and carpets, exists a reality of simple or complex behaviours of individuals deserving of respect. The tired mother, the lovelorn teenager, the worried business person, the curious searcher after antiquity – these are the subject matter of the tourism researcher – and no matter how learned the discourse about the nature and techniques of research, the analysis of the nature of society and the role of tourism within it, it is a privilege to partake in such lives, however brief the moment and the nature of the understanding derived from it.

THE EXPLICIT RESEARCH VALUES

If this view is accepted, then the gap between this section and the preceding discussion of the nature of research is not unbridgeable. Implicit in the previous discussion there lies the concept that relativity and subjectivity are important in understanding the issues surrounding tourism. That the inherent nature of tourism as a dialectical process between the escape from the normal and the 'pull' of the extraordinary on the one hand, and the security of the familiar and the risk of the new, combine to form a dynamic and complex relationship that cannot be fully understood by conventional empirically based studies. In order to understand, the researcher must partake, must engage in the subjective, must immerse themselves in an experience as well as measure and observe from a neutral point. Additionally, it is implied that no one research method is better than another, and that indeed there is no one truth about tourist behaviour.

Yet this section will almost entirely ignore this approach, and assume a set of absolutes that are to be obeyed by the researcher. The existence of such 'absolutes' can only arise from a viewpoint about values associated with the integrity of being 'human', and the need for self-respect on the part of the researcher. Yet, there is almost as much consensus on the following list of absolutes as there is a recognition that problems are fuzzy, and the behaviour of both researcher and studied is complex and difficult to define. So, what are these absolutes?

Honestly and fully report findings

For many students there is often a sense of disappointment or failure when the data fails to support a hypothesis, and hence there arises a temptation to engage in sophistry, that is, the reporting of those findings that tend to the proposed hypothesis, and a non-reporting of those findings that do not support the hypothesis. But do not consider that data that fail to support a suggested relationship are without value. Often knowledge advances as much by knowing what does not work, as by knowing what might work.

In many cases of student research the sample size is small, and again there is a temptation to 'hide' this by use of such expressions as '25 per cent stated that ...'. If the total sample involved was, for example, only 20 in number, then the findings are being 'supported' by only 5 respondents. It is much better to report that '5 of the 25 respondents stated that ...'. In many cases, for example at final year undergraduate level, the student project is designed not so much as a means for discovering new 'truths', but as an exercise in developing research expertise. It is legitimate for a student to use statistical tests as an illustration of the illustration of knowledge as to how to analyse data by using a given technique, but it is not legitimate to place undue weight upon those results. Indeed, the use of caveats as to the validity of findings shows a much greater awareness of the limitations of the technique.

The same warnings apply to research in a more practical setting. Even with quite large samples of, say, 200 or more, sub-samples of, for example, a given age or income group might be quite small, and hence again it is misleading to use percentages if the size of the sample is small. The purpose of research is to illuminate, not mislead.

Carefully consider the confidentiality of the data and the respondent

In many cases assurances are given to respondents that they will not be identified. It is imperative that such confidentiality is respected. In cases where qualitative data is being sought, and there is a wish to report this, it must be done in such a way that there is no means by which the respondent can be identified. A common way in which this is done is simply to use the impersonal pronoun, or refer to a respondent by a number.

Researchers must be sensitive to this issue. If qualitative data has been generated through a small number of focus groups, and there is an attempt, for example, to distinguish the attitudes of unmarried single mothers towards holiday arrangements compared to married mothers with young children, then care must be taken that no unmarried single mother can be identified by reporting comments that relate to that respondent's personal situation. Given small numbers of respondents, the chance of such an identification by the other respondents who might have access to the findings is increased.

From a commercial viewpoint, if, for example, data have been obtained from a postal survey where names and addresses have been elicited for purposes of ensuring the representative nature of the survey, if confidentiality has been promised, it should be obvious that it is not now appropriate to sell the list of names and addresses to a list broker.

In replying either to direct questioning or by questionnaires, respondents are giving their time, and revealing data about themselves. There is already concern about 'sugging' and similar practices where sales people seek to create a 'lead' by pretending that they are undertaking market research, and such practices make it more difficult to undertake future research. It can raise some serious issues for the researcher. As will be later discussed, there is always the problem that significant differences might exist between respondents and non-respondents. If the survey is seeking to undertake some attitudinal measurement, then there might be differences between those who are willing to give information, and those whose suspicions predispose them to non-response. The betrayal of confidentiality can thus have a range of implications for the individual researcher, subsequent researchers, or the process of social science studies.

The same issues, albeit perhaps in a different format, arise where a focus group or other forms of interview are filmed. In the commercial world it is quite common for such groups to be videoed from behind a one-way mirror. Under such circumstances it is the norm that respondents are informed that this is going to be the case. In the area of tourism research there are no equivalents to the ethics committees that characterise much medical research, yet ethical questions can arise in any observation of human behaviour. It can be hypothesised that observations of, say, beach behaviour, or the use of aerial photography to assess crowding measures, could reveal people engaging in intimate behaviour. This raises questions of ethics relating to the right to enjoy privacy. Certainly, if it were possible to identify individuals, the conventions of research would assume that confidentiality was to be respected.

Unethical research is morally wrong

This is a strong statement to make, and is indeed absolute in its terminology. It must also be noted that it is, in the experience of most tourism researchers, extremely rare that tourism research will be of such a nature. In some cases, it is possible to imagine circumstances where it could occur, although it is most unlikely to be encountered by students or researchers working at the majority of tourist attractions. However, in many parts of the world tourism is associated with criminal activity. For example, tourism might be associated with the sex 'industry', the laundering of money and drugs, the forced purchase of property from those either in no position to appreciate the commercial value of sites once developed for tourism, or in no position to oppose such sales. Research that is commissioned to show that there are no negative implications of such processes is very likely to be unethical. It is probably going to be unethical in its commission, in its implementation, in its results, and eventually in the policies that might stem from it.

It must be emphasised that it is difficult to envisage such research in the area of tourism, but should this issue arise it will do so in a complex guise where it is difficult to assess where the boundaries lie between what is or is not ethical. For example, in the area of impact assessment the economic impacts of tourism are often of benefit in generating jobs and incomes. But who benefits from such jobs, and who is paying the cost of those jobs? The development of tourist resorts in areas previously sparsely inhabited will attract labour, change the nature of the landscape, and will, of course, significantly change the previous pattern of life of the inhabitants. Tourism development, as already noted, will have a cultural impact. Ethical questions are apparent. To what extent does one group have the right to change the life style of another group? What rights have the majority over the wishes of the minority? These are not questions unique to tourism, and have been debated for several hundreds if not thousands of years. But even the most positive, empirically determined researcher should be aware that research findings might be incorporated into political processes with ethical outcomes.

Ensure that research findings are analysed appropriately

It may seem to be quite a jump from the ethical to consider the mechanistic aspect of research, but it is possible for the two to be linked. Appropriate analysis has a number of components:

(a)   selection of methods appropriate to the nature of the problem;
(b)   appropriate selection of the sample;
(c)   appropriate design;
(d)   rigorous implementation of the research design;
(e)   selection of methods appropriate to the problem, nature of the sample and research design.

Poor research design, sample selection and analysis of data might lead to invalid recommendations and hence, albeit inadvertently, inappropriate policies might result. The researcher has a duty of care to the user and reader of the research findings, and to the respondents. A careless use of analytical techniques can be construed as being unethical. It should also be evident from the earlier discussion of the role of objectivity and subjectivity in research that the selection of any one method contains within it a value judgement as to the nature of the problem and the means by which that problem can best be analysed.

The questions of research design, sample selection and analysis will be discussed more fully in the following chapters. However, for the purpose of illustration, a common mistake in undertaking an analysis is the use of parametric tests where a normal distribution of results is assumed. In many cases relating to attitudinal measurement in tourism this distribution is not the case. As generally enjoyment arising from touristic experiences is high, the data are skewed, and hence a non-parametric measure might be more appropriate. In many circumstances it is unlikely that significantly different results will result from the use of one rather than another test of significance, but that potentiality always exists. Indeed, it may be the case that the researcher is rejecting a hypothesis as a result of the more rigorous assumptions of parametric tests when the finding might, in fact, be significant if, for example, a Mann–Whitney test is used to assess inter-group differences.

In this example, the parameters of testing are quite well known, but the problems associated with qualitative data are often much more subtle. On the one hand it might be a simple form of content analysis that is being undertaken in terms of counting the frequency of a given response. Here the issue can be one of categorising a type of response. On the other hand, assessing the nuances of meaning that have arisen within, for example, a focus group, where one respondent is picking up and developing an idea from another, can be a complex matter. In many cases it is better that such interpretation is not left to one researcher alone, but that results are checked by others independently, and subsequently compared to assess consistency of interpretation.

SUMMARY

Research implies a set of values that relate first to underlying constructs of the nature of reality. Is there an objective reality existing that can be 'discovered', or is there simply a set of complicated patterns existing for unknown periods of time, random at the individual level, but which nonetheless possess meaning for that individual, and which form a totality that can be assessed at some level or other, for some time, however long or short?

Yet there is a further set of values about research that require rigour on the part of the researcher in expressing their assumptions, and applying pertinent techniques and methods. There is a tension between the 'world view' of the nature of phenomena and the disciplines of research. After all, if the world is chaotic, why is structured research appropriate? Why seek to make explicit assumptions? In short, no researcher should escape the implications of the debate surrounding research by simply not being aware of the values implicit in research.

Those values cannot help but be present in research design. The empirical traditions of the past have helped to set a series of guidelines in an attempt to ensure that findings have both reliability and validity – both concepts which imply an underlying consistency in behaviour. The steps of research design from the empirical tradition require the researcher to undertake a reiterative process between the nature of the problem and the techniques used to approach the definition of the research problem with a view to ensure clarity of thinking. Whatever the approach adopted by the researcher, it must possess an inherent logic that is sustainable in producing outcomes that make some addition to understanding.

Chapter 2

Research design – an overview

INTRODUCTION

However complex the issues relating to the nature of tourism, or the norms associated with research methodologies, there comes a point where the researcher must actually commence the process of research planning. It is conventional to describe the process as a series of steps beginning with the formulation of a problem and ending with a report (e.g. McDaniel Jr and Gates 1993:35–51). This convention will be followed (see Figure 2.1). The steps are therefore:

1 Identification of the problem.
2 Assessment of value of the research process.
3 Development of the research proposal.
4 Development of the research design.
5 Determination of data collection methods and procedures.
6 Determination of analytical procedures.
7 Evaluation of results.
8 Final report including results, evaluation and recommendations.

Posed in this way, it appears that each stage is sequential, but in practice this is not the case. The nature of the problem and the way in which it is defined should obviously indicate the methods to be used, but if the cost of such methods is too great, then the problem may be redefined in such a way that some information of value is collected that is consistent with the available methods of data collection. Indeed, in designing the research the problem could be defined with reference to the available methods, resources and theories applicable to the issue. For example, in tourism research a common problem is the collection of data relating to tourist perceptions of, or satisfactions with, attractions, destinations, accommodation or some similar type of facility. The value of the findings will be significantly enhanced if the researcher uses a model of attitude measurement rather than simply a tick list of what are thought to be the important variables. Again, there is a difference as to the quality and type of information that is to be gained from the use of scales in questionnaires as against simple frequency

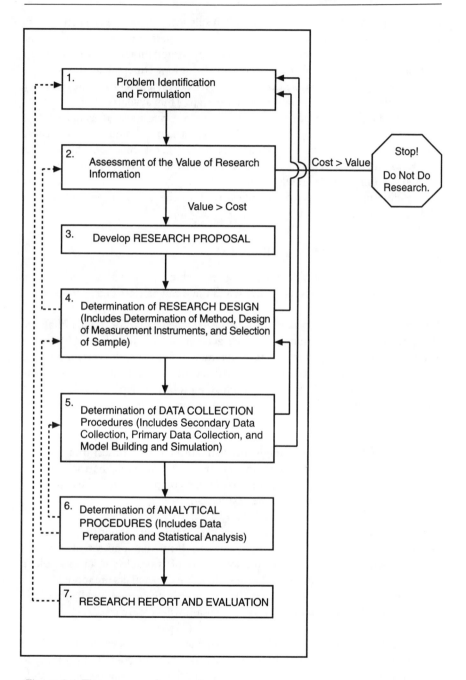

Figure 2.1 The process of research

counts. The use of qualitative data will result in a different perspective from merely adding up numbers derived from a questionnaire. In short, the methodology selected is not independent of the formulation of the problem, nor is it necessarily sequential to the problem definition. Different methods create different data, different costs of collection of that data, and, in turn, the relevance of that data helps to formulate research design. Thus available designs help to formulate the definition of the problem. However, care must be exercised. It is very important that a problem is not 'squeezed' into a technique simply because the researcher is conversant with that approach. What is important, however, is that research is perceived as a systematic, rigorous, structured and honest process whereby assumptions are made explicit and continually tested in order to assess the validity and reliability of outcomes. Each of the above stages can now be addressed in turn.

IDENTIFICATION OF THE PROBLEM

The identification of a problem requiring research can arise within tourism from a number of different potential sources, and these can be classified as follows.

Observation   That is, perceptions of events, behaviour or trends that are thought to possess importance or which generate a basis for action. Hence, the validity of the observation needs to be examined. For example, certain patterns of tourist behaviour might be observed which generate some questions as to why that behaviour arises. Or, within a business, a problem emerges that is affecting the performance of the business. Possibly an opportunity for new products, or the expansion of an existing product might require research.

A need to test facts   Facts might be distinguished from observations on the premise that facts are what are thought to be true. It might be thought that satisfied clients are more likely to re-book with a company. Is this the case? Why is it true? Do clients revisit the same destination?

A need to test a hypothesis   A hypothesis is a conjecture about the nature of a relationship between variables; usually in the form that one set of variables determine changes of behaviour in another (set of) variable(s). For example, a travel agent might propose the hypothesis that holiday-makers are more likely to select brochures that are at eye height on the racks in an agency, and hence this in turn increases the probability that those holidays will be purchased.

The initial definition of a problem in a generalised manner is not in itself sufficient to initiate a research process. The problem must possess importance to the researcher, or to the organisation or person that is sponsoring the research. Importance of the problem is a precondition for research, but must not in itself predetermine the outcome. While this might not be the deliberate intent, there is some danger that the prioritisation of variables thought to be important determines the questions used to the exclusion of other potentially important factors. If, for any reason, only a small number of questions are being used, there is a possibility that a correlation between factors results – but such a correlation might be a function of research design rather than the reality that is being sought. For example, if the travel agent argues that clients select holidays from brochures at eye-level height, and accordingly asks questions as to whether or not they purchased holidays from those brochures – a high correlation might result. However, if the clients were price sensitive, and those brochures happened to contain the cheaper holidays, the wrong conclusion might be drawn from the result of the study if questions about price were omitted.

DEFINITION OF THE PROBLEM

Thus, a further precondition for successful research is not simply the identification of a problem, but also the definition of the problem. The definition draws upon the above processes in that observation, facts and hypotheses lead to model building where the nature of the relationships between determined variables (the outcome) and determining factors (the causes of change) is defined. The nature of the relationship between observation, facts, hypotheses and models is often classified as arising from three processes.

The deductive

This is where conclusions are reached as the result of reasoning from initial premises. It is an inferential process. For example, it has been observed that levels of holiday-maker satisfaction are generally very high, even where problems occur in the holiday. A deductive theory might state:

Premise   Holiday-makers have high emotional involvement in their holidays.

Premise   Regardless of the nature of the holiday, holiday-makers report high levels of satisfaction.

Conclusion Holiday-makers adapt behaviour patterns to achieve their goals.

The outcome of high satisfaction that has been observed is 'explained' by adaptive behaviours designed to overcome the deficiencies in the resort area or hotel and to seek satisfaction, because holiday-makers have a high emotional investment in the need to secure satisfaction while on holiday. This presents a series of testable items by asking questions about the expected benefits to be had from a holiday, what happened on holiday, and what was the final level of satisfaction derived. The relationships between the three sets of data can now be explored.

This example also raises another question. It was assumed that the model lent itself to questions that could be asked; in other words, the data existed or could be collected. Any theory that is constructed must be in a form where it can be tested. In the case of some student projects, given the restraints of time and financial resources, it is probably important that any hypotheses developed are done so with reference to the ease of access of the information. Such model building can be undertaken in descriptive terms.

The inductive

The inductive method results in a series of postulated relationships that are deduced from rigorous and systematic repeated observations of reality. The same sort of relationships between the above premises and conclusions could have been reached by a study of holiday-makers over a period of time where they had been observed and questioned.

The functional

In practice, what occurs is a mixture of both the above where there is dialectical process between the conceptualising of the deductive method and the observation of the inductive. A process of reiteration occurs as outcomes from different stages are fed into the evolving model in order to refine it.

From one perspective, this reiteration can be applied at two levels. First, it can be applied within the one research project, as the researchers seek to refine their models and explanations by testing the outcomes against observation, and feeding the observations back into the model. But reiteration can also be understood as occurring within a discipline of study, as researchers build upon the results of others in defining and redefining their own research. Researchers are part of a community of scholars that incorporates those working in both the private and public sector, and reiteration hence occurs between different research projects. Ideally, within the field of tourism literature this process of reiteration should be continuing as one researcher seeks to replicate the findings of another, and in doing so refines the theory. Arguably, there are not many examples of this in the sense of tourism researchers using the same research tool or methods in order to continually test their viability. Indeed, albeit in a slightly different context relating to comparative research, Pearce has noted:

> The comparative approach has yet to emerge as a distinctive, readily recognizable methodology in tourism research despite its application to a wide variety of problems during the last two decades.... When a comparative approach has been adopted by tourism researchers there has generally been little elaboration on its use, with at best only passing mention of methodological issues or fleeting reference to other work (Pearce 1993:20).

Others have been even more critical of the way that tourism research has been reported. For example, Reid and Andereck wrote:

> Much research either ignores or fails to clearly report useful descriptive statistics ... many readers may be aware that ANOVA is used, but others might profit by a brief description of the statistical method and reasons why its use is appropriate in a particular context. A short technique description also forces researcher accountability and allows readers to evaluate the appropriateness of statistical tests used (Reid and Andereck 1989:24).

ASSESSING THE VALUE OF THE RESEARCH PROCESS

Research is costly in terms of time, emotional investment and money. In the case of many student projects there is often little choice as to whether research must be undertaken, but there is a choice as to topic, and the emotional commitment and time involved in research must not be under-estimated. Nor should the cost. Research based on interviews of even a small number of people implies travel costs. The time involved in undertaking the research has an opportunity cost in that time so spent is not being spent on other activities. What is true for the student, is also true for the commercial world. While it is comparatively easy to assess the costs of undertaking research by calculating the cost of hours spent, the costs of postage, computer time, printing, travel, equipment and the other factors involved, it is difficult to assess the return on the investment, for, by definition, the outcome of the research is not known. Lord Russell expressed this very strongly when he wrote:

> Research, in its very nature, is a form of gambling, for the researcher does not know what he is going to find out. If research is a form of gambling, the financing of it must be a form of gambling also. It is no use asking researchers, ... to estimate the benefits of their projected research in terms of discounted cash flow on an annual basis over 20 years. Any researcher who answers this question should not be funded at all. He knows what he is going to find out, and therefore is not engaged in genuine research, but a form of sophisticated fraud, in which his results will be dressed up to produce a predetermined result. If he is not in fact aiming at a predetermined result, but merely pretending he is in order to get the money, then he is only engaging in a different fraud (Russell 1993:29).

In the pharmaceutical industry the gambling nature of research is recognised by undertaking a large number of projects in the belief that the one successful outcome is able to pay not only for its own research costs, but also subsidises the costs associated with the unsuccessful initiatives. Further, a loss mitigation strategy might be undertaken, where some research is not of a 'blue skies' nature, but is seeking a refinement of an existing product. In tourism, the same costs and issues are not generally present, and data collection costs are generally far lower than those associated with industries such as the pharmaceutical industry. Yet for the small operator, the cost of a research project into client perceptions, wants or levels of satisfaction might nonetheless represent a significant percentage of their marketing budget. The relationship of the value of the research and problem definition is closely allied to each other. A distinction needs to be made between the 'nice to know' and the 'important to know', and only those commissioning the research can make the judgement. It follows therefore that research will, at least in the field of tourism, generally lead to a number of recommendations for action. However, such is the nature of research that it is always possible that the recommendation might simply be to continue that which is being done. Yet even this is not enough, for what is satisfactory in the past, and the present, is not by definition, necessarily the case in the future. Continuous monitoring is a cost that the tourism industry needs to bear, even if it is difficult to assess the tangible values of that monitoring.

DEVELOPMENT OF THE RESEARCH PROPOSAL

In most research communities, whether in academia, government, industry or commerce, those seeking to undertake research need to submit a research proposal. While there is no predefined method of presenting a research proposal, it is evident that many of the above mentioned problems need to be addressed. Any evaluation of a research proposal would include:

(a) Identification of the problem
    Is the background of the problem explored?
    Can the researcher define the problem by reference to an identification of key factors and relationships between those factors?
    Can the researcher show the necessary degree of familiarity with the complexities of the problem? This might be demonstrated by a brief review of pertinent literature, findings relating to similar problems elsewhere, or past findings.
(b) Identification of research strategy
    Is the research strategy presented in a succinct fashion?
    Is the design pertinent to the problem?
    Is the sampling frame pertinent?
    Can strategy, design and sample be suitably justified?
    Are the indicative modes of data collection appropriate?
    Are the indicative means of analysis appropriate?
(c) The nature of the resultant information
    An indication of the types of information expected.
    Is the anticipated type of output appropriate to the problem?
(d) Schedule and costs
    Is the time frame realistic given the objectives of the research?
    Is the budget appropriate?

	Nov	Dec	Jan	Feb	Mar	Apr	May	June	July	Aug	Sept	Oct
Conduct secondary literature search	*----*											
Design questionnaire		*----*										
Obtain feedback and qualitative data		*----*										
Determine sample	*----*											
Test questionnaire		*--*										
Redraft questionnaire			*-*									
Commence background write up		*------*										
1st round of data collection			*--*									
Code results				*--*								
Input data into computer				*--*								
Analyse data					*--*							
Commence 1st round write up						*------*						
2nd round of data collection									*--*			
Code results										*--*		
Input data into computer										*-*		
Analyse data											*--*	
Commence write up											*--*	
Present results												**

Figure 2.2 Research schedule for residents' attitudes research

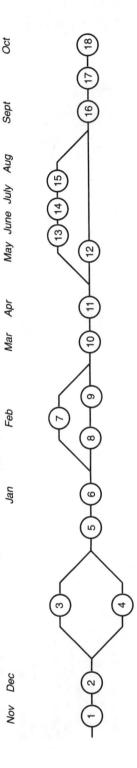

Nov Dec   Jan   Feb   Mar   Apr   May June July Aug   Sept   Oct

Key:
1 Conduct secondary literature search
2 Design questionnaire
3 Obtain feedback and qualitative data
4 Determine sample
5 Test questionnaire
6 Redraft questionnaire
7 Commence background write up
8 1st round of data collection
9 Code results

10 Input data into computer
11 Analyse data
12 Commence 1st round write up
13 2nd round of data collection
14 Code results
15 Input data into computer
16 Analyse data
17 Commence write up
18 Present results

Figure 2.3 A critical path analysis

(e) Experience of the researchers
   Do the researchers possess the expertise, qualifications and experience necessary for the work to be done?

The preparation of a research proposal is a necessary part of the discipline of undertaking research, even if it is not required by a commissioning agent, as the process of considering the above list enforces a structured approach. The list actually begins to establish a plan of action for the research, and indeed this can be taken further by drawing up some form of time schedule. Two common ways of doing this is by use of a Gantt Chart or simplified Critical Path Analysis (CPA).

   For example, a study of attitudes of residents towards tourists might take the better part of a year, and the simple Gantt Chart could appear as in Figure 2.2. This chart is based upon actual research undertaken in Bakewell, Derbyshire, as a contribution to the Peak Partnership Initiative, part of which was concerned with the reaction of local people living in a village located in an area of very high tourist traffic. The research was aimed at assessing the level of support or otherwise for tourism, and local people's attitudes towards how successful tourism planning was. It was thought important to assess attitudes at both an off-peak period and during the season so as to see whether they were consistent, or whether they varied during the year. Hence the study took most of the year, and covered the 1993 season.

   In this study certain key dates were important. Obviously the first round of enquiry had to occur before Easter and the commencement of the tourist season, while the second had to be completed prior to the end of August. Also, there was a requirement to complete the task by the end of November. It can also be noted that after the second round of questionnaires, the process of writing up the results and the analysis of the data was, to some extent, a simultaneous activity, as the writing up of a result caused new questions to arise that had to be confirmed or checked. Having identified the key periods within the research schedule, it then became a question of identifying what other activities needed to take place, and when.

   An alternative approach is to construct a critical path analysis, which takes the same items and traces out the sequence of events as shown in Figure 2.3.

DEVELOPMENT OF RESEARCH DESIGN

The development of research design in tourism is normally of the type where the researcher is unable to exercise any control over the variables involved in a situation. Such a situation is often described as requiring an *ex post facto* design as opposed to an experimental design where the researcher is able to exercise some control over independent variables. *Ex post facto* studies are generally of two types:

1   A field study that covers a literature search, experience surveys, structured

observation, and case studies. Often such a study is regarded as an exploratory phase in research, and in many case studies can be descriptive. The purpose of such research is to examine a situation in order to identify key variables in any given situation, and to discern factors which could be important elsewhere.

2   A survey which often, but not always, includes the use of a questionnaire. Here the researcher still possesses no control over the independent variable, but rather seeks to assess the relative level of importance of the isolated factors.

An example in tourism of how a field study might lead to a survey is in the case of the development of destination life cycle theory. Many have observed the processes of change in destinations as they grow over time, and in consequence, the changing usage patterns of properties. For example, Young (1983) develops further the theory of Butler (1980) by making more explicit the changing land-use patterns. For example, former fishing cottages on the quay front become holiday homes or souvenir shops. From these concepts have subsequently emerged further refinements based on surveys such as those of Kermath and Thomas (1992) and Di Benedetto and Bojanic (1993). Kermath and Thomas identified a distinction between the formal and informal tourism industry sectors in a resort in the Dominican Republic, each with its own life cycle. Di Benedetto and Bojanic undertook statistical modelling of visitor numbers to assess the impact of new attractions and environmental effects.

Experimental designs are not common in the tourism literature, but in one way they are common in the industry. If an experimental design is defined as being a situation where the 'researcher' controls a variable, and by changing that variable seeks to assess its affect upon the determined variable, it could be argued that many marketing practices are quasi-experimental field studies. For example, a travel agency might wish to assess the impact upon his business by offering no deposit bookings, by actually offering such a scheme for a period of time.

THE NATURE OF THE VARIABLE

However, in such field experiments there are significant problems in defining the role of the different variables. Not all variables can be categorised as determining or determined variables, and indeed, not all variables might consistently play the same role. Variables can be classified as follows:

(a) An independent (or determining) variable – a presumed cause of an event, it precedes the changing outcome.

(b) A dependent (or determined) variable – the factor that changes as a result of change in the determining or independent variable.

For example, if wages increase, holiday expenditure might increase. Wages are said to be the determining variable, and holiday expenditure the dependent variable. But, it is possible that wages do increase, but holiday expenditure remains static. That may be due to the presence of intervening or moderating variables.

(c) An intervening variable – a function of the independent variables that helps to explain the behaviour of the determined variable.

So, in our simplified example, if increasing wages cause a faster increase in retail prices (or inflation), then holiday expenditure might not increase because other costs borne by household budgets have increased faster than income. In this example, inflation caused by the independent variable, wages, in turn influences the dependent variable, holiday expenditure. Inflation could be said to be an intervening variable. But it might be the case that although consumer price inflation increases to offset any increase in income, holiday expenditure still increases. This might be due to a factor having a strong effect upon the independent–dependent variable relationship. So while wage increases are mitigated by inflation, holiday expenditure might increase if holiday-takers feel so much in need of a holiday that they substitute holiday expenditure for, say, savings. From this perspective, the psychological need can be defined as a moderating variable that acts upon the linkage between inflation and holiday expenditure. Diagrammatically, the relationship can be shown as in Figure 2.4.

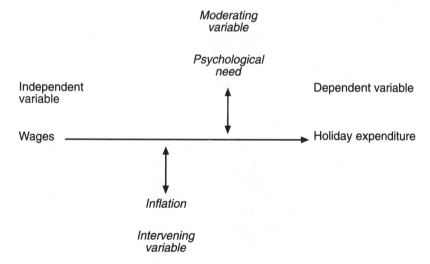

Figure 2.4 The role of variables

Figure 2.4 also indicates the importance of modelling and identifying the actual role of variables. From the economist's perspective the model might possess a prima-facie validity, but alternative scenarios using the same variables are possible. For example, a psychologist could well argue that the psychological need is the independent variable, and that wages are an enabler which facilitate the meeting of the need, that is, in the language of variables, wages are an intervening variable. Given that the same factors have been identified as being important, the actual modelling process that is engaged upon would have very important implications for the actual research design. The economist might engage in a process of measurement of economic variables using regression analysis, with the residual being a measure of psychological need. On the other hand the psychologist might engage in a series of interviews with little reference to economic data. So the presumed functions of the variables as independent, intervening or moderating variables have significant implications for research design.

QUANTITATIVE AND QUALITATIVE RESEARCH

One of the implications of the above example is that research can be designated as being qualitative or quantitative in its nature. The use of the word 'and' in the above sub-title is important. Although the topic has often been approached as one of qualitative versus quantitative, most practitioners perceive both as valid, both complementing each other, and yet both having different objectives and problems. The detail of some of the techniques are explored in the following chapters, but an overview of the two is appropriate here as emerging naturally from the previous points.

The distinction between the two is indicated in Table 2.1. Some observations might be made about specific components of the table. For example, many with psychological training would also possess good statistical knowledge, while many who utilise decision models are also fully conversant with consumer behaviour modelling and the psychological theories upon which they are based. Equally, the table implies that statistical interpretation is entirely 'objective', but this is not always the case. For example, Everitt and Dunn (1991:110) concede that the procedure of estimating the number of clusters resulting from dendograms may 'be rather subjective'. The statistical technique of factor analysis has been attacked as being a technique that permits investigators to rotate data until they get the answer they are looking for. Chatfield and Collins (1980) feel that in most practical cases factor analysis should not be used. Such processes do involve decisions based as much upon experience and under-standing of the purpose of the technique as 'rigid' statistical rules. In this the expertise of the researcher is important, just as it is in attributing value to spoken statements by interviewees.

Nonetheless, as a generalisation it can be said that qualitative research is concerned with the subjective component of research. It offers many advantages to the researcher. The comments of respondents and the in-depth interview can produce a richness of information and feeling about attractions, travel, places and the experience of holidays. Given that holidays can be cathartic experiences which have the potential to change peoples' lives, the reduction of such an experience to a few ticks on a five-point scale is obviously insufficient. Qualitative research can be a source of ideas, insights and new perspectives upon

Table 2.1 Qualitative versus quantitative research

Comparison dimension	Qualitative research	Quantitative research
Types of Questions	Probing	Limited probing
Sample size	Small	Large
Information per respondent	Much	Varies
Administration	Requires interviewer with special skills	Fewer special skills required
Type of analysis	Subjective, interpretive	Statistical, summarisation
Hardware	Tape recorders, projection devices, video, pictures discussion guides	Questionnaires, computers, printouts
Ability to replicate	Low	High
Training of the researcher	Psychology, sociology, social psychology, consumer behaviour, marketing, marketing research	Statistics, decision models, decision support systems, computer programming, marketing, marketing research
Type of Research	Exploratory	Descriptive or causal

Source: McDaniel Jr and Gates 1993: 188.

a problem. Hence, in spite of all the doubts that are expressed as to the ability to generalise from its findings, the problems inherent in interpretation of the meanings and comparative importance of respondents' comments, and the possible invalidation of responses because of the social dynamics that can occur within small groups, techniques such as focus groups, role play and projection techniques are all commonly used within the commercial sector of the tourism industry. Tour operators have intensively used focus groups to assess the reaction to their brochures, to the nature of destinations, and to help in the formulation of television advertising.

Quantitative research, however, brings other advantages, notably some reassurance about the validity and reliability of findings. It can also be very much cheaper in terms of being able to poll the views of very large numbers of people relatively quickly if, for example, postal questionnaires are used. Additionally, there is an increasing sophistication of analysis possible given the increasing power and reduced cost of computerisation.

From this quick review it is evident that the simple distinction between non-quantitative qualitative research and non-subjective quantitative research is a simplification. Those conducting focus groups count the numbers who agree with a statement, and statisticians use their judgement when compiling clusters of holiday-maker types. It is also true that where possible many research designs will seek to use both approaches. Conventionally, quantitative research is preceded by qualitative research in an attempt to confirm the validity of the questions being posed, or to ensure that all the key variables within a situation have been identified. However, this is to imply that the role of qualitative research is secondary to that of quantitative (i.e. its function is to ensure the validity of the questions to be asked in a questionnaire). This is to underestimate the functions and roles of qualitative research, and these will be more fully discussed in Chapter 4.

DIFFERENT RESEARCH DESIGN STRUCTURES

Many examples of tourism research that are reported in the journals and undertaken in practice might be called 'snap-shot' research. In other words a group of people are interviewed at one period in time, often after they have visited an attraction. Although this is valuable in the sense that some information is better than no information, there are deficiencies in such an approach. For example, in one study a survey of the attitudes of those visiting a swimming pool was commissioned by a leisure-centre operator. The purpose of the survey was to increase the rate of usage, and visitors to the swimming pool were duly questioned as to why they came, the frequency of visit and their attitude towards the pool and its facilities. However, such an approach omits an important consideration – what of the attitude of the non-visitors? In many senses the potential to increase business lies much more with converting 'reluctant' users into users, than it does in attempting to increase the frequency of use by existing users.

Now, assume that a survey of non-users was undertaken, and as a result some promotion was aimed at that group. What would be their attitude after they had visited the swimming pool? Was it similar to the 'experienced' group of visitors? What distinguished these new users from those that still did not patronise the pool? In what ways had experienced users changed their behaviour after the promotion had taken place, and perhaps increased the number of users or rate of usage? In other words, for the study to have greater validity, it is helpful if comparative studies can be undertaken between groups, and over a period of time. This gives rise to different research designs, which can be applicable to both quantitative and qualitative research. These different research designs can be classified as below.

One-shot case study

This is the simplest of all designs, and consists of asking a population or sample a series of questions on one occasion only. It therefore has the advantages of being comparatively cheap and simple to administer, but it suffers from several weaknesses. As indicated in the above example of users of a swimming pool, what is not known is the history of behaviour and attitude. Also, with possibly only one sample, it becomes difficult to assess the degree to which even being selected as a member of a sample begins to change perception. Research in tourism often requires people to make explicit those things that previously they have undertaken without necessarily too much thought. The actual process of thinking about a topic, of perhaps justifying actions, begins to change perception of the topic under consideration, and perhaps influence the answer. Without comparative groups it is difficult to identify the extent to which this is happening, although, this is a problem with many forms of research design.

It is also problematical as to when the questions are asked. If they are asked after an event, say a visit or a holiday, the interviewer is seeking recall of an event, and that recall may or may not accurate. In turn, this raises the question of the importance of the accuracy of recall. One approach is to argue that what respondents think is important, is as important as what actually did occur. On the other hand, asking holiday-makers questions about their expectations before they visit a place puts respondents in the position of having to make judgements about something they have not actually experienced. Hence responses are coloured by degrees of familiarity with comparable places and experiences.

Also of importance for the one-shot study is the nature of the preparation prior to asking the questions. There is a danger with one-shot questions that respondents reply to an agenda determined by the researcher as to what is thought to be important, rather than what the clients believe to be important. Additionally, any researcher must pay attention to questions of internal validity of the responses, something that is possibly more difficult to do with the small samples associated with qualitative research.

Simple longitudinal designs

This is a development of the one-shot design in that the same sample is revisited on more than one occasion. With a series of interviews it becomes more possible to assess the consistency and validity of responses. Strictly speaking, a longitudinal study requires responses from the same sample in each case, but in tourism there are many cases where the same questions are used but with different respondents over time. For example, the data prepared for the United Kingdom Tourism Survey is based on surveys of approximately 2,000 respondents each month. The questions over the short to intermediate term remain unchanged, and hence a monitoring of changes in holiday-taking patterns is built up over time. Similarly, with the International Passenger Survey a longitudinal picture is developed even though on each occasion different respondents are approached. These and other changes can be more formerly classified as follows.

One group pre-test–post-test

This is a development of the longitudinal study in that the series of questions take place over a period of time that is defined with reference to a specific event, occurrence or happening. In a sense it might be described as a quasi-experimental design in that while the researcher does not 'control' the event as it is understood in conventional physical science research, a measurement before and after an occurrence is undertaken in order to assess the influence of the event. In tourism this can happen in a number of situations. For example, it would be associated with research that seeks to measure the impact of tourism. A study might be done as to resident attitudes prior to the opening of an attraction, and then after the attraction has opened. Visitor attitudes before and after visiting a tourist development might be measured and compared and any change might be attributed to the new attraction. The comparison with traditional physical sciences research is obvious if the research is concerned with the impact of tourism development on water quality and usage. Measures of pollution might be taken before a resort is built, and then after, and any change in water quality might be attributed to the tourist development.

The question is to what extent is any difference between the two periods actually due to the supposed determining variable? For example, suppose a resort was developed and the environmental authorities were concerned about the disposal of resultant sewage and its effect upon the quality of water in a defined area. The water quality might be measured before the opening of the resort, and after the resort is built. If it is found that, by whatever measurement used, water quality has deteriorated by 10 per cent, can it be argued that the resort has led to a deterioration in water quality? In part, an answer to the question can only be given by a longer time series of studies prior to the event under study. For example, a monitoring of water quality over time prior to the opening of the resort might have found that water quality had diminished by, say, 7 per cent due to various agricultural practices prior to the opening of the resort. It might then be argued that the resort has added to the deterioration in water quality, but is not responsible for all of it. In other words, to improve upon the simple one group pre-test–post-test design, additional comparative groupings and measurements are required. These can be developed in a number of ways.

Static group comparison

This is a quasi-experimental alternative to the one group pre-test–post-test situation, but is not a full response to the deficiencies of that design. In the static group design two groups are surveyed to assess the effect of an event occurring. In the case of one group they have experienced the event, place or happening, while in the case of a second, matched population or sample, they have not been to the place, event or happening.

For example, suppose that an airline introduced a new in-flight service and it wished to assess whether this had any impact in establishing favourable attitudes towards the airline and hence, in turn, the likelihood of generating repeat business. It might survey those passengers that had flown on the new service, and compared their responses and subsequent behaviour with a group that had not flown on the new service.

In this case, the comparison might be said to be a post-test comparison only. To begin to overcome the deficiencies of the pre-test–post-test single group design, a longitudinal element can be built into the surveying of both groups. The resultant pre-test–post-test control group design, as it is known, consists of two samples:

1   Sample A is questioned before the event, they experience the event, and are subsequently questioned again after their experience.
2   Sample B is questioned before the event in parallel in group B, and are interviewed a second time in parallel with sample A, but do not experience the event.

The purpose of this procedure is to identify the change that was already existing in a system, as identified by sample B, and thus be able to distinguish that amount of change which is solely due to the event and independent of any existing trend. In other words, any change measured in sample A before and after the event might be composed of two sources of change: the change due to the event experienced; and a process of change already existing in the system. The data now available from sample B permits the change due to the event itself to be identified.

One area where this might occur is in terms of attitudes towards tourists. The Doxey Irridex indicates that host communities affected by tourists begin to demonstrate annoyance and subsequently antagonism towards tourists. But it might be queried just how much of that attitude is due to direct experience of interaction towards tourists, and how much of it might be due to general cultural attitudes derived from other sources (e.g. the news media). A pre-test–post-test control group design might be one way of trying to disentangle the influence of general factors from tourist specific items.

Solomon four group design

The most complex experimental research design is the Solomon four group design. This is used in research based upon the physical sciences such as pharmaceutical or medical research, but is not normally found in tourism. It consists of four samples and is a combination of all the above systems. The groups are:

1   Sample A is questioned prior to the event, experiences the event, and is then subsequently re-questioned.
2   Sample B is questioned in parallel with sample A, but does not experience the event.
3   Sample C experiences the event, and is questioned after the event. In other words, they are not questioned before the event.

4   Sample D is simply questioned in parallel with the above three groups without any prior questioning or experience of the event.

Why adopt such a seemingly complex pattern of questioning? Essentially, in using this research design the researcher is attempting to control for a number of potential complicating factors that could reduce the validity of the findings. These include:

(a) a control to assess general trends that might be occurring anyway independent of the effects caused by the event, happening or visit that is being specifically assessed;
(b) a possibility that any group that is questioned more than once gains experience as a respondent. This might change their perceptions in such a way that they become less representative of the general population, or they begin to respond to the interviewers and learn what they think is 'approved' behaviour;
(c) over time, respondents are themselves subject to changes due to factors such natural ageing or changes in life stage. In the shorter term they may simply be fatigued with the exercise.

The Solomon four group design overcomes these problems in a number of ways. The two longitudinal groupings permit assessment of changes in the general system as described in the pre-test–post-test control group design, but samples C and D allow for any learning experience that might arise through retesting. Sample D permits a testing of sample B to indicate whether sample B's second results are representative of the wider population that has not experienced the event (so testing for any learning or maturation affects that might influence answers). In a similar way, sample C is a validation of sample A's results.

Such research design can obviously be applied in the case of questionnaire response, but the same process can also apply to qualitative research involving, say, focus groups. However, two caveats can be raised. The gain in certainty about results is purchased at a cost of time, effort and money. Second, by their very nature, qualitative processes generate problems of replication of results; yet it can be argued that in such cases attempts to analyse the source of discrepancy can be quite fruitful.

Additionally, there is a third issue. The process can also raise serious issues if the results raised by the additional samples for purposes of installing checks within the research indicate a lack of desired consistency. How might such inconsistencies be explained? One potential source of such discrepancy is that the research instrument is itself faulty? The cynic might comment that one reason why the more rigorous research designs are not adopted is that they avoid such questions arising.

DETERMINATION OF DATA COLLECTION METHODS AND ANALYTICAL PROCEDURES

The methodologies of data collection are examined more carefully from Chapter 4 on, and for purposes of this general review, can be connected with the assessment of analytical procedures. It should already be obvious that however much care is taken over the design of the research, errors arising in collection will cause difficulty. Errors in collection can lead to errors in data, which in turn can lead to further problems in analysis of the data. The nature of the problem can be illustrated by Figure 2.5.

While the cells indicate that an error in research design or collection indicates a need either for redesigning or undertaking again the data collection process, in practice the researcher is not so easily able to make the distinction. If results do not support a hypothesis, then that may be due to:

(a) the hypothesis being false;
(b) the research design being inadequate;
(c) the data collection process being inappropriate;
(d) a combination of items (b) and (c).

The question of the composition and size of sample is thus very important, and is duly considered in detail in Chapter 7. Figure 2.5 also utilises the terms 'validity'

Research design

	Appropriate	Inappropriate
Appropriate (Data collection)	Research has validity and reliability	Research lacks validity, but requires redesign and implementation
Inappropriate (Data collection)	Research lacks reliability and needs to be implemented again	Research lacks reliability and validity

Figure 2.5 Errors in research

and 'reliability' in their general sense, but in statistical research they have very specific meanings, especially with reference to the developments of measurement scales. Validity implies that the research instrument measures what it is supposed to measure. The sources of validity are threefold, namely:

Content validity   The research design is based upon a correct hypothesis, and thus has led to scales of measurement which are pertinent measures of the problem under examination.

Construct validity   The scale is a true representation of what is being measured; that is it behaves in a manner analogous to that which it purports to measure. From a statistical viewpoint construct validity might be measured in two ways. First, the researcher would look for a high degree of positive correlation between associated variables. Thus the score on a statement such as 'I believe leisure pursuits are important' would be expected to correlate highly with a score of indicating agreement with a statement like 'my holidays are important to me'. This would be noted as having a convergent validity. On the other hand, a questionnaire may have an item seeking agreement with the view that 'work is a very important aspect of my life'. It might be expected that this statement would have an inverse relationship with the statement that holidays are important. If this was the case then a discriminant validity would be said to exist as the two items were able to discriminate between the work and the holiday orientated.

Criterion-related validity   Here the validity of the research is based upon the ability of the variables to predict another variable. For example, suppose it was hypothesised that there was a correlation between levels of satisfaction derived from a holiday and the levels of repeat booking with the same tour operator. In this case the criterion-related validity of the construct would be shown by the subsequent levels of repeat booking by the highly satisfied holiday-makers.

Reliability can be differentiated from validity quite easily. As might be expected, reliability is concerned with the consistency of the results obtained; that is, repeated testing yields the same results. However, a scale might be consistent, but if it lacks validity, the scores are of little help in achieving an understanding of the situation. However, the question of reliability implies that respondents are questioned more than once; that they are subjected to a test–re-test situation as indicated in some of the research designs noted earlier. This is, of course, not always possible, but it is sometimes possible, if the sample is sufficiently large, to divide respondents into two groups, and to assess the difference between the two groups. If the correlation between the two groups is high, then this split-half testing as it is known, is said to indicate reliability. The statistical techniques associated with this testing is discussed on page 254.

The issue of research design generating validity and reliability is important for researchers who want to avoid what are termed type one and type two errors.

These errors arise from a fundamental assumption adopted in testing for statistical relationships. This is known as the Null Hypothesis, which states that any relationship possesses no significance, or that any value does not significantly deviate from the 'average'. It is akin to the assumption in law that no-one is guilty of deviate behaviour unless found otherwise guilty.

The type one error can be defined as: the rejection of the null hypothesis as being false when it is in fact true. In other words, a relationship is thought to be significant, but in fact it is not.

The type two error is: the null hypothesis is not rejected when it is false (i.e. the researcher thinks a relationship is 'ordinary', and does not reject the hypothesis that the relationship is 'ordinary', but in fact the finding is significant).

The importance of avoiding these areas is self-evident, and in quantitative research a number of techniques are available to the researcher to ensure that hypothesis testing can be carried out. These are based upon the expected variance around a mean average score, and the nature of this distribution is discussed in Chapters 7 and 8.

THE EVALUATION OF RESULTS

The statistical processes involved in interpreting the data are an important part in generating information from data in quantitative research, but it is not entirely a mechanistic task. As indicated previously, the researcher must be familiar with the nature and purpose of the tests available, and be able to interpret their findings accordingly. Judgements are being made continually as to what is, or what is not an appropriate test. Data evaluation must take into account the nature of the information available. There is, for example, little point in using sophisticated methods of analysis if the sample is too small to support such techniques, or if the basis of data used in, say, economic modelling changes during the time period being considered. This latter point is particularly important in comparative studies seeking to compare data from one country with another. For example, if inflation is thought to be an important variable in determining disposable income and attitudes towards holiday-taking, then the researcher must be familiar with the different constructs of price indices between different countries. To say that inflation in country A is 10 per cent, and in country B 5 per cent does not automatically imply that those in country A are twice as badly off than those in country B. Countries will differ, for example, in their treatment of housing costs and questions relating to the imputation of a rental value when considering the effect of housing costs on home owners. Again, different countries have different levels of home ownership, and hence the weighting of housing costs within the different indices of inflation might again mean that like is not being strictly compared with like. Different types of research require specific levels of expertise if the results are going to be meaningful.

THE PRESENTATION OF THE REPORT

All the care about research design, testing, and evaluation of results will be of little avail if the report is unclear, obtuse and unreadable. There are some practices that can help in the writing up of research, whether it be for academic or commercial purposes. It is not possible to discuss all the requirements of report or thesis writing within this review, but some observations can be noted. Academic research is often quite specific in requiring detail about the context of the research in terms of the existing literature, and an important discipline for any researcher is to develop care about correctly recording their references as they progress. Much time can be lost in seeking out a lost reference when someone else has the book or report that you want when seeking simply to confirm a quotation or a reference. The guidelines for referencing are usually quite straightforward. What are required are the names of the authors, the year of publication, the title of the book, article, journal or conference proceeding as appropriate, the volume, part number and pages if it is a journal or, in the case of a book, the place of publication and publisher. When noting down specific words as used by an author when reading a book or article, it is excellent practice to note the actual page where the quotation occurred. This is because it is customary when quoting the precise words of an author to note the specific source including page number.

In commercial research, although the requirement of an extensive review of past literature is not present, a bibliography might be appended to a report, and hence again the need for maintaining a correct bibliography and list of references is important. From the commercial viewpoint it can be expected that those commissioning the research are not always those who have to implement in detail the recommendations that might be made. A good practice therefore is to list in a preamble the key findings and recommendations. Busy executives can quickly read these to familiarise themselves with the issues, and then either pass the report to those delegated to act upon it or, if they wish, read the further detail. It is good practice when listing these key points to reference them to the appropriate pages or sections of the report. Hence, if executives wish to read further as to why the researcher has made a particular recommendation, they are able to access the key part of the report immediately.

In both reports and academic studies, it is important that a consistent approach is adopted as to titles, sub-titles and headings. Lists of contents, figures and diagrams should be included and the language should be accessible and appropriate to the audience. Thought must also be given to whether or not it is appropriate to break up the text at various stages with perhaps a list of items, rather than running them through as a single line of text. Finally, it is important to state clearly the outcomes of the research in two senses: what has been found, and what are the implications. In commercial studies these implications are usually interpreted as meaning specific recommendations for future action; in academic work this might be the case, or it might be a discussion of how the findings affect thinking about a specific issue.

The same process can be used within an academic report, although in this case it might be called a synopsis. Nonetheless, the synopsis serves a useful purpose. It prepares the reader for what is to come, it sets the scene, and can set to rest the concern of the reader from the outset that, when developing an argument, certain aspects are not ignored, because it is known that they are dealt with elsewhere in the study.

SUMMARY

Research design has been shown to require a systematic appraisal of variables, the way in which they interact, and the need to distinguish between the existing trends and those that might be solely due to the events being considered. Even where it is not possible to undertake more complex research designs, researchers will need to consider carefully how they might best identify these other factors.

Research design is not only structured in terms of its identification of key variables, but also in the need to enforce a self-discipline on the part of the researcher. This relates to the planning of time when various stages of the research need to be completed, and the sequence of events.

The next issue to be considered when researching tourist satisfaction is the context within which such satisfaction occurs, and the state of mind of the tourist. This forms the subject matter of the next chapter.

Chapter 3

Tourist satisfaction – concepts and research issues

INTRODUCTION

Within tourism research a significant amount of the primary analytical data that is generated refers to the attitudes of tourists. This is not to say that little else is researched. For example, any review of the leading tourism journals will indicate articles on topics like spatial analysis, the impacts of tourism, strategic implications of computer reservation systems, case studies of resort development, and tourism forecasting by use of econometrics, Delphi forecasts and *ad hoc* measures to mention but a few topics. Nonetheless, questions of tourist behaviour and attitudes are important. The first volume of the *Journal of Travel and Tourism Marketing* (1992) contained 18 main articles. Of these, 10 were specifically concerned with measures of attitudes or behaviour, utilising diary analysis, factor and cluster analysis and descriptions of the role of culture to mention a few of the techniques used. Accordingly, and also acting on the premise that many student projects are concerned with obtaining reactions of visitors to attractions, and that the majority of sizeable tourist attraction operators and tour operators also monitor client satisfaction, the main emphasis of this and the following chapter will relate to the measurement of tourist attitudes. These chapters will discuss a number of issues pertaining to researching tourist attitudes and behaviour including: components of attitude and behaviour to be considered in research design; types of motivation for holiday-takers and resultant tourist segmentation; multi-attribute models and measures of tourist attitude; issues of consistency in attitudinal measurement; means of measurement of tourist satisfaction.

FACTORS INFLUENCING TOURIST SATISFACTION

In this section a review of concepts relating to tourist attitudes and their measurement is undertaken:

(a) to provide a theoretical framework for subsequent analysis of attitudes;
(b) to indicate the issues that need to be considered in research design.

⫟ It can be argued that the attitudes, expectations and perceptions of the holiday-maker are significant variables in setting goals, influencing behaviour and determining final satisfaction. In undertaking any study of tourist behaviour and attitudes a number of considerations must be addressed, including:

(a) the perceived importance of the activity in terms of self-development, self-enhancement, ego, meeting perceived roles, and responding to perceived requirements of significant others;

(b) the importance of the activity being evaluated not only by need, but also by expected outcomes. Thus questions relating to perceptions of both need and outcome need to be considered;

(c) the intervening variables such as the skill brought to the recreational activity by the participant are also important. Skill may be a function of innate ability, experience and learning. Utilising the terminology of Csikszentimi-halyi (1975), it can be argued that the relationship between the challenge posed by external conditions and the ability to handle them contributes to the 'flow' experienced by the participant, and hence the degree of satisfaction gained;

(d) other intervening variables that might include the presence of significant other individuals or groups, and the importance attached to their presence or absence;

(e) the degree to which the participant adjusts expectations, experiences cognitive dissonance, and engages in displacement activities and the role of these in determining final satisfaction if initial expectations are not met within any given situation.

The above is, at best, a partial listing of potentially important factors that must be considered systematically in any research of tourist attitudes. Equally, any brief consideration of this area should take into account some theories of consumer behaviour. If satisfaction is seen as the congruence of need and performance, then dissatisfaction can be perceived as the gap between expectation and experience. Therefore, some form of gap analysis might be helpful in analysing tourist satisfaction. Equally, if cognitive dissonance is thought to play a role, then it is arguably 'triggered' by some event, some 'critical incident' in the holiday-taker's experience of place or activity. Research would apparently indicate that such events can serve as powerful 'confirmers' of positive experience (Bitner et al. 1990).

Within the UK, approximately 40 per cent of stays away from home are associated with visiting friends, family and relations (VFR), and are included in tourism statistics produced by the tourist boards, even though the pattern of visits may have more in common with day-trip activity than with other forms of holidaying. One incidental aspect of viewing tourism as an experience of place would be to put day-trip activity within the gamut of both academic and commercial tourism research. To do so would also require an assessment of the role of familiarity with destinations to a more central position in assessing the determinants of tourist choice and satisfaction. Nonetheless, holidays requiring travel away from home do generate contextual differences for leisure activity.

Indeed the fact that the trip is away from home may be the very rationale of the holiday. In the terminology of tourist literature, holidays are motivated by 'escape' and 'pull' factors. Yet, it can be pointed out that while tourists may return to a favoured location, the holiday experience is never entirely duplicated. Prior knowledge of an area changes search activity, different tourists staying at the place generate new patterns of inter-tourist interaction while some familiarity of the place might change tourist–host relationships. Consequently, repeat visits cannot generate an experience which duplicates the original. Actions may be the same within the same place, but prior experience changes the nature of the satisfaction to be derived from those actions. Past experience also changes expectations of the place, and inasmuch as expectation shapes motivation, and the motivation to enjoy becomes a goal, behaviour on repeat visits might also be affected. From this viewpoint, the theories of flow and arousal (Csikszentimi-halyi and Csikszentimihalyi 1988) are important in helping to distinguish between those repeated actions that generate positive satisfaction and those that are the cause of boredom.

There are many issues involved in assessing attitude and motivation, of which the obvious one is the determination of what exactly does motivate a holiday-maker in the selection of a holiday. There have been a large number of studies that have sought to identify these factors, or to classify tourists on the basis of their holiday motivations. Reviews of these motivations can be found in books by Matthieson and Wall (1982), Murphy (1985), and Ryan (1991b), to list three. However, the linkage between motivation and behaviour is not automatic, and in many cases the actual holiday is long enough to permit a range of different activities, each of which might meet different needs, some of which may not have been considered at the time of actually booking the holiday. Any model of, and research into tourist behaviour must allow for serendipity – the knack of making the unexpected, but happy, finding. Motivations can also be experienced at different levels of intensity, and from some perspectives it is this difference of intensity that needs to be carefully considered at the stage of research design into tourist attitudes. Simply identifying a motivation or attitude is only a partial answer. How important is that attitude or motivation; what is the nature of its contribution to the setting of goals and objectives required of a holiday? And, at a more basic level, to what extent are goals and motivations made explicit in the mind of the holiday-maker? In many cases of research pertaining to tourist attitudes, these fundamental questions are often overlooked. The result is that little is known about the importance of the discovered attitude, or the duration or 'sustainability' of that attitude, or the degree of involvement which the tourist has with the place, experience or interaction that has occurred. Therefore, the issues that need to be considered include:

(a) The nature of involvement – it can be argued that the more committed a person is to a course of action, the higher the degree of success.

(b) The role of risk – going to new places generates a degree of risk, and some are more likely to take risks than others.

(c) The role of stress – travel involves 'travail' (i.e. some stress is felt).

(d) Boredom and frustration – holiday-making can involve both of these feelings, although in the final assessment of the holiday they may be overlooked.

(e) A sense of flow – when the holiday-maker feels capable of handling things, there is a sense of achievement.

(f) Mindlessness – in many cases things are so easily handled that there is little recall, things are dealt with automatically.

(g) Needs analysis – holidays are motivated by a need to achieve certain goals.

Arising from a consideration of these points there subsequently results a need to consider some of the practical research issues in terms of adopting some motivational theories, and these are then considered.

THE NATURE OF INVOLVEMENT

Expectation, and the motivation to enjoy the goals of the holiday, would lead to the hypothesis that the tourist has a high degree of involvement with holiday activity. Laurent and Kapferer (1985) and Dimanche *et al.* (1991) argue that involvement is an important antecedent of satisfaction in leisure situations. Ryan (1994) argues that a strong tourist motivation to derive enjoyment from the holiday experience becomes a determinant of behaviour, so that negative experiences give rise to displacement activities or cognitive dissonance to achieve the goal of enjoyment. Involvement is thus both a motivator and a goal.

Laurent and Kapferer (1985) argue that involvement is a multi-dimensional function with four attributes – importance, pleasure, self-expression and risk. Risk can itself be divided into:

(a) perceived importance of negative consequences in case of a poor choice; and

(b) perceived probability of making such a mistake.

(Dimanche *et al.* 1991)

Following multi-attribute theory, it can also be noted that risk must entail the perceived consequences of a positive choice (benefit) and the associated probability. However, while recognising the significance of involvement as a determinant of satisfaction to be gained from either a leisure or holiday experience, it can be seen as an indirectly derived dimension. The importance of the act determines the degree of involvement, but this gives rise to the question, what are those factors that generate importance? The derivation of pleasure and self-expression might be argued to be determinants of the importance of involvement. (This presents some difficulties in that it questions whether the four attributes identified by Laurent and Kapferer are independent or interdependent variables). But pleasure-seeking can be denied, or delayed, as items of more importance take precedence, and sensitivity to self-expression may be dependent upon degrees of self-actualisation (Maslow 1970). Thus, from the viewpoint of humanistic psychology where self-expression and awareness are significant motivators of human behaviour, the results of Dimanche *et al.* (1991) derived from their factor analysis, whereby a factor, self-expression, accounts for the greater part of the explained variance, (38.3 per cent) and pleasure and importance items form a second factor are not surprising. Such results, arguably, support the notion that while involvement is a determinant of satisfaction, it is itself dependent on more fundamental variables, e.g. personality, and/or possibly the opportunity to become involved due to economic or social factors, to mention but two other reasons.

THE ROLE OF RISK

The role of risk may also be linked with that of self-expression. One of the characteristics of 'self actualisation' argues Hampden (1971) is that the self-fulfilled person is more prepared to expose themselves to psychological risk. Obviously, psychological risk is not to be necessarily equated with physical risk, although overlaps between the two dimensions can exist; but in the field of tourism it can be argued that those prepared to take psychological risk are those who travel to new and unfamiliar destinations.[1]

Such is the characteristic of the allocentric tourists described by Plog (1977). The concept has been criticised, notably by Smith (1990) who found in his survey of tourists from different nationalities there were no significant differences in destination choice by allocentrics, psychocentrics or mid-centrics. However, Plog (1990) has refuted Smith's findings, arguing that Smith has not replicated his concepts due to the use of different items on the questionnaire, different scales and a non-representative sample. Smith does, however, make a pertinent point when he notes that:

> I suggest that future research does not focus on the relationship between personality types and *destinations*, but rather focus on examining possible relationships between personality types and travel *styles* (Smith 1990:51).

Support for this viewpoint is provided by Laing (1987). In analysing reasons given for independent holiday-making, 'freedom' and 'independence' were the most quoted reasons (by 50 per cent of the sample (ibid.)), while the primary reason for selecting a package holiday was that little planning was needed, and, in 16 per cent of cases the primary reason was that 'no risk was involved' (ibid.:173). Laing also found that for package-holiday-takers, the lack of risk was the most frequently quoted secondary reason for taking package holidays, and concludes 'perceived risk ... seems to play an unique role as an enforcer rather than a prime motivator to stay at home' (ibid.:146).

Laing also notes that 25 per cent of his sample of package-holiday-makers revisited familiar destinations, and that those who visit familiar destinations with previously used tour operators are much more likely to book longer in advance – all of which can be seen as risk avoidance strategies. However, one must be careful to avoid over-stressing the importance of risk aversion, for other variables were found to correlate significantly with package-holiday choice (notably low school-leaving educational qualification). Laing concludes his discussion by stating that the reason for package-holiday-taking:

> is less easily explained than as first thought ... for many people package holiday taking is an habitual action – they rarely consider the reasons behind the preference ... [the] preference for packaged travel may be more an outcome of personal and highly individual factors which demand particular detailed analysis. Information of this ilk might be assimilated by extensive qualitative research into holiday aspirations, felt need, and how this is satisfied by the package holiday. A closer grasp is needed of the individual's perception of package tours and their associated meaning (Laing 1987:179).

and again:

> the holidaymaker visiting recent seaside resorts is more likely to be a relatively inexperienced traveller than is the visitor to traditional, scenic locations, or in particular, to special activity centres. Holiday experience thus seems one means of fostering more specific holiday intentions (Laing 1987:331–2).

THE ROLE OF STRESS

Exposure to risk can involve the generation of stress, and while recreational tourism is motivated, in part, by the need to escape stress, holidays can be generators of stressful circumstances. The sources of stress are potentially many for the holiday-maker in a foreign country with a different culture, a language which the holiday-maker might not speak, and customs which are unfamiliar. Stress can be defined as levels of arousal which are so high as to induce feelings of anxiety, and where further arousal begins to induce lower levels of effective performance. The Yerkes–Dodson 'Law' (1908) argues for an inverted U-shape relationship between performance and levels of arousal (see Figure 3.1, p. 47). This may be particularly true for the less experienced foreign traveller. It is of passing interest to note that Norton (1987), when discussing the decline of trans-Atlantic traffic in 1985 and 1986 after aircraft hijacking and other terrorist action, comments that the American market was particularly affected because of the inexperience of the American tourist in travelling outside the USA. Gray (1987) proposes a categorisation of four components of stress that is applicable to recreation and tourism. The 'stressors' are:

(a) intensity – the demands of the task and self-assessment of ability to cope with those demands;
(b) social interaction – the relationships incurred in being part of a group;

(c) novelty – the creation of concern by being in a new and unfamiliar
      environment;
(d) specific situations – the development of perceived threat within a specific set
      of circumstances.

Each of these reasons might be seen as possessing the nature of a continuum.
Intensity may be associated with concepts of challenge which can be overcome;
social interaction poses opportunity as well as threat, novelty of environment has
long been regarded as a motivation for travel, while specific situations might well
pose opportunities for significant satisfactory experiences. It has also been
recognised that stress is a facilitator of performance under certain situations.

    Thus two questions arise:

(a) Is there evidence that these 'stressors' are experienced within a recreational
      setting?
(b) What are the characteristics of a situation that produce arousal so that the
      negative aspect of the continuum comes to the fore rather than the positive?

Robinson and Stephens (1990) utilised the concepts of the stressors within the
context of a canoeing trip across Canada, and concluded that:

> although each of the four stressor types were shown to influence state anxiety,
> the modest size of the accounted-for variances (13% in the pre-test; 20 to 46%
> in the field tests) suggest that the stressor categories of intensity, social inter-
> action, novelty, and specific situations do not fully define the antecedents of
> stress which operate in this type of setting (Robinson and Stephens
> 1990:229).

They suggest that essentially two components exist:

(a) the first is the types of situations which generate common response patterns;
(b) the second is concerned with inter- and intra-personal concerns.

As noted above, within the context of holidays, the four stressors might be
deemed to be part of continua, namely intensity of experience, positive or
negative, novelty, positive or negative, social interaction, positive or negative,
and special situations, positive or negative. With reference to the question, what
are the characteristics of a situation that produces debilitating arousal, the
suggestion made by Robinson and Stephens might be said to change the nature of
the argument. Rather than defining the components of stress, it becomes a
categorisation of situations and response patterns. Such response patterns might
be said to be dependent upon variables such as the situation, the personality of
the participant, and the perception of the situation by that participant.

BOREDOM AND FRUSTRATION

It is consistent with the Yerkes–Dodson 'Law' (see Figure 3.1), and with the
concepts of 'flow' as advanced by Csikszentimihalyi (1975), that an absence of

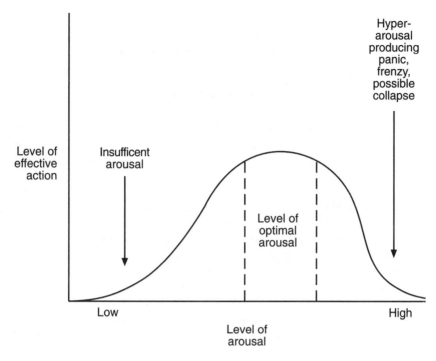

Figure 3.1 The Yerkes–Dodson 'Law'

sufficient levels of arousal can generate boredom. The distinction between relaxation, a common motivation for holidays, and boredom is, from this viewpoint, dependent upon a level of arousal that is sufficient for relaxation, but is not so low as to induce boredom. Iso-Ahola and Weissenger (1990) define boredom within the area of recreation in terms of available leisure time – too much time for the task in hand generates boredom, as can too little time. Allied to this is the nature of the task and the challenge it presents in relation to the skill of the participant. Research would seem to indicate that factors associated with boredom include skill, challenge, habituation and familiarity, novelty, and available time (Hill and Perkins 1985; Iso-Ahola and Weissenger 1990; Voelkl and Ellis 1990). Patrick (1982) describes boredom as being a sense of dissatisfaction, disinclination to action, longing with an inability to designate what is longed for, a passive expectant attitude, a sense that time hangs heavy or stands still, and a sense of emotional bankruptcy.

Hill and Perkins (1985) associate boredom with frustration, noting that frustration occurs when a constraint of either time or challenge exists, or is perceived to exist, thereby limiting the availability of an optimally satisfying behaviour. It can be argued that frustration is associated with higher levels of arousal, and with a sense of helplessness arising from an inability to exercise control, which may be a stage that precedes apathy whereby the inability to influence events leads to a lapse of action. Within the holiday industry it can be suggested that this mode of behaviour is exhibited in the case of delayed aircraft, particularly in the case of returning home from a package holiday where the tourist is in a foreign milieu. Iso-Ahola and Weissenger (1990:5) define boredom as 'a mismatch between desired arousal-producing characteristics of leisure experiences, and perceptual or actual availability of such leisure experiences'. This is in evidence when holiday-makers encounter a delayed charter flight on the return from their package holiday. The holiday-maker on a package holiday is collected by the coach at the expected time, arrives at the airport, and after an expected wait is told that there is a delay. In many cases there is little information as to the length of that delay. Faced with uncertainty, arousal increases, annoyance is exhibited. Further delay exacerbates the annoyance, but the couriers are notable by their absence. Annoyance leads to action as the holiday-maker seeks information, attempts to find the couriers, and demands some form of immediate compensation, perhaps in terms of a free meal. But if the hours drag by, and there is the realisation that the holiday-maker can do little, the annoyance lapses into apathy. There is indeed, to slightly misquote Iso-Ahola and Weissenger, a mismatch between the initial arousal-producing situation and the perceived ability of generating desired change.

Two elements are immediately obvious from this approach – the first is that satisfaction derived from an experience may be dependent upon the level of original expectation (i.e. it is a form of gap analysis), and secondly, satisfaction may be a factor of personality in that different people react to the same environment in different ways.

Iso-Ahola and Weissenger (1990) have developed a sixteen-item Leisure Boredom Scale which has been applied in at least three studies and found to have good reliability. But, when subjected to factor analysis, only one factor emerged. Close analysis of the scale also shows its high correlation with single items such as 'boredom frequency' and 'depth of boredom'. It might be suggested that, given the number of items, possibly leisure boredom is a reasonably homogeneous concept, and thus the scale is of a unitary nature.

THE CONCEPT OF FLOW

In the literature relating to recreation the work of Csikszentimihalyi (1975) has been pivotal for developing a concept of 'flow', which has initiated significant research. Much of this research has emanated from North America, and was initially restricted to outdoor and wilderness recreation. More recently it has been applied to other recreation pursuits. For example, Mannell *et al.* (1988) applied it to retirees undertaking exercises in Ontario, while Chick and Roberts (1990) used the dimensions of challenge and skill and resultant 'flow' in a study of Americans playing in pool leagues in bars on a Monday night. However, the concept has hardly received a mention in the literature relating to tourism. Pearce (1988:26) makes reference to Csikszentimihalyi, but does so within the context of 'flow' being an aspect of Maslow's (1970) 'peak' experience. Ryan (1991b:44) also briefly mentions the concept, and at a descriptive level applies it to the holiday-maker experience, but does not provide any empirical evidence. Yet the concept would certainly appear to be applicable as an aid to understanding tourist behaviour, and the sources of satisfaction and dissatisfaction. (See Figure 3.1.)

Csikszentimihalyi (1975:36) defines the 'flow' experience as 'one of complete involvement of the actor with his activity' and identifies the following seven indicators of its frequency and occurrence:

(a) the perception that personal skills and challenges posed by an activity are in balance;
(b) the centring of attention;
(c) the loss of self-consciousness;
(d) an unambiguous feedback to a person's actions;
(e) feelings of control over actions and environment;
(f) a momentary loss of anxiety and constraint; and
(g) feelings of enjoyment or pleasure.

(Csikszentimihalyi 1975:38–48)

However, for the flow experience to be felt there are four prerequisites:

1   participation is voluntary;
2   the benefits of participation in an activity are perceived to derive from factors intrinsic to participation in the activity;
3   a facilitative level of arousal is experienced during participation in the activity;
4   there is a psychological commitment to the activity in which they are participating.

Generally speaking, it can be assumed that these four prerequisites are present within a vacation setting. Incidentally, with reference to the prerequisite of facilitating level of arousal being present, this is not the same as stating an absence of stress. As previously noted, stress can be both facilitating and debilitating – the difference being determined by an individual's ability to cope with a given situation – which ability is in part determined by past experience, skill level, and predisposition to disenabling degrees of arousal. These factors are in turn a function of an interaction of learning and biology that establishes personality.

Arguably the potential for a flow experience exists within work as well as leisure situations, and three questions arise.

1   Is it possible to distinguish between the individual prerequisites and attributes of the flow concept as envisaged by Csikszentimihalyi?
2   Is there relative dependence between the prerequisites and attributes?
3   Is there a difference between the work and leisure situation?

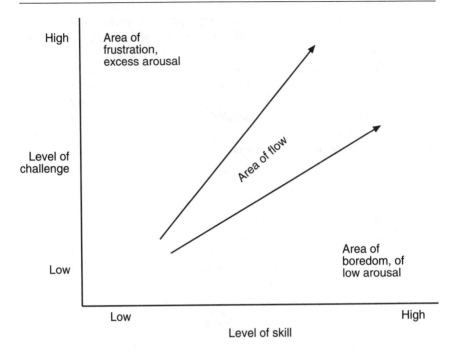

Figure 3.2 The concept of flow

These issues have been examined in a series of studies. Tinsley and Tinsley sought to establish the importance of the quality of leisure experience in self-development when they stated: 'The increased self awareness and personal growth associated with participation in leisure activities are the result of leisure experience' (1986:39). In a later and more detailed study, Baldwin and Tinsley (1988:266) concluded that: 'there is evidence to support the notion that the four requisites of leisure experience are more readily perceived in leisure rather than in work'. They also noted that the results for the prerequisite 'commitment' are 'troublesome'. The F-score for this factor between work and leisure situations had a value of 1.37 (compared to 136.01 for perceived freedom), and hence was not significant (p = 0.25). They propose three possible explanations – the theory is incorrect, the items used did not measure the variable as intended, and third, both work and leisure require commitment. They tend to the third explanation based on the mean scores of respondents.

Equally, correlations are found between the prerequisites and the attributes, but inasmuch as the prerequisite conditions must be present prior to an individual experiencing leisure, this is not surprising. They comment, 'correlations may be expected between such dimensions as increased sensitivity to feelings and increased intensity of emotions or total absorption and lack of focus on self.' (Baldwin and Tinsley 1988:266).

The relationship that Pearce (1982, 1988) draws with the 'peak' experience described by Maslow (1970) as part of the process of self-actualisation is self-evident, but it can be postulated that 'flow' can be experienced in a holiday activity such as wind-surfing. As the concept has been developed by Voelkl and Ellis (1990), and others, it is situation and activity specific and relates to dimensions such as challenge and skill. Thus, an experienced windsurfer will gain 'flow' from a balance of challenge and skill presented by sets of wind and wave conditions unsuitable for a beginner. The conditions suitable for the beginner pose inadequate conditions for the expert, and thus generate boredom, while the conditions that are invigorating to the expert generate stress and feelings of risk for the beginner. The attraction of the concept for researchers studying satisfaction to be derived from sports and outdoor recreation is thus obvious.

However, it has been argued (Mannell *et al.* 1988) that the concept has a wider application. For the concept of 'flow' to be more fully understood, it has to incorporate a role for expectation and purpose (motivation). In the case of the windsurfing example, if the expert windsurfer wishes to practice freestyle sailing, then high winds would inhibit this, thereby generating dissatisfaction. Equally, therefore, placed in a context of holidaying activities, it is the balance between challenge, skill, motivation, and expectation that determines the experience of flow. Mannell *et al.* found that 'there was strong evidence for the prediction that higher levels of flow accompany freely chosen activities ... freely chosen activities are not only more likely to be labelled leisure, but to be accompanied by higher levels of flow' (1988:299). The process is also evident in many of the more 'passive' aspects of holiday behaviour. For example, sightseers at places of historic interest often derive greater satisfaction when given some information about what to look for. The provision of 'expertise' informs the activity of 'looking' into one of 'seeing' and 'understanding' – thereby generating greater satisfaction.

Mannell *et al.* also raise the question that the concept of intrinsically motivated behaviour poses a problem as to the direction of causality. Does the satisfaction come from the act of participation, or from the result of participation? They clarify their distinction by reference to a parent playing with a child – a sense of the need to play generates an extrinsic reward that gives rise to intrinsic satisfaction. In this instance, an extrinsically imposed constraint (the child's insistence for play), which is normally associated with lower levels of satisfaction, can actually generate high satisfaction levels (the sense of well-being arising from play with the child). They pose the question – is it a cause or an outcome that is being discussed?

One question that has arisen is whether gender is a factor determining the level of flow. Arguably feminine traits are those of nurture and warmth; as emotionally expressive and environmentally receptive, they might arguably score higher on some items used to measure degree of flow. Other more masculine traits such as those of dominance, aggression and control could score higher on items relating to competition and control of environment. Hirschman (1984) points out that allocation of male–female traits on the basis of gender alone is, in any case, too simplistic. She argues that while people are born male or female, it is through the process of socialisation that male and female roles are learnt. Consequently there may be congruence or otherwise between gender identity and psychological sexual identity that gives rise to confirmation of sex type, cross-sexing, or androgynous-undifferentiated roles. In a study of 440 adults she reports that gender was not a predictor of ability to engage in 'absorbing experiences', and was only significant in predicting levels of competitiveness. Sexual role as measured by the Personal Attributes Questionnaire and Sex Role Inventory was a predictor in dimensions of the flow experience such as levels of involvement, alertness, competitiveness, and attitudes to adventure.

From the viewpoint of this study, the significance of Hirschman's findings is the hypothesis that gender is not a determinant of holiday satisfaction where it is deemed to be the outcome of a flow experience. But it can be contended that psychological sexual identity is partly a tautological, or possibly definitional question for it is subsumed by the wider issue of self-perception. For example, some females may value competitiveness as a statement of self-value, and its categorisation of it being a male trait as simply a secondary consideration.

From this review, what does appear to matter is that the flow concept has a validity for recreational pursuits, and hence, by implication, for vacations. Both prerequisites and attributes of the flow concept are to be found within holiday circumstances. Hence the concept may also help in the understanding of what constitutes a satisfactory holiday experience.

NEEDS ANALYSIS

So far a behaviourist approach has been adopted whereby behaviour is perceived as goal directed, and thus motivation is an important determinant of tourist behaviour and subsequent satisfaction derived from the experience. Yet one of the most quoted theories of motivation is that of Maslow (1970), and inasmuch as recreation and tourism are concerned with re-creating self, finding self, and in short are related to the spiritual objectives referred to by Smith and Godbey (1991), as supported by the work of Tinsley (1986), it seems appropriate to consider motivation towards self-actualisation within the holiday experience as an alternative approach (see Table 3.1).

Within the field of recreation and tourism, Maslow's work has been seminal. His hierarchy of needs, stemming from the basic wants of bodily survival to the establishment of healthy psyches through a process of self-knowledge and fulfilment of potential, has been the basic model for a number of theories. In spite of its popularity it should be noted that 'his need hierarchy has received little clear or consistent support from the research evidence' (Witt and Wright 1990). Nonetheless, it is possible to develop hypotheses from the basic formulation that have been subjected to testing, and two that need to be considered in some detail in that they relate to tourism are the Leisure Motivation Scale associated with

Table 3.1 Maslow's need hierarchy

Basic needs	
Physiological needs	Hunger, thirst, sex, sleep, air.
Safety needs	Needs freedom from threat or danger; a secure, orderly and a predictable environment.
Love (social) needs	Feeling of belonging, affectionate relationships, friendship, group achievement.
Esteem needs	Self-respect, achievement, self-confidence, reputation, recognition, prestige.
Need for self-actualisation	Self-fulfilment, realising one's potential.
Higher needs	

Source: Adapted from Maslow 1943.

Ragheb and Beard (1982), and the concept of a travel career postulated by Pearce (1988).

THE LEISURE MOTIVATION SCALE

From this stance, the Leisure Motivation Scale of Ragheb and Beard (1982) represents a significant starting point as its constructs can be related to the literature that refers to tourism satisfaction as reviewed by Mathieson and Wall (1982), Pearce (1982, 1988) and Ryan (1991b). Beard and Ragheb (1983:225) argue that four motives determine satisfaction to be gained from leisure pursuits. These are:

1   The intellectual component, which 'assesses the extent to which individuals are motivated to engage in leisure activities which involve ... mental activities such as learning, exploring, discovering, thought or imagining'.
2   The social component 'assesses the extent to which individuals engage in leisure activities for social reasons. This component includes two basic needs ... the need for friendship and interpersonal relationships, while the second is the need for the esteem of others'.
3   The competence-mastery component assesses the extent to which 'individuals engage in leisure activities in order to achieve, master, challenge, and compete. The activities are usually physical in nature'.
4   The stimulus-avoidance component of leisure motivation 'assesses the drive to escape and get away from over-stimulating life situations. It is the need for some individuals to avoid social contacts, to seek solitude and calm conditions; and for others it is to seek to rest and to unwind themselves'.

It can be argued that these components echo closely tourism literature relating to tourist motivations. Iso-Ahola (1982) has referred to two motivations for touristic activity, the desire to leave behind an environment, and to seek an intrinsic reward. However, both motivations interact with personal or inter-personal areas of activity, thus giving rise to a dynamic dialectical process as the tourist seeks and avoids push/pull motivations and interaction with others. The stimulus-avoidance, the intellectual and social factors discussed by Ragheb and Beard (1983) are present, albeit within a different framework. For Iso-Ahola, the attributes of the experience are interactive and holistic in nature, while Ragheb and Beard disaggregate them.

Many of the studies that utilise the Beard and Ragheb scales seek to relate them to specific periods of activity, and in this respect the research of Loundsbury and Hoopes (1988) is potentially important in that it sought to establish its stability of motivational factors. Stability can be assessed in a number of ways (e.g. mean scores, rankings, and the persistence of factor weightings). Loundsbury and Hoopes utilised rankings of factors over a five-year period, including the factors taken from the Leisure Motivation Scale, and concluded that:

> The present results indicate a most encouraging and even surprising level of stability over a five-year period for leisure activity participation as well as, to a lesser extent, the leisure motivation variables studied' (Loundsbury and Hoopes 1988:130).

In short, there appears to be at least some medium-term consistency, while arguably such consistency is not inherently opposed to the concept of a longer-term 'holiday career' as proposed by Pearce (1988:78–81) and Laing (1987:195–200). However, there have been few studies applying the Leisure Motivation Scale to holiday-taking, although Ryan (1993) reported that: (a) the scale had validity when applied to a UK sample; and (b) it was possible to construct a holiday motivation scale from it that led to specific clusters of holiday-takers who valued different attributes of holiday destinations.

THE CONCEPT OF MINDLESSNESS

One factor that must be taken into account by any researcher is the notion that those participating in recreation and tourism are not necessarily processing their motivations and sources of leisure in any conscious manner. As already quoted above, Laing (1987) has commented upon the habitual response in the booking of the package holiday. Langer and Newman (1979) and Langer and Piper (1987) have argued that there is a predisposition by researchers to attribute to people rational, logical, and goal orientated behaviour in situations where all too often actual behaviour is characterised by 'mindlessness'. This is behaviour that is governed by rules and habituation and is opposed to mindful behaviour that is rule forming, and thus is 'engaged in creating categories and distinctions'.

It can be argued that 'mindlessness' will be associated with many of the tourist activities that are essentially passive in their nature. There is perhaps a danger that the terms 'mindful' and 'mindlessness' will attract normative interpretations, but this is not what is meant by the terminology as used by Langer and subsequent writers such as Pearce (1988). Relaxation by the swimming pool may be characterised by 'mindlessness', yet functionally it is important for 'relaxation' is required by the holiday-taker. However, in the reporting of the satisfaction to be derived from the experience, unless the requirement for the relaxation motivation is very high, it is likely that there will be little recall of the events of the day, and compared with 'peak' experiences, will be scored as a source of only moderate satisfaction. Yet, it is a common mode of behaviour for tourists, and hence must fulfil some need.

Pearce (1988) refers to the work of Argyle, Furnham and Graham (1981) who categorised eight features of social situations. These are:

1   Goals – purposes or ends of social behaviour.
2   Rules – shared beliefs that regulate behaviour.
3   Roles – duties and obligations attending social positions people occupy.
4   Repertoire of elements – sum of behaviours appropriate to a situation.
5   Sequences – ordering of the repertoire of behaviours.
6   Concepts and cognitive structure – shared definitions and understandings needed to operate in social situations.
7   Environmental setting – props, spaces, barriers, modifiers that influence the situation.
8   Language and speech – the codes of speech inherent in language.

From this Pearce refers to the importance of 'scripts' (1988:38–42) in tourist situations. There are many situations, from ordering a meal in a restaurant to sightseeing in groups, where expected behaviour patterns are conformed to, and opportunities for generating 'remembered' experiences are comparatively few. Thus, in one research study undertaken by Pearce, caravan travellers in Australia who undertook a 320-kilometre drive were generally only able to remember 4 or 5 features of the journey – in a sense it was a 'scripted, mindless' experience.

Obviously scripted behaviour and mindlessness as defined by Langer and her associates are closely related concepts. Ryan (1991b:159–60) lists the variables that are associated with drunken behaviour by 'lager louts' on the Spanish Costas. It is observed that one variable is 'holiday destinations that are not "foreign" – i.e. the general milieu is in fact a familiar one to this type of tourist, and is primarily one of pubs, clubs and discos'. Allied to the expectation of a specific type of holiday experience, a 'scripted' experience occurs whereby the norms of peer cohesiveness are enforced, and rule-governed behaviour can be observed. Yet, in this instance, the achievement of the expected 'script', the sense of cohesiveness felt, generates highly satisfactory experiences for the participants, and recall of various events may be good. Thus, it can be contended that 'scripted', 'rule governed, mindlessness' is not necessarily associated with poor recall, and by implication, only moderate levels of satisfaction. What distinguishes this type of situation from that described by Pearce and Langer?

Arguably, the expectation of a specific type of holiday experience has a role to play, plus the environmental setting. This latter factor has two functions to perform. First, in the sense defined by Argyle *et al.* (1981), it permits certain forms of behaviour (i.e. a repertoire and sequence). Second, it is permissible because it is not home. Once again, the role of the holiday as a means of irresponsibility, as recognised by Cohen (1979) and others, needs to be acknowledged.

THE CONCEPT OF A TOURIST CAREER

This concept is relatively new within tourism literature. The fullest statement of the concept appears in Pearce (1988); quoting Hughes (1937:409–10), he adopts the definition of 'career' as being:

> the moving perspective in which the person sees his life as whole and interprets the meaning of his various attributes, actions, and things which happen to him (Pearce 1988:27).

Pearce agrees with Hughes that it has both objective and subjective components, but in view of the previous section on 'mindlessness' it has, arguably, further components. It is 'mindful', that is, operates at a conscious level, and possesses a temporal component. The 'mindlessness' of the moment, or rather the actions and experiences of that time, are subsequently interpreted as a factor contributing to a sum of experience, which accumulatively affects the needs of the tourist and hence determines the ability of any one destination or attraction to satisfy the tourist. Pearce appears to argue that the tourist career takes a form of progression that follows Maslow's needs hierarchy. Evidence is provided from work undertaken by Mills (1985) whereby multi-dimensional scaling of responses made by skiers yields a fourfold classification of safety needs, esteem needs, affiliation needs and self-actualisation needs. An implication is that the more experienced skier moves from concern about safety towards the self-actualisation process. Pearce also seeks to progress the concept further by arguing that prior to self-actualisation, the needs have both an external and internal orientation (this can be seen as a refinement of a concept introduced by Iso-Ahola in 1982 when he introduced the same considerations). However an apparent weakness might exist at the safety need stage (Pearce 1988:31). The self-directed need is orientated towards self-preservation, the external orientation is categorised as a concern over the safety of others. Arguably, action prompted by the wish to save others that involves the placing of self at risk is not an action conducted at the same level of Maslow's need hierarchy. Certainly, Hampden (1971) would consider the risking of self as a sign of 'radical', or 'self actualised man'.

An additional factor to be considered is that the actual data provided by Mills (1985) is possibly not as strong as Pearce implies. Indeed, Mills himself provides many caveats to his data. For example:

The analysis revealed the existence of a second dimension which produces a 'radex' theoretical structure instead of a simple hierarchy. The two-dimensional radex corresponded to the prior defined mapping sentence. Admittedly, the portrayal of the radex structure in the resulting space diagram was *somewhat weak* due to the marginally significant coefficient of alienation (0.21).

The smallest space diagram showed evidence of the self centred/non self centred distinction operating for safety needs as well as esteem needs. More than merely being an aspect of one type of need, results of this study indicated that the self centred/non self centred dichotomy constitutes a second dimension which *modulates esteem and safety needs*. Groves *et al.* (1975) suggested this second dimension may also operate for self actualization in the sphere of work.

The content validity in terms of numbers of items and diversity within some of the operational measures in this study is admittedly weak. However, the operational measures are valid in other respects (Mills 1985:197). [Emphasis added]

On the other hand weak evidence does exist in a study of 488 visitors to the Australian theme park Timbertown (Pearce 1988:81). On the basis of seven questions relating to different stages of the Maslow hierarchy, and cross-tabulating results with the number of previous visits, Pearce argues that 'repeat visitors show more interest in relationship and self-esteem levels' (ibid.:78). However, it would appear that this is not at statistically significant levels. With reference to the satisfaction derived from the visit, the mean scores vary from 5.30 to 5.83 on a 6-point scale by level of need, and the only statistically significant finding would appear to be: 'Scheffé post hoc comparison indicates that the principal difference in the means lies between the self actualisation mean and the family and friends [affiliation] mean'. However, it may be pertinent to query why it is expected that satisfaction should be greater for those motivated by self-actualisation needs. Satisfaction, it can be argued, is a function of the congruence of need and experience (i.e. a need met by an appropriate experience generates satisfaction). Yet, this too may be simplistic. Ryan (1991b) in his model of linkages between expectation and satisfaction, stresses the adaptive ability of the tourist:

The interpretation of the travel experience and the nature of the resort area with the personality generates both perceptions of gaps between the resort zone and expectations, and governs the nature of interactions with others, but then certain social and psychological skills also come into play in the sense of being able to perceive authenticity, suspend disbelief when required, and conduct positive sets of relationships. These attributes help shape travel and activity patterns which permit the fulfilment of the original or amended expectations and hence create satisfaction (1991b:47–9).

The concept of a travel or tourism career can also be questioned in the sense that experienced tourists are capable of selecting various types of holidays for differing needs – something that is possible with multi-holiday taking within appropriate time scales. Thus, one holiday might be directed at meeting needs of family bonding (affiliation needs in Maslow's terminology), while a second holiday within the same year might be motivated by a wish to exercise specific skills (status or self-actualisation needs). The sequential pattern of such holiday taking is determined not by psychological development but by other more prosaic matters such as, for example, school holiday periods. On the other hand, a longitudinal study over a period of several years could, it can be contended, begin to show an increased frequency of holiday type orientated towards self-actualisation needs. But again other variables would intrude in interpreting these data. Life stage *per se* would indicate a reduction of holidays orientated towards bonding child and parents.

Laing (1987) states that tourism literature relating to motivation reveals 'a muddle and lacks cohesion', and adheres to Iso-Ahola's models whereby there is a separation of initial travel desire from specific motivation, and, in consequence, there is some mental conflict experienced by the traveller. Laing also queries the concept of a travel career, by referring to the work of Young and Wilmott (1960:15) where it is argued that older people do not walk more often than younger people because they are old, but rather because they always walked more. One of the hypotheses tested by Laing is that holiday choice can be explained by reference to a leisure career, and Laing tends to find evidence not of a developing nature of holiday-taking, but rather a confirmation of past experiences found to be satisfactory. Age, he comments (1987:195) is a predictor of familiarity – in his sample of 303 holiday-makers originating from Hull, 80 per cent of those between 16- to 29-year olds visited new destinations, whereas less than 50 per cent of pensioners selected new locations. Older holiday-takers like taking coach trips; not, argues Laing, because of an intrinsic fear of flying, but simply because when they started their holiday careers air flight was not commonplace. Further, he comments:

> older travellers tend to involve themselves with the host environment because this is the type of behaviour with which they have become accustomed – it represents habits that pre-date the rush to the sun soaked coast line ... behaviour on holiday is also an outcome of previous holiday experience ... confidence as a function of previous experience determines the types of activity pursued once on holiday (1987:230).

For purposes of simplifying the argument, it appears that two viewpoints of holiday career can be said to exist. On the one hand there is the developmental viewpoint argued by Pearce, where holiday-makers learn and so progress along the Maslow hierarchy towards higher needs, and second, the process of early habits becoming ingrained, whereby tourists repeat that process found to be satisfactory on earlier trips. Both viewpoints stress the importance of the holiday experience as a determinant of future behaviour. For example Laing comments:

the holidaymaker visiting seaside resorts is more likely to be a relatively inexperienced traveller than is the visitor to traditional, scenic locations, or in particular, to special activity centres. Holiday experience thus seems one means of fostering more specific holiday intentions (1987:331–2).

This latter comment by Laing would imply that he also recognises that a developmental process is possible, and this indicates why the two extreme viewpoints of holiday career are seen as simplistic. The process of development or confirmation of behaviour arises from the satisfaction gained from the holiday trip. Thus, the process of confirmation/development is a function of:

(a) actual experience;
(b) perception of the experience as satisfactory or unsatisfactory;
(c) personality in terms of whether that experience is a trigger for returning to the destination, or for exploring new places.

A further factor to be considered is whether personal development can be observed from behaviour. On a macro level, this reopens the question of whether a person returning to the same destination is in fact simply repeating past experiences. From the viewpoint of Maslow's model, there is nothing inherent in the process towards self-actualisation that requires a change of venue. At a micro level, the repetitive actions might be interpreted differently by the participant at different times. For example, a factor motivating repetition of a visit might be a wish to reminiscence.

In the studies undertaken of travel career the methodologies used were not sufficiently sophisticated to permit analysis of these questions. Not, it must be added, because the researchers were necessarily unaware of these issues, but because there is, at this embryonic stage of the concept, a need to assess whether there is prima-facie evidence for the concept to merit further analysis of its working. Indeed, Laing reports that the linkages between former holiday experience and holiday choice were weak. Even combining it with occupation, former holiday choice only correlated with current holiday choice at a probability level of 0.02 (Laing 1987:269). A further consideration is that those operating at a higher need level may also seek actions that confirm lower order needs for both self and others. For example, the self-actualised parent will engage in behaviour that confirms bonds with young children, while simultaneously meeting the infant's needs for security and love. Holidays are frequent occasions of such behaviour. Additionally, it can be argued that the self-actualised may be less in need of the 'escape' patterns provided by the holiday – or even the provision of the new and unfamiliar. The self-actualised person, after all, is able to find that which is new in the familiar object or event. There is a wonder in the miracle of the daily rising and setting of the sun.

IMPLICATIONS OF THESE FACTORS

In conclusion, therefore, while the concept of travel career is important in linking past and future holiday behaviour, and while past experience is important in determining expectations of any one holiday occurring in the immediate future, it is perhaps a secondary factor that meshes with more immediate primary factors as a determinant of holiday satisfaction, and is itself, an outcome of that interaction.

Additionally, it has been shown in a number of studies that attitudes, especially with relation to items considered important, can be quite durable. Reference has been made to the way attitudes towards leisure motivation as measured by the Ragheb and Beard Leisure Motivation Scale have been shown to have been sustained for periods of at least five years. In the area of resident attitudes towards tourism, there is, for example, some evidence that these change little between off-peak and high season periods. For example, Montgomery and Ryan (1994) found little significant change between clusters of residents in a study of residents of Bakewell, Derbyshire.

More significantly, both in the sense of measuring attitudes that are fundamental to personality and perception of life, and in terms of the duration of these studies, Diener and his associates have found consistency of attitudes towards general satisfaction and perception of quality of life. Diener argues that life satisfaction is emotive and judgemental, is subjective, may be positive or negative, and 'resides in the experience of the individual'. Further, these feelings of well-being include a global assessment rather than a 'narrow assessment of one life domain' (Diener, 1992:4). In general measures of well-being and satisfaction, Headey and Wearing (1989) found correlations of 0.5 to over 0.6 during a six-year period. Costa and McCrae (1988) report $r = 0.57$ between spouse and self-rating over a similar period of 6 years. Evidence for the sustainability of such attitudes across work and leisure is provided by Diener and Larsen (1984), which found correlations for pleasant and unpleasant affects of 0.70 and 0.74 respectively across such life domains.

Feelings of well-being and satisfaction can diverge (McNeil *et al.* 1986), and this can be seen in holiday situations. In the short term the queasy stomach, the mosquito bite and other such holiday experiences can produce unpleasant feelings of a distinct lack of well-being, yet the holiday experience can still be judged satisfactory. The important point, however, is that a general sense of well-being and perception of life being 'satisfactory' can be important in determining the general satisfaction that is derived from a holiday, even where events within that holiday might be less than ideal.

With reference to the impact of the cathartic experience which Pearce and others have noticed on the holiday, and which from a Maslowian viewpoint might be considered as an important function of the holiday, it is of interest to note that Diener *et al.* (1991) note that it is the frequency of the positive experience, rather than the intensity of experience, which generates higher scores on measures of well-being and satisfaction with life. One interpretation of some of their findings is that humans perhaps seek a homeostasis of emotional life, because it is noted that the moments of intense, positive, affective emotion seem to follow periods of negative psychological experience, and it is perhaps the net effect rather than the totality of the peak experience which is added to the general perception of life.

Although Diener's studies and those of co-workers in this field have not been concerned with the impact of holidays *per se*, it does seem that these views are of importance to the researcher into holiday-maker satisfaction. Some of the satisfaction that is expressed by holiday-makers is due to this general sense of well-being, and hence if this is strong, a single measure of 'holiday satisfaction' may be primarily composed of general 'life satisfaction' rather than a refection of the specifics of the holiday experience.

SUMMARY

By its nature, the above review has omitted many of the subtleties of the arguments advanced by their proponents, but nonetheless it is sufficient to indicate a number of issues relating to research into tourist satisfaction. It would appear that any such work is aided by:

1   Not only a conceptual basis of the construction of attitude as discussed in the following chapter, but also a construct of satisfaction that recognises:
    (a) the gaps and congruence between expectation and perception of the reality of the holiday destination;
    (b) the ability of the holiday-maker to cope with life in 'non-home' environments; to be able to generate 'flow'. Such flow can be generated by either risk avoidance or risk enhancement policies by the selection of the milieu of the holiday;
    (c) the importance of past experience as a learning mechanism, either in terms of a developing tourist career as proposed by Pearce (1988), or in a Skinnerian response as confirmation of positive feedback.
2   An awareness of the scripted situation. Holidays may offer opportunities for 'peak' experiences. However, the reality of much holiday time is not one of catharsis, but of situations nearer to 'mindlessness'. Is 'mindlessness' a facet of relaxation? If so, holidays might be classified as 'memorable' or 'unmemorable' – but the latter does not signify any lack of satisfaction if 'unmindful relaxation' was the goal.
3   Holidays involve the fulfilment of motivations – but motivations become goals, goals determine behaviour, and, in the search for a satisfying holiday, holiday-makers engage in adaptive behaviours to secure the success of a satisfying holiday.

Chapter 4

Attitudes and measurement

INTRODUCTION

Chapter 3 reviewed a number of concepts relating to psychological components that affect the frame of mind of the tourist. Questions of risk, arousal, and the ability to meet the challenges posed by travel were briefly discussed. It was concluded that satisfaction was possibly a consequence of the perception of these events as dictated by the individual's interpretation of the interaction entered into at the destination. Such perceptions are born of the holiday-maker's personality, and the goals that they deem to be important.

In this chapter the concept of lifestyle is introduced. This is an important concept in contemporary marketing, and results in classifications of personalities, and holiday-makers, in terms of their attitudes, opinions, behaviour and demographics. Based in many instances on cluster analysis (described in Chapter 12), it is a pragmatic proxy for personality. Inasmuch as these classifications are based on attitude, and if it is accepted that the tourist career is based on the evolution of attitudes towards holiday-making, then it behoves the researcher into tourist satisfaction to be aware of at least some concepts of attitude measurement. Additionally, a brief review is undertaken in this chapter of some of the issues surrounding different measures of attitude and whether possibly each approach examines another facet.

Another approach to the tourist career is to link it with life stage. Holiday requirements vary as people mature and as their responsibilities to other family members change. Additionally, they may seek to carry through with them the results of past learning derived from holidays, notably those activities that gave them the highest levels of satisfaction. Lawson (1991), Bojanic (1992) and Ryan (1994) all argue that a family life cycle strongly influences tourist behaviour, especially if a 'modernised' cycle is studied whereby the traditional life cycle is extended by the addition of single parents and middle-aged couples without children.

WORK–LEISURE RATIOS

The concept of lifestyle is important in current marketing practices. Market researchers no longer seek to predict consumer behaviour solely on the grounds of socio-economic background or life stage. The advent of cheap computing combined with the introduction of such items as postcodes has led in the 1980s to the emergence of geo-demographics as an important marketing tool. Evolving partially from these practices, and as a development from earlier work which sought to identify consumers on the basis of psychological profiles, psychographics is being allied with the geo-demographic databases to establish the potentially powerful marketing tools that lie behind targeting clients.

It can be argued that lifestyle is related to work–leisure ratios. What people do and the way in which they divide their time between work, non-paid work time and leisure and touristic activities is a significant determinant of the lifestyle cluster to which they may be allocated. The work–leisure ratio has been the subject of extensive sociological research for over sixty years. A fourfold classification of possible relationships between occupation and its daily realities with recreation and touristic behaviour can be discerned. These are, briefly:

(a) *The trade-off hypothesis.* Under this scenario people specifically select between more time spent at work, or time spent in leisure. An inverse relationship between income and time available for leisure results. Grafton and Taylor (1990) and Ryan (1991b) apply an indifference curve analysis to analyse partially the changes in holiday behaviour whereby an upward sloping demand curve perhaps describes some types of contemporary holiday-taking.

(b) *The compensation hypothesis.* The premise here is that the deficiencies that arise in the work life of an individual motivate compensating behaviour during recreation and leisure time. Those with boring work fulfil their needs for excitement through active leisure pursuits.

(c) *The 'spill-over' hypothesis.* In part this has its origin in Durkheim's concept of anomic societies, whereby the depressing nature of work removes the ability to initiate, and in consequence those with boring work are not able to generate compensatory activities. By the same token, those with active, fulfilling work lives are more likely to have similar leisure lifestyles.

(d) *The 'neutralist' hypothesis.* This states that there is no relationship between work and leisure – they are different spheres of action which generate their own patterns of expectations and behaviours without reference to either set.

At an intuitive level both compensation and spillover hypotheses have much to recommend them. Prima-facie evidence exists for compensation theory at a community level in the 1930s as mining communities in South Wales and Yorkshire developed a tradition of an active political and cultural life outside the mines. Support comes for the spillover theory in the studies of boredom referred to above, where Patrick (1982) analyses boredom as consisting of dissatisfaction, disinclination to action, passive expectant attitude and an inability to escape meaningless routines. The concept of flow is strongly associated with the ability to make choices. Tinsley and Tinsley (1986) reviewed the literature relating to leisure satisfaction and identified 23 studies where life satisfaction and leisure satisfaction appeared to be correlated.

However, the position is far from clear in that there is also significant evidence to support the neutralist position. Zuzanek and Mannell (1983) incline to the neutralist position, but conclude that there is a 'multi-faceted and multi-dimensional nature of the work–leisure relationship'. Loundsbury and Hoopes (1988) also contribute to the discussion in their finding that life-satisfaction scores were more stable than non-work satisfaction over a five-year period. By implication this would imply potential changes in the work–leisure ratio, although the nature of the change is far from clear. Also, what needs to be considered in this finding is that the term 'non-work' cannot automatically be equated with 'leisure and recreational time'.

In fact, as changes of occupational activity take place, arguably the work–leisure ratio is becoming less important for many, and indeed the work/non-work divide becomes less clear. The business lunch and entertaining on the golf course are perhaps extreme examples of where work is not devoid of some leisure, while the use of non-work time for educational purposes has potential implications for current and future work patterns and careers. As early as 1975 Bacon commented that 'work has lost its former hegemony and centrality in most people's lives and has become a much more marginal experience'. For many people in the 1980s this may have become increasingly true, but by the end of the decade in both North America and Europe attention was being drawn to the 'harried leisure classes' (Shaw 1990; Kay and Jackson 1990). It has been noted, for example by Kay and Jackson, that it is the most active who complain most of the lack of time. Perversely, as the distinctions between work and leisure become more difficult to demarcate clearly, so work begins to re-establish a prime role in some people's lives, thereby affecting the demand for the type of, and time of holiday taken. Mintel reports on the short break overseas market, for example, indicate a heavy demand from AB groups living in the south-east of England; it is tempting to hypothesise that much of this demand is originating from income-rich but time-short executives.

GEO-DEMOGRAPHIC SYSTEMS

The debate on work–leisure ratios has a long history, but within that time the nature of society has changed. Arguably it is the breakdown of a homogeneous society into a more heterogeneous one where socio-economic and life stage variables are no longer good predictors that has motivated the search for lifestyle clusters that can predict consumer behaviour.

For academic researchers in the field of tourism this has represented problems. The type of data based on the detailed lifestyle clusters of the commercial market analysis companies such as CCN Marketing with its MOSAIC and Persona geo-demographic and 'behaviourgraphic' database has not readily been available to academic researchers. Essentially this has been due to the limited budgets that have characterised academic research into personal holiday activities and motivations, but, as discussed below, these database systems are now becoming available on microcomputers.

Geo-demographic systems incorporate socio-economic data into not simply a listing of people's addresses, but also a description of the neighbourhood in which they live. The basic data that most geo-demographic databases will hold are drawn from the census of population updated in the case of Britain by the annual electoral register, which permits an identification of areas characterised by stable or rapidly changing populations. Consequently the database is likely to hold records of the names of people at a given address, the size of house in terms of number of rooms, whether the residents own or rent the house, the occupation of the members of the household and their educational level. In addition, the systems will contain descriptions of housing areas, for example, MOSAIC type 25 – smart inner city flats with few children, an area of Victorian high status housing, or MOSAIC type 31 – a high unemployment estate with the worst financial problems occupied by those with low income and a high incidence of inability to pay credit.

MOSAIC is the database of CCN Systems, Nottingham, and contains 60 elements in the construction of 58 classifications of neighbourhoods. In addition to the above data it also contains information on the incidence of use of credit cards and other forms of credit, and the levels of county court judgements on debt. MOSAIC, ACORN, PinPoint and other systems all offer similar types of data, and mapping facilities, but differences do exist reflecting the basis of group determination and additional data sources used.

The English Tourist Board now offers a database of over 400,000 names and addresses of people interested in British holidays, and combines this with socio-economic classifications, size of family, car ownership, responses on a holiday lifestyle questionnaire, newspaper readership, and types of holiday preferred.

LIFESTYLE FACTORS

Researchers have begun to apply psychographic and other detail to problems associated with the tourism–work ratio relationship. However, very little of this has been published, and most studies use comparatively broad categories or groupings of population. Faced with this, it is perhaps not surprising to find that, contrary to the intuitive hypotheses that linkages do exist between lifestyle, life satisfaction and types of holiday experiences and satisfactions gained, it is the neutralist hypothesis that tends to be supported. Utrecht and Aldag (1989) examined vacation characteristics against criteria that included trade-off between vacation time and increased income, work-related characteristics and liking to be away from home, but found low alpha coefficients, implying a lack of inherent consistency in the measures used, and possibly doubt over the concepts. Laing (1987) discusses the relationship between work and holiday-taking in some detail, and finds a rather 'mixed bag' of relationships. He writes that 'there is little cause to readily dismiss the role of the quality of work', but later on the same page comments:

> though plausible, each of these connections [variables relating to quality of work] is rather tenuous, for in the present sample no significant associations are uncovered. However, log-linear analysis reveals rather specific links. For example, a greater proportion (19%) of manual workers in strenuous occupations take a holiday than those who don't perceive their work presents such physical demands (11%). It is interesting to reflect that this trend is reversed amongst managers. This hardly qualifies as substantial evidence however, and the realistic conclusion is that work lifestyle measures fail to assist significantly in the identification of the non-holidaymaker (Laing 1987:140).

If it is argued that lifestyle affects holiday behaviour, then it is at the more detailed psychographic level that this evidence must be sought rather than simply in terms of broad work–leisure–tourism ratios. Here there is some evidence relating to basic predisposition actually to taking holidays. Both Laing (1987) and Mazanec (1981) argue that there is a distinction to be made between those whose lifestyle is home orientated and those who are socially orientated. Mazanec states that:

> the leisure type mapping endorses the view that leisure life style barriers to continuous market penetration of travel and tourism are real: some incompatibility exists with certain leisure life styles. It becomes particularly pronounced if 'home-orientedness' combines with low cultural/educational aspiration level (Mazanec 1981).

Laing (1987) comments that the clusters 'home-care' and 'solitary-restful' were more represented amongst non-holiday-takers, and under-represented in holiday-takers than was the case for 'social mixers'. He also notes that there was a higher incidence of passive pursuits amongst non-holiday-takers than is the case for holiday-takers, and argues that the evidence 'helps to substantiate the view that active leisure participation is similarly reflected in holiday participation' (ibid.:141). On the other hand, Ryan and Groves (1987), when they sought to confirm a similar type of relationship for a sample of high income groups corresponding with MOSAIC types M45 and M46 (above average income groups with high levels of educational attainment), were unable to replicate such findings.

LIFESTYLE – A VALID BASIS FOR CLASSIFICATION?

From the commercial viewpoint, the cross-categorisation of geo-demographic groups with holiday-taking behaviour has proven useful in identifying key groups for certain types of holidays. If there is evidence of the intuitive relationship between lifestyle and holiday-taking behaviour existing in an unambiguous manner, it is not to be found in the academic literature, but in the commercial world. Companies such as Hoseasons, Center Parcs, Warners, and Saga are amongst those who utilise such databases to know their clientele better. Data are drawn not only from the geo-demographic databases against which client lists can be checked, but also from cross-referencing such information against returns from omnibus surveys such as the Target Group Index and the National Shoppers' Survey as well as company specific data.

Within the field of market research there has been a long debate about the usefulness of geo-demographics and psychographics compared with more conventional predictors of consumer behaviour such as age, sex, socio-economic class and life-cycle stage. It is not the intention of the author to review this debate in any detail, but some pertinent points need to be borne in mind. The arguments against the continuing use of traditional classifications of consumers are primarily based on the concept that as British society becomes less homogeneous, so these measures become less pertinent. First, it is argued that there is a lack of stability in social class membership. For example, in March 1987 BARB reported that apparently 32 per cent of their panel changed social class over a 12-month period, although this was subsequently amended to 4–7 per cent (BARB, 1987b). In a review of Granada's television panel O'Brien and Ford (1988) reported an apparent change of social class membership by 41 per cent of respondents in a 6-month period. On closer examination, this was corrected to 10 per cent of all respondents. Thus, it seems that forecasts of consumer behaviour are bedevilled by both social class movement and mistakes in class attribution.

Figure 4.1 The conventional life-stage scenario

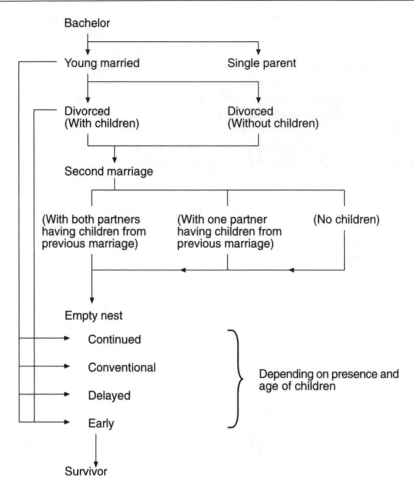

Figure 4.2 The new life-stage complexity!

It is also argued that life-cycle classifications become less dependable when the increasing rates of divorce are taken into account. Consequently, as people have children from their second marriage, the empty nest stage is delayed, and thus age alone becomes less of a predictor of consumer expenditure. Other factors such as delayed childbearing might create the 'squeezed generation', as females find that they have as dependents both elderly parents and young children. Other factors include growing rates of illegitimacy and single parent families. Others have indicated that for those within stable income and family groups, the diversity of products and services now available itself creates a less homogeneous lifestyle. It is therefore against this background, which reduces the predictive power of conventional socio-economic variables, that lifestyle marketing becomes attractive as a means of targeting consumers and reducing advertising costs per sale. (See Figures 4.1 and 4.2.)

On the other hand, Cornish and Denny (1989) argue that social grade often underperforms as a predictor of consumer behaviour because 'individuals will often be graded in the field on a shortened and subjective version of the measure'. A combination of socio-educational grade, income and life stage is, they argue, a powerful predictor of consumer behaviour, while they also point out (based on data drawn from the National Readership Survey) that for package holidays disposable net household income is a strong discriminator.

Alexander and Valentine (1989) suggest age cohort effects exist, whereby shared lifetime experiences common to a particular age group shape their world view, and that over time this becomes more important and possibly absorbs the style clans of the teenage world. They comment:

> at the younger end we are strong on style-clanning and weak on age cohorting; then, as we get older, the polarities reverse – and when we're old we become better age cohorters and less effective style clanners.

In the field of recreation and holiday marketing, at an intuitive level, the use of lifestyle marketing is appealing. Holidays are expenditure drawn from discretionary spending, and hence are most likely to be reflections of personal interests, and an expressive symbol of lifestyle. For example, Baker and Fletcher (1987) maintain that the psychographic system, 'Outlook', was a better predictor than Social Class in areas relating to leisure activities such as pub-going and taking package holidays. There have, however, been few attempts to compare 'predictors' of consumer behaviour in the literature relating to holidays. O'Brien and Ford (1988) did include holidays as a purchase item in their survey of the effectiveness of alternative predictors of consumer behaviour. They assessed social class, life stage, lifestyle, and disposable income (through two groups they called 'acquisitors' and 'big spenders') across 20 items by 4 methods of discrimination. They concluded that:

- social grade *does* discriminate
- no alternative classification provides *consistently* better discriminatory powers
- no *one* classification works best across all product fields,
  but, we would add that
- sometimes other classifications discriminate *more*, and frequently they are *just as powerful* as Social Class.

> In short, *Social Class as a discriminator, is not dead. However,* we can also conclude that the other classifications we have looked at *should always be considered* when designing surveys and analysing data (O'Brien and Ford 1988:309) [italics are original authors' emphasis].

In the case of holidays the scores achieved by the predictors (on an index constructed by the authors) were as follows:

Life stage	83
Lifestyle	88
Social Class	87
Acquisitor	86
Big Spender	79

(O'Brien and Ford 1988:297)

This indicates the 'correlation' between predicted and actual purchases of various household items and services. In taking these findings into consideration it must be noted that the holiday behaviour analysed was simply the purchase of a 'main holiday'. It can be contended that lifestyle categories can be even more important when seeking to assess the type of holiday that is undertaken. On the other hand, Lawson (1991), Bojanic (1992) and Ryan (1994) have all argued that life stage is still a powerful predictor of holiday activities and needs. Each, has argued, either implicitly or explicitly, that in spite of the current heterogenous nature of contemporary society it is, at least for the moment, too early to reject more conventional socio-economic/life stage approaches as explanations of holiday-taking behaviour.

HOLIDAY-MAKER CLASSIFICATIONS

This has not stopped individual researchers from using lifestyle to analyse market segments with reference to general holidaying behaviours. Mazanec (1981) analysed the German market using factor analysis, and concluded that on the basis of responses to 16 statements such as 'I would do without a lot of things, but never without my holiday trip' or 'Travelling is no longer a pleasure, for everything gets more and more expensive everywhere', the German population could be divided into a total of 12 categories (7 male and 5 female), which, on the basis of attitudes towards leisure and travel, could predict the propensity to travel. Yiannakis and Gibson (1992) were able to distinguish 14 types of tourist based on their reactions to three motivational dimensions. The types were:

1 Sun lover – interested in relaxing and sunbathing in warm places with lots of sun, sand and ocean.
2 Action seeker – mostly interested in partying, going to night clubs and meeting the opposite sex for uncomplicated romantic experiences.
3 Anthropologist – mostly interested in meeting local people, trying the food and speaking the language.
4 Archaeologist – mostly interested in archaeological sites and ruins; enjoys studying history of ancient civilisations.
5 Organised mass tourist – mostly interested in organised vacations, packaged tours, taking pictures and buying lots of souvenirs.
6 Thrill seeker – interested in risky, exhilarating activities that provide emotional highs, such as skydiving.

7 Explorers – prefers adventure travel, exploring out-of-the-way places and enjoys challenges in getting there.

8 Jetsetter – vacations in élite world-class resorts, goes to exclusive night clubs, and socialises with celebrities.

9 Seeker – seeker of spiritual and/or personal knowledge to better understand self and meaning of life.

10 Independent mass tourist – visits regular tourist attractions but makes own travel arrangements and often 'plays it by ear'.

11 High-class tourist – travels first class, stays in the best hotels, goes to shows, and dines at the best restaurants.

12 Drifter – drifts from place to place living a hippy-style existence.

13 Escapist – enjoys taking it easy and getting away from it all in quiet and peaceful places.

14 Sport lover – primary emphasis while on vacation is to remain active engaging in favourite sports.

The three underlying motivational dimensions were identified as being:

1 Tourist environments – high to low structure.
2 Stimulating – tranquil environments.
3 Strange – familiar environments.

The findings, as is the case of many of these studies were based on responses to questionnaires subsequently subjected to factor and cluster analysis, which techniques are discussed in Chapter 12.

NATIONAL TOURIST BOARD EXAMPLES

Visitors to North America

These techniques are also utilised by large scale studies sponsored by major national tourist organisations. Two such examples are provided by Tourism Canada and the United States Travel and Tourism Administration and the New Zealand Tourist Board. In an analysis of the Swiss market, a threefold segmentation of the market was developed by Tourism Canada and the United States Travel and Tourism Administration in 1988. These three segments were:

1 Travel philosophy – a basic orientation towards travel.
2 Benefit segmentation – the motivation for travelling and the type of travel experiences being sought.
3 Product segmentation – the choice of specific features within a location.

Each of these three segments were likewise divided into groups.

Travel philosophy

(a) Premium package travellers (20 per cent of the market).

(b) Premium independent travellers (21 per cent of the market).
(c) Guarded package travellers – preferring familiar destinations (28 per cent of the total).
(d) Budget independent travellers (30 per cent of the market).

Benefit segments

(a) Adventure travellers (32 per cent of the total).
(b) Luxury travellers (38 per cent of the market).
(c) Social safety travellers (30 per cent of the market).

Product segments

(a) Developed resort travellers (16 per cent of the total market).
(b) Nature and culture travellers (18 per cent of the total).
(c) Rural beach travellers (21 per cent of the total market).
(d) Culture and comfort travellers (22 per cent of the market).
(e) Sports and entertainment travellers (23 per cent of the total market).

Visitors to New Zealand

In 1992 the New Zealand Tourist Board completed a study of the Malaysian market, and categorised the tourist market as consisting of six groups:

1   Reserved short haulers – less interested in going to new and different places, less interested in planning travel than other segments, and often travelling to visit friends and relatives.
2   Dreamers – prefer package and guided tours, and rely on travel agents. Planning is important to them, and travel provides an escape from family, stress, noise, pollution and crowding. They seek safety, relaxation, and excitement within structured tourist venues.
3   Young well-educated adventurers – travel provides an opportunity to widen their knowledge and experience. They have higher than average interest in adventure, aboriginal peoples, wildlife, natural wonders, peace and quiet.
4   Traditional Malays – they prefer new places but do not want to encounter language difficulties. They have a strong interest in safety, beaches, resorts, family travel and inexpensive places.
5   Mature travellers – an older segment, these like to see and do lots of different things, and experience different lifestyles. They have below-average levels of interest in beaches and small towns, but would like to visit historic sites.
6   Indifferent travellers – well and widely travelled, they are primarily interested in young singles, good sunbathing and hot weather. They have comparatively low levels of interest in safety, shopping, history, scenery, restaurants, educational experiences or package tours.

DIFFICULTIES WITH LIFESTYLE SYSTEMS

The use of factor analysis to generate such typologies is undoubtedly useful, but a number of practical and conceptual difficulties exist. The first practical difficulty is that many academic tourism studies relate to comparatively small samples and for specific purposes. As noted in Chapter 1, there is little comparative work using academic created lifestyle systems, and in consequence, from the commercial viewpoint, little in the way of any database linking such attitudes to other aspects of consumer life that will enable any form of direct marketing to take place. Increasingly, therefore, reference will be made to those psychographic profiles that do possess these advantages. Within North America one of the longest established is the VALS (Values, Attitudes and Lifestyles) index. Now into a second version, VALS 2™, it was originally constructed on the premises underlying Maslow's (1943) hierarchy of needs.

Within Britain there are two similar indices, *Outlook* and *Persona*. '*Outlook*' has six categories: the Trendies, Pleasure Seekers, Indifferent, Working-Class Puritans, Sociable Spenders and Moralists. This system arises from work done by Baker and Fletcher (1987) utilising the 20,000 responses made to the British Market Research Bureau's Target Group Index. This monthly survey not only includes questions about purchases of products, but also includes responses to over 190 attitudinal/lifestyle questions, and covers respondents' use of media. Consequently, the correlation of *Outlook* with use of media presents opportunities not only for identifying types of tourist, but also the newspapers they read and the television programmes they watch. *Persona* has many more categories and is based on an analysis of almost 3 million respondents to the National Shoppers' Survey. This has been of specific use in the analysis of clients at holiday centres within the UK (Ryan 1991e). The use of psychographics in tourism planning is comparatively new, although segmentation policies based on vacation preferences, demographics and personality types were described in detail by Crask (1981), Bryant and Morrison (1980) and Mayo and Jarvis (1981) amongst others in the early 1980s.

Further caveats about lifestyle systems emanate from the use of factor analysis and related techniques. Bagozzi comments:

> One drawback with this procedure is its atheoretical character. Rather than proposing a structure of perceptions based on conceptual arguments and prior research, the researcher relies on the pattern of responses found in the particular data under scrutiny to arrive at perceptual dimensions. This can lead to fortuitous, but erroneous, solutions and tends to promote a multitude of variables and interpretations, since little consistency results across studies. A second drawback is that principal components and common factor analysis can sometimes generate many dimensions within any particular study and thus yield cumbersome models (Bagozzi 1988:166).

The former problem to which Bagozzi alludes perhaps has some foundation in the case of the *Outlook* and *Persona* systems in that they are utilising items not devised with the establishment of lifestyles in mind, although the size of samples lends initial credibility to the systems. Indeed, it can be argued that contrary to Bagozzi's viewpoint, the greater problem is where the researcher does have a specific model in mind, and constructs questions accordingly. The use of factor analysis to 'discover' the factors that compose the model is then not a proof of the model, but of a tautology. What has been shown is the existence of a series of correlations between items as having a statistical validity, but the problems remain as to the relationship between the 'model' and the 'reality'. This does present real problems for any researcher. In constructing a model that is tested by such statistical techniques, the researcher is seeking for high levels of correlation in order for the model to pass the initial screening in testing its validity. But what if the results are 'satisfactory'? Does that necessarily support a hypothesis, or is it little more than a correlation between items arising from the parameters of the process of questioning? Hence the need for careful processes of hypothesis design, testing, and the development of research expertise whereby little more than tautological exercises are avoided.

MULTI-ATTRIBUTE MODELS OF ATTITUDE MEASUREMENT

The discussion has already been wide ranging, starting from a description of the states of mindlessness that sometimes characterise tourist behaviours, to the listing of some tourist typologies based on motivations and attitudes. The question of the relative importance of itemised attitudinal components that might be listed upon a questionnaire has also been noted, and any researcher into tourist attitudes should be aware that various research approaches do exist to take this into account. Specific marketing models have been alluded to and now need to be examined in more detail. These include the expectancy-value or multi-attribute models, and the gaps analysis of models such as the 'Servqual Model' of Parasuraman, Zeithaml and Berry (1988).

The use of Personal Construct Theory has a number of advantages, one of which is that it permits the construction of semantic differential or Likert scales that utilise variables that reflect attributes considered important by actual or potential users of a resort or tourist zone. Fishbein (1967) initially argued that there were two important components of attitude, the evaluative component, and the importance of that belief. In the formation of an attitude, a number of beliefs might be involved. Accordingly this can be written as:

$$A_o = \sum_{i=1}^{n} B_i a_i$$

where A_o = attitude towards destination o
  B_i = strength of belief i about destination o
  a_i = evaluative aspect of belief
  n = number of beliefs

On this basis it becomes possible to devise a two-part questionnaire. The first would consist of a number of questions asking respondents to indicate the degree of importance they attached to specific variables when selecting a holiday destination. A 5-point Likert-type scale ranging from 'very important' to 'of no importance' could, for example, be used. The second part of the questionnaire could relate to a specific destination, the respondents being asked to indicate the degree to which a destination possessed a specific attribute, and again a five-point scale might be used. This technique has been widely used (e.g. Scott *et al.* 1978) with reference to New England states, and by Tourism Canada (1988). In the Tourism Canada study the results were presented in a manner that reflected the methodology. This disaggregation of the total score implied in the Fishbein formula overcomes a number of objections, at least in part, namely:

(a) Can it be said that within the attitude the relationship between the component parts is a multiplicative one?
(b) To what extent is the process of summing together factors to produce an univariate (and possibly uni-dimensional score) valid?
(c) Does the approach fully document the processes of compensation that occur between the various components that create the attitude?

Thus, in the example of Hong Kong residents' perceptions of Canada as a tourist destination, resort areas and budget accommodation are viewed as being of equal importance, but whereas Canada is perceived as offering good resort areas, the question arises, as to whether this offsets to any degree the perceived lack of budget accommodation? To some extent the answer is partly answered by the total score arrived at for Canada compared with scores achieved for competing destination areas. Each of the cells shown could be said to represent four different positions as shown in Figure 4.3.

Saleh and Ryan (1992) used this simple model to analyse the attributes applied by business users to assess the attractiveness of competing hotels and, for example, found that guests paid little attention to facilities such as gymnasia and swimming pools (i.e. these factors were found in the bottom right-hand cell of Figure 4.3).

Fishbein extended his theory to discuss the concept that attitude is a precursor of behaviour in that any person does not simply construct an attitude, but also considers the expected results of pursuing a course of action. This can be expressed as:

$$A\text{-act} = \sum_{i=1}^{n} b_i e_i$$

where A-act = the individual's attitude towards performance of the action
b_i = the belief that action will lead to consequence i
e_i = the evaluation of consequence i
n = the number of salient consequences

It is possible to hypothesise a summation of the two aspects of the attitude as being:

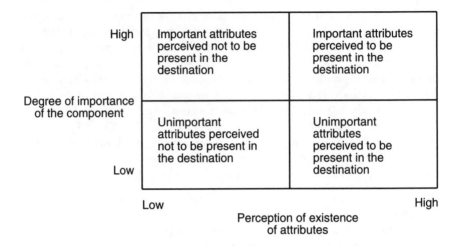

Figure 4.3 The four cells of the Fishbein measurement of attitude

$$\text{Strength of conviction} = \sum_{i=1}^{n} B_i a_i + \sum_{i=1}^{n} b_i e_i$$

In terms of holiday destination the consequences of going to one destination are at least twofold. The first is that the simple fact of going on holiday means expenditure on vacations is not available for expenditure on alternative pursuits. Second, it means that the selection of one destination means the foregoing of another or, at the least, a delaying of the opportunity to visit the competing location. Assuming that holiday-makers allocate within their budgets a sum for going on holiday, it does raise the question as to whether or not individuals form attitudes towards a holiday destination that are independent of their beliefs about the attributes of other resort areas. It has already been noted that the scores for Canada have meaning only if the scores for competing destination are known. Taking the initial Fishbein formulation, this implies an extension of the model:

$$BI_{ij} = A_{ij} = \sum_{j=1}^{m} \sum_{k=1}^{n} (B_{ijk} V_{ik})$$

where $i =$ holiday-maker
$j =$ holiday destination
$k =$ attributes of holiday destination
$n =$ number of attributes
$m =$ number of holiday destinations
$BI_{ij} =$ holiday-maker i's behavioural intention towards destination j
$A_{ij} =$ a unidimensional measure of consumer i's attitude toward brand j
$B_{ijk} =$ the strength of holiday-maker i's belief that attribute k is possessed by destination j and
$V_{ik} =$ the degree to which attribute k is desired by holiday-maker i

However, in considering a range of holiday destinations the holiday-maker does not consider every destination, but only those which are thought to hold some appeal. Thus, the consumer is considering only those that they are aware of, and from these, only the destinations which evoke positive images (i.e. the evoked set). In the terminology of Howard and Sheth (1969) the inert and inept sets are not considered, only the evoked set of alternatives. Scott, Schewe and Frederick (1978) postulate that if this is the case, then a 'proportionality of product knowledge' exists, and this can be calculated as:

$$PPK_{ij} = \frac{PK_{ij}}{\dfrac{1}{m} \sum_{j=1}^{m} PK_{ij}}$$

where   i = holiday-maker
         j = destination
         m = number of destinations in the evoked set
         PPK_{ij} = proportional knowledge of holiday-maker i of destination j
         PK_{ij} = knowledge of holiday-maker i for destination j

Hence, this can be added to the previous formula to give:

$$BI_{ij} = A_{ij} = \sum_{j=1}^{m} \sum_{k=1}^{n} (B_{ijk} \, V_{ik} \, PPK_{ij})$$

Witt and Wright (1990) have adopted a closely related but slightly different approach by using Vroom's theory of valences. They adopt Lawler's definition that the premise of such an approach is:

the strength of a tendency to act in a certain way depends on an expectancy that the act will be followed by given consequences (or outcomes) and on the value or attractiveness of that consequence or (outcome) to the actor (Lawler 1973:45).

The formulations are closely akin to those given above, and arguably differ only by reason of the emphasis given to comparison of outcomes arising from different actions. They conclude from their review of the theory that:

Because it provides a framework for the analysis of tourist motivation rather than suggesting specific reasons for travel, expectancy theory enables a much more sophisticated and more realistic view to be taken of tourist motivation (Witt and Wright 1990:25).

In practical terms the implications for research into the attitudes and perceptions of the image of any given holiday destination must involve not simply an identification of attributes thought to be important, but an assessment of the degree to which competing destinations are thought to possess such attributes weighted by degrees of knowledge about such destinations as possibly measured by familiarity with resorts. Familiarity might arise from previous visits to given destinations, or destinations thought to be similar. Thus questionnaires must include questions that elicit responses as to frequency of holiday trips undertaken, and places visited within a given period of time, and cover a number of competing holiday destinations. The inclusion of other destinations (within reason) also has advantages in overcoming problems involved in analysing responses such as acquiescence sets, or predispositions to score low or high, in that the presence of alternatives may help to cause a distribution of scores and perhaps avoid bunching around the mean. Some of the practical aspects of this approach to questionnaire design is discussed in Chapter 6 when aspects of questionnaire design are looked at in detail.

HOLISTIC OR DISAGGREGATED MEASURES OF ATTITUDE?

As already noted, the multi-attribute model is a decompositional measure, and implies that judgements are made on a combination of independently evaluated attributes associated with a product or service. Toy *et al.* note that the method includes:

> a strong and thoroughly tested conceptual foundation, ease of operationalisation, and relatively high levels of predictive and interpretive validity (Toy *et al.* 1989:277).

On the other hand, it might suggest a sophistication of decision taking that does not exist in fact. One of the criticisms associated with multi-attribute models is that it is objected that holiday-makers do not in fact separate the individual components of a holiday destination, but rather when making choices, compare concepts of the total image of place. Marketing research has devised means of measuring such responses, and one approach is that of conjoint measurement (Green and Rao 1971; Johnson 1974; Hair *et al.* 1987). The basis behind the approach is that the respondent might be given a number of possible destinations and asked to rank them in order of attraction. The research problem is one of specifying the relationship between the product attributes and the preference rankings, and thus 'utility' values will need to be placed for each attribute level to 'explain' the consumer preference rankings. The normal method for doing this is to use a computer statistics package and apply values derived from a monotonic analysis of variance (MONANOVA), but general linear models have also been shown to work (Cohen 1968; Hair *et al.* 1987).

June and Smith (1987) have utilised this method in a study assessing levels of service in a restaurant, while Carmichael (1992) used it to measure attitudes of Canadian skiers in British Columbia. In her study skiers were asked to evaluate 29 resorts on the basis of their ratings of the snow conditions, variety of runs, lift lines, value for money, staff, and accessibility to home. It was found, not surprisingly, that snow condition was the major determinant of the decision to go skiing. However, the study revealed much more in terms of the ranking of the resorts, and the problems involved with the approach.

In an important sense conjoint measurement is also a disaggregated or decompositional model in that it seeks to identify the importance of components of attitude, but it approaches the questioning from the reverse viewpoint of the multi-attribute model. The latter requires responses as to the particular so as to calculate the whole; conjoint measurement assesses the whole to identify the particular. Theoretically, however, its relationship with the multi-attribute approach can be shown by the formulation given by Timmermans (1984:203) whereby

$$U(x) = \sum_{i=1}^{i} \sum_{k=1}^{M_i} V_{ik}X_{ik}$$

where $U(x)$ is an overall utility of preference measurement
V_{ik} is the part worth contribution associated with the kth level of the ith attribute
and X_{ik} is the presence or absence of the kth level of the ith attribute.

From this perspective it can be argued that both multi-attribute and conjoint measurement, in theory, are uni-dimensional in the sense that both can produce a single or holistic score purporting to be a measure of the strength of attitude. Bagozzi has summarised this viewpoint by stating:

> Attitude is thought to be a single entity. Indeed, the unidimensionality of attitude is taken by assumption, and measurements are selected and scaling techniques applied so as to produce an unidimensional scale. In the case of $A_{object/act}$ single factoredness is maintained as the *sine qua non* of its measures, whereas for the b_ie_i unidimensionality is accomplished by definition (i.e. by summing the product terms to arrive at a single, *a priori* specified construct) (Bagozzi 1988:169).

Bagozzi, like many other researchers, favours a multidimensional expectancy-value attribute model, of which he states there are two kinds – the molecular and the molar. The molecular is really little more than the disaggregated Fishbein formulation – that is each individual belief/evaluation product is a single dimension. This author would argue that, in practice, this is how the Fishbein (and Vroom) formulations tend to be used in practice. Thus, in a sense Bagozzi has set up in the above quotation something which, while technically correct, is in practice, little used. However, he does make the valid point that each individual dimension can be correlated with the total score, and thus three benefits accrue. These are:

1   it is possible to represent random error explicitly and to correct for unreliability in measurement;
2   the molecular multi-dimensional attribute model reveals detail; and
3   the multi-dimensional model can circumvent multicollinearity problems.

The molar multi-dimensional attribute theory is simply a variant upon the molecular, and is closer to the basic b_ie_i formulation in that it does not seek to correlate separate item scores with the total product. Bagozzi comments 'no one-to-one correspondence exists between each dimension and its respective b_ie_i measures' (1988:172). The advantage of this approach is that molar multi-dimensional attribute scores can be measured and used for predictive purpose by use of partial least squares regression – the procedures are 'distribution free and can be used even where sample sizes are quite small.' (ibid. 1988:173).

If this latter technique is valid it raises some interesting possibilities. The simple Fishbein models noted above tend to look at attitude as an outcome of evaluation and beliefs – the process by which that outcome emerges is not explicitly stated. Traditionally, criticisms of the Fishbein model have been made on the grounds that it describes reasoned behaviour, and not that behaviour which is routine or mindless. Yet, it has already been noted that at least some components of holiday-taking behaviour are both routine and mindless.

Bagozzi and Warshaw (1988) have formulated a theory of goal-directed behaviours and outcomes (TGBO) which is a variant of the basic Fishbein model in that it emphasises the attempt to perform a behaviour or achieve a goal. That is, it concentrates on the trying rather than the achieving of the goal. Beliefs and evaluations are thus in part outcomes of the frequency and recency of past attempts to achieve the goals. Evaluation of consequences is, it is argued, part of a multiplicative process with attitudes towards success and failure. Bagozzi and Warshaw (1988) were able to demonstrate that using regression analysis where the variables were attitudes towards success, failure, the process of trying, the intention to try, trying, control, frequency and recency of past attempts, and behavioural performance, high percentages of explained variance could be found to support a hierarchical model of goal-directed behaviour.

THE IMPLICATIONS FOR TOURISM RESEARCH

The application of this model to holiday-taking is particularly appropriate for a number of reasons. First, Bagozzi and Warshaw (1988) argue that it is pertinent 'especially to situations where the goal or outcome of consumption is intangible'. Second, the emphasis on trying and past experience lends itself to work done from an entirely different direction by Jackson and his co-researchers. In a series of papers Jackson (1983, 1988, 1990a,b), Jackson and Dunn (1988), Jackson and Searle (1983) have explored the nature of constraints upon leisure and recreation participation. Third, the importance of trying implies gaps between performance and expectation, and thus might have linkages with consumer gaps theories as, for example, expounded by Laws (1990) and Laws and Ryan (1992).

Jackson has argued that much of the research into leisure constraints has been too narrowly focused on the outcome that constraints negate performance by those who have expressed a wish to participate. Inasmuch as non-participants are comprised of two groups, those who express a wish to join in, but do not, and those who show no inclination to partake in a given activity, research into non-participation has tended to focus only on the former group. He has therefore developed a concept of antecedent constraints which interact with leisure preferences rather than participation. This concept has been developed by feminist literature that has studied, primarily in the USA, the nature of constraints on female participation in leisure activities (e.g. Henderson *et al.* 1988). Such antecedent constraints include 'prior socialisation into specific leisure activities, kin and non-kin reference attitudes and other factors' (Jackson 1990b:133). In the case of holiday-making, it is of interest to note that within the UK for more than a decade, according to ETB data, consistently approximately one third of the adult population have not taken long holidays away from home. The normal conclusion that is drawn is that this is due to economic factors (intervening variables in Jackson's terminology). In the case of the 20 per cent of the AB group who do not take such holidays, this is probably not the case, and thus other antecedent conditions exist. Psychographic profiling reveals part of the answer by reference to home orientation on the part of respondents. One implication of this is that any research into general holiday-taking behaviour would require recognition of such antecedent conditions.

Two other considerations can also be found in the literature. The first is further refinement and development of the technique, and the second is to assess reliability by comparison of findings with other measures of attitude.

Hagerty assesses means of improving the predictive power of conjoint analysis by allying it with factor analysis, and in doing so addresses the question as to whether, in the comparison of choices, there is in fact an overlap between clusters. He notes that 'is the assumption of non-overlapping clustering valid – the answer seems to be that it is almost never true' (Hagerty 1985:169).

One of the advances in conjoint analysis has been the development of hybrid models. These might be said to be characterised by attempts to calculate desirability values for the levels of each attribute separately, in short, to retain the advantages of complete image comparison, but produce the detail associated with multi-attribute disaggregation. Green (1984) describes the objective of this approach 'as being the idea to develop individual utility functions in which some aspects of the resulting part worths are measured at the individual level and other aspects at the total sample (or subgroup) level'. The rationale for the approach is that respondents may find it difficult to estimate desirabilities and self-explicated importance weights, while he adds:

> additive combination rules may not be appropriate ... respondents may be sufficiently heterogeneous that a single origin and scale unit change is not accurate, and ... the function that transforms the Us (individual utilities) to Ys (overall responses) may not be linear (Green 1984:155).

Toy *et al.* (1989) also note that hybrid conjoint analysis possesses the advantage that for large numbers of successive attributes it reduces quite dramatically the number of stimulus profiles to which respondents have to reply.

Within the debate over predictive abilities, problems still abound. For example, the findings of Stewart (1981) on the use of optimal weighting are not replicated by Hagerty (1985). Green (1984:167) notes, 'however, whether hybrid models offer any advantages in smaller scale studies entailing for example five or fewer factors with two to four levels per factor is a moot point'.

MULTI-ATTRIBUTE OR CONJOINT MEASUREMENT – THE LEVEL OF CORRELATION

An important question is whether the methods of conjoint analysis and multi-attribute measures of attitude actually measure the same thing, or do they measure different things. The question is important in terms of research design. If they measure different things, then the researcher must ensure that the methodology used is appropriate to the task in hand, and that the resultant questionnaire is appropriate to the methodology. There have been very few studies that have sought to compare the results of the different methodologies of measuring attitudes of the same respondents, partly because of the very real problems of respondent fatigue when faced with a series of differently posed questions about the same subject.

One of the seminal studies in this area was that of Jaccard *et al.* (1986) who compared six measures of attitude, namely elicitation, information search measures, importance ratings, conjoint measurement, subjective probability measures, and Thurstone scales. The information search method is one whereby respondents could ask for information about items presented to them in a list, while the subjective probability measures used involved measures of a 'willingness to consider'. Subjects were asked, on an eleven-point scale, their willingness to consider a purchase and the score was the difference between reversed questions, which served as an index of importance. One of their results referring to purchases of cars is shown in Table 4.1.

The authors note that:

> Overall, strong evidence for convergence was not apparent in the data. This result raises questions about consumer research that relies on a single measure for inferring attribute importance (Jaccard *et al.* 1986:466).

Clearly the correlations between most of the different methods are weak, and this poses a set of questions which fall into at least two main categories:

(a) Do the results arise from faults in the research instruments?
(b) Does the variation arise due to the different techniques actually measuring different things?

There have been very few comparative studies in the field of tourism, but that of Lego and Shaw (1992) found many of the same problems. They studied 1,600 Australian travel agents and their attitude to CRS (computer reservation systems). Four methods were utilised:

Table 4.1 Comparison of attitude measurement scales (correlations between scores)

Indices	e	sp	f	o	dr	c
Elicitation (e)	–	0.19	0.15	0.22	0.19	0.28
Subjective probability (sp)		–	0.28	0.25	0.62	0.68
Frequency (f)			–	0.78	0.22	0.19
Order (o)				–	0.25	0.15
Direct rating (dr)					–	0.58
Conjoint (c)						–

Source: Jaccard *et al.* 1986.

1   elicitation – travel agents were asked to express opinions in their own words;
2   selective ranking – travel agents ranked attributes of CRS in order of importance;
3   direct rating – travel agents rated attributes on a 6-point scale;
4   conjoint measurement – respondents evaluated 16 profiles of CRS.

The authors additionally generated what they termed a self-explicated model described as 'essentially a Fishbein-type model' and concluded that:

> the ability of the self-explicated model to match the conjoint profiles at the individual level was weak. However, at the aggregate level, the correlation was quite high between the self-explicated scores and the actual conjoint profile scores (Lego and Shaw 1992:392).

RESPONDENT FATIGUE

One obvious problem with undertaking this type of methodological research is the very length of either the time or questionnaire the respondent is faced with. The implication is that respondents face questionnaire fatigue, and this induces a reduction in consistency of response. Jaccard *et al.* met this question head on, and note 'it can be just as easily argued that subjects tried to be consistent across tasks and, if anything, that the current data overestimate the convergence' (1986:467). In short, respondents are more inclined to be conscientious when faced with this task. Arguably, both hypotheses are open to question on the premise that the truth is more complex. It has been noted that samples have been divided on grounds such as 'yea sayers' and 'nay sayers', and it can be contended that some respondents will attempt to maintain consistency, while others will more rapidly tire of the task. Both in terms of means of analysis, and in types of research design, there is simply not enough evidence to propose anything but a series of potential hypotheses, but certainly no answers. For whatever value it carries, this author feels that questionnaire fatigue would probably be an important factor, and this implies that more care must be given to research design. Rather than attempt to complete different means of attitude assessment in one session, what may be required is a series of questionnaires, but under conditions where individual respondents are in receipt of a feedback of their own previous results. Another factor might simply be one of a lack of apparent consistency in held opinions.

SALIENCE, IMPORTANCE OR DETERMINANCE?

One reason why such a lack of consistency can arise is related to the actual techniques. Direct elicitation requires an opinion based on a holistic view of the variables under consideration, while rating methods require a serial consideration of those variables, and perhaps a series of comparisons are being forced (this is certainly the case under ranking). Sometimes the distinctions between variables may be fine, so fine, in fact, that while possibly close in scores, differing levels of importance may be attributed to variables over different trials. Myers and Alpert (1977) argue that elicitation methods generate responses based on salience, while rating scales tap importance, and correlational techniques identify determinance. It can be argued that conjoint measurement requires a specificity not normally associated with decision-making, in that consumers might adopt decision-making techniques which would, in practice, exclude from consideration, many of the choices they are being asked to rank. Yet, because of the nature of questionnaire design, such choices are being awarded values. While conjoint measurement subsequently rates the contribution of the variables to final choice, it might have a possible overstatement of less important considerations where they have been combined with an item that is attractive to the respondent.

Conjoint measurement might be considered as an appropriate technique by a researcher wishing to consider such issues of salience, importance and determinance. The technique can be used to assess attitudes at a segment level rather than at an individual level, but as Kohli indicates:

> the major application of conjoint analysis is in product design settings, it is useful to assess attribute significance at a segment level rather than separately for each individual. However it is not desirable to base the testing on 'average' segment preferences, which ignore the information on preference heterogeneity *within* a segment. The difficulty of developing testing procedures that retain idiosyncrasies across consumers, has been the ... major impediment in the development of significance testing methods for conjoint analysis (Kohli 1988:124).

TECHNIQUES AND QUESTIONNAIRE DESIGN

The above discussion highlights an important aspect of questionnaire design. That is, what is the underlying conceptual framework to be adopted in analysing data? This question has at least two components to it. First, what is the model or framework of relationships that is being hypothesised. The second question relates to the methods of analysis to be used. The design of a questionnaire will appear very different depending on whether multi-attribute analysis, conjoint measurement or other methods such as multi-dimensional scaling are to be used. Failure to consider this at an early stage in the questionnaire design creates a proclivity towards a series of questions that are unrelated, thus leading to a loss of richness and diversity in the analysis.

Attempts to create a questionnaire where it becomes possible to utilise more than one attitude measurement tend to generate overlong questionnaires, or force compromise whereby it becomes uncertain what is actually being measured, or indeed may generate inconsistency of results. The danger of at least apparent inconsistency of results has been discussed with reference to the work of Jaccard *et al.* (1986). Compromise emerges if, for example, the rankings required by conjoint measurement are imputed to respondents based on product scores derived from multi-attribute measures. If, arguably, the one method assesses importance, and the other determinance of decisions, what does this hybrid actually measure?

While the different means of attitude measurement require a different mode of questioning, there are obvious overlaps in the statistical techniques associated with each measure. For example, hybrid conjoint measurement employs regression analysis in determining part-worths at various stages to reduce the number of selections presented to respondents. Toy *et al.* note that:

> the regression weights in this model may be thought of as a derived set of importance weights that are fitted at the total sample level. This allows for statistical tests of goodness of fit and predictor significance to be applied to the model so that the relationship between variables can be more accurately assessed (Toy *et al.* 1989:281).

Similar overlaps between techniques can be identified in other areas. Thus, the items associated with multi-attribute analysis might permit either factor analysis or multi-dimensional scaling to be used. The two techniques are related. Both multi-dimensional scaling (MDS) and factor analysis attempt to identify the inherent structure with data. However, factor analysis requires the variables to be measured on at least an interval scale, whereas MDS does not require this condition. Fenton and Pearce (1988:237) also note that 'the researcher using MDS usually finds relatively fewer dimensions than would occur if the data were analysed through factor analysis', because the latter utilises rigid assumptions of linearity.

In assessing the means of analysis to be used, the researcher must also take into account the wording of the questions to be used. For example, if MDS is to be used it must be appreciated that it is based upon measures of proximity, and that the conventional mode of questioning is for respondents to make pair-wise comparisons between how similar, or dissimilar items elements are. Another method is to rank order items on the basis of how similar they are to a predefined standard. One problem with this is that the number of questions required increases rapidly. For example, with 8 items, 28 paired comparisons are required; with 12 elements, 66 paired comparisons are needed. This was one of the reasons why many researchers do not use a complex multi-dimensional scaling method. Nonetheless, it should be noted that MDS has been used successfully in a number of tourism research projects, and some of these are summarised by Fenton and Pearce (1988). Additionally, one of the advantages of MDS is that it permits a visual description of inherent data sets through its mapping process, but this is not unique to MDS, and many factor analysis programs (e.g. that of NCSS) also permit mapping of factors.

THE CRITICAL INCIDENT

This chapter now seeks briefly to review some of the concepts relating to services pertaining to tourism, and the assessment of quality of service. It is the viewpoint of the author that much of the debate about distinctions between services and products is sterile. In many cases, for example, the process of branding is concerned with the creation of intangible benefits that become associated with use of the product. Similarly, it matters not whether the product is a holiday, a credit card or washing machine – the practical problems of scheduling advertising to achieve high viewing by the target market are common to each of these and other products and services.

One of the conventional distinguishing features between the marketing of services and products has been the notion that both provider and user of the service are in close proximity (Booms and Nyquist 1981). An implication of this relationship is that consumer satisfaction is, at least in part, determined by the consumers' perceptions of the service and attention they receive from the representative of the service company with whom they are dealing. Indeed, Bitner *et al.* (1990) refer to the 'critical incident' in the sequence of events that make up the service. These are categorised as being employee response to service delivery system failures, employee response to customer needs and requests, and finally unprompted and unsolicited employee actions. For each of these categories there may be a positive or negative experience.

However, the critical incident occurs within a context of expected service and within a physical space, both of which serve to achieve a desired end. In short, the critical incident may reinforce and occasionally change the existence of a positive or negative gap between what is expected and what is delivered. Laws (1986, 1990) argues that it is the direction of this consumerist gap that is the determinant of satisfaction. On the other hand, the Servqual model proposed by Parasuraman *et al.* (1988) is based on the notion that this is but one of a number of potential gaps, and that others have to be taken into account. Such gaps would include management perceptions of customer expectations, and management perception of staff performance. (See Figure 4.4.)

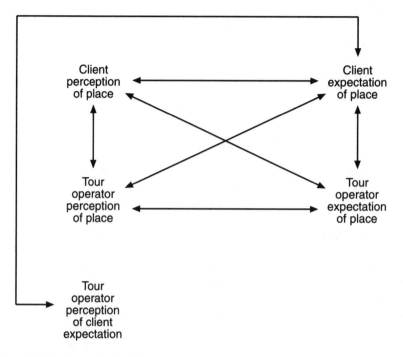

Figure 4.4 A gap analysis of tourist destination

Note: Each line represents a potential gap that affects tourist satisfaction. The model can be extended by creating new pairings and adding tourist intermediaries such as hoteliers and employees.

From a general viewpoint, the components of a service may be divided into three. Gronroos (1978) describes these variables as being of a technical, functional or image creation nature. Lehtinen and Lehtinen (1982, 1991) also propose a similar classification, namely physical, interactive and corporate qualities. With reference to a hotel, its physical (technical) features would include the tangibles of reception area, bedrooms, restaurants, while the functional, interactive processes relate to the expressive performance/usage of the tangibles. Courtesy, promptness of attention and empathy are features identified by Lewis and Klein (1987) as being, arguably, the core of the interactive process. Any image that clients possess of a hotel will be determined by a mix of marketing messages to which they have been exposed, the tangible components they view, the interactions they have experienced with staff, and the degree of familiarity they have with a specific hotel, chain of hotels, or competitors. In short, the factors identified by Lehtinen and Lehtinen (1982) and Gronroos (1978) are not independent variables, but are interacting variables that define a dynamic process.

The nature of this dynamic process is illustrated by the concept of the critical incident. Bitner *et al.* (1990) indicate how failure of components of the technical process of the service can be offset by corrective action by representatives of the service provider. Rapid and courteous action can generate customer satisfaction, overcome the potential dissatisfaction caused by service failure, and may even enhance corporate image. Laws (1990), in his analysis of airline service, also refers to the importance of management blueprints indicating structured reactions designed to respond quickly to customer needs in the event of technical failure. In such situations, the quality of the interaction between customer and the representative of the service provider is of paramount importance. This interaction should comprise at least three components – corrective action, information to the customer and a correct form of personal approach.

The expressive performance of the action is, of course, not simply important in cases of technical failure. As already referred to, for many authors it is the key distinguishing feature between products and services. Consequently it is pertinent to examine the nature of this expressive service or interaction between client and provider. Parasuraman *et al.* (1985) identified ten components. Briefly, these are: reliability, responsiveness, competence, courtesy, communication, credibility, security, knowledge and understanding of customers and their needs, and finally tangibles representing the physical evidence of service. Such a tangible would include the appearance of staff. Subsequently, in 1988, the same authors tested these variables and reduced them to five factors – tangibles, reliability, responsiveness, assurance and empathy.

SATISFACTION – A GAP BETWEEN EXPECTATION AND 'REALITY'?

The performance of the service occurs within a context of not simply a physical environment, but rather an environment which is managed. It is therefore possible that a service may be carefully conceived and performed, yet fail to generate client satisfaction because the managers or entrepreneurs have failed to assess correctly the needs of the customer. In another situation, management may correctly identify customer needs, but incorrectly perceive the ability of staff to implement the specifications. Lewis and Klein (1987) illustrated this process when they found that management tended to overestimate the level of service required by customers, but in doing so underestimated the importance of some individual factors such as the need for quietness and staff friendliness. Parasuraman *et al.* (1988) comment:

> In essence, service firms' executives may not understand: 1) what features connote high quality to consumers in advance; 2) what features a service must have in order to meet customer needs; and 3) what levels of performance on those features are needed to deliver high quality service.

In their study of Canadian hotel management Saleh and Ryan (1991) also lent support to the above observations. Looking at five gaps between the perceptions of management and guests, and their expectations, they argue that the gap concept is of practical use for management to monitor its own performance and that of staff. They also found that satisfaction was highest with the tangible components of the service, but lowest with the empathic and responsiveness elements. This would seem to confirm a general consensus of many commentators (Bateson 1989) that the easiest management problems within services marketing relate to the tangible components, but the training, monitoring and evaluation of staff is more difficult.

Saleh and Ryan (1992) also indicate some structural factors that must be taken into account when viewing gaps between performance and expectation. They note:

> it can be argued that management over-estimates guests' expectations, guests record their perceptions of service being below their expectations, while both management and guests share the same perceptions of service delivery. The implication of this is that management is involved in a process where they condone the provision of a service that is thought not to meet client needs. One possible explanation may be that management have to seek a series of second best solutions within the resource constraints that exist. Their perception of guests' needs becomes the optimal target, the provision of a service that 'satisfies' exemplifies a process of target satisficing. The gap between guest expectation and guest perception of actual service might be part of the same process. Expectation might be partially based on a marketing message that is itself a representation of an ideal, whilst the actual experience is one that is based on degrees of tolerance of service that is satisfactory, but which does not quite meet expectation.

This approach might indicate some problems in assessing levels of customer satisfaction. If customer tolerance of some deviation from expectation exists, and thus a level of service less than the ideal does not generate dissatisfaction, then it implies that the boundary between what is acceptable and what is not is 'fuzzy'. It further implies that the analysis of client satisfaction has to be conducted in terms of what Laws (1990) has defined as 'the just noticeable difference'. There is evidence that 'the just noticeable difference' is not only a factor of past consumer experience, but also of structural components within the service delivery process. Outside the hotel industry, Quelch and Ash (1981) suggest that in cases where the service provider possesses high degrees of expert knowledge clients may be intimidated, may not possess sufficient knowledge to be aware of poor service or may have poor sets of reference within which to assess quality.

The Servqual model of Parasuraman et al. (1985) has attracted considerable attention. As indicated above, there is much to recommend it in terms of creating monitoring systems of performance, but there are also problems. Saleh and Ryan (1992) comment:

> A further factor that may be operating is a process akin to threshold effects. The presence of certain factors may be insufficient to raise levels of

satisfaction because the client is habituated to them, or expects them. On the other hand, the very absence of those factors is quickly noticed by hotel guests. Equally, on the other hand, the performance of staff that is significantly above expectation, i.e. a level that is 'noticeable', becomes a significant determinant of satisfaction.

Swartz and Brown (1989) also note from their research into the provision and perception of medical services that 'threshold effects exist, even where expert knowledge is possessed by the service provider and not the user'. They note:

> The discrepancies just noted can and often do result in client dissatisfaction. In mild cases of disappointment, the consumer may continue to participate in the exchange. With increasing levels of dissatisfaction, however, he/she may tell other existing or potential clients about the unsatisfactory experience, seek the services of another professional, or, in extreme cases, initiate a professional liability suit (1989:193).

Carman (1990) also sought to replicate the findings of the Servqual questionnaire within three situations, a tyre store, a placement centre and a dental clinic. The dimensions that emerged with eigenvalues greater than one were:

> Tyre store – tangibles, reliability, responsiveness, security, courtesy, access.
> Placement centre – tangibles, reliability, responsiveness, security, personal attention, access and convenience.
> Dental clinic – tangibles, reliability, security, convenience, cost.

Carman notes:

> PZB combined their original Understanding and Access dimensions into Empathy. Our results did not find this to be an appropriate combination ... when one of the dimensions of quality is particularly important to customers, they are likely to break that dimension into sub-dimensions. For example, many retailers would find location and parking to be key and separate dimensions in the customer's perceptual map. Thus it is recommended that items on both Personal Attention and Access (or Convenience) be retained until it is determined that some items are not important (1990:39–40).

He also raises the topic of 'nay-saying', noting that 9 of the 26 items from the PZB scale are negatively worded to avoid nay saying, halo effects and maintain alertness. 'In a long questionnaire, many respondents find this change in wording difficult to comprehend, and thus they misread the scale.' (Carman 1990:42). In an additional noteworthy comment he states:

> In pure service situations, such as an airline journey ... the customer is involved in a number of service encounters, and the quality of each might be evaluated. How much does each of these contribute to an overall evaluation of quality and how can these quality perceptions be measured? The literature suggests that Tangibles and Personal Attention weigh most heavily in

customer perceptions of store quality and that store quality weighs more heavily on customer loyalty than does the quality of the product (Jacobsen and Olsen 1985). Thus the dimensions under analysis here are the correct ones (Carman 1990:43).

Another criticism that has been made of the Servqual questionnaire relates to its implementation. Parasuraman   *et al.* asked respondents to complete the questionnaire in one setting, there was no before and after experience. 'All respondent beliefs were entirely ex post. These expectation responses can be of little value' (Carman 1990:47). In the case of the placement service an expectation questionnaire was set as the client started to use the service, and a satisfaction questionnaire some five weeks later. 'The results were not satisfactory ... Only two-thirds of the items loaded the same way on the expectations administration as they did on the perceptions administration' (Carman 1990:47).

To most service providers the importance of a particular service attribute seems more relevant than its expected level (e.g. the competence of the surgeon is more important than the art on the hospital wall). Parasuraman *et al.* use the concept that:

$$Q = \Sigma I_i(p_i - e_i)$$

where I is the importance of the service attribute i; and p_i and e_i are the perception and expectation of the attribute i. Thus importance, expectation and perception are all important, and there is a need to collect data on all three. Arguably, Parasuraman *et al.* infer values for I. This raises a series of questions about attitude measurement from the viewpoint of expectancy models, and some of the issues are discussed in much further detail below. Carman's conclusion is also worth noting:

Based on criteria of face validity and factor analysis eigenvalues greater than one, it is recommended that items on seven or eight of the original ten PZB dimensions (rather than 5) be retained until factor analysis shows them not to be unique. Items on some dimensions should be expanded if that is necessary for reliability (1990:50).

A major shortcoming of the SERVQUAL procedure as presented by PZB concerns the treatment of expectations. There appear to be serious problems with the value of the expectations battery as proposed, the ability to administer it, and the factor analysis of the difference between perceptions and expectations. Expectations are important, and the service marketer needs to collect information about them ... A complete attitude model of service quality must measure the effects of the importance of individual attributes on perceptions of quality (1990:51).

Carman was not alone in making these comments. Babakus and Boller (1992:259) also observe on the basis of their survey that 'the proposed dimensionality of SERVQUAL is problematic'. Saleh and Ryan (1991:339) noted that 'The factor analysis shows that the questions relating to the tangibles explained little of the variance' and that one factor accounted for 62 per cent of the variance. Brown *et al.* (1993:137) noted that their factor analysis also indicated that the items 'might represent a unidimensional construct, and certainly not a five dimensional one'. In the former case, however, part of the problem may have emanated from deviance of the original wording of the SERVQUAL questionnaire in an attempt to more specifically meet the needs of the hotel industry. The problem of wording questions specific to a service industry have been noted by other authors, including Babakus and Boller.

Babakus and Boller (1992) and Brown *et al.* (1993) also comment upon problems of reliability and discriminant validity. The latter argue that using the gap between expectation and perception generates problems due to the nature of the correlation of the gap to the expectation and perception scales. They argue that 'the perceptions component of SERVQUAL alone performs about as well as SERVQUAL itself' (1993:134).

Such criticisms have been noted by Parasuraman *et al.*, and in response, they refined the SERVQUAL model (1991). Subsequently, in reviewing the work of Brown *et al.* they stated:

> it is noteworthy that the difference-score formulation displays somewhat stronger discriminatory validity that the non-difference score formulation (i.e. using Brown's own data) ... while the difference between the two average correlations is small, it is similar to the differences on several other criteria (e.g. reliability, nomological validity) that BCP invoke to claim psychometric superiority for the non-difference score formulation (1993:142–3).

The SERVQUAL model has not only generated a significant amount of literature, but has also been used in many practical situations by management consultants. It is certainly an approach that holds promise for analysing aspects relating to the tourism experience and industrial sectors of the tourism industry. Thus studies have been undertaken relating to hotels (Saleh and Ryan 1991) and travel agents (Cliff 1994), to mention but two. For any researcher who is seeking to undertake any form of gap analysis, the literature is also worth examining as it highlights many problems relating to the assessment of reliability and validity, and the way in which such gaps correlate with the original two scales – an important question because it relates to whether the 'gap' can be treated as an independent variable in its own right.

HOLIDAYS – A SERIES OF RELATIONSHIPS AND EVENTS?

The above discussion has been restricted to a consideration of the concept of service and perceived gaps between expectation and perception of service in the terms of the research into service provision in hotels and similar establishments. It is therefore context bound in a way that the wider holiday experience is not.

The use of the hotel creates, in Pearce's (1988) terms, a series of scripted encounters. The holiday is far more dynamic in its creation of much more complex interactions. Such interactions include:

(a) the relationship between holiday-maker and accommodation provider;
(b) the relationship between tourist and tourist;
(c) the use of the tourist destination zone by the holiday-maker;
(d) the relationships between tourist and agencies of the tourist industry;
(e) the relationships between tourist and members of the host community not employed in the tourist industry.

This discussion began by noting that one of the properties of a service as distinct from a product was that it required the presence of the service provider. The holiday certainly meets the service requirement of 'intangibility'. At the end of the holiday the holiday-maker has memories, but no tangible possessions of note. Those tangibles purchased, the souvenirs, have as their function, the evocation of the intangible. The tangible items used such as, the hotel room or the hire car, were used but not owned. That is, the holiday-maker has engaged in a contract of usage, not of purchase. In this sense the holiday is a classic 'service'. But was it necessary for the service provider to be present? The classic definition of the tour operator as provided by Holloway (1990) is that they are a wholesaler of services, a 'packager' of flight, accommodation and other services, but a representative of the tour operator is not on the beach with the holidaymaker! Arguably the holiday-maker consumes place – the tour operator provides means of reaching the place, but cannot be said to supply the place. Distinctions might therefore (and have been made) between services such as a holiday, a financial service, a hotel or, a meal. Uhl and Upah (1983:238), for example, introduce the concept of 'pure' and hybrid services.

From this perspective the role of the tour operator as simply a means of reaching the place to be consumed does raise some important issues with reference to holiday-makers' perceptions of the service called a holiday. Just as the tour operator provides components which create a product, and just as the holiday-maker consumes a product composed of some elements within management control, and others outside that control, so it can be argued that the holiday is experienced as a series of events rather than as one event.

Laws and Ryan (1992), in an examination of flight experiences based on diaries and examination of unsolicited letters to an airline, concluded that there is little to support the hypothesis that passengers perceived flights as one event. Rather, there were a series of events and part-encounters, and indeed it was possible to distinguish phases within events. The same, it can be hypothesised, is true of holidays. To what extent can there be a sense of satisfaction or dissatisfaction with an entity called a holiday, if in fact, the holiday is a series of events that may be unconnected? Each event gives rise to an opportunity for satisfaction or dissatisfaction. The answer in part lies in the type of analysis inherent in the multi-attribute theories considered previously, and that is, holiday-makers attribute varying degrees of importance to the events that comprise the experience and evaluate each accordingly to come to a judgement.

A NEED FOR A PLURALITY OF PARADIGMS

However, reference to such theories must take into account criticisms of the fundamentals inherent in such approaches. From the view of classical and operant conditioning, affective theorising is an attempt 'to move the environment into the head' (Skinner 1977). It is argued that cognitive and affective theories of consumer behaviour offer explanations that merely infer alleged inner causes from observation of the very behaviour they seek to explain. However, in the field of psychology, the 1970s and early 1980s saw the emergence of 'radical behaviourism', which sought to explain behaviour in terms of reinforcement schedules, but recognised the role of pre-behavioural components. Thus, Hirschman (1984) postulates the existence of inherent novelty seeking as a pre-behavioural internal process. In the domain of consumer behaviour 'actualised innovativeness' may be evident in three ways – vicarious innovativeness (learning about new products not yet acquired); adoptive innovativeness (purchase of new products); and use innovativeness (use of new products). Skinner refers to the innovator as 'a place in which certain genetic and environmental causes come together to have a common effect.... It is not some prior purpose, intention or act of will which accounts for novel behaviour; it is the "contingencies of reinforcement"' (Skinner 1972:352).

Needless to say, this contains echoes of the view that tourism can be explained as a dialectical process characterised by a search for the new (novelty seeking in Hirschman's terms), but constrained by a wish for the familiar. Hence the emergence of holiday complexes located in foreign countries but preserving the familiarity of daily modes of living.

In short, a number of potential approaches exist as to how to research holiday-maker behaviours and attitudes, but such paradigms must recognise the constructs of a dialectical process such as that of risk aversion and risk taking inherent in travel. Perhaps the researcher in tourism must be prepared to adopt more than one perspective, and indeed Foxall refers to the erosion of paradigms as psychologists have sought to refute, incorporate or improve understanding of human behaviour. He comments:

> A comprehensive plurality of paradigms is inescapable if authentic understanding of consumer behaviour is preferable to the doctrinaire parochialism that would follow the domination of consumer research by one ontology and associated methodology (Foxall 1990:174).

SUMMARY

Holiday-taking is an important aspect of human behaviour. This is evidenced by the fact that for many families it is often the largest single repeated expenditure that occurs at frequent intervals. After the infrequent purchase of a house, and a car, the holiday is, for at least two-thirds of the population, an annual experience. In addition it has both a temporal as well as a spatial component. It is anticipated prior to departure, and arguably the process of destination and activity choice is itself part of the total holiday experience. It is savoured after return. Thus, although an intangible purchase, it is important. It also reflects lifestyle and personality, albeit subject to the constraints of family and income.

At times it is a mindless experience, where the holiday-maker enacts a scripted role. At other times it offers opportunities for self-actualisation. It consists of not one, but a series of experiences, but is evaluated as an entity. Given the importance of the holiday, and if the assumption is accepted that personality is partly determined by experience, then holidays are important in the process of personality formation. It is a cliché to state that the holiday fortnight is different from the rest of daily life, that it is a reflection of aspirations, fantasies, an escape from realities, a search for new realities. It is worthy of examination. It is also worth taking great care in the design of research. It has been shown to be a complex matrix of emotions, hopes and fears on the one hand, and yet, in many cases, perhaps quite simple on the other as tourists report that they simply want to relax, to get away from it all. Like many other aspects of human behaviour, there is a need to consider carefully a series of paradoxes, and in doing so the selection of a theoretical approach is important in determining and designing the research approach, and ensuring that that approach is pertinent to the problem being studied.

Chapter 5

Qualitative research

INTRODUCTION

There is a significant debate about the role and assumptions underlying qualitative research. On the one hand there is the viewpoint that qualitative research is not a science. Wells is perhaps an extreme protagonist of this view when he states:

> it (qualitative research) does not produce truths, factual, data-based results; nor does it lend itself to being conducted in a series of clearly defined and separable steps – ... – although this does not mean that it should be conducted in a well-planned systematic way. I see qualitative research as living and evolving, a source of insights and ideas, continuously arising, at any time (Wells 1991:39).

On the other hand, does qualitative research, in its requirement for a systematic approach, and in the requirement that its findings aid in understanding a phenomenon, need its own tests of reliability and validity?

From one view qualitative research lends itself to a deconstructionist perspective where objectivity is unobtainable. But this process of relativity might be seen as twofold. There is what might be termed nihilistic validity, where each man is the measure of all things; where all claims to knowledge are equally valid, and there is no basis upon which to make judgement. This view has had its adherents at least as far back as the Greek philosopher Protagoras of Abdera (500–430 BC). Protagoras was in a position that is not without its parallel in today's academic debate about the nature and validity of objective reality. In a reaction to the early physicists, Protagoras postulated a theory of individualist ethics and politics in *Truth of the Throwers*. This theory was tempered by that which is 'normal'. As Barker (1967:70) comments, 'Protagoras was not a mere individualist, but an empiricist who believed in the normal common sense of man'. Common sense perhaps gives us four tests for assessing the validity of findings derived from qualitative research, namely credibility, transferability, dependability and confirmability. Do people accept the interpretation (the test of normal common sense!)? Does research among similar groups reveal identical results? If so, then perhaps it is possible to transfer findings (i.e. make some form of guarded generalisation). Do the results permit some forecast of outcome, which is confirmed? So, in a second sense, there is a relative validity wherein given processes possess validity within certain frameworks, and which might help in understanding others through generalisation.

Finally, before beginning to debate the methods of qualitative research as they might be used within the context of tourist attitudes and behaviour, it is worth noting the strictures of Myrdal (1970:74). He argues that no social science can pretend to be 'amoral' or 'apolitical', and that research is 'always and by logical necessity based on moral and political valuations'. It thus arises that research can be attacked on these grounds, but Myrdal emphasises that 'value relativism is ... emphatically *not moral nihilism*' [original author's emphasis]. After making these comments Myrdal continues with a chapter entitled 'The Respect for Life', and for any researcher an essential element must be respect for the respondent. This is particularly important given the nature of the techniques employed in qualitative research.

This chapter will therefore cover the following issues:

1   categorisations of qualitative research and problems;
2   unstructured research such as complete participative research;
3   the problems of content analysis;
4   techniques associated with more structured qualitative research such as focus groups and projective testing.

CATEGORISATIONS

Qualitative research can be categorised in various ways. For our current purposes it can be divided into two broad categories; first field research, and second open-ended interviewing techniques. The first includes methods such as participant observation and case studies, and can include format-free methods such as the use of conversations. The second ranges from more structured methods such as the use of Kelly Grids, to the less structured like focus groups and projection techniques including Murray's Thematic Apperception tests. The reason for these approaches has already been covered in Chapter 1, but essentially they exist to develop a sense of the emotion that is associated with the subject being researched. In the area of tourism research Moutinho (1989:522) has stated that such techniques are 'designed to find the "emotional hot buttons" of the tourist in relation to a particular subject, by bringing hidden stimuli up to the level of conscious awareness'. But such a process is very different from the detached one of simply keying in data from the completed questionnaire. In many cases the researcher is not simply acting as a 'detached observer' receiving data, but plays a real part in the creation of that data through direct interaction with respondents.

QUESTIONS POSED BY SOCIAL AND CULTURAL STUDIES

Arguably this is particularly so in areas such as the impact of tourism upon host communities, especially when the hosts belong to cultures other than that of the tourist. It may be even more important with the growth of a type of 'eco-tourism' which threatens to increase the level of interaction between tourists from western cultures and hosts from groupings of indigenous peoples with very different cultural frames. The tourist is derived from a culture where leisure, recreation and tourism has been institutionalised, even while it is used at an individual level to escape 'institutionalisation'. The host might come from a society where the dualism between work and leisure is not recognised or discussed in the same terms. While bound by traditions and norms, such native societies exhibit many approaches to work and relaxation that are different to their western counterparts. Heron (1991) discusses many of the issues involved, and their implications for research. Native societies are often characterised by different perspectives of time – not only in terms of the passing of time in a linear pattern, but also in the division of personal time combined with concepts of the metaphysical and sacred (Hall 1984). Often the development of tourism is advanced for reasons of economic growth, but such growth cannot help but create social change. In this context, Thompson has commented:

> For there is no such thing as economic growth which is not, at the same time, growth or change of a culture; and the growth of social consciousness, like the growth of a poet's mind, can never, in the last analysis, be planned (1967:77).

Given that tourism has social impacts it might be asked, how can the researcher best understand such issues unless he or she immerses him or herself into the norms of the host society? If the researcher comes from the hosts, then there is a need to understand the dynamics of the tourist and their needs. From this perspective, the hegemony of rationality as a process of understanding and undertaking research needs to be carefully questioned. Three sets of questions are posed for the researcher:

1   The ontological – that is, what is the nature of the interaction between tourist and host – the process is an expressive one as native peoples seek adaptation within a framework of meaning for themselves to cope with the 'official' demands of a western-led process based on dualisms of personal/ institutional time, work/place, family/career roles that are not defined by them in the same way.
2   The epistemological – how is understanding to be sought.
3   The praxiological – the questions of 'whose practices for whom?', and 'by whom?'. Such questions of necessity precede discussions as to the values inherent in the answers that might be forthcoming. Qualitative research is, to reiterate Myrdal's comments, not free from normative questions.

It is contended that in matters relating to cultural change induced by tourism, field research has a valuable role to play as it is a means by which understanding at the intuitive level can be gained. This is not necessarily to imply that there is a dichotomy between the empirical-rational mode and the descriptive, ethnographic or phenomenological approach – certainly, to follow Augustinian tradition, man is both body and soul, and research based upon questionnaires alone that are subjected to statistical analysis is unlikely to uncover all of the nuances of such situations. There is, therefore, a need for qualitative studies to discover the 'soul' of both the tourist and host if the impact of tourism is to be understood. How, then, might such studies be approached?

UNSTRUCTURED SITUATIONS

Participative-observer field research

Field research in tourism poses many dilemmas for researchers, most of whom have been tourists and gained significant experience. The process that is being researched may have personal significance for the investigator as respondents echo the researcher's own beliefs or experiences. Additionally, the researcher may deliberately immerse him or herself into a situation so as to be at one with the group that is being studied. Much may depend upon the role that the researcher is playing, and the type of holiday being examined. Gold (1969:30–9) identifies four roles that the participant researcher might play:

1   Complete participant.
2   Participant as observer.
3   Observer as participant.
4   Complete observer.

The *complete participant* becomes a genuine participant. For example, suppose behaviour of 'The Club'[1] holiday-makers was being examined. This would require the researcher to be of an appropriate age group, and to indulge in discos, beach games, drinking, participating in team games, 'chatting up' members of the opposite sex and generally exhibiting extrovert behaviour. The ethical questions discussed in Chapter 1 are obvious under such circumstances. At what stage, if at all, do researchers reveal that their intentions are to research such behaviour. Yet, if they are to participate, they must actually participate; and that could include fulfilling the roles expected of a successful 'The Club' holiday-taker.

The *participant as observer* resolves this dilemma by participating, but actually making it known that they are doing research. This, of course, then raises the question as to what extent is the research compromised by the revelation. Perhaps the researcher might not be invited to certain events by participants, or equally, those holiday-makers might now feel that they have to live up to a set of (their own?) expectations as to what is deemed to be an appropriate behaviour.

The *observers as participants* also reveal themselves as researchers, and will participate in normal social process, but make no pretence at being participants.

They are generally present at events as part of the group in the sense that they are known to the group members, but do not actually play any role in the group's happenings. This form of research role is separated from the *complete observer* in the sense that the latter simply observes without being part of it in any way. They might be the sunbather on the beach who observes 'The Club' members playing their games. They might be the solitary drinker in the bar when 'The Club' members hit the town. They are present, but are not known to the group. The novelist David Lodge (1992) describes the tourism researcher thus:

> Roger Sheldrake hears but is not distracted by the noise of the ambulance. He has been up for hours, out on the balcony of his room, high up in the Wyatt Regency, with his notebook and binoculars and zoom-lens camera, hard at work, observing and recording and documenting ritual behaviour around the swimming-pool in the big hotel across the street.... The pool, however minimal, is a *sine qua non*, the heart of a ritual. Most of the sunbathers take at least a perfunctory dip. It is not so much swimming as immersion. A kind of baptism.
>   Roger Sheldrake makes a note.

Thus Roger projects his deconstructionist Ph.D. thesis of tourism as the new religion of a non-religious age upon the unsuspecting tourist! How can the researcher avoid the pre-judgement of a Roger Sheldrake, wearied by the 'seen it, done it, been there' syndrome which loses contact with the feelings actually experienced by the tourist?

Of course, if the researcher is aged between 18 and 30, then they might more easily identify with the activities of 'The Club' holiday-makers than if they are over 45 years of age. Equally, the academic researcher might feel more at one with a group of 'explorers' on their holiday. The higher the level of congruence between the particular vacation interests of the researcher and the type of holiday under examination, the greater is the danger of a loss of 'objectivity'. But, as defined in Chapter 1, if holidays are essentially about experiences, then is not the reality of the holiday a question not of objectivity, but sharpness of emotional understanding? How does the researcher convey this, while at the same time ensuring the validity of what is conveyed?

Stephenson and Greer (1981) point to five issues that affect the researcher as an understanding participant/observer. These are:

Problems arising from familiarity

Holiday-taking researchers have been absorbed in the experience of their own holidays, which meet their needs of relaxation and exploration. In viewing others, do researchers fully recognise the patterns existing in situations that possess such high levels of familiarity for them? Do they project generalisations of motivations based on their own personal experience on to other holiday participants? Is this danger not intensified by their own levels of awareness of the academic literature, because it is a literature with which they can identify not only at a professional level, but also at an inherently emotive level?

Writing of what the tourist sees at heritage attractions Heron comments that:

> What the tourist sees and feels comfortable with is the fundamental message of the program which is the agency's belief in its distinctions between professionals, administrators and labourers, in its hierarchy of control ... in its expertise, and in the goodness and beneficence of itself (1991:181–2).

His argument is that the tourist is exposed 'not only to a foreign interpretation of the local culture but also to the beliefs and values of a foreign agency', namely that which heritage interpretation staff regard as their own professionalism established within an international context. How does this bear upon the problem of being a researcher in tourism? By extension it can be argued that the expert, or indeed, the student of tourism, by reason of being aware of implications of tourism, begins however unconsciously to project reasons and motives upon the tourist of which the tourist might perhaps be only slightly aware. Or, at the other extreme, the motivations seem so obvious that the thought that anyone would wish to examine them would seem to be equally strange. The danger of projection is perhaps even greater where the tourist researcher is grappling with the normative issues associated with sustainable tourism. Eco-tourism, as Wheeller (1990) wryly observes, is a question of 'the good guys in a good guise' – it is writ through with values and ethical judgements, and hence again there may be problems for the researcher to maintain the needed distance and objectivity.

The nature of the relationship between researcher and informant

In the example of the researcher looking at 'The Club' holidays, it might be argued that the nature of the response given to a 22-year-old researcher, and that given to someone of over 40 might be very different. The former might find it easier to get a response because the respondents more easily identify with the researcher.

To what extent does local knowledge gain rapport and access to data?

In the field of anthropology, it can be argued that the researcher familiar with the locale, and who speaks the local dialect can gain more than one who does not possess those advantages. Does a researcher into holiday behaviour in Spain gain from having a higher knowledge of Spain than the holiday-maker? The researcher might have the support of Spanish hoteliers, which gains access, but does this knowledge actually inhibit understanding of the respondent who has a more limited network of influence at the local level?

Ethical and political questions

If the researcher does possess specific advantages, do these create personal, ethical and political questions? Do their insights make them more sensitive to issues by reason of being more informed. How does this affect their research attitudes?

Subsequent responsibilities to respondents

If researchers are familiar with the holiday experience and the holiday-makers, are there any special problems likely to arise after the research has been completed? For example, if a researcher into 'The Club' finds someone who has drunk too much, engaged in casual sex, and who makes a series of statements about this experience, to what extent does the researcher, as a confidant, have an continuing responsibility to support the respondent? Does the nature of responsibility differ if the field researcher has adopted the complete participant role as against one of the other roles?

In many senses these questions are a further reinforcement of the points discussed in Chapter 1. They would be familiar to many researchers. Additionally, the role of any researcher, even those involved in field research, is to adopt the role of the stranger even as they seek to understand the emotion of the holiday. It is by finding the familiar unfamiliar that the researcher begins to discover the nuances and realities of a situation. It should also be noted that these issues are even more pertinent when a researcher is seeking to assess the impacts of tourism upon a host community. Finding out how local people feel about tourism is an obvious example of a situation for which participant observation is a pertinent technique. It might say something about the nature of tourism research that such studies are not reported more often in the tourism journals. But such studies have been undertaken. For example, Lever (1987) demonstrates from a number of visits to a Spanish village, how tourism changed the role of women in a traditional male-orientated family structure.

Such techniques can also be used to discover how tourists feel. In an as yet unpublished study Hebditch (1994) gained a significant richness of data by booking herself on to coach tours visiting places that were capitalising upon being the location of British TV series. These included 'Inspector Morse's Oxford', 'Spender's Newcastle', 'Bergerac's Jersey' and a visit to 'Coronation Street'. By actually going on the coach trips, some of which included overnight stays, she was able to experience the holiday from the perspective of the holiday-takers. Additionally, by being a member of the group, she was able to converse easily with the holiday-makers in a natural setting to obtain their views. In another study, Laws and Ryan (1992) report the results of a diary exercise made by Laws arising from his trans-Atlantic flights. Here, there is the example *par excellence* of the researcher being the participant, and the subject of the research, as Laws attempted to develop a means of measuring the nature of a travel experience.

Perhaps one of the longest examples of participative-observer research is that of Cohen's experience of *soi* (lane) life within the slums of Bangkok, and his observations of tourist-oriented prostitution during the summers of 1981 to 1984. In a series of articles Cohen has reported on the nature of the relationships between *Thai* girls and *farang* (foreign) men (1982, 1986) as he observed the pattern of hopes and fears that these often transitory relationships generated. Equally, Cohen's work (1983, 1992) on the impacts of tourism upon the hill tribes of Thailand in the early 1980s also shows the benefit of detailed observation arising from field research methods. It is doubtful if more conventional empirically based quantitative methods could have generated such insights, and Cohen's articles are recommended to any student who has interest in the anthropological approach to tourism research.

SAMPLING

In quantitative research, sampling to ensure the representativeness of the sample is an important consideration. It should also be important to the field researcher, although if the researcher is a participant-observer within a tour group there is a sense in which no sampling takes place at all. Those who react with the researcher are the sample. In many instances the research will adopt a non-probability sample, that is, there is no way of estimating the probability of respondents being included in the sample. The common ways of categorising such samples are:

Judgement and opportunistic sampling

The researcher interacts with those who provide information. This would be the norm in participant-observation. In the case of the observer as participant however, the researcher might be making more judgements as to whom to approach for information on the basis of previous observation.

Snowball sampling

Here researchers approach some respondents, and ask to be put in touch with other respondents. The resultant chain follows a population of social relations. This could be used, for example, in assessing the views of residents to the impact of tourism upon their daily life. One example of this approach was in the study undertaken for the Peak Tourism Partnership in 1993 by BDOR Ltd. The Partnership wished to establish Community Groups for a series of workshops to be held in the Hope–Edale–Castleton area of the Peak National Park in the UK. The consultants established such groups by talking to residents and asking them to identify people who they thought would be interested and who represented their concerns. Such exercises can be effective, but may also have political implications as it implies a recognition that existing processes of local democracy may be failing to obtain a genuine representation of local views (Prentice 1993; Montgomery and Ryan 1994).

Theoretical sampling

Glaser and Strauss suggest a third category of sampling, which they term theoretical sampling. They define this as:

> the process of data collection for generating theory whereby the analyst jointly collects, codes and analyses his data and decides what data to collect next and where to find them, in order to develop his theory as it emerges (Glaser and Strauss 1967:45).

The research is thus a reiterative process where each stage informs the next. Thus, if it is found that the nature of 'The Club' holiday activities are being dictated by the couriers, then the researcher might want to interview in more depth the attitude of the couriers as to how they define their role, and what they think are the needs of their clientele.

QUESTIONS AND CODING

As already noted, there are significant difficulties in wording questions in a manner to avoid the question itself determining the response, rather than the respondents' own feelings or thoughts dictating the reply. In the case of field research, however, the researcher has the advantage (and the problems) that many questions arise in conversation, and can therefore be amplified, embroidered upon, and the issue discussed at length. Of course, in normal conversation the process is two-way; both express views and an interchange of views, opinions and experiences occurs. In this sense the researcher colours the perception of the respondent, and the question arises as to the extent to which this produces a bias in the responses. Do respondents simply feed back the researcher's own prejudices? In circumstances other than the participant-observer, this danger should be less likely.

Whatever the nature of the question, the golden rule for any researcher must be to record the answer. Do not depend upon memory. If it is not possible to record a reply by the use of video or recorder, it is essential that the response is written down as soon as possible. It is vital that the researcher develops the discipline of maintaining a research journal. If the notes are taken during the day, then almost certainly they will consist of hurried scribbles with the use of an abbreviated form of words. It is important that they are written out in full each day (or night) while the memory is fresh as to:

the acts that were being performed, however brief;

the activities, that is, the context of the acts;

the participants, the people involved and the nature of the relationship;

the participation, the level of participation by participants, the level of adaptation to a situation;

the meaning of the act, the verbal statements of participants that define the action; and

the entire setting under study as an unit of activity.

(Lofland, 1971)

From this it becomes obvious that it is possible to plan a journal page ahead of an action so as to more quickly aid the collecting of data (see Table 5.1). Equally, it is obvious from the above list that some elements of the data are of a longer duration than other components. So, to take an example, let us suppose that our group of 18–30 holiday-makers are meeting at the bar of their hotel prior to going out in the evening. The page in the journal might look something like Table 5.1, for example.

In practice, at the time of collection of the data, the researcher will have developed their own notation of abbreviations. Participants may be noted by initials, venues by numbers if the researcher is familiar with them. The nature of the activities may be referred to by codes as the researcher becomes increasingly

Table 5.1 Sample journal page

| Setting | 18–30 holiday-makers – Group A, Magalluf, Hotel Le Club, Rafter's Bar |
| Date | 22 August 1994, 4th day of holiday |

Time	Participants	Action
10.00 pm	Arrive in hotel bar. Henrietta only one there.	Buy drink – H comments still too early – place not worth going out till 11.30 but thought Jane and Helen were going to be down by 10.00.
10.05	John arrives	Kisses H – buys us all a drink.
10.15	Helen and Jane arrive.	Girls go off together to washroom – John makes derogatory comments to me about them – says fancies Jane, but can't prise her from Helen.
10.22	Peter, Jason, Gareth arrive – been drinking next door.	Loud entry, Peter wolf-whistles. Helen goes up to Peter, share cigarette.
10.28	All seated at table with drinks, couriers arrive with Mark, Ann, Lesley, 'Skinner', Paul, 'Bonkers' and Andy. Complaints about Janine not being ready. Janine arrives in micro-skirt. Plenty of comments about 'looking for action'.	

Table 5.2 Sample journal report of conversation

Researcher	Commented that Jane was early in the bar tonight.
John	Yer, thought was onto a good thing there as I said I would be there early, but she came with Helen. Why do girls stick around in pairs?
Researcher	Guessed that was the way it generally was.
John	Yes, but he and Paul were going to try to split them up – Paul liked Helen.
Researcher	What was he hoping would happen?
John	Getting fed up with all this keeping together – wanted to get Jane somewhere a bit quiet so they could talk a bit more. They had gotten on well together on the beach etc. etc.

familiar with the milieu. Later the notes will be accompanied by reports of conversation (see Table 5.2). Even in the example in Table 5.2 it is notable that the researcher has posed questions and made fairly neutral comments that progress the conversation, but in a natural way. Nonetheless, questions dictate the path of a conversation, and the question can arise as to what extent would this conversation have developed if it had occurred between two 'ordinary' male holiday-makers.

In this form it quickly becomes obvious that the researcher is going to compile copious notes, many of which are far from rivetting, when considered in isolation. But at the time of compiling notes the researcher does not know what is, and what is not important. Will John succeed? What will be the nature of the relationship? How long will it last? To what extent will it be typical of holiday relationships? Does it matter – if so, to whom, and why? The answer to these and other questions are simply not known at the time of recording the data. Should the relationship develop, then of what significance is it that it did not occur until say the fifth day of the holiday? It is not known if this is significant unless other cases exist for comparative purposes. What is the meaning of the holiday for the individuals? This is not known at this stage of the holiday – and perhaps a follow up after the holiday is required.

It should also be clear that many of these notes are not going to see the light of day in any report. In a sense they are the ore from which, hopefully, the gold will be extracted. The notes are the data in the same way in which individual questionnaire returns provide the basis for the statistical interpretation that occurs in quantitative research. However, the task of entering data from responses to scales is quite easy. For their part, field researchers have to develop their own units of assessment.

CONTENT ANALYSIS – A CLASSIFICATION SYSTEM

The researcher has to determine a means of analysing the content of the reports as to their meaning, the frequency of events occurring, the importance of these happenings, to whom they happened, what was thought about them, how they shaped behaviour, what the implications of that behaviour was – the questions are easy to think of – the means of analysis less so.

One solution is to devise a catalogue of classifications. But while each catalogue may be specific to the situation being studied, in order to be of help to other researchers wishing to undertake a comparative study, or wishing to have some reference point from which to interpret their own research, it is useful if the study can draw upon some more general process. Within sociology, many researchers have found the work of Talcott Parsons (1951, 1952) of use, with the emphasis being on the difference between instrumental and expressive values and orientations. In tourism, however, there could be some problems in utilising this distinction – tourist activities are expressions of wish fulfilment, but it can be argued that they are also instrumental in living out the wish fulfilment. If a tourist seeks adventure, whitewater rafting becomes the instrument by which the expression of self as an adventure seeker becomes operationalised. The act is both expressive and instrumental. Such a problem was tackled in a different context by White (1951), and it might be that his classification can represent a starting point in tourism field research. Adapting White's approach a little, the following classification can be suggested (see Table 5.3).

Table 5.3 Components of content analysis

Instrumental	A sense of achievement Cognitive satisfaction Economic value
Expressive	Self-expression Meeting affiliative needs Showing concern for others Defining purpose – the religious-philosophical needs
Other Aspects	Individualistic Physiological Political Miscellaneous

Source: White 1951.

Instrumental

Achievement

Values that produce achievement motivation for the individual holiday-maker can be assessed through the completion of some task perceived as a challenge. It might require some degree of commitment or work. The holiday-maker who completes a long-distance walk such as the Pennine Way has achieved a measurable goal requiring commitment. The tourist who secures a PADI award by taking a scuba-diving course while on holiday has a tangible sign of the achievement, namely a certificate.

Cognitive

A drive for learning as an end in itself as well as the means of achieving a given end – the sightseer who visits the ruins of Ephesus in Turkey absorbs an experience that might help to understand the Roman world. Curiosity was a motive for the visit, the satisfaction of curiosity is an addition to knowledge. How that knowledge is put to use becomes another instrumental process.

Economic

White's work can be interpreted as the economic values existing at a collective level rather than an individual level. Thus, the paying of admission fees to a museum is an economic transaction of value to the museum, but the individual may obtain a cognitive gain.

Expressive

Self-expressive

These are important in many holiday situations. It has been noted that holidays are a period of freedom from normal constraints imposed by work or family; they are a period of fun. Holidays are a sanctioned 'escape route'. Podilchak (1991) examines the meaning of leisure and fun, and argues that there is indeed a distinction. Fun is perceived as being:

(a) doing things on the surface, being silly, laughing;
(b) as growing out of an activity, being purposeless;
(c) exciting, exhilarating – unique, not everyday.

Fun, according to Podilchak's informants, was qualitative; it also entailed the need to be with others with whom one was relaxed, open and carefree. Self-expression can also be seen through the process of discovery, and the appreciation of art.

Affiliative

The affiliative needs refer to behaviour associated with interaction with others, belonging to groups, expressing loyalty, fulfilling a need for belonging. Again, this is an important part of the holiday process for many, as evidenced by the example of 'The Club' holidays referred to above. But the holiday is partially artificial in the sense that the affiliation to a group is for a short period of time, and furthermore holiday groups are often composed of those who have not previously known each other, and who may subsequently never see each other. The social dynamics of holiday groups are therefore of significant interest. The quality of those dynamics is an important determinant of the success of the holiday. They are formulated from a shared experience of place and activities, often by like-minded people in the sense that the type of holiday attracts some but not others.

Concern for others

White (1951) argues that this is different from an affiliative need in that it is more generalised; this category focuses on attitudes towards specific groups and humanity in general. Again, in some types of holidays this can be an important motivating force for participation. An example would be holidays based around specific projects designed to help communities, rebuild historic buildings, be involved in archaeological digs or like activities. From another perspective, holidays are periods of strengthening bonds between family units or friends, and hence could be said to be about concern for immediate others.

Religious-philosophical

Defined as a concern with the ultimate meaning of life, and an assessment of the meaning of self, relationship with the deity, this expressive behaviour is both historically and currently a key factor in tourism. Rinschede points out that the pilgrimage is as old as civilisation, and that among the Celts 'holy groves and burial sites were places of great gatherings' (1992:53). Today visits to Mecca or Lourdes attract tens of thousands at any one time. But like Lodge's (1992) protagonist, there are those who consider tourism to be a secular pilgrimage. Certainly, for those who seek solitude in the hills, the experience can surpass being merely a passive viewer of scenic beauty to being something more philosophical.

Other

Individualistic

Concerned with expressions of the importance of the individual, this category covers activities that nurture individual personality and personal fulfilment.

Physiological

This category is concerned with activities based upon physiological drives such as eating and drinking.

Political

This relates to activities associated with collective goals and group decision-making. In White's (1951) work this category is meant to apply to institutionalised processes.

Miscellaneous

This category covers any behaviours or goals not listed above such as modesty or manners.

A number of comments can be made about this categorisation. First, it poses some difficulties for the holiday situation in that being generalised the classifications are overlapping. The individualistic, in a holiday context, can overlap with the self-expressive, for example. Second, the very generalised nature of the categories present potential problems of reliability. In practice, therefore, researchers will often undertake independent categorisation, thereby requiring the research to be undertaken by a team. Third, the distinction between the instrumental and the expressive is itself difficult to maintain in practice within the holiday context.

On the other hand, it is of interest to note that this model of content analysis, developed without reference to the tourism and leisure literature, has, nonetheless, significant parallels with that body of literature. Earlier reference was made to the categories of the Ragheb and Beard Leisure Motivation Scale (1982) (see Chapter 3, p. 53), and it is evident that there are parallels. The needs for affiliation, intellectual pursuits and self-expression through relaxation are evident in both classifications.

For any researcher undertaking field research of this nature there are advantages in being able to develop a method of content analysis that can work back from the specific to the general. The situation that is being analysed can be context bound, and hence it becomes difficult to assess the wider implications of the results. On the other hand, being able to redefine categories into a more generalised schema does permit comparisons to be made – comparisons that can inform the project under study, and that permit future researchers to test any findings. This process might therefore require a two-stage approach from the researcher. The first consists of developing a classification for coding events at the specific level, the second requires receding this series into a more generalised model. In this way the researcher can retain the richness and detail of the specific, and additionally generate a model for wider testing.

For example, in an analysis of behaviours of an 18–30 holiday group, this hierarchical process might include:

Specific level	beach activities	bar activities	disco activities
Generalised level	AFFILIATION NEEDS		

It is very difficult to be prescriptive – each project requires its own classification systems. But, for findings to have a wider value, it is advantageous for any researcher to be able to develop categorisations that refer to other studies derived from the literature.

CONVERSATION AS A SOURCE OF DATA

For the student or other person undertaking research into tourism, while there may be a wish to undertake the participant-observer roles noted above, time may not always be present. There may therefore be a temptation to use question-naires, but as will be discussed in Chapter 6, while there are undoubted advantages, there are also problems. Can conversations be used to derive some of the richness of data referred to above, and to what extent can the data be regarded as possessing validity and reliability? The first point to make is that the use of conversation as a research method has a long and honourable tradition in social research. In 1851 Mayhew drew upon such conversations in his report *London Labour and the London Poor*. In 1948 Zweig commented:

> I tried a new and unorthodox technique … and, as far as I can judge, it was not unsuccessful. I dropped the idea of a questionnaire or formal verbal questions put forward in the course of research; instead I had casual talks with working-class men on an absolutely equal footing and in friendly intercourse. These were not formal interviews but an exchange of views on life, labour and poverty (Zweig 1948:1).

Here the researcher becomes a confidant and a friend. However, such a process should not be as unstructured as at first sight appears. There is a preparation in terms of the themes that might be discussed, a knowledge of the daily reality of the respondent, and in the selection of a respondent. Possible respondents are observed, they may be sampled to match a sampling frame, their behaviour might have been recorded. Preparation can also include experiencing aspects of the type of holiday under question. Thus, to return to the work of Hebditch (1994), conversations arose naturally because she was a member of the group. To intrude a personal note, I became better at understanding the impact of children upon tourist behaviour when I became a father. Experience, preparation of an agenda, establishing a friendly rapport, determining a discipline whereby the results of a conversation are quickly recorded are necessary skills in the use of conversation as a means of conducting research. Additionally, there is a need to develop a skill in using questions as prompts, as shown in example of 'The Club' holiday-maker above. However, one of the self-disciplines that a researcher must adopt is to

Table 5.4 Conversation as a source of data

Researcher	Did you enjoy that trip to the taverna?
Holiday-maker	Well, it was all right.
Researcher	I thought the food was rather good (*prompting for reason as to why the trip was just 'alright'*)
Holiday-maker	Yes.
Researcher	Says nothing (*This can be useful in obtaining a longer response – many people are not 'happy' with longer periods of silence in conversation*)
Holiday-maker	Pass me that mat will you please.
Researcher	I thought the waiter was a bit surly. (*Trying to redirect the conversation*)
Holiday-maker	Did you – I didn't notice.
Researcher	Yes – I had to ask him twice for my beer.
Holiday-maker	Yer – it happens sometimes.

accept the negative as a valid strategy by the respondent. For example, consider the exchange in Table 5.4.

In this short example, it can be seen that the researcher is pushing for an answer where the respondent is not, in probability, rating the visit to the taverna as being anything of any importance. In many senses, therefore, the researcher can draw upon conversation as a valid source of information, but needs to develop many of the skills associated with running a focus group.

The above discussion also implies that conversations, for purposes of research, can be categorised as being of two types: the unplanned and the planned. The former is where the researcher absorbs information from the incidental intercourse of everyday life. It is pertinent perhaps in the early stages of research where the researcher may have only a hazy notion of the research topic and the direction of research. It can occur where the student is perhaps on holiday, talking to friends and fellow tourists, and subsequently draws upon the memories of such conversations either to define a research project, or to elicit evidence for a viewpoint. Such conversations are unplanned; there may be doubt about the veracity of recall, and little is known about how representative the viewpoints may be. Yet such conversations have made a contribution to the research.

The planned conversation is akin to interviewing in that the process is part of the participant-observer function discussed above. Respondents may have been selected on some basis, however general. The researcher has a framework of interests that might be drawn upon. Such conversations lie between the 'free-for-all' of daily communication, and the interview where set questions may be posed. The conversation is planned in the sense that the researcher has an agenda in mind, but that agenda is not known to the other party.

As well as conversation, a similar source of research data is the use of letters. This has rarely been used as a source of tourist research, but one interesting example is to be found in Cohen's analysis (1986) of personal letters produced by Thai girls engaged in tourist-oriented prostitution. Grey comments about the love affair with the exotic as follows:

> Excessive love for the exotic can destroy the white European in the Orient. Many men think they go away from here with their soul's intact – but they find in their own countries they've been profoundly changed by their experiences without knowing it. They become outcasts among their own people because everything at home seems insipid in comparison with the East. Then usually they're lured back by the siren call of what has already ruined them (1983:254).

Cohen is well aware of the lure of the exotic and of the problems associated with the use of letters – do letters 'objectivise the subjective'; do 'letters render the interpreter real access to the writer's self' (Cohen 1986:117), or indeed, in this context, are letters a means of manipulation? The letters he uses to illustrate his arguments show the frustrations, the self-delusion, the hopes, the deceits and the loves that the tourist trip to Thailand has created. In this sense, the analysis has provided rich data as to the nature of the tourist–host interaction.

POSTCARD ANALYSIS

Postcards can also be studied by the researcher and can be approached from a number of different angles. There is the interpretation of the message; there is also the interpretation of the picture. In a study of the hill tribes of Thailand, Cohen reviews the postcards from the area and states:

> The way people are perceived and labelled is not of purely intellectual significance; it has its repercussions upon the manner in which they are dealt with by the state and wider society (1986:122).

He argues that the portrayal of the hill tribes perpetuates an ambiguity and uncertainty about the role of hill people within Thailand. One is tempted to ask, in another context, what do Spanish and Greek people think of Northern European tourists who buy postcards of topless women to send as 'souvenirs' of their holiday? How do such cards fit into the categorisations or means of content analysis proposed by Cohen? (See Figures 5.2 and 5.3.)

Cohen suggests a simple matrix for first establishing the nature of the representation, and this is reproduced in Figure 5.1. This matrix not only identifies who is represented, but also who, or which company, is taking the photographs and controlling the depiction of the scene.

The actual image can then be further analysed along five dimensions:

(a) beautiful images: structured so as to elicit a serious appreciation by the viewer according to aesthetic criteria familiar to them;

Who is represented

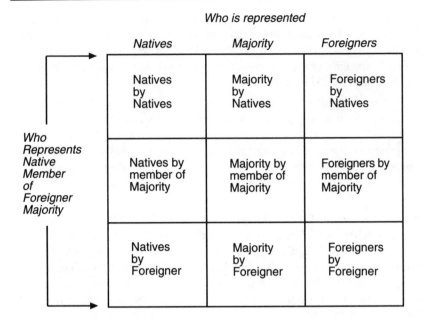

Figure 5.1 Image content analysis

(b) exotic images: designed to elicit serious consideration on the premise of that which is unfamiliar to the viewer;

(c) cute images: a portrayal of familiar traits of sweetness or prettiness designed to elicit a ludic sense of enjoyment;

(d) comic images: designed to generate merriment through exaggeration or incongruence;

(e) neutral images: which Cohen describes as being 'common in most journalistic and scientific representations ... [but] infrequent in touristic images owing to the symbolic functions of such images' (1993:43).

However, it can be commented that symbolic functioning is not confined to the neutral or metanymic image – the metaphoric image of exoticism or cuteness also conveys attitude and symbolises an approach to the matter portrayed on the card. The pictures upon postcards can act as effectively as symbols of attitudes as the messages that are written upon them; and again, as with the above examples, the researcher needs to categorise and interpret such symbols. The traditional 'saucy' postcard of the British seaside coveys the comic, but also says something about a society that finds the image both familiar and comic. See Figures 5.2 and 5.3. The dates of both of these cards are not known, but are probably prior to the mid-1950s. They indicate that certain attitudes towards tourism are therefore at least 40 years old!

Figure 5.2 'There's a lot to see down here!' The conventional appeal of scenic beauty of the holiday destination is given a sexual flavour, but who is the figure of fun? The 'gentleman' is salacious, but a caricature. The wider implication of the card as a perception of tourism is that bathing provides an opportunity for an encounter with a sexual flavour – but in this card what is the nature of the 'encounter'. Is it purely passive as the gentleman can only passively stare? Does he invite retribution judging from the looks of the two ladies in the caravan? Their looks appear not to invite further attention. Is this how young ladies are supposed to behave? The lady stepping out into the water is certainly free from the encumbrances of normal dress. Holidays allow freedom? In fact, the more one looks at the card, the greater the number of interpretations that come to mind

CASE STUDIES

Case studies are common in tourism, but in many instances are applied to descriptions of spatial change of destinations, the management of tourist flows through resort or attraction areas or assessments of physical change due to tourist developments. They are less commonly used in studies relating to tourist attitudes, although some work on behaviour patterns have been reported. For example, Jordan (1980) in a study of a Vermont Vacation Village describes the attitudes of residents towards tourists through the various months of the year. For example, in late October and early November he records the attitudes of the residents towards the hunters in these terms:

> Hunters are considered to be the most unprofitable, even dangerous type of tourist and there is little inter-personal contact.... These amounts (of expenditure) are judged to be inadequate in consideration of their behaviour,

Abraham's Humorous Series, Keswick,
No. 2 (copyright).

Honister Pass and Crag.

Ye simple tourists, who *so* cheerful
    pay
O'er Honister Pass to drive in "four
    horse shay,"
This painful truth experience will
    tell,
It's mostly walk and pay your fare
    as well.

Figure 5.3 Honister Pass and Crag. The tourist appears as a simple trusting soul – again seeking the delights of the countryside. The so-called ride to the crag in practice becomes a walk – and apparently from the fact that there are about 17 figures drawn, it is a walk not done in solitude. Here tourism is indeed travail. On the horizon stands a building – a pub perhaps, or some place where tourists will willingly part with their money for a drink. So, is this an example of hosts being in the 'superior' position? One only hopes that the downhill return trip is without incident!

when by day they terrorize the neighbourhood with their careless gun fire or, by night, when their loud drunken parties are disruptive (1980:39–40).

Again, however, as in many such case studies, the report is the result of a period of observation. In this instance Jordan spent many periods of time as a participant observer in the village concerned.

Can case studies be more than simply a description? The answer must surely be yes. Tourism case studies are often the result of informed looking, that is a process of observation informed by a theoretical framework. Again examples can be given. Doxey (1975) developed his by now much-quoted Irridex as a result of observation of tourist and host interaction in Barbados and Niagara-on-the-Lake. In turn, his model has been developed by those who have used it to inform their own observations. Milligan (1989) used Doxey's Irridex in her study of Portuguese workers in the Guernsey hotel industry as a means of analysing resident attitudes towards migrant workers dependent upon tourism. Yet again, this study resulted from a period of participant observation while she was working within the Guernsey hotel industry as a casual summer season worker.

In other cases the literature may lack comparative development, and hence initial work might be descriptive in nature as it seeks to identify variables that pertain to a given situation. Arguably this might be the case in studies relating to the relationship between crime and tourism. One such example might Elliot and Ryan's (1993) work on the effects of terrorism on Corsica's tourism. The nature of the topic makes measurement of impact very difficult to assess, and hence the authors are restricted to a description of flows of tourism and levels of terrorist action. The same is true of Buckley and Klemm's (1993) study of tourism in Ireland. However, Ryan (1993) works upon these studies in an attempt to begin model building, albeit still at a descriptive level. In short, it is possible to observe developments of thought within the literature commencing from case studies. Nowhere is this perhaps more obvious than in the case of the tourist destination life cycle. From a descriptive process of tourist types and spatial development, this is now beginning to be reiterated in the form of quantitative analysis, as evidenced by di Benedetto and Bojanic (1993).

STRUCTURED SITUATIONS

The focus group

So far the discussion has centred upon comparatively open, free-flowing structures where the researcher exercises, on the whole, comparatively little control over the situation. Qualitative research also permits more structured situations where the researcher can play a more proactive role. Even here, however, that role is generally designed to be more facilitative rather than directive, as is evidenced by the use of the focus group.

A focus group is usually fairly homogenous in character (i.e. of the same age group, sex, or income group), as is required. It normally numbers 8 to 10, rarely more than a dozen. People are selected by field workers, and it is important that those selected have little or no experience of working in a focus group. People acquire knowledge of social structures, and the important thing from the researcher's viewpoint is to obtain views representative of a wider population; not from expert 'opinion givers' accustomed to the dynamics of a focus group. People are usually put at ease with coffee or tea, introduced to each other, told the purpose of the interview, and then the conversation begins, aided by the researcher in the role of a moderator or facilitator.

The focus group has undoubted advantages as a means of obtaining views. These can arise from the social dynamics of the group, which can be categorised as being:

(a) synergism – a cumulative group effect produces a wider range of ideas than is possible from just interviewing individuals;

(b) snowballing – a single comment can elicit a whole range of additional confirmatory or modifying statements;

(c) security – the social ease generated by the situation reduces the sense of insecurity or defensiveness that some might feel, allowing such people to make their views known;

(d) spontaneity – more spontaneous, but possibly more unconventional views might result;

(e) stimulation – the members of the group can stimulate each other.

In practice, the above processes are obviously over-lapping and confirmatory, but the researcher gains an originality of insight and a richness of data not usually forthcoming from individual interviews. Additionally, although the process is a qualitative one, there are advantages to be derived from the homogeneity of the group. In a sense the respondents are representative of clusters of pertinent experiences – but this does presume that care has been taken over the selection of the group. The researcher also gains time – one hour with a focus group can generate more ideas than several hours of individual interviews. On the other hand, it can take several hours for a group interview to be analysed, and such analysis often requires independent confirmation.

There are various techniques that the researcher can use to prompt conversation should it flag. One is by simply returning to a topic that the researcher might want to re-open, although care must be taken not to lead the conversation into conclusions. Other techniques have an element of game-playing, but can nonetheless produce interesting results. One common one is to ascribing a personality to a place. The process might go something like the conversation illustrated in Table 5.5. By ascribing a personality to a place, it becomes possible to elicit an image of the place.

Other techniques commonly used include the use of prompts to elicit comments. Showing photographs of places, obtaining comments to video extracts, using brochures – all are means of prompting conversation. The dangers of such techniques are perhaps equally obvious. There is a danger that one

Table 5.5 Focus group conversation, ascribing personality to a place

Reseacher	Let's compare some destinations. Let us suppose there was a person called Miami, what sex would that person be?
Respondent	Well, I guess Miami might be female?
Researcher	Why do you think that?
Respondent	Um, I'm not sure; er . . . I guess Miami is like one those mutton dressed as lamb places. You know the type. Well, she's seen better days, but wants to keep on seeming young.
Researcher	How old do you think Miami is?
Respondent	Definitely not young, but not too old. I don't know . . . I suppose about late 30s.
Researcher	So we have this late 30s female; how would you describe her?
Respondent	Oh – a bit 'blowsy' – a bit 'tarty' – you know, trying to entice the men.

member of the group begins to dominate proceedings; and hence the skilled researcher must try to ensure that other views are expressed. There is the danger that a group can spend a long time on trivial points, and less on matters of substance because group members may feel less knowledgeable on these. Again, there might be a need to prompt such a discussion, especially if what is thought to be important are views; and views can be distinguished from informed comment, but can be just as important in determining individual's actions.

Interpreting such conversations is difficult, and requires the skills discussed in content analysis above. It is usually wise to have independent assessment of contents; otherwise there is possibility of the subjectivity of the researcher

Table 5.6 (Mis)interpretation of focus group interaction

Moderator's Report	*Interpretation*
There was a strong minority view.	One person made what I thought was a very good point.
A consensus emerged.	After a lot of debate one respondent bullied the others into agreement.
There was a lack of agreement.	One person refused to change their views.
The group divided into two.	Actually, out of the 8, there were two groups, one of 4, another of 2, and 2 others who would not express an opinion.

intruding. One agency produced an interpretation of moderator's reports on focus groups; see Table 5.6. One way to avoid such problems of interpretation when producing a report is to videotape the proceedings. However, it is for the researcher to interpret the results – simply passing over a videotape is avoiding responsibility for interpretation.

Focus groups are commonly used in commercial research, especially with reference to developing and monitoring advertising campaigns. In this sense they have also been used for political campaigns. Various refinements have been developed. For example, in political campaign monitoring respondents are shown a political broadcast and are asked to press a button indicating levels of support or disagreement with statements – thereby producing frequency counts which profile the 'trigger' phases that can be used as future 'sound-bites'. The world of tourism research has not generally gone as far as this, but focus groups are used for obtaining feedback on holiday brochures. Various groupings are asked to respond to the layout, pictures, text, and typeface of brochures to find those that appeal most to the market niches. Brochures are important sources of information, are expensive to produce, and an important tool in the development of market brands. The term 'market brand' is deliberately selected because a company is, in some sense, not simply selling a destination, but selling the tour operator. The holiday-maker is not likely to wish to return to the same destination on their next holiday, but the tour operator would like them to choose the same tour operator for arranging travel to another destination.

Finally, it is interesting to note the conclusions of Robson and Wardle (1988) on the impact of the presence of an observer at focus groups. In many cases of commercial research the client company wishes to have a representative present at the interview. Robson and Wardle argue that this acts as a catalyst for a series of unwanted effects on both the moderator and the focus group members. They therefore propose that:

(a) at least half of the groups in any-one project should not have an observer present;
(b) at most there should be only one observer;
(c) observers should match the group, especially in sex;
(d) respondents feel more at ease when moderator and observer clearly know each other;
(e) where possible, observers should be out of sight of respondents. If this is not possible, they must be clearly in everyone's view;
(f) there is evidence that respondents withhold negative views if the observer is from the client company. This needs to be debated as to what should be done, which debate to include discussion of the ethics of withholding the identity of the observer;
(g) the group should be told what the observer will be doing;
(h) observer passivity seems more intrusive than some form of participation;
(i) sporadic note-taking can be distracting.

Interviews

Interviews can be structured, unstructured, or a combination of both. The unstructured interview is akin to a planned conversation as noted above, but differs from the conversation in the sense that both parties are aware of an agenda of question and answer. Thus, while it is unstructured to the extent that the researcher does not follow a set sequence of questions or issues, and the conversation may go backwards and forwards over a topic, it possesses a plan in the sense that the respondent has been asked to an interview, and may have prepared for it in having checked on information prior to the meeting.

The structured interview involves a number of skills, some of which refer to questionnaire drafting skills such as determining the sequence of questions, and their precise content. As such, this discussion is left to Chapter 6. Other abilities relate to the inter-personal skills involved in conversation, such as winning trust, relating to the respondent, speaking the language, and generally being able to elicit information in a way which, if not entirely friendly (depending upon the circumstances) at least ensures respect by both sides for each other.

Where the structured interview can differ from the questionnaire is in the type of answer of that is given, and the way in which it is treated. By its nature the researcher has little control over the answer and the form in which it is given. The respondent is not replying to a check list of items or values, but is giving an opinion – the questions are open-ended. As before, therefore, the researcher has to develop the skills of recording accurately the answers, and being able to determine the major themes.

The conventions of an interview can depend upon the circumstances, the subject of the research, and the nature of the respondent. Drawing upon the author's experience, it is suggested that in the case of research involving responses from individuals in organisations, either commercial or from the public sector, a series of courtesies can be followed. These include:

(a) Making the appointment. An initial contact has to be made which:
    explains the purpose of the research;
    suggests a proposed date for the interview, but invites the respondent to change the date to one which is more convenient;
    clarifies the situation as to whether the respondent is answering in a personal capacity or as a representative of their organisation;
    clarifies the position as to confidentiality.

(b) After the date has been set:
    send a list of questions or topics. This permits respondents to obtain the necessary data prior to an interview, and collect any necessary materials. It also allows a respondent to determine what degree of confidentiality may be required.

(c) During the interview:
    if a respondent makes an especially pertinent point which the researcher

may wish to use as a quotation, ensure that this can be done. Confirm that the quotation will be sent for checking.

(d) After the interview:

   send a letter of thanks;

   send any statements that may be quoted in verbatim so that the respondent can amend if this is felt necessary;

   it might also be appropriate to enclose a transcript of the conversation if this is thought necessary.

The important thing is that your respondents have given of their time to help you, and that should be respected; this respect should be shown in a tangible form by letters of thanks and confirmation of quotations.

Kelly Triads

At the initial stages of research there may be a need to follow up conversations, and, if the research is to generate quantitative data, to develop items for scales to be used on a questionnaire. Hence, there is a need to clearly identify the constructs that comprise the attitudes towards the specific destinations, behaviours or experiences that are being surveyed. One simple and time effective method is to use Kelly Triads, so called because respondents are required to select from groups of three items.

Kelly (1955), in his theory of Personal Constructs, claimed that just as few traits are needed to explain most components of personality, so too only a few dispositions are needed to explain the construction of an attitude. His process of the construction of Kelly Triads has been used in research relating to perceptions of recreational destinations. For example, Bowler and Warburton (1986) used it to assess the attributes of attractiveness in the case of water resources (lakes and reservoirs) in Leicestershire. Ryan (1991a) used it to identify attributes of a conservation area in order to assess those factors that contributed to the effectiveness of an environmental education programme a year after students had visited the site. It was also used at a pilot stage in the series of studies that Gyte (1988, 1989) made of British tourists in Majorca.

The process is essentially a simple one in its initial stages. If, for example, research is being undertaken into attitudes about tourist destinations, a list of at least 20 destinations might be presented to respondents, and they are asked to select 4 destinations they would like to visit, 4 they would not want to visit, and 1 about which they are unsure. The destinations that the respondents would like to visit are numbered 1, 3, 5, and 8; those they would not like to visit 2, 4, 6 and 7, and the 'unsure' destination is labelled number 9. The researcher then presents the destinations to the respondents in groups of three. The groupings are made up in the following ways:

1, 2 and 3
4, 5 and 6

7, 8 and 9
1, 4 and 7
2, 5 and 8
3, 6 and 9
1, 5 and 9
3, 5 and 7

If the respondent is particularly articulate, other combinations of three destinations can be presented. Looking at the above list it will be seen that in the majority of cases the Triad consists of two of a type plus a third (e.g. two 'wanted' destinations to be compared with an 'unwanted'). The remaining Triads consist of a 'wanted', 'unwanted' and an 'unsure' item. The question posed to the respondent is along the lines of 'looking at the three destinations, which do you think is different, and why?' The object is to elicit the basis of comparison.

From reported research in tourism and other consumer studies, what seems to happen in practice is that respondents, after approximately seven or eight responses, begin to repeat themselves, albeit perhaps using different words to describe the same characteristics. Equally, it has been found (Harrison and Saare 1975), that comparatively small sample sizes can produce valid constructs. Often, perhaps with as few as twenty respondents, the number of constructs being used by members of any given group tend to be repeated. For example, one destination may be seen as too hot, and hence others are not too hot, one is too crowded, and the remaining two are not. Bi-polar constructs are thus elicited, and as such can be used in the construction of semantic differential question-naires or Likert scales. With such scales, factor analysis may be used to identify or confirm constructs used in the formation of attitudes.

Bowler and Warburton (1986) found that constructs varied between different groups based on sex, age, social class and degree of usage of water facilities, but characteristics such as beauty, character, attractiveness and usage rates were of importance to the respondents. Gyte (1988) and Denis (1989) in studies of attitudes towards holiday destinations found that constructs such as the price of the holiday, the beach, friendliness of hosts, attractive scenery, history and culture were among the determinants used in selecting holiday destinations. Riley and Palmer (1975) used these techniques to assess seaside resorts, and concluded that resorts could be grouped on the basis of six components, including the following items:

(a) expensive, exclusive, warm with good scenery;
(b) good hotels, foreign, more sunshine, different food;
(c) quiet, less commercialised, mountains;
(d) family resorts;
(e) for young people;
(f) good for touring.

Another advantage of the system is that it lends itself easily to mapping of perceptions and attitudes using repertory grid analysis and associated statistical techniques, some of which are discussed in Chapter 12.

Projection techniques

The constructs underlying an attitude can be revealed in other ways, one of which is the use of projection techniques. In the discussion relating to the focus group the example was given of respondents being asked to describe a destination as a person. This is a form of projection technique. Another method is to develop a 'mini' profile and ask respondents to describe what sort of person answers to that profile. For example, let us assume there are two respondents being questioned. One respondent might be presented with profile A, which is not revealed to the second respondent (see Table 5.7). The second respondent might be given profile B, which is not shown to the first respondent (see Table 5.8). Both respondents are then asked to describe what sort of person is being described in these profiles. The difference between the two profiles obviously rests in the different holiday destination, and in this way the perceptions of the holiday destination is revealed. Such a technique contains the potential for eliciting quite detailed responses, although such responses are subject to the criticism that they are very respondent dependent – that is dependent upon the experience, the degree of articulacy and possible education of the respondent. Also, care needs to be taken in the selection of the other items included on the list. They need to be 'neutral'.

Another projection technique is to show the respondent a picture or cartoon

Table 5.7 Projection techniques – profile A

Profile A	
	Male, aged 30
	Married, has one child
	Earns £25,000 pa
	Likes going to the cinema
	Goes to Torremolinos for his holiday

Table 5.8 Projection techniques – profile B

Profile B	
	Male, aged 30
	Married, has one child
	Earns £25,000 pa
	Likes going to the cinema
	Goes to Santorini for his holiday

representing a particular situation, and to ask the respondent to state what they think is actually happening, or what one cartoon character is saying to another.

The concept behind many of these projection techniques is that respondents tend to give socially acceptable answers, but by asking them not to give a direct answer which is 'their' answer, but rather the answer of another 'character' they are able to project on to that character those socially unacceptable feelings that they may actually be feeling. For example, research might be undertaken to assess the feelings of tourists towards host communities, and the nature of their interaction. An open-ended, unstructured question might be, 'how friendly do you think local taxi drivers actually are to tourists?'. This might elicit the desired response, but there is a danger that the response is what one might term diplomatic. A questionnaire might pose the question along the lines of 'On a scale of 1 to 5 where one means 'not at all friendly' and five means 'very friendly', how would you rate local taxi drivers that you have met?' Here the response is simply a number.

Now, however, imagine a cartoon showing a local person and a 'tourist' beside a taxi. The tourist might be opening his wallet. The respondent can be asked – 'what do you think is happening here?' Answers can simply range from, 'well, he's going to pay for a taxi ride' to 'the local person is overcharging the tourist'. The frequency of such latter answers is, it is argued, a closer approximation to the way that tourists actually perceive local taxi drivers than could be gained from either of the above methods.

The techniques are based in Freudian psycho-analysis in that reality anxiety is easily dealt with by the ego if the anxiety is projected and attributed to some external part of the respondent's world. In a simple example, one tends to say 'he hates me' rather than 'I hate him'. However, Freudian analysis has been subjected to significant degrees of modification and challenge over this century. Many of the projection tests used today derive from Murray's Thematic Apperception Test (1938, 1943), which he developed in the post-Second World War period. Murray categorised projections as twofold, supplementary projection, that is where the subject endows objects with attributes that he, the subject possesses, and complementary projection, which is where the subject projects attributes to his or her environment in order to make it congruent with their own needs, affects or impulses. His work shows that the latter tend to be more malicious in nature. Thus the question arises in the above taxi driver example – is the answer saying in fact much more about the respondent than simply indicating an attitude towards local people?

Allport was very critical of such approaches, and commented:

At no point do these (projective) methods ask the subject what his interests are, what he wants to do, or what he is trying to do.... The argument, of course, is that everyone, even a neurotic, will accommodate himself fairly well to the demands placed upon by reality. Only in an unstructured projective situation will he reveal his anxieties and unmasked needs.... Has the subject no right to be believed? ... This prevailing atmosphere of theory has engendered a kind of contempt for the 'psychic surface' of life. The individual's conscious report is rejected as untrustworthy (1953:108–110).

It can be concluded that any student or market researcher who wishes to use such techniques in their research must be entirely conversant with the concepts and the problems surrounding them. But that is just as true of any research technique. However, arguably the nature of these thematic apperception tests and other projection techniques make them more vulnerable to problems of interpretation, and the value that can be placed upon such interpretation. It may be wise not to use such tests alone, and unsupported by other means of research. Such methods do have their uses, and are used within the commercial world, but often as part of a creative advertising campaign rather than in situations designed to plan or manage tourism impacts at a social, economic or physical environmental level.

SUMMARY

The techniques inherent in qualitative research bring to the fore the ethical questions initially discussed in Chapter 1, and confirm many of the issues debated in Chapter 2. What does emerge, however, is that while qualitative techniques may seem to concentrate upon the subjective, that is no excuse for a lack of meticulous groundwork and analytical thought in trying to understand what has been said. Content analysis requires very careful preparation of categories, and the testing of those classifications. Prior testing using others to help is strongly advised. If responses are to be coded into defined categories, the coders must be trained, and the levels of agreement they produce carefully ensured by discussion and working together. Four tests were mentioned to help assess the validity of findings, namely credibility, transferability, dependability and confirmability. While these terms lack the specificity associated with terms such as 'the mean' or the 'standard deviation', they are in their own way guides to the validity and reliability of results that any researcher should take note.

Chapter 6

Quantitative research and questionnaire design

INTRODUCTION

Quantitative research brings its own problems of preparation and interpretation, and nor are these simply the technical ones of, for example, determining which tests to use, and how to interpret the results. (These subjects will be dealt with in subsequent chapters.) Whereas qualitative research can fully utilise inductive and functional approaches by reason of the interactive process between researcher and subject, in many cases quantitative research tends to be typified by the one-off questioning discussed in Chapter 1. This is particularly so where postal questionnaires are used. It is therefore essential that any questionnaire is carefully designed, and such design incorporates many considerations, including:

(a) care over the sequence and wording of questions;
(b) developing a questionnaire that accurately reflects the conceptual framework of the research idea;
(c) in the case of attitudinal research, developing a questionnaire that uses an analytical framework of attitudinal measurement within the context of the subject matter of the research;
(d) developing a questionnaire that permits analysis to develop a richness of data. This requires, for example, consideration of how sub-samples might be categorised to permit comparisons, or how scales might be composed to permit additionally fine levels of analysis.

There is also a need to think about the nature of the sample that is required, or is available, and its implications for the research concepts that are being tested.

Not all quantitative research results from questionnaires. Some of it can arise from qualitative research where the counting of frequencies and the construction of rankings might have been involved. Additionally, desk research can lend itself to the assessment of correlations between factors affecting travel – for example, seeking relationships between economic variables as measured through various statistical series, and the proclinivity to travel to any given destination. It might be thought that such research has little to do with tourist attitudes, but if behaviour is the outcome of attitudes, then travel in reaction to economic trends reflects the perceived importance of the economic variables as a determinant of travel. So, to some degree, time series and regression analysis can be incorporated into discussions of attitudinal measurement.

SECONDARY DATA – PROBLEMS OF ACCURACY

Earlier chapters have discussed the relationship between the subjective and the objective. As previously noted there is a danger that qualitative approaches are perceived as the subjective approach to tourism research, and quantitative with the objective. But this assumes a number of things. First, it implies that numbers are either accurate and/or pertinent measures of the values being analysed. Tourism and economic statistics are actually notorious for being subject to quite significant levels of error. Recent data are not always the most accurate. A suitable exercise for any student of numbers is to look up the GDP for, say, 1986 in the latest series of economic figures, and then compare it to estimates of the 1986 GDP in 1987. In the case of the British economy, for example, the difference is significant in terms of actual cash!

Problems exist too with tourism data. Within the EC in 1992 a working party was attempting to ensure some compatibility between EC member states as to how they collect their data. Comparing published data between countries requires awareness as to how those data are defined and collected. Practices differ, for example, as to calculations of day visitors. To acknowledge this is not new. For example, in 1973, the European Travel Commission published a *European Programme for Travel Statistics*. In 1981 the World Tourism Organisation published *Guidelines for the Collection and Presentation of Domestic Tourism Statistics*, to be followed in 1989 by the *Harmonisation of Household Surveys on Pleasure and Holiday Travel*. A working party was set up in 1989, and in November 1990 the EC Council of Ministers agreed that EUROSTAT should undertake a two-year programme examining the co-ordination of travel and tourism data and methodologies between the EC member countries. The European perspective is, however, just part of a global problem in this area. In June 1991, at the Ottawa Conference on Travel and Tourism Statistics, a radical statement with wide implications for the practical collection of data was agreed by representatives. It stated:

> The Conference recognised that the initiating event that ultimately defines tourism is a demand side concept, the act of consumption, and it was agreed that the core concepts of tourism would be expressed in those terms (WTO 1991).

Recommendations are subsequently to be made to the UN.

The problems associated with data collection from the supply side of the tourism industry can easily be illustrated. Within the UK alone, Middleton (1992) estimates that there are approximately 200,000 individual providers of services. He notes that 'supply side measures based on questionnaire returns would lead to a nightmare of bureaucratic activity which would never produce adequate results'. While it might be noted that, for example, the 'bureaucracy' of the UK Office for Population and Census Surveys (OPCS) is more than able to cope with the Census of Population derived from over 21 million addresses, of more concern might be the quality of information that is gathered from the tourism industry. Small businesses have many concerns besides being collectors of information for the government, and experience derived from the UK Survey of Hotel Occupancy would indicate that considerable care has to be taken in collecting such data.

Attempts to undertake statistical collection from both the supply and demand side of the industry run into problems with deriving suitable sample sizes – a problem to be discussed in Chapter 7. Even with the International Passenger Survey (IPS), as presently comprised in the UK, error rates associated with visitors from some countries are quite large – well in excess of the normally accepted plus or minus 2.5 error rate. The problem is compounded when data are broken down into regional analysis. For example, while UK data for national levels of tourist spending derived from the IPS and other sources are estimated as being accurate within plus or minus 2.5 per cent, at the regional level the figures may be accurate to plus or minus 7 per cent and in some cases much worse.

PROBLEMS OF CAUSATION

Quantitative data are often sought to answer not only questions of a descriptive concern, but also issues of a causal nature. Thus, at one level a survey might seek to establish who visits a destination, where they come from, and how much they spend. In other words a descriptive analysis is undertaken. But the same data that are collected for such a survey might be used to develop answers to relational or causal issues. For example, the survey data might include information about the age, marital status, presence of children, and occupation of visitors, and such data might be reassessed to determine the degree to which these factors 'explain' the probability of a visit to a given attraction. This might, for example, be used to support a theory that a given attraction appeals to people at certain stages of the life cycle (e.g. parents with young children). Hence, the success of an attraction may be thought to lie in the 'fact' that it appeals to such groups. The research might attempt to assess whether this hypothesis is true, and if so, then subsequently seek to examine the nature of the appeal to a given group. In short, patterns of cause and effect are being sought.

Such modelling is characteristic of quantitative approaches and is, furthermore, quite parsimonious in its approach. This means the model seeks to explain as much of the behaviour of as many people as possible with the smallest number of determining factors. For example, a study of why people visit Disneyland could adopt a qualitative approach where tourists are interviewed in depth. A single tourist might advance any number of reasons. For example, they had business in 'LA' so they took a few days holiday and brought the children. They had wanted to go to the Great Universal Studios tour, but thought their youngest child might be frightened, so instead had opted for Disneyland. Also, they had friends coming out from England who had booked a stay in a hotel at Anaheim, so it gave them a chance to meet these friends. The quantitative approach, on the other hand, would simply describe the respondents as being at a stage where, having young children in the family, there was a fairly high probability that they would visit Disneyland. The difference between the two approaches is conventionally described as:

(a) the idiographic model – that is behaviour is explained by the enumeration of many considerations. Some of these may be idiosyncratic. It is an attempt to achieve fullness of explanation;
(b) the nomothetic model – that is the isolation of a few key variables that provides a partial explanation for as many aspects of behaviour of as many people as possible.

In the idiographic approach the researcher might find 30 reasons why a person visited Disneyland. If another person was found who shared those 30 reasons, there would be a very high likelihood that that person would also visit Disneyland. In the case of the nomothetic model where the probability of a visit to Disneyland is forecast on the basis of a few variables, it is also probable that someone sharing those few reasons would not visit Disneyland. The model and its efficacy is measured by the levels of probability associated with an outcome resulting when a number of factors are found to be present.

The nomothetic model is often felt to be dehumanising. It is accused of reducing human behaviour to a number of symbols. But is it any the less dehumanising than the idiographic approach. The only difference is the number of reasons being advanced. If the tourist who has 30 reasons for visiting Disneyland finds themselves in a situation where all 30 reasons are satisfied, is a visit to Disneyland the automatic result? To borrow a phrase that has been used to describe chaos theory – a butterfly flaps its wings and a hurricane results over Florida. The phrase seeks to illustrate the holistic nature of the natural world, and how the seemingly insignificant can set in motion a series of events which accumulate to produce the significant. The apparently random has been reduced to a series of deterministic sequences. But the sterility of the argument can be illustrated by asking why did the butterfly flap its wings at that particular time. Perhaps there was a hurricane over the Pacific which caused an air movement that in turn caused the butterfly to flap its wings. Was that hurricane over the Pacific due to a butterfly flapping its wings because of a hurricane over Florida? Where does the game of causality begin and end. The sequence reminds one of the cartoons of the American, Rube Goldberg, who worked in the 1950s. In one of his cartoons he drew a sequence whereby a glass of milk is tipped off the table to set in motion a series of misadventures leading a nanny to let go of a pram, which bumps into a table causing a glass of milk to spill, thereby completing the

Figure 6.1 Logical sequence of cause and effect – cartoon in the style of Rube Goldberg

logical sequence of cause and effect, but, of course, with no identifiable beginning and end. See Figure 6.1.

Lazarsfeld (1955) suggests three criteria need to be present for causality to be established:

(a) the cause precedes the effect in time;
(b) the two variables be correlated with one another;
(c) the empirical relationship cannot be explained away as being due to the influence of some third variable causing both of them.

One of the problems relating to research into tourist attitudes and behaviour is that, as already discussed, the direction and sequence of causality is not always clear. Thus, tourist satisfaction might be thought to be consequential upon the event. But if the event is described as a visit, then this can be broken down into a series of happenings, and if the initial experiences are satisfactory, this satisfaction predisposes the tourist to enjoy themselves further. If the initial events take place within a background of an expectation of 'having a good time', then the expectation of satisfaction prior to the event creates satisfaction, 'everything else remaining the same'. The event becomes not a cause but a confirmation, retaining the potential to disappoint. In a sense therefore, the sequence of causality becomes different in the case of dissatisfaction than in the case of satisfaction, although the observed sequence of events are the same. The cause of satisfaction is not the event itself, but the expectations surrounding the event, and the perception of it. A thread of potential cause and effect may be discerned, but is less clear than might first be thought.

Because quantitative research deals with parsimonious explanations of behaviour that are of a probabilistic nature, it also needs to distinguish carefully between causes that are necessary and those that are sufficient for an outcome to occur. A necessary cause needs to be present, but does not in itself cause the outcome. To state the obvious – to be satisfied with an attraction it is normally necessary that the tourist actually visits the attraction. The visit is necessary for a satisfactory experience, but in itself is not sufficient to cause satisfaction. Sufficient conditions are those that, if fulfilled, create the outcome. But the distinction can be difficult. Consider buying a ticket for Disneyland. If you are not a guest of the Disney Corporation or an employee the ticket is a necessary thing for acquiring entry, but possession of a ticket does not cause entry. Other things have to be present. However, if the ticket is perceived as the means of acquiring permission to enter Disneyland, then the purchase of that ticket is sufficient to acquire permission to enter for the period stated on the ticket. The same act can be interpreted as being necessary or sufficient dependent on how the problem is stated.

However, from a pragmatic viewpoint, life is not always so difficult, and the example can be rightly regarded as a question of semantics. In practice the tourism researcher is not concerned with permission to enter, but rather with actual entry. However, the example still possesses a valid warning – namely, the act of purchasing a ticket is not a sufficient although it is a necessary factor to precede the outcome of entering an attraction.

THE INTERCHANGEABILITY OF INDICES

One of the problems of quantitative research is what Babbie (1979:436) terms the interchangeability of indexes. If the researcher is seeking to establish a pattern of causality, the nature of the problem can be stated as $Y = f(X)$; that is, the event Y is due to the presence of X. In the language of Chapter 1, Y is the determined variable, and X is the determining, independent variable. But a concept such as satisfaction may be measured by many proxies. For example, a researcher might construct a series of questions which can include the direct, such as, 'on a scale of 1 to 5, where 5 is "very satisfied", how satisfied were you with the holiday?'; or the indirect such as, 'to what extent would you recommend this holiday to a close friend?' Or the researcher might seek to assess satisfaction of the holiday by a series of questions relating to the location, hotel, events, courier, and other experiences the holiday-maker is likely to come across. A series of indices might be possible. Some might even be the summation of scores. The problem therefore is that instead of measuring $Y = f(X)$, the researcher is really measuring $y = f(x_1)$, $y = f(x_2)$, $y = f(x_3)$ and so on. Babbie states the problem thus:

> If following the traditional view of the scientific method created the problem that the single empirical association might not be perfect, now we may be faced with several empirical associations, none of which will be perfect and some of which may be in conflict with one another (1979:436).

Let us suppose that x_1 is a measure of the courier's performance, and that x_2 a measure of the scenic value of the location, and x_3 a measure of the friendliness of fellow tourists. It could be conceived that the level of satisfaction (Y) is the function of (is dependent upon) the values of x_1, x_2 and x_3. However, it might be found that the correlation between the scores of these three variables is lower than expected, and the sum of the satisfaction scores not as high as anticipated. Why might this be? Closer examination of the data might show that some of those who score high on appreciating scenic value are scoring low on an appreciation of the courier, while some score high across all three variables. One hypothesis to explain this is that our sample of tourists is not homogeneous. There are some who enjoy the solitude of the scenery, and who wish to be left alone to enjoy it; while others are more sociable, and while rating the scenery highly, see it as a nice backdrop to the social interaction created with other tourists, with the courier acting as a facilitator of such relationships. The disaggregation of the casual variable (the holiday) has thus actually enriched the results.

It can also be argued that if the concept of the holiday experience can be broken into component parts, so too perhaps can the concept of satisfaction. Instead of $Y = f(X)$, or indeed of $y = \Sigma(x_1 \dots x_n)$, perhaps it is a situation of $y_1 \dots y_n$ being measures of satisfaction. So, in our earlier example, the response to questions about how satisfied were the tourists, and would they recommend this holiday to a friend (y_1), or other variables like, would they want to come again to the destination (y_2) – all of these can form measures of satisfaction (that is $y_1 \dots y_n$), while the measures of courier performance, scenic beauty, and other tourists form a series of determining variables, $x_1 \dots y_n$.

This means that a series of relationships can now be examined. To what extent is satisfaction as measured by a desire to repeat the holiday determined by couriers (x_1), scenic value (x_2) and other tourists (x_3). This question can be

Table 6.1 The expanding of a hypothesis

The question
　Is holiday satisfaction determined by activity can be written as

　　$Y = f(X)$

　where holiday satisfaction is Y and activity is X
But the question can be restated as
　Is holiday satisfaction determined by
　　　sightseeing (x_1)
　　　sports activities (x_2)
　　　dancing (x_3)
So the question is reformulated as

　　$Y = f(x_1, x_2, x_3)$

But holiday satisfaction can be redefined as
　　　positive feelings to self (y_1)
　　　positive feelings to spouse (y_2)
　　　positive feelings to others (y_3)
So the question is formulated as

　　$(y_1, y_2, y_3) = f(x_1, x_2, x_3)$

This can lead to a number of relationships being explored
for example

　　$y_1 = f(x_1), y_1 = f(x_2), y_1 = f(x_3)$

or

　　$y_1 = f(x_1, x_2, x_3)$

Hence the question is now HOW is holiday satisfaction determined by identified
factors?

---

symbolically represented as $y_2 = f(x_1)$, $y_2 = f(x_2)$, $y_2 = f(x_3)$, and equally there are the question sets of $y_1 = f(x_1)$, $y_2 = f(x_2)$, $y_2 = f(x_3)$, and $y_3 = f(x_1)$, $y_2 = f(x_2)$, $y_2 = f(x_3)$. At this stage the researcher needs to examine more carefully their data, taking advantage, if at all possible, of the ability of the computer to examine quickly, and, if need be, to discard options. It might be decided that satisfaction is best measured by some combination of variables, say the 'wish to return' and the direct response to the question, 'to what extent were you satisfied by the holiday?' while the characteristics of the holiday were best measured by a combination of scenic value and interaction with other tourists. Thus, the researcher reaches a point where $Y_i = f(X_j)$, where i and j represent the range of appropriate factors variables.

In short, the researcher has to retain a flexibility of thought and a wish to re-examine data rigorously. Furthermore, the above example shows a shifting from the original question of 'is Y a function of X?' to, 'how is Y a function of X? It also shows that the process of measurement is closely associated with what is being measured and what is the nature of the association that is being measured.

Additionally, the development of a hypothesis lies upon the way in which appropriate questions have been identified and worded. See Table 6.1.

QUESTIONNAIRE DESIGN

To repeat the opening comments, successful questionnaire design must therefore include consideration of:

(a)   the subject matter of the questions;
(b)   the lay-out and design of the questionnaire;
(c)   the actual wording and sequence of questions;
(d)   the underlying theoretical constructs with reference to both
       the nature of the investigation and
       the methods of analysis to be used.

All too often discussions of questionnaire design emphasis the first three points, and possibly too many questionnaires pay little regard to the fourth item, with the consequence that the design of many questionnaires inhibit a richness and diversity of findings. The limitations of analysis arguably arise from too little attention being paid to how resultant data are to be analysed at the time of questionnaire construction.

In discussing issues relating to questionnaire design there is also value in drawing upon studies that relate to the means by which questionnaires can be improved upon, either in terms of increasing response rates, or in refining the levels of data interpretation. Although there are few such studies emanating from tourism research, there are many that pertain to the problems of measurement of tourist attitudes and behaviour. Any review of the literature will reveal a number of problems.

Questions of comparability

Studies relating to, for example, the usefulness of pre-notification of a survey as a means of increasing response rates often refer to different subjects and types of samples. Much of the work relates to commercial market research, and thus might not be applicable to academic research in that respondents might have different perceptions and attitudes towards the two types of surveys. This relates to a further problem.

Questions of methodology

These issues are also divisible as follows:

(a)   research into the same issue can utilise different methodologies;
(b)   research utilising the same techniques when examining the same issues may
       not be a replication of the original due to minor, but important differences.

For example, it will be noted that studies relating to the effectiveness of labelling and the number of divisions in scales might refer to different types of scales. The problem of comparison is often further compounded by inherent differences in methods being studied. Where the methodologies are uniform they can differ as to a third consideration, i.e. questions of interpretation.

Questions of interpretation

Statistical tests used can vary considerably in their sophistication, from the simple use of percentages to express differences, to complex methods of measuring significance of those differences. Schlegelmich and Diamantopoulos (1991) also draw attention to what they call a 'balance' problem, where some reports of studies omit cases that are contrary to the researcher's theme. In some cases, they note, transcription errors arise.

LAYOUT AND DESIGN

General concerns

Questionnaire design is important. In part, results can be no better than the way and means in which the question is posed. Once respondents have replied, there is generally little opportunity to go back to them to clarify responses, or to correct possible misinterpretation of questions. This highlights the importance of a pilot questionnaire.

A number of general statements might be made about questionnaire design. In short, it can be contended that a questionnaire must fulfil the following criteria:

(a) Be interesting to the respondent, and be able to maintain that interest. Alternatively, a benefit might be offered to the respondent.
(b) Logical development of the subject matter aids both interest and consistency of reply.
(c) The questionnaire must not be so long as to fatigue respondents.
(d) Individual questions must be clear and address a single issue.
(e) Questions must relate to the respondent's ability to provide data.
(f) There must be a means of classifying respondents that is pertinent to the study – this usually entails personal information, and conventionally is left to the end of the questionnaire. However, if there is a need to filter out certain types of respondents, such questions may occur early in the questionnaire.
(g) Simple language must be used – this requires the avoidance of technical terms, while also avoiding ambiguity. The search for specificity can, however, give rise to overlong questions as the questionnaire seeks to specify a particular set of circumstances. In short, there is a need for care. A common occurrence where specificity is required arises when seeking in-

formation about frequency of events where there is a need to specify a time period. For example, the questions:

how many holidays do you take a year on average?

how many holidays did you take last year?

are superior simply to asking 'how many holidays do you normally take?' but each could produce different responses. In practice, it is thought that the responses to both questions are likely to be similar (Belson 1964).

(h) Avoid leading questions.

(i) Carefully consider the order of questions – for example, if there is a need to assess the frequency of an event, it is better to insert this question before eliciting opinion about the event. To elicit opinion prior to requesting information about frequency of behaviour can often lead to an over- or under-recording due to the respondent answering by reference to perceived norms of social acceptance, social status or possibly the levels of enjoyment associated with the event.

(j) Questions must be realistic in terms of the ability of the respondent to recall behaviour.

A number of other questions relating to questionnaires must also be considered. For example:

(a) Are questions going to be closed or open-ended? The debate about the relative merits of each has been well rehearsed in a number of standard texts (e.g. Oppenheim 1966; Moser and Kalton 1989). Pre-coded questions offer advantages in terms of computer analysis, but may generate a loss of qualitative information. Much depends on whether or not the range of alternative answers are known prior to the questionnaire being constructed.

(b) What scales are going to be used? As noted above, three related questions are involved – the type of scale, the number of its divisions, and how it is labelled. Broadly speaking, commonly used scales include graphics like *visual analogue scales* such as the 'ladder', 'hour glass' or 'pyramid' (Crimp 1991) where respondents draw a line to indicate the strength of feeling, *itemised rating scales* where descriptors are used on a continuum, *Likert Scales* where the respondent indicates varying degrees of support for a statement, and *Semantic Differential Scales*. Various forms of comparative rating might also be used.

Having listed some of the considerations involved in questionnaire design, it is now pertinent to cover some of them in more detail.

THE WORDING OF QUESTIONS

Asking questions is an art. Thus, there is a fundamental paradox within the quantitative method, which is that the apparent objectivity of the statistics is based upon the complexities of language, the perceptions of the question's meaning by both interviewer and respondent, and the mental framework that both bring to the task at hand. Additionally, the development of that art is important but difficult. Gallup (1947) concluded that survey results were influenced more by question design than by sample composition. In the intervening years it has been difficult to develop specific rules about how to ask questions, but there are some equally fundamental points about questioning, which include:

(a) Do you need the question? Why is it being asked? What is its purpose?

There is a need to review continually the questions being asked. Nor is this simply a matter of avoiding overlong questionnaires, even though this is an important consideration. Each question must carry some purpose in the analysis of the data.

(b) Is the question clear? Does it avoid ambiguity?

There are some obvious pitfalls that can be avoided. One is to ask two questions within one sentence. For example, the question 'how important is climate and culture important in choosing a holiday destination?' is really asking about the importance of (a) climate and (b) culture. As both will have very differing degrees of importance to different types of tourists the question is very difficult to answer.

Another danger is that the researcher devises questionnaires that use the language of the researcher rather than that of the respondent. It pays to use simpler language than that associated with academic or even commercial reports. For example compare:

How important is price in determining your purchase of a holiday?

with

When buying a holiday, how important is price?

Gowers (1954) mentions many words where there are simpler variants, some of which are listed:

Assist	Help
Consider	Think
Determine	Decide
Purchase	Buy
Reside	Live
State	Say
Sufficient	Enough
Vacation	Holiday

Today many word-processing packages include a thesaurus, which is useful for checking whether simpler terms exist. Ambiguity can easily arise. Consider the question:

If entry prices are increased, will you come again?

This seems simple enough as a question, but further consideration quickly shows some difficulties. How does one interpret the answer 'no'. Is it a 'no' because price increases are a real deterrent? Or does the 'no' arise because the visitor is from overseas and not likely to return in any case (there is a need to cross-check the response with other data as to place of residence)? Or does the 'no' really mean 'yes' if the undefined price increase was, say, 5 per cent? Thus, ambiguity is not only a function of the wording of the question, but also the context of the answer.

DEALING WITH A LACK OF KNOWLEDGE

Another problem is the answer that is prompted by the layout of the questionnaire, but where the respondent has little knowledge upon which to base an answer. Consider the question where the respondent has to reply on a 5-point scale. See Table 6.2. As laid out in Table 6.2 the questionnaire assumes knowledge by the respondent of each of the services. But what if the informant has not used, say, the gymnasium. If that respondent circles the figure 1, does this mean that they really rate it as very poor, or does it mean it is of no importance. Under such circumstances respondents might resort to coding an item as a 3 – and this reinforces a tendency to the mean score, where a mean score (3 on the 5-point scale) is used to convey an uncertainty of response. Hence it becomes doubly difficult to interpret a score of 3 if it also includes a response which really means no knowledge.

It is therefore good practice to provide informants with a specific instruction as to what to do if they feel unable to provide a response due to a lack of knowledge. One method to overcome this is to provide an option as shown in

Table 6.2 Questions based on a 5-point scale

Using a 5-point scale where:
Very good	= 5
Good	= 4
Neither good nor poor	= 3
Poor	= 2
Very poor	= 1

How would YOU rate the following services:
(a) early morning call	1	2	3	4	5
(b) daily change of bed linen	1	2	3	4	5
(c) mini bar in the room	1	2	3	4	5
(d) gymnasium	1	2	3	4	5
(e) room service	1	2	3	4	5
(f) bar service	1	2	3	4	5

Table 6.3 Revised question based on a 5-point scale

Using a 5-point scale where:

Very good	= 5
Good	= 4
Neither good nor poor	= 3
Poor	= 2
Very poor	= 1
Don't know	= 0

If you feel unable to comment, please code the item as 0

How would YOU rate the following services:

(a)	early morning call	1	2	3	4	5	0
(b)	daily change of bed linen	1	2	3	4	5	0
(c)	mini bar in the room	1	2	3	4	5	0
(d)	gymnasium	1	2	3	4	5	0
(e)	room service	1	2	3	4	5	0
(f)	bar service	1	2	3	4	5	0

Table 6.3. The questionnaire as shown in Table 6.3 now begins to overcome the problem of respondents selecting a score where they have no knowledge of the item in question, but now poses other problems in turn. How is the item '0' treated in the analysis of the data? This will be discussed when considering the calculation of mean scores and their meaning on such scales.

Another way of dealing with the problem is to use filter questions, or cross-checking questions. For example, in another part of the questionnaire it would be possible to ask the questions as shown in Table 6.4. This now permits a cross-checking with the rating assessments. In addition it now permits a much more useful analysis based on potential differences of assessment by frequency of use. The problems of how to set up scales, and the different types of scale are discussed later in this chapter.

Often there is a need to find the frequency of some action. But while the question 'how often do you go on holiday?' can elicit responses on a scale such as 'rarely' or 'very often', these lack a degree of precision. One person's 'often' may be another's 'not often enough'! To obtain greater accuracy, there is a need to define a time period. Thus the question might be redrafted as 'how many times did you go on holiday last year?' How does the respondent interpret the phrase 'last year'? Does it mean the last twelve months from the date of questioning? If the question is asked in September 1995, does it mean the year 1994? So the researcher might attempt to be more specific by asking 'how many times did you go on holiday in 1994?' But if the time of questioning is September 1995, there can be problems of recall. If the question becomes 'how many times have you been on holiday in the last twelve months?', does it then make a difference if, for any reason, respondents do not all answer the questions within the same short time period. So, for example, one respondent might answer at the beginning of July before they go on holiday, while another responds two weeks later, having

Table 6.4 Cross-checking of questions

On a scale where:				
Very frequently	= 4			
Frequently	= 3			
Infrequently	= 2			
Not at all	= 1			

How *often* have YOU used the following services:				
(a) early morning call	1	2	3	4
(b) mini bar in the room	1	2	3	4
(c) gymnasium	1	2	3	4
(d) room service	1	2	3	4
(e) bar service	1	2	3	4

just come back from holiday. Both respondents might actually take the same number of holidays in a year, but it would not necessarily show from their answers to the question.

The answer to how the researcher might actually phrase the question becomes not simply an issue of drafting the appropriate words, but also a matter of the time the research is being implemented.

USING POSITIVE OR NEGATIVE WORDING

Consider the questions following a preamble as shown in Table 6.5.

It is obvious that the statements in Table 6.5 differ in two respects:

(a)   they are posed in positive or negative manners;
(b)   they are posed with or without an emotive phrase ('a good time').

What differences result? There is some evidence to suggest that there is a significant level of stability in responses to questions when worded in positive or negative manners, although when differences do occur it is not always possible to identify when, or with what result, the deviation from stability of response occurs. In a study of the use of positive and negative statements, Gendall and Hoek comment:

Although some of the differences between the equivalent responses to the different versions were quite large ... there was no discernible pattern to these differences and no evidence to support the hypothesis that a positive or negative set of statements has a predictable effect on respondents' answers (1990:30).

Certainly, the study of Labaw (1980), in which responses to differently worded questions about Americans' attitudes towards the Panama Canal over the period May 1976 to June 1978 were analysed, indicates little variation in response to the different wording. However, both the Labaw study and that of Gendall and

Table 6.5 Use of positive and negative wording in questionnaire

I'm going to read you some statements about taking holidays. Please tell me whether you agree or disagree with each statement. If you have no opinion, just say so. Would you agree or disagree that . . . ?

Comfortable accommodation is important in having a 'good time' on holiday; or

Comfortable accommodation is not important in having a 'good time' on holiday; or

Comfortable accommodation is important when on holiday; or

Comfortable accommodation is not important when on holiday.

Hoek (amongst others) do show that the introduction of qualifying phrases, particularly if they are of an emotive type, can significantly change responses. The Labaw study included one question where, in January 1978, an NBC poll asked if Americans would favour a revision of the Panama Treaty, 'specifically giving the United States the right to intervene if the Canal is threatened by attack'. Whereas in every other poll those favouring a revision of the treaty was between 24 to 30 per cent, in this case those wanting a revision was 65 per cent.

Researchers have also to be aware of the emotive nuances involved in words such as 'allow' and 'forbid', 'in favour of' and 'opposed to', 'allow' and 'prevent', and to be 'in favour of' and 'not in favour of'. Generally speaking people are more prone to 'allow' than to 'forbid' (Converse and Presser 1986), and the phrases do not work as logical opposites in terms of getting a stability of response. The pair 'in favour of' and 'opposed to' tends to produce a similar response pattern, but as one works towards the final pairing of 'in favour of' and 'not in favour of' the pattern becomes less marked.

It seems, therefore, that where possible questions should avoid qualifying statements and, in particular, emotive terms. In undertaking holiday research, however, the nature of the topic makes it difficult to avoid the value-laden question. However, it can be argued that the values associated with holidays are less important than those associated with issues such as racism or abortion. Accordingly, it can be argued that stability of response might be greater, the less important is the issue. The evidence is not clear. Gendall and Hoek (1990) found differences in responses to items about racism and rabbit meat having waste depended on how the question was posed, while responses to items about abortion remained constant however the issue was worded. The question about abortion used the 'allow/forbid' and should/should not rubrics, while the question on rabbit meat related to 'factual' components (i.e. does rabbit meat have a little or a lot of waste). It can only be concluded that questions are examined with reference to their wording, context within a questionnaire, and the subject under investigation!

UNPROMPTED OR PROMPTED RECALL

From this it follows that great care should be taken over the wording of the question. Similarly, care must be taken over the sequencing of questions. Ideally the sequence must be:

(a) logical;
(b) not lead the respondent;
(c) retain interest for the respondent;
(d) where necessary, carefully filter respondents;
(e) not create unnecessary hostility or reluctance to answer questions.

In developing questionnaires about holiday behaviour and attitude there is often a wish to question attitudes and past behaviour. There might be a problem about prompted recall. In many situations people are able to give fuller answers if provided with something that prompts recall of a situation – but such recall might lead to a modification of the original opinion. Which opinion is the more valid if this occurs?

For example, suppose a researcher was wishing to assess the level of satisfaction derived from a holiday, and sought to use a multi-attribute approach. This requires asking respondents how important various aspects of a holiday trip are to them, and then asking them to assess their last holiday trip by those aspects. It is probably better to pose the questions in this order. If a respondent is asked about their last holiday, the process of recall of that holiday might influence the weighting they give to the importance of attributes associated with holiday-taking. To be more specific, suppose that a respondent had a holiday in the UK last year, and the weather was exceptionally warm. When asked about this holiday, they might recall that the weather was very good. In moving to the second stage of the questionnaire when the respondent is asked to assess the importance of factors that make up a good holiday they might now stress the role of weather more than they would otherwise have done.

Generally it is better not to evoke a memory of something if some general attitudinal statements are being sought. However, in seeking to measure the impact of behaviour, for example, there can be very good reasons for wanting to evoke memory as to past behaviour and what prompted it. Questioning without evoking recall might elicit responses about the more important or 'top of the mind' attitudes, but in the case of impacts arising from actual behaviour, there could be a need to obtain as full a picture as possible. One way in which to do this is to use prompt cards on which there is list of activities, and the respondent is asked to state which of these activities they undertook. Obviously the list has to be carefully considered beforehand, and usually tested in pilot studies. Second, it is a good idea to ask the respondent if there were any other activities undertaken.

Prompt cards also have a second use besides eliciting fuller answers. They can also serve to clarify thought in matters of detail. For example, suppose a researcher was interested in traffic densities around and inside a tourist destination. There are a number of ways in which this can be done, including tracking studies where a sample of visitors are followed by a researcher who records the places visited, the activities undertaken, and the time spent on those activities. However, such studies are time consuming, and, if resources are limited a researcher might wish to use a questionnaire in order to increase sample size. Asking people, for example, which road they used to approach an attraction can lead to problems. Visitors from far afield might not actually know the name or number of the road, or the town through which they came. Passengers in a bus or car in particular are less likely to have identified such things. The use of a stylised map can solve the problem; respondents can identify the entrance they used and the direction from which they approached it. Additionally, the same approach can be used to identify places visited within the tourist zone. This method was used quite successfully by Groves *et al.* (1987) in a study of Staunton Harold Hall. This clearly stated the numbers visiting the craft workshops, the lake and other parts of the site by the simple means of showing respondents a map of the area, with points marked A, B, C, etc., and asking whether or not they had visited them.

CLOSED OR OPEN-ENDED QUESTIONS

Another form of prompting a reply is to devise the 'closed question' whereby a respondent is asked to state which is, for example, the most important factor about an attraction. Is there a difference between asking the questions shown in Table 6.6.

The evidence from past research by Gendall and Hoek would seem to be that:

1   the pattern of response to open and closed versions of the same question are likely to differ, and
2   the pattern of responses to closed questions is heavily influenced by the choices presented to respondents (1990:29).

What is good practice is to be able to combine open and closed questions to achieve response at different levels. To revert back to Gallup (1947) his five types of questions are:

1   Is the informant aware of the issue at all?
2   What are the respondent's feelings on the topic?
3   What are the informant's view on specific components of the issue?
4   What are the reasons for these views?
5   How strongly are these views held?

Of the above list, closed, pre-coded questions are suitable for item 3, and possibly item 5, while open-ended questions are suitable for items 2, and possibly for items 1 and 4. The final choice must refer to the purpose of the research, while the length and the layout of the questionnaire must also be considered.

Table 6.6 Open and closed questions

What do you think is the single most important factor that attracts visitors to Disneyland?

---

or

Would you please look at this card and tell me which of these you think is the single most important reason why people visit Disneyland?

Variety of rides
Good entertainment
Value for money
Good for all ages
Family-based fun   etc., etc.

CONFIDENTIALITY

Generally, in the case of questionnaires relating to holidays, it is the experience of the author that people are more than ready to voice their opinions. Questions of the confidentiality and sensitivity of data are less of a problem than in other areas of social research, but it is still wise to remove doubt on the part of respondents as to the nature of the questionnaire by not initially asking questions of a personal nature. Such questions are often important in being able to classify respondents by age, gender, marital status, and possibly income, occupation and social class. Such classification then becomes a source of analysing potential differences based on these criteria, or some combination of them. On the other hand, one reason for introducing such questions at an early stage in the questionnaire would be if there was a need to filter out respondents. Suppose, for example, a researcher was interested in the attitude of couples with young children to the development of play areas within a tourist attraction, there would be a need to ensure that respondents met the criteria of having young children. While locating themselves by the side of the play area increases the likelihood of identifying a suitable sample, not all adults accompanying young children may be parents. Some might be grandparents, aunts or uncles, or older siblings to mention but a few possibilities. The researcher will have to decide whether the opinions of such people are part of their research design for comparative purposes, or whether they are to be excluded. If they are to be excluded, the researcher might have to ask respondents initially if they are parents of young children. It is probably advantageous, if the filtering questions are not at the first stage of the questionnaire, to leave, at this point, questions relating to socio-economic variables. The researcher can now pursue questions relating to safety concerns, variety of equipment, suitability for age groupings or whatever aspects form the focus of the research, and then return to the socio-economic questions at the end of the interview.

Two advantages accrue from this. First, by this stage a process of rapport will have been created and the respondent will be less likely to withhold such information. Second, should a respondent not wish to answer these questions, the researcher now possesses some information about the play area and attitudes to it. The same considerations exist in the case of postal questionnaires. As a general rule therefore, personal data can be safely left to the end of the questionnaires.

CLASSIFICATION OF RESPONDENTS

With reference to classifying respondents, real problems exist when trying to classify respondents by occupation. Asking for self-description produces information of limited use. For example, the self-description of 'engineer' is notoriously difficult to interpret. To define more carefully occupational grouping can require a series of questions which might include items such as:

(a) job title;
(b) qualifications;
(c) level of pay;
(d) title of person/manager to whom employee reports;
(e) number of people who report to job holder.

There is a real danger, however, that these socio-economic variables become too time-consuming in obtaining data, or extend unnecessarily the length of the questionnaire so that it becomes a deterrent to completion. In addition to the above questions, there may be questions about age, gender, marital status, and number of children to mention the obvious. Thus, like many other parts of the questionnaire, the researcher must carefully consider why these questions are being asked, and what their function is in the analysis.

An important consideration for some forms of analysis is to be able to identify the life-cycle stage that respondents might have reached. Researchers such as Bojanic and Lawson have argued that life stage is an important determinant of holiday choice, and researchers might want to use life stage as a possible variable for analysis. The life cycle consists of stages such as dependent young, independent young, young marrieds without children, marrieds with children under five (full nest 1), marrieds with children over five (full nest 2), marrieds without children (empty nest), marrieds with retired partner, retired couples, and survivors. Due to the increased incidence of divorce and subsequent remarriage on the one hand, and the increased degree of childless, career couples, Bojanic (1992) and Lawson (1991) suggest use of an extended life-stage model which adds two further groups, namely single parent and middle-aged couples without children.

Hence, to identify these groups, questions need to be posed about age, gender, marital status, existence of children under five and under eighteen (or perhaps even older who are living at home), and employment (to identify retired persons).

The question of marital status needs to be considered. The full range of possibilities can extend from being single, young, unmarried, to being divorced, widowed, separated, or co-habitating with a partner of the opposite sex who is not married, to possible other combinations of same sex relationships. Again, there is a danger of creating apparently overlong questionnaires if the full range of options is given, and again researchers must ask themselves if this detail is required. Often it is sufficient to ask if a respondent is single or has a partner/ spouse. This can be combined with other information to identify life-stage grouping. There can be problems however. For example, a single, retired, female of over 60 might be either widowed, divorced or never married. The researcher has to ask whether there are, for the purposes of the research, likely to be significant differences between divorced, widowed or never married females over 60 for the research project. If there are, then additional questions on marital status to covered widowed or divorced will need to be present.

SCALING

Scales are frequently used in attitudinal research, and can be categorised in a number of ways. The list below gives a general introduction, and then the questions of the uses of scales, and the problems associated with them are subsequently discussed. Scales can include:

Graphic rating scales

Having selected the appropriate wording, the informant is asked to draw a line along a graphic indicating the degree of agreement or disagreement with the statement. Such graphics are illustrated in Figures 6.2, 6.3, 6.4 and 6.5. Respondents simply draw up the line to indicate their level of agreement in all four examples.

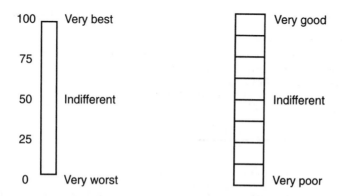

Figure 6.2 The thermometer   Figure 6.3 The ladder

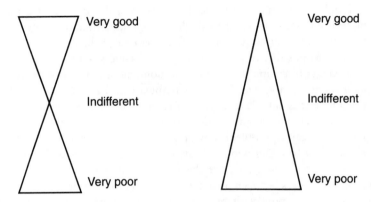

Figure 6.4 The hourglass   Figure 6.5 The pyramid

Proponents of such scales argue that they permit respondents to indicate a judgement that is more detailed than that given by a range of numbers – for example, if a respondent is unsure whether on a numeric scale, an item is a 4 or 5, on the line drawing they can more easily indicate their predisposition towards say, the 4, rather than the 5. On the other hand, such scales might be implying a fine distinction that does not exist in practice – the respondent is not always as careful as is assumed in drawing the line. Second, there are problems in actually reading and coding the data, although with Optical Character Recognition (OCR) the problem is less than was once the case.

Itemised rating scales

Very commonly used, itemised rating scales require a respondent simply to tick against the appropriate entry. An example is shown in Table 6.7.

Table 6.7 Itemised rating scale

How interested are you in purchasing a holiday in Bermuda?	Very interested	—
	Somewhat interested	—
	Not interested	—

Comparative rating scales

Here the informant is asked to make a comparison between items, and to rate them in order of preference, as shown in Table 6.8.

Table 6.8 Comparative rating scale

Please rank the following holiday destinations in terms of their attractiveness to you. Assign 1 to the most attractive, 2 to the next, 3 to the next and so on for as many of the places as you can.

Hawaii	....
Majorca	....
Greece	....
France	....
Scotland	....
New Zealand	....
USA	....
Bali	....

The problems associated with such scales are fairly evident. There is no way of knowing the difference between the ratings. For example, a respondent might be quite clear in their mind that Greece is their number one choice, but Majorca, France and Scotland are close together, while Hawaii is perceived as being by far the least attractive, while opinion about Bali is unclear because of a lack of knowledge. The rating system fails to catch such nuances.

Likert scales

Likert scales are very commonly used because they lend themselves so easily to many forms of statistical analysis, as will be discussed in Chapter 8. Examples of Likert-type scales are given in Tables 6.2, 6.3 and 6.4 concerning the rating of hotel services. See Table 6.9.

Table 6.9 Likert scales

Using a 5-point scale where:

Very good	= 5
Good	= 4
Neither good nor poor	= 3
Poor	= 2
Very poor	= 1

How would YOU rate the following services:

	1	2	3	4	5
(a) early morning call	1	2	3	4	5
(b) daily change of bed linen	1	2	3	4	5
etc., etc.					

SEMANTIC DIFFERENTIAL SCALES

Semantic differential scales are similar to the Likert scale in that 5, 7 or more points are used, but in these cases the judgement is made on a bi-polar scale with opposing statements at each end of the scale. An example is shown in Table 6.10; the respondent circles a response on the 5-point scale.

Much of the theory upon which semantic differential scales were developed stems from the work of Osgood *et al.* (1957). They suggested scales whereby the extremes of the continua are described by opposite adjectives (e.g. good vs bad, hot vs cold, fast vs slow). Analysing their results, Osgood and his colleagues concluded that the most dominant factor had high loadings on polar adjectives such as good–bad, positive–negative and true–false – that is, they were evaluative in nature. A second factor emerged, entitled potency, and was described by adjectives such as hard–soft, strong–weak and heavy–light. The third factor was activity and referred to the continua active–passive, fast–slow and hot–cold. With reference to attitude measurement, they argue that the evaluative factor is the most important, and hence an attitude scale can be devised by use of bi-polar adjectives incorporating evaluative criteria.

The choice of 'anchors' in such questions is also important. Ursic and Helgeson (1989) report that:

> More extreme anchors lead to less positive decision-making. This might be increased because the mental space between the ends of the scale forces people into a middle more neutral zone and thus reduces the number of positive remarks (1989:237).

In terms of measuring attitudes, the most commonly used scales are the Likert and Semantic Differential Scales. They possess the advantages of easily lending themselves to descriptive statistics. It is possible to compute average scores for the sample and required sub-samples that not only permit comparisons but also allow the use of techniques such as t-tests and F-tests to assess the significance of differences. Response and acquiescence sets can also be allowed for by the use of t-tests where a 'universal' mean is calculated. For example, if there have been a series of questions relating to assessments of the importance of say, accommodation, then the mean of that set can be calculated and used as the comparative statistic when assessing the significance of scores on the individual

Table 6.10 Semantic differential scales

In describing Torremolinos would you say that it is:						
Hot	1	2	3	4	5	Cold
Friendly	1	2	3	4	5	Unfriendly
Busy	1	2	3	4	5	Quiet

components of the set. This is important in that there tends to be a bias towards central tendency in scales. For example, on a 5-point scale, scores tend to be within the range of 2 to 4. An item mean score of 3.1 against an assumed mean of 3 as the mid-point of the scale might not therefore show as being statistically significant, but if the 'universal' mean for the questionnaire is found to be 2.85, then a score of 3.1 might be statistically significant when using t-tests.

Thurstone scales

There are other scales that have been used in research. For example Thurstone scales are described by many authors on research methods, but such scales require specific skills, and from a review of the literature relating to tourism, do not seem to be used very often. Moser and Kalton (1989) comment:

> Another criticism of Thurstone scaling is its laboriousness. The judges' task requires careful application and a certain level of skill, and it may not be easy for the researcher to gain the co-operation of a large number of persons able and willing to do the work. A point in favour of the other scaling methods ... is that they do not need the services of judges (1989:361).

The method requires a large number of 'judges' to rate approximately one hundred statements according to their assessment of 'favourableness' on an attitude in question, on an eleven (seven or nine) scale. The process can go through various stages.

THE NUMBER OF DIVISIONS AND LABELS

At least two further aspects of scaling need to be briefly considered. The first is the number of divisions used and the second is the labelling of such divisions. In order for any calculation to be undertaken the scales must be other than nominal in type, that is the scale does more than simply categorise groups. As noted above, the conventional criticism of ordinal scales used for ranking is that they do not indicate the intervals between the units. For example, in scales that seek to rank attributes, the respondent may have little difficulty in identifying the most popular location, but the choice between second and third might, from their viewpoint, be difficult. A simple ranking of 1, 2 and 3, gives no information as to the nature of such thought processes. Within an attitude scale indicating degrees of agreement with a statement, the same problem can arise for respondents who may have difficulty indicating the degree of agreement should the scale possess too few divisions. Consequently studies have been undertaken on the differences of results that arise if researchers use 5, 7 or more points on a scale.

Moser and Kalton (1989:359) review the traditional concerns as follows:

> A decision to be made with rating scales is the number of scale points to use: if the scale is divided too finely the respondents will be unable to place

themselves, and if too coarsely the scale will not differentiate adequately between them. Often five to seven categories are employed, but sometimes the number is greater. The choice between an odd or even number depends on whether or not respondents are to be forced to decide the direction of their attitude; with an odd number there is a middle category representing a neutral position, but with an even number there is no middle category, so that respondents are forced to decide to which side of neutral they belong. Another factor to take into account in fixing the number of categories is that respondents generally avoid the two extreme positions, thus effectively reducing the number they choose between.

Two additional comments can be made. If the researcher is seeking to replicate previous research findings then it may be necessary to repeat the previous researcher's questionnaire, even if it is felt that it unnecessarily restricts respondent choice. This may be important in, for example, comparing scores or establishing reliability by use of alpha coefficients or other similar measures.

Second, there is the problem that the use of the 'neutral point' in an odd-numbered scale reinforces the central tendency through respondents using it to record what in effect is a 'no-opinion' response as distinct from a genuine neutral stance. Arguably there is a real distinction between some one being knowledgeable about the subject, and the item being perceived as being of a 'neutral weighting', and the respondent who has no experience of the product and scores the mid-point because there is no other option open to them. The score of 3 on the 5-point scale thus represents very different realities, yet is interpreted as being the same for statistical purposes. Furthermore, if a sizeable minority of the sample is 'inexperienced', it can reinforce the tendency to the mid-point. Therefore there need to be either clear instructions indicating to respondents that they may omit items if they feel unable to comment, or there is a column which they might use to record a 'not appropriate'. Yet, even this strategy is also open to problems for it might encourage a nil response where attitudinal responses are required. This could be important if perceptions are being sought on the basis that what is perceived is as important as the 'objective reality' of the situation being examined.

One problem to be considered is what descriptors should be used. A New Zealand study by Gendall et al. (1991) examined this topic. The interesting aspect about this study is that it compared labelling over an 11-point scale with responses gained from a non-verbal, probability-only scale. A sample of 1209 households was used, with the Juster Scale being used to predict consumer purchases. The sample was followed up three months later to ask which consumer durables had been purchased over the intervening period. Ten consumer durables were being considered. In seven of the cases 'the standard Juster Scale produced lower predictive errors than the probability-only scale' (Gendall et al. 1991:259). The authors conclude:

The standard Juster Scale produced slightly more accurate purchase

Table 6.11 Three types of semantic differential scale

The numerical adjective	1	2	3	4	5	adjective
The unlabelled adjective	( )	( )	( )	( )	( )	adjective
The labelled	very	quite	neither/ nor	quite	very	
adjective	( )	( )	( )	( )	( )	adjective

predictions than the probability-only scale, although the evidence for the former's superior predictive power was not conclusive. However, responses to the standard scale were more evenly distributed and non-response levels were consistently lower for the standard scale than for the modified scale. Furthermore, it was clear that at least some respondents were not entirely comfortable with pure numeric scales (Gendall *et al.* 1991:262).

These results are consistent with those of Garland (1990) in his comparison of various sematic differential scales, some of which contained descriptors and others which did not. He concludes:

> if you are surveying a sample of numerate people then the numerical form may be the best; if you are surveying people familiar with abstract thinking then the unlabelled semantic differential should be considered; but if you are surveying the general public, or in any doubt about comprehension of the task by your respondents, then the labelled semantic differential is the best compromise (1990:22).

The three types of semantic differential scale to which Garland is referring can be easily demonstrated. These are shown in Table 6.11.

In many cases it is obviously possible to combine the numerical with the labelled scale for either a Likert-type or semantic differential as shown in Table 6.12.

THE PROBLEM OF ACQUIESCENCE SETS

The question of acquiescence sets has been considered for at least fifty years. Since Cronbach's work of 1951, experimenters and test designers have been aware of the possibility of a response set operating that creates a general tendency for the subject to accept or reject items. Acquiescence is a response set that may determine a reply to a question where that reply is, to some extent, independent of the content of the statement. Indeed responses to a particular

Table 6.12 Combination of numerical and labelled scale – Likert scale and semantic differential scale

---

Likert scale
Using a 5-point scale where:

Very good	= 5
Good	= 4
Neither good nor poor	= 3
Poor	= 2
Very poor	= 1
Don't know	= 0

If you feel unable to comment, please code the item as 0.

How would YOU rate the following services:

	Very good	Good	Neither good nor poor	Poor	Very poor	Don't know
(a) early morning call	1	2	3	4	5	0
(b) daily change of bed linen	1	2	3	4	5	0

Semantic differential scale
Please circle the rating that you think is appropriate. For example, if you thought the room service was very fast, please CIRCLE the Number 1.

How would YOU rate the following:
The room service was

	very	quite	neither/ nor	quite	very	
fast	(1)	(2)	(3)	(4)	(5)	slow

---

statement can be determined by many factors, for example, the content, chance, alternatives available, mode of testing, external stimuli, and juxtaposition of items.

Of all response sets the acquiescence factor is probably one of the more difficult to quantify, and Berg (1967) indicates why in a series of figures. In Figure 6.6, A will signify agreement on the basis of personality trait, while B does so on the basis of belief or knowledge. D could misrepresent the respondent's 'true' position as to content. C is finely balanced by a tendency to agree on the basis of content, counterbalanced by a trait towards disagreement. Such a respondent may therefore show low test-retest reliability. Arguably, if respondents' content and response style differ, it is not legitimate to collapse the two into one score.

Couch and Heniston (1960) indicate that personality differences do exist between what they term as 'yea sayers' and 'nay sayers' – the former are impulsive, emotional, under-controlled, stimulus accepting and extrovert – while nay-sayers are cautious, rational, intellectually controlled, stimulus rejecting introverts. On an F-scale for dogmatism they found that 'yea saying' accounted for 14 per cent of the variance in scores.

One method for attempting to assess how important acquiescence might be is to use reverse questioning for part of the sample for comparative purposes. But reversal poses three sets of problems. The first is to identify a logical opposite. In some instances this is quite easy. For example, 'I like going on holidays', can easily be reversed into 'I do not like going on holidays'. However, in many examples the simple insertion of the word 'not' does not suffice. Thus the second problem of difficulties of syntax and semantics might emerge – in short the problem of trying to propose a statement that is logically opposite may create increasingly complex questions.

Third, in addition to being logically opposite, the question needs to be 'psychologically' opposite. As one seeks to assess more complex sets of attitudes and emotions, the more this problem emerges.

There are reasons for believing that the verbal content of questions is, however, a much more important determinant of responses than any form of response set. For example, Christie *et al.* (1956:155) comment that:

> although the weight of evidence indicates that responses to the F scale are affected by response set, it does not support the notion that response set is the primary determinant.

Such a finding, albeit specific to the F-scale developed by Adorno *et al.* (1950), is generally significant for attitude questionnaires as the scale measures degrees of dogmatism and stereotyping in thinking patterns. If, within measures of a lack of flexibility of thinking where response sets might be thought to be problematical,

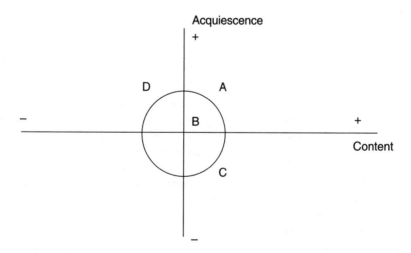

Figure 6.6 The problem of acquiescence sets

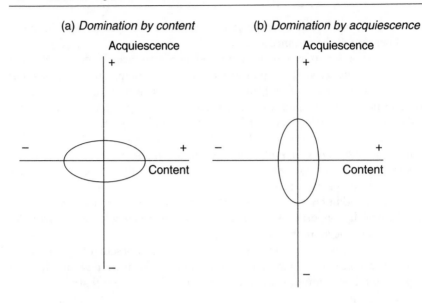

(a) *Domination by content*   (b) *Domination by acquiescence*

Figure 6.7 Domination by content or acquiescence – a diagrammatic representation

it appears (albeit contrary to Couch and Heniston 1960) that acquiescence is unimportant, it is likely to be even less important on less emotionally sensitive topics.

Another method of seeking to assess the extent to which subjects are agreeing for reasons other than an evaluation of the content of the questionnaire is simply to change the order of items on the questionnaire. However, Berg (1967) suggests that:

> the data suggests that reversing the sequence in which items are presented has little or no effect on the agreement responses produced to them ... the conclusion is rather inescapable that the most likely explanation of these response patterns is the verbal content of the item.

It can be contended that a factor contributing towards the development of acquiescence sets is simply the wording itself. In short, difficult and ambiguous items are required to elicit the acquiescence set. It would appear that the weight of evidence would suggest that where respondents are conversant with both the subject and wording of questionnaires, their responses tend to those shown in Figure 6.7a. That is, response set is determined primarily by the content of items themselves. If, however, the questionnaire is either about subjects with which they are unfamiliar, or expressed in a language with which they are not comfortable, or possibly where the topic is perceived as being sensitive, then responses might come to be dominated by acquiescence sets as indicated in Figure 6.7b.

A question related to acquiescence sets is whether the location of favourable adjectives on semantic scales affects responses. Holmes (1974) reports that in a sample of 240 beer drinkers, comparing left–right with right–left scales, there was a definite bias towards the left side of the scales. Friedman *et al.* (1988), examined three situations:

(a)   where favourable adjectives were placed on the left-hand side of the page;
(b)   where the favourable adjectives were consistently located on the right-hand side of the page;
(c)   where a mixture of locations were used.

The sample was one of university students asked to assess features of their university life. A 5-point scale was used, and there were no significant differences between the overall mean scores, although significant differences did occur on individual items. The authors concluded:

> Randomly mixing right-to-left and left-to-right scales had the effect of reducing the inter-correlations among ten items in the semantic differential scale. On the other hand, placing all the favourable descriptors on the left side of the semantic differential scale had the effect of shifting responses to the left, that is, toward the more favourable side of the scale. Placing all the favourable descriptors on the right side of the semantic differential scale appeared to produce less than consistent results.
>
> Thus placing all the favourable descriptors on the left side of the scales would seem to have a possible biasing effect. Researchers are advised to use 'mixed' scales in order to minimise this bias (Friedman *et al.* 1988:480).

The complete questionnaire is not included in their report, but the semantic differential scales appear to have been applied to ten items. One of the customary reasons why consistency in either left–right or right–left scales is used is that while mixing scales may produce logically valid results, they also tend to confuse respondents. To that extent, the Friedman *et al.* study seems to invalidate this argument, except that the number of scales used seems to have been limited, while the sample used is not representative of the wider population. Arguably, confusion can be avoided by consistency of scale direction, but reliability can be assessed by replication of the topic. The problem with this procedure is that it may unduly lengthen the questionnaire.

SUMMARY

This chapter has reviewed a number of issues relating to the construction of a questionnaire. It must again be emphasised that the creation of questionnaires is not a task isolated from the process of developing a hypothesis nor carried out without reference as to how the data are to be subsequently analysed. It is all part of a coherent whole. The choice, for example, of ranking or Likert-type scales has an important implication for the statistical tests that are appropriate. Ranking or

Likert-type scales also have implications for the way in which the researcher is choosing to measure attitude, as previously noted. Thus, the construction of a questionnaire is not simply a matter of technique related to question-setting, important though this is, but is part of a much wider research process.

Chapter 7

The implementation of the questionnaire

INTRODUCTION

Chapter 6 considered the construction of the questionnaire. Before data are obtained, a number of other questions have yet to be discussed. What strategies can a researcher utilise to ensure as high a return as possible, especially when a postal questionnaire is being used? And how is the sample selected? These issues will be the main focus of this chapter.

RESPONSE RATES

The marketing literature contains a number of articles concerning means by which response rates to postal questionnaires can be increased. Postal questionnaires contain many advantages with reference to implementation. It is possible to specify carefully the sample profile by utilising geo-demographics and/or psychographic profiles based on postcode databases. They are easy to undertake, and can be very time-effective in obtaining data from large sample sets quite quickly. They are also effective in terms of labour; a single researcher can quite easily and quickly obtain a sample that is both valid in size and composition. They can be cost-effective in obtaining quantitative data. For example, a postal questionnaire, including printing and mailing costs can be less than £2 per person mailed, and given a 20 per cent response rate, still cost less than £10 per response. The use of a field interviewer undertaking individual surveys would normally cost a minimum of £10 per respondent.

These advantages of postal questionnaires are nullified if the response rate is too small and unrepresentative. A number of methods to increase response rates have been used. Dommeyer (1989) found that 'offering mail survey results to respondents in a cover letter or lift letter does not increase the rate or speed of response, and has only a minor effect on reducing the number of item omissions' (ibid. 1989:406). He comments that while having no effect on response rates, it does increase the number of requests for results! In an earlier study in 1985 the same author hypothesised that the level of interest of the questionnaire was a factor in determining response rates. In constructing a 'boring' and 'interesting' questionnaire, and randomly distributing them to university students, he found no effect on the response rates.

Another method used is some form of monetary award. Since most researchers struggle for funds, it is interesting to note the results of offering inducements. Dommeyer (1988) undertook a comparison between a control group with no monetary inducement, the use of a 25c coin, a 25c cheque, a 25c money order, a promise of refunding post paid costs to respondents, and the chance to enter a sweepstake. (25c was the relevant cost of postage.) The response rates to each of these methods were 37 per cent, 50 per cent, 37 per cent, 38 per cent, 33 per cent and 30 per cent. Mosher (1968, 1979) would argue that the success of the coin was due to the fact that people experience feelings of guilt when they violate internalised standards of proper conduct.

One of the commonest methods used to increase response rates is pre-notifying respondents of the survey. Murphy *et al.* (1991) report that in two cases, the use of a postcard pre-notifying potential respondents of the survey increased response rates from 10.67 per cent to 16.51 per cent, and from 19.54 per cent to 27.60 per cent – the measures of significance being $p = 0.07$, and the second, $p = 0.046$. While having a significant effect on response rates, they note that 'pre-notification by postcard did not significantly increase response speeds nor did it significantly influence response quality' (Murphy *et al.* 1991:341)

Peterson *et al.* (1989) assessed the effect on response rates of the varying numbers of contacts made with respondents. These contacts included pre-notification (either by postcard or letter), follow up (once or twice, again by postcard or letter), as well as the actual sending of the questionnaire. Their results are indicated in Table 7.1.

It can be argued that pre-notification is a crude means of establishing what has been termed the foot-in-the-door approach (Kamins 1989). Kamins describes the foundation of this method as follows:

> With a basis in self perception theory ... and Kelley's discounting principle, the foot-in-the-door technique involves gaining a subject's compliance with a small request (the foot) with the goal of obtaining subsequent compliance with a much larger request.... The idea is that people make self attributions

Table 7.1 Effect of number of contacts on response rates

No. of contacts	Response rate %	Cost/response $
1	10.0	6.27
2	13.6	8.03
3	17.6	8.56
4	21.6	8.82

Source: Peterson *et al.* 1989.

conditional upon observations of their own behaviour and the situational context in which the behaviour occurs. Hence, if a person willingly agrees ... to perform a small request ... he/she is likely to develop a self perception of being helpful and compliant (Kamins 1989:273).

In his study five experimental conditions were observed. In each case the main questionnaire was of a postal self-completion type.

(a) The solicitation control group – subjects were telephoned and simply asked if they would complete a questionnaire. The response rate was 48.51 per cent.
(b) The simple foot condition – respondents were asked four questions on the telephone and then asked if they would respond to a questionnaire. The final response rate was 52 per cent.
(c) The probe foot condition – this was the same as in the simple foot condition, except that respondents were asked their reasons for their replies. The response rate to the questionnaire was 60.78 per cent.
(d) The labelled probe foot condition – in this case the same procedure was followed as for the probe foot condition, but in the follow up postal questionnaire a covering letter made specific reference to the respondent in the following terms: Thanks for your help, you are a very cooperative and helpful individual. I wish that more people would be as willing to participate in important research studies as you were (Kamins 1989:278). Under these conditions the response rate increased to 71.57 per cent.

Kamins subsequently examined the hypothesis that such an approach might generate differences in the actual response patterns, and concludes that:

> only one importance measure out of 69 comparisons ... revealed a significant effect at $p < 0.05$ ... it can be concluded that the pre-contact conditions administered did not differentially affect the subject's actual response and hence resulted in no significant response bias (Kamins 1989:281).

Fern et al. (1986) examined the hypothesis that the response rates of the foot-in-the-door approach are also the function of at least four variables, namely:

1   The relative magnitude of the initial request; as it increases, so too does the response rate.
2   If the initial request behaviour is performed as opposed to be agreed to be performed, then response rates increase.
3   There is an inverse relationship as to the time delay between initial and subsequent requests, and the response rate.
4   If each request is made by a different requester, the response rate falls.

Fern et al. report (1986:145) that the first hypothesis is not supported, but there is evidence to support the remaining contentions. What then can be concluded from this review? Basically it would seem that pre-notification does increase response rates. The nature of the pre-notification is also important. Offers to forward results have little effect on response rates. Small inducements have limited effects. From the practical viewpoint of a lone researcher attempting to undertake a postal questionnaire with limited funds, the ability to undertake pre-notification by letter or telephone is obviously limited. However, 'foot-in-the-door' techniques can be used, albeit to a limited effect. What Kamins (1989) does show is that the message of the covering letter can be important in increasing response rates. However, what he does not cover is whether or not the nature of the sample is itself changed by the foot-in-the-door methods he advocates. While, in his study, this could be controlled by the researcher in terms of the selection of respondents to match a sampling frame, this is not open to the user of a one-shot postal survey. Alternative strategies can exist however. The first is the use of a targeted mail shot. Ryan (1989–90) found this to be effective when seeking to assess the attitudes of a specific geo-demographic group, and obtained a response rate of 54 per cent. An alternative strategy that can be used in the case of student research is to use the 'foot-in-the-door' approach by accessing the parents of students – hence permitting an appeal to a common interest, that is the request from the institution where their children are being educated. Cross-referencing with a sample frame drawn from geo-demographics or other sources can then proceed based on an analysis of their post code. The questions involved in ensuring that the sample is appropriate are discussed later in this chapter.

APPROACHING RESPONDENTS

Many of the above considerations apply where respondents are being approached in the street, or at a tourist attraction. Interviewers need to:

(a) be polite and friendly. This requires the use of expressions such as 'excuse me' and 'please'. The interviewer should smile. Such an approach is more likely to create a more positive response akin to the feelings caused by pre-notification or a 'foot-in-door';

(b) try to select appropriate moments for interviews. If you are trying to research attitudes towards a location, then generally, there is a need to question people after they have experienced the place. This implies questioning people at the point of departure, but there are problems with this in that some people will not want to be detained. One possible strategy is to question people when they have made significant use of the facilities, but have yet to leave. Opportunities can present themselves in cafeterias or airport lounges where people have to wait prior to flights being called;

(c) ensure confidentiality;

(d) identify themselves.

Those working under the auspices of organisations belonging to the Market Research Society should identify themselves as such. Students should also have some form of identification. When working on private property such as shopping centres, airports, tourists attractions and the like, always obtain the permission of the owner or the owner's representative. Prepare schedules of attendance and stick to them.

These are common-sense rules, but certainly help in establishing better response rates. Another strategy that the researcher might wish to consider if time and finance are short is simply to spend as much as possible on sampling as many people as possible within the shortest time possible, rather than spending time and money doing a follow up. This has undoubted administrative advantages, but might create problems of various sub-groups being over- or under-represented.

SAMPLING

A sample is a representative group drawn from a given population. The population might be the total number of inhabitants of a nation. It might be the total number of visitors to a tourist attraction. A statistic is a summary description of a given variable in the sample. As such it is an estimate of a parameter within the population. For example, a survey might find that the average age of visitors to the American Adventure Theme Park is thirty-five. The average population of all visitors to the theme park might actually be thirty-six. Ideally, the researcher will want the characteristics of the sample to match closely those of the population. In many cases, however, the true nature of that population might not be known. The probability that any given sample matches the population therefore rests upon a number of factors:

(a) definition of the population;
(b) selection of sampling units;
(c) selection of sampling frame;
(d) selection of sample design;
(e) selection of sample size;
(f) selection of operational procedures;
(g) selection of the actual sample.

Definition of the population

The nature of the population to be sampled depends upon the nature of the research topic. Earlier, in Chapter 2, the survey of users of a swimming pool was mentioned. The problem described was one where the operators of the pool wished to increase the level of usage. Given this problem, a survey of both users and non-users was required. But the problem could have been restated in a number of different ways. For example, the operators may have wished to increase the level of retail spending within the pool area. From this perspective the population has to be the current pool users in order to assess their spending habits, and the factors that deterred additional spending.

Visitors to any tourist attraction are far from homogeneous. There are many ways of categorising them. Many may be day-trippers, coming from within a distance of two hours travel time. Others will be tourists from further afield, and yet others will be foreign tourists. Tourists might be sub-divided by age, by whether they are accompanied by young children; in short, by any number of permutations. It becomes important, therefore, to define carefully the research problem. Whose attitude or behaviour is being examined, and why that particular group? Equally, it can become important to assess whether particular groups have behavioural or attitudinal factors that are characteristic of that group alone – in which case it is necessary to ensure that proper comparative studies can be made. With whom is the target group to be compared?

It is evident that in some areas of research data exist about the nature of the population. For example, if one was wanting to survey holiday-taking activities of the British population, data exist as to the nature of that population from the Census of Population. The data also exist at regional, local and, to an extent, at neighbourhood levels of analysis. Accordingly it becomes comparatively easy to devise a sampling frame from these data. This is not the case when seeking to assess views of a particular attraction. The numbers of visits might be known, but not the composition of those visitors. Hence recourse has to be made to sampling methods that represent the population. The techniques are now discussed.

The sampling unit

The sampling units are the individual units of analysis. In most cases of tourism research they are the individual tourists, but they need not be so. For example, it is possible to undertake research where the sample units are actual destinations or events. For example, a comparison of expenditures by festivals would mean that the festivals form the sample units.

The sampling frame

The sampling frame is the list of sampling units used in the actual sample. In practice the size of the sampling frame will be inhibited by available resources, both of finance and time. Kish (1965) classifies the problems associated with a sampling frame as being three.

Incomplete frames

Samples based on the Census of Population, for example, will become incomplete over time unless the records are updated. New housing estates may be constructed, or inner city areas reconstructed. The population ages. Obviously, without updating, the Census becomes incomplete over time, and becomes less viable by itself as a basis for devising a sample of the population.

Samples of visitors to attractions may also be subject to problems of incompleteness. The study may be based upon a careful sample of the visitors present at the time of the survey, but tourism is prone to seasonality. Hence the question arises as to whether a sample of visitors during peak seasons is really representative of visitor profiles during the 'shoulder' months or the off-peak season.

Clusters of elements

Samples might not be based on individuals but on clusters. Tourism research is prone to this type of problem. For example, Montgomery and Ryan (1994) in their study of the attitudes of residents in Bakewell comment:

> There was an apparent skew towards older respondents.... Three comments can be made. First, Bakewell has a skewed population distribution towards older people in that it has a high proportion of retired and older people.... Second, questionnaires of this nature are generally skewed in this way because they are often completed by one of the older members of the household. Third, it was suspected that even higher levels of older people might have been sampled if the collection of the questionnaires had been undertaken during the day because older people were more likely to have been at home at that time. The Census data indicates that 73 per cent of the economically 'inactive' are retired people.

This demonstrates the problems that arise from sampling based on households and not individuals. The survey was undertaken by leaving, and subsequently collecting, questionnaires at households. Inevitably the questionnaires were completed by the older members of the household, meaning therefore that the younger members were under-represented.

The same problem can occur when questions are posed to groups of visitors. In many cases the visitors are in family groups, and answers will be provided perhaps by one member of the group, perhaps by either parent. To what extent is the response common to all members of the cluster (visitor group)? To what extent is the answer characteristic of all wives, husbands or other similar members of other groups? And, does it matter that differences might exist?

Blank foreign elements

This can occur when sampling units are not present in the original population. For example, a survey might include large numbers of a given type of visitor because on the day of the survey a series of coach parties might be present. This creates a difference between sampling frame and actual population.

The problems with the nature of sampling frames are well known, particularly in the case of political opinion polls. The most famous case was probably that of the 1936 USA presidential election, when opinion polls prior to the event predicted an overwhelming win for the Republican candidate Alfred Landon.

The democratic nominee, Franklin Delano Roosevelt won. It seems that the poll of 2.4 million individuals was based on telephone directories and club membership lists, and thus excluded those too poor to own telephones or belong to clubs. The lower income groups voted overwhelmingly for Roosevelt. In the 1992 UK general election the Conservative party was returned to power even though opinion polls gave a constant lead to the Labour party under Neil Kinnock. One possible reason for the error was that the opinion polls were based on samples of the British electorate, but not of those who actually voted. Certainly 'don't knows' in political opinion polls can cause problems for pollsters. The 1993 New Zealand polls gave a constant figure of about 38 per cent for the National party and about 34 per cent for the Labour party. In the event both parties polled an almost equal share of the votes, and the Nationals retained power with a one-seat majority. However, prior to the campaign the percentage of 'don't knows' and 'not telling' was at times as high as 25 per cent.

Such mistakes are not so evident in tourism research, perhaps because surveys are not subjected to the same expression of the popular will. However, any survey that has high levels of non-compliance must be suspect. One of the necessary disciplines that any researcher must follow is to check that there are no differences between respondents and non-respondents. In the case of mailed questionnaires where addresses are known, it is possible to undertake a follow-up survey by telephone. An abbreviated version of the questionnaire might need to be used, but it permits comparison between the two groups to assess whether or not differences existed.

SAMPLE DESIGN

Sample design is the means of selecting the sample units. These means fall into two main groups – probability and non-probability. The former permit calculations of possible error estimates because of known sampling distributions. The latter possess the advantages being less costly and taking less time, but are less valid in terms of being able to generalise from their results. Each of the two groups can be further sub-divided.

The basis of probability samples

Samples drawn from populations generally possess three characteristics as to their frequency distributions. These are:

1   normal distributions;
2   binomial distributions;
3   multinomial distributions.

In most cases the researcher is dealing with normal distributions, especially if the data are derived from scale or interval measures. Thus, scores on the Likert-type or semantic differential scales referred to in Chapter 6 will often, but not always,

Table 7.2 Sample variance

Respondent	Score	Difference from mean	Square of difference
1	4	+0.8	0.64
2	2	−1.2	1.44
3	4	+0.8	0.64
4	3	−0.2	0.04
5	3	−0.2	0.04
sum	16		1.80

mean 3.2
sample variance = 1.80/4 = 0.45

fall into a pattern of a normal distribution. The characteristic of a normal distribution lies in the characteristics of its measures of central tendency and dispersion; that is to what degree will sample scores cluster towards the centre of the distribution, and towards the average mean score. To be more precise, to what extent will they centre around the arithmetic mean. The mean is the sum of all the observations divided by the number of observations.

Suppose there is a population of five people. If these 5 value accommodation with scores of 4, 2, 4, 3 and 3, the sum is mean is $(4+2+4+3+3)/5$; namely 3.20. The measure of dispersion measures the amount of variation in the sample. It can be seen in our simple example that the values range from 2 to 4. The variation can therefore be calculated by the difference from the mean. However, those differences, when added together, will cancel each other out; so to overcome that the differences are squared. This removes the positive or negative sign. The sum of these squared differences when divided by the number of respondents less one is known as the sample variance. See Table 7.2.

However, the normal measure of dispersion used is not the sample variance, but the square root of the variance. This can be crudely regarded as returning to the same units as the difference from the mean. For example, if the researcher was calculating the average age of the respondents, the variance is actually 'squared years' (years^2). It can also be seen from the illustrative example that the result of squaring differences from the mean yields a far greater weighting to those scores that are furthest from the mean. In the final column of Table 7.2 those respondents with a score of 3 have a square of difference of but 0.04, while the informant with a score of 2 carries a weighting of 1.44. The more spread out the sample scores are, the larger is the value of the variance and standard deviation. The more concentrated the scores are, the lower the value of the variance and standard deviation. The actual standard deviation is the square of 0.45 (i.e. approximately 0.678).

The above calculation has deliberately used simple values to illustrate the process. Obviously populations are greater than five in number in most cases. It should also be obvious that just as the mean, variance and standard deviation of a population is calculated, so too can the mean, variance and standard deviation for a sample be calculated. If the sample is representative of the population, then the sample mean and the population mean should be similar, as will the standard deviation of both dispersions. The relationships between samples and populations are quite well known, and some detail is given in Appendix 7.1 for those who are interested. It should also be clear that if the nature of the relationship between sample and population is known, the researcher should be able to generalise from the results of the sample to make comments about the behaviour of the population.

One problem that can occur frequently in attitudinal research relating to holidays is that because generally people enjoy themselves, scores on a Likert-type scale or semantic differential are not normally distributed. They tend to be skewed towards the top end. For example, on a 5-point scale the mean score would not be 2.5, but perhaps something like 4.1, even though the range of scores will vary from 1 to 5.

The binomial and multinomial scores are more likely to occur where the questionnaire is based upon nominal or ordinal data. Nominal data means simply categories or classifications. For example, the distribution of gender cannot be 'normal' in that gender is categorised as male or female. Nominal data are simply labels, and one can only count the frequency of such data. Gender is an example of a binomial or dichotomous variable – there is an absence of variant. Ordinal data, on the other hand, results from the ordering or ranking of variables. For example, if there is a list of desired attributes of a holiday, the frequency of mention would produce an order or ranking of those attributes. Ordinal data can therefore be treated in two ways, as binomial or normal. Strictly speaking ordinal data should not be treated as possessing a normal distribution. Davis and Cosenza sum up the debate in the following way:

> What is the most appropriate use of ordinal scales? Well, you can find proponents and opponents of each of the uses given. We take the view that if ranking procedures are used, they are strictly ordinal in nature and should be treated that way. On the other hand, complex scales and indices of an ordinal nature are useful in certain situations and allow us to use the more generally more powerful parametric statistical techniques. As a result, we side with the view of Fred Kerlinger who states, 'The best procedure would seem to be to treat ordinal measurements as though they were interval measurements but to be constantly on the alert to the possibility of gross inequality of measurement' (1988:148).

Generally, it is suggested to researchers that if they wish purposely to seek to use rankings, then they should do so within a research design that utilises techniques specifically designed to measure rankings.

The terms parametric or non-parametric primarily refer to the presence or otherwise of normal distributions. If they exist, the classical tests of hypothesis testing are valid (i.e. parametric tests can be used). The tests concerned are described in the following chapters. Binomial tests rest upon the fact that if data are classificatory in type, then an object has a calculated probability of belonging to that group. One of the earliest examples of this approach lies in the leisure activity of gambling. There are calculable odds of the ball landing on a red or black number, or on any given number.

The concept of a binomial distribution is important when seeking to create a sample drawn from a population, for there is a need to ensure that the sample consists of the same proportion of those of a given gender, age or whatever the required characteristics are as are present in the population. The binomial distribution consists of four properties:

1   Observations are selected from either an infinite population without replacement, or a finite population with replacement. To illustrate the difference, consider drawing a sample of three people from a population of ten. In the former case an individual is selected at random, so there is a one in ten chance of being selected. The second is then selected, but now there is a one in nine chance of being chosen. The third person has a one in eight chance of being picked – so the probabilities of being chosen change. In the latter case, if, after being picked, the selected individual was 'returned' to the population, the chance of being selected remains at one in ten. In most cases, for all practical considerations, the former situation exists, even where, by definition, a population is not infinite.

2   Each observation can be classified into two mutually exclusive and collectively exhaustive categories, success and failure.

3   As noted in (1), for practical purposes, the probability of being a success, p, is constant from observation to observation. Hence the probability of being a failure, $1-p$, is also a constant over all observations.

4   The outcome of success or failure of any observation is independent of the outcome of any other observation.

Thus, if 60 per cent of the population go on holiday, then a sample of the population must consist of a number for whom there is 0.6 probability they will be on holiday, and 0.4 $(1-0.6)$ probability of not being on holiday.

TESTING THE LEVEL OF BIAS IN A SAMPLE – AN INTRODUCTION TO CONFIDENCE LEVELS

From the above comments a number of implications result. One of the more important can be illustrated by reference to a simple random selection. Suppose one wished to calculate the average age of a 18–30 holiday-maker. To simplify, suppose the population consisted of 4 18–30 holiday-makers who were 18, 22, 26 and 28 years old. Thus we have 23.5 as the mean population age. Suppose that a sample of two was taken. If we assume non-replacement of the first

Table 7.3 Range of mean scores

Ages of sample	Mean
18 and 22	20
18 and 26	22
18 and 28	23
22 and 26	24
22 and 28	25
26 and 28	27
mean of means	23.5

selected individual, there are now a number of possible samples, each with its own mean. These are shown in Table 7.3.

It will be seen that the sample can vary quite significantly from the actual mean age of the population, but the average of all of the samples is, in this example, identical with the population mean. The table of the sample means is technically known as the sampling distribution of the mean. It is important to note that although each sample is randomly drawn it can result in a bias. It is possible to estimate from any one random sample how big the sample fluctuations are going to be. It has been noted that the spread or distribution around a mean is the standard deviation – the square root of the sum of the deviations from the mean. In our example this is the square root of

$$(23.5-20)^2+(23.5-22)^2+(23.5-23)^2$$
$$+(24-23.5)^2+(25-23.5)^2+(27-23.5)^2,$$

namely 5.43.

This figure is known as the *standard error of the mean*, and is thus the standard deviation of a sample. In our example, the standard error has been calculated from six samples; it is also possible to calculate the standard error from one sample. Given a normal distribution, then by definition that distribution has specific properties, namely:

68 per cent of values will lie within the mean plus or minus the value of one standard deviation.
95 per cent of values will lie within the mean plus or minus the value of 1.96 multiplied by the value of the standard deviation.
99 per cent of values will lie within the mean plus of minus the value of 2.6 multiplied by the value of the standard deviation.

Thus, if the sample mean is 24.0, and the standard error is 5.4, there is a 95 per cent confidence level that the actual population mean lies between the values of 19.6 and 29.4. Many statistics books contain tables that are also a feature of computer programmes that permit the precise probability of an event to be calculated. The use of such features will be discussed in Chapter 9.

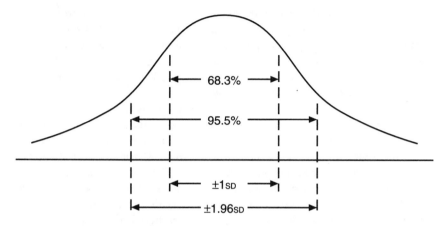

Figure 7.1 The normal distribution curve

Note: 68.3% of cases fall within the range of the mean plus or minus *one* standard
deviation.
95.5% of cases fall within the range of the mean plus or minus 1.96 standard
deviation.

This description is meant to serve only as a very basic introduction to the concept of random samples and levels of confidence. There are many books of introductions to statistics that develop the concepts in much more detail in cases where population means and/or standard deviations are either known or not known. The basic premise, however, is that given any random sample of a population, the mean of that sample will be equal to the mean of the population within definable limits. It should also be noted that as the sample size increases, the sample mean becomes closer to the population mean, subject to the variance of the standard error of measurement.

PROBABILITY SAMPLES

Sample design is thus a concern about ensuring as close a match as possible between the sample and the population, but subject to some constraints. These constraints will sometimes emerge because the researcher will wish, for example, to over-represent sub-groups within the sample in order to ensure that there is a large enough sample of that sub-group for statistical purposes. The main types of probability research design are now described.

Random sampling

Random sampling is where each element of the population has an equal chance of being selected. Thus the process begins with a listing of the specified population. Divide that population (P) by the size of the required sample, n, and then select every (P/n)th name on the list once a randomly selected starting-point is chosen. Alternatively use a random number generator to select the required number of respondents. If the former method is used, then it might be said that a *systematic random* method is used, and if the population is ordered with reference to a specific property, this can give a stratification effect which reduces variability compared to the second method.

In many areas of tourism attitudinal research this is a common method of undertaking research. It is, for example, the method used in the International Passenger Survey where field researchers are asked to select every *n*th passenger that crosses an imaginary line. The important thing is that any field researcher must be disciplined to maintain such an approach. The temptation to deviate on the grounds that the *n*th person does not look likely to be particularly sympathetic is strong, but obviously any such deviation means that the random nature of the sample is being distorted. However, there is the likelihood that a potential respondent may not wish to provide information; researchers will have to have a coherent strategy under such circumstances. These problems will be discussed on page 180.

Multistage random sampling

This method is used when a selection of a sample possessing specific properties is sought. Suppose that one wanted to examine the causes of dissatisfaction with a tourist zone. This would require two stages.

1   Take a sample of visitors and apply some measure of satisfaction.
2   Of those recording high levels of dissatisfaction, select a sample for further questioning.

In samples of the population a multistage random sample is quite common. For example, the country may be divided into electoral areas. From the list of electoral areas a random list might be generated. From the selected constituencies, a random selection of wards might be made. From these wards, a random list of voters is generated as potential respondents. This has the advantage of minimising travel to obtain a large enough sample. Such multi-stage samples based upon geographical proximity are generally referred to as *cluster sampling*.

Stratified sampling

The population is separated into non-overlapping groups called strata, and from each stratum a random sample is drawn. For example, if data exist about types of visitors to an attraction, and the respective volume of each grouping, then the sample might be required to reflect this. One consideration might be to ensure that various groups are represented and hence weights can be attached to each group to ensure a large enough sample. The method of calculation is outlined in principle in Appendix 7.1.

Stratified sampling does possess several advantages for anyone who is planning research and using field researchers. It permits the researcher to define carefully the nature of the sample so that, for example, a field interviewer might be given a schedule which requires them to interview, say, 4 females under 25, 4 females over 25 but less than 35, 4 males under 25 and 4 males between the ages of 25 to 35. It also possesses the disadvantage that the chance of failing to interview representatives of certain groups that exists under simple or systematic random sampling is averted; and additionally less variability will occur.

While an extremely efficient method of determining sample composition, it does of course require detailed knowledge of the population. If holiday habits of, say, the UK population are being studied, then that knowledge exists through the Census of Population and other means including geo-demographic databases. The use of such databases is considered below, because they offer an increasingly cost effective manner of creating samples based on data which are updated annually. On the other hand, samples of actual visitors to any attraction pose greater difficulties because the nature of the visitor population is not known. Under these circumstances the researcher might have to use simple or systematic random sampling, but strictly speaking such samples are only representative of the populations at the period of data collection. The process of seasonality that is characteristic of tourism poses very real difficulties for any researcher. For example, during the offpeak period there is a real possibility that the population is biased towards day visitors drawn from a local catchment area, whereas visitors may be coming from further afield during the peak period. To sample a population fully on an annual basis therefore requires selecting sample periods throughout the year, and engaging in a process of monitoring.

One such example, albeit on a national level, is the UK Tourism Survey. This is undertaken on a monthly basis because it is possible that holiday-taking patterns can vary between sub-groups on a seasonal basis. For example, parents of school-aged children will generally be taking holidays during school periods; hence others might deliberately avoid taking holidays during such periods. Higher income groups can take more than one holiday; low income groups might only take one or no holidays. Periodic monthly sampling therefore helps to detail more accurately these types of patterns, besides having the advantage of avoiding the problems of recall that are associated with annual surveys.

Stratified cluster sampling

This design, as might be guessed from its name, incorporates the features of both stratified and cluster sampling. Basically, it involves the stratified cluster sampling using clusters at random from pre-specified strata. In this way all strata are sampled, but are done so through randomly selected clusters.

Repetitive: multiple or sequential

Essentially these can be described as combinations of two or more samples drawn from stratified and cluster samples. Such sampling tends to be complex, and is driven by a need to create samples with highly specific characteristics. In a sense, therefore, each sample design is a 'one-off' driven by the needs of the research project.

NON-PROBABILITY SAMPLES

Additionally there are non-probability sample designs. These are described as follows.

Judgement samples

Basically this is a sample based upon what the researcher feels is representative. Often it is a form of convenience sample. One such form of sampling is where a researcher wishes to examine the differences between those who, say, are satisfied or dissatisfied with a visitor attraction, and wishes each sample to be of equal size. The problem with this is that the errors introduced by this process are unknown.

Snowball

This is essentially a situation where a respondent is selected on the basis of known characteristics, and then asked to identify another with the same characteristics.

Key decisions

Underlying the process of sampling is a series of key decisions, plus the inherent facts that research design affects the type of inferences that can be made from the data, even while probabilistic sampling is no guarantee that any results so derived are accurate. The key decisions include:

1   Has the population been identified in a way consistent with the research problem?
2   Does the sample frame accurately represent the population?
3   Given the research objectives, is the sampling design chosen appropriate?
4   If particular levels of precision and confidence have been selected does the design generate estimators with the required characteristics?
5   If a non-probability design has been selected, does it provide the required type of information?

THE USE OF GEO-DEMOGRAPHICS FOR GENERATING SAMPLES

As noted above, questionnaires that are based on households rather than individuals possess some disadvantages. Such disadvantages are simply characteristic of a number of problems associated with many forms of quota surveys. Marsh and Scarborough (1990) forward nine hypotheses commonly maintained in the marketing literature. These are:

1   Quota samples are biased towards the accessible.
2   Quota samples are biased against small households.
3   Quota sampling is biased towards households with children.
4   Random samples are biased against employed people.
5   Random samples are more biased against men than quota samples.
6   Quota samples are biased against low status individuals.
7   Quota samples are biased against workers in manufacturing.
8   Quota samples are biased against extremes of income.
9   Quota samples are biased against the less educated.

Marsh and Scarborough then report their findings with reference to each of these contentions, and conclude, broadly speaking, that the position is in fact more complex than it appears at first sight. Certainly, it would seem that it is more difficult to contact males, but otherwise many of the above contentions cannot be supported, or if so important caveats need to be made. They comment:

> Our general conclusion, then, is that random and quota samples are different, but not entirely in the way predicted in the literature. And if our experiment suggests that the existing literature does not give a definitive account of the performance of quota sampling, there may be other methodological questions which, similarly, need to be kept under review (Marsh and Scarborough 1990:502).

They conclude that it is therefore important that survey researchers should use their surveys to answer methodological questions. From the viewpoint of any study, an important consideration has to be the nature of the actual respondents as against the sample frame, and a comparison with what is known of the socio-economic background of holiday-makers. What is evident from the geo-demographic data provided by CCN Marketing (see Chapter 3), and from the surveys undertaken by the national tourist boards as reported in the United Kingdom Tourism Survey (UKTS), is that the market for holiday-taking is significantly skewed towards higher income social classes.

In cases where there is a known bias within the population, Baker (1989) argues that while not the 'universal panacea', geo-demographic systems offer significant advantages as a tool for disproportional sampling. He notes that 'the sampler is free to over-sample areas of high product potential while having the facility to calculate the likely effects on standard errors' (1989:41). From the viewpoint of the subject matter of this work, it is also worth noting his argument that geo-demographics are of significant help in minority product sampling – a factor which might be of interest to those concerned with market research into niche holiday products. Sleight and Levanthal (1989) also make the same point, 'geographic targeting can be a highly effective tool for identifying the likely members of a minority population' (1989:82).

From a practical viewpoint the advantages of using geo-demographics for constructing a sample has been demonstrated in the development of the Businessman Readership Survey and the National Readership Survey. Cornish (1989) notes that in 1986 ACORN was used for the first time with a resultant improvement in discrimination. From 1988 MOSAIC was used as it proved to be an even more powerful discriminator (ibid. 1989:47).

Humby (1989:55) offers further evidence of the ability of geo-demographic systems to generate highly effective sample sets. Seeking, say, high income AB groups by using a random sample, then one would expect that if 10 per cent of the population is sampled, 10 per cent of those so sampled would fall into the target groups. Using ACORN, he argues, it is possible to select 26 per cent of the target market from a sample of 10 per cent of the population, and 44 per cent of the target AB groups can be reached from sampling 20 per cent of the population.

What is worth noting is his point that geo-demographics omit one important variable that would significantly improve sample construction, and that is age. He notes that if age is added to geo-demographic data, then on a sample of 10 per cent of the population, it becomes possible to increase penetration of American Express holders from 30 per cent to 44 per cent. An intermediate stage in improving accuracy was the construction of MONICA by CACI, but this has been bypassed by more recent techniques. Many market research companies such as BMRB are now able to offer an analysis of product purchasers by not only geo-demographics, but also by psychographics. In the case of BMRB they offer not only ACORN but also OUTLOOK classifications, while CCN Marketing, drawing on the National Shoppers Survey of CMT Ltd, offer MOSAIC overlaid by Persona. Persona is a psychographic, or in their terminology, a 'behaviour-graphic' profile of consumers based on conventional psychographic variables. These include data as to behaviour, opinions, values and demographics. In discussion with personnel from CCN, it would appear that at present, selection of a sample based purely upon Persona would not be recommended, but overlaying MOSAIC with Persona profiles, which can be mapped on a geographic basis, does represent significant advances on solely geo-demographic data. Currently it is being used primarily for catchment area assessment for retail and financial services.

The size of the sample

A common question is how large a sample is required. This is particularly true of projects being undertaken with constrained funds, as is often the case with student projects. But the same can also occur in the commercial world of many tourist attraction operators where profit margins might be low, and operators may be only too aware of the cost involved in generating research data. From one perspective a crude answer would be the larger the better, but it is not simply the numbers in the sample that is important, but also the composition of the sample; size itself is not a guarantee of degree of representativeness.

In the case of tourism research the situation normally falls under one of two categories – establishing a survey where the size and variance of a population is either known or not known.

In the case of a finite population where the population size is known, the formula for calculating the sample size is:

$$n = \frac{Ns^2}{\dfrac{(N-1)B^2}{z^2} + s^2}$$

where n = sample size
N = population size
s = standard deviation or estimate
B = allowable error
z = z score based on desired confidence level

Suppose we wished to undertake a survey of package holiday-makers, of whom there are 10 million in the UK in any one year. Where the variance and hence standard deviation is not known, an estimate can be calculated based on Tchebysheff's Theorem, which states that the standard deviation is the value of the range divided by four. So, for example, if it is estimated that generally most holiday-makers spend between £200 and £2,000 per head, then the range is £800, and hence the standard deviation is £450 (£1,800/4). Generally speaking, market research will seek to work to a level of confidence of plus or minus 2.5 per cent. As it is known that 95 per cent of all cases fall within the range of the mean plus or minus 1.96 standard deviations, the z value is customarily 1.96. If the basis of the estimate of the standard deviation is visitor expenditure, then allowable error will also be based upon expenditure, and it might be decided that the allowable error will be £15. This is to cover problems that might be thought to exist when estimating expenditure. Much will depend upon how the data have been derived. If they derived from an analysis of revenue accounts and cash flow, then the allowable error may be small. If, on the other hand, they result from a pilot study, then the allowable error will be generally higher.

Therefore, if it is known that 10 million took package holidays, the desired sample size is:

$$n = \frac{10,000,000(450)^2}{\dfrac{(10,000,000-1)15^2}{(1.96)^2} + 450^2}$$

$$n = 3,456$$

In the case where the variance and hence standard deviation is not known, the formula is:

$$n = \frac{NPq}{\dfrac{(N-1)B^2}{z^2} + Pq}$$

where n = sample size
 N = population size
 P = population proportion or estimate
 q = 1−P
 B = allowable error
 z = z score based on desired confidence level

Obviously the formulation requires some decision about what population proportion to use. If there is no *a priori* inclination, then the value of P = 0.5 is often used, but in most cases researchers have some idea, albeit that the proportion is based upon a pilot study. For example, suppose a pilot study found that 90 per cent of holiday-makers expressed satisfaction with their visit, then a survey of visitors could use P = 0.9. The allowable error by convention is normally estimated as being 3 per cent, but this should be carefully assessed in light of the nature of the derivation of the population proportion and other aspects of the initial data. Again, convention would dictate that z = 1.96 as explained above.

Under these circumstances the sample size is thus:

$$n = \frac{10,000,000(0.9)(0.1)}{\dfrac{(10,000,000-1)(0.03)^2}{(1.96)^2} + (0.9)(0.1)}$$

$$= 3,838$$

In the case where the size of a population is not known, the size of the sample can be calculated from:

$$n = \frac{z^2 s^2}{B^2}$$

where z = z score based on desired confidence level
 s = standard deviation
 B = allowable error

So, if the number of package holiday-makers was not known, but using the 95 per cent level of confidence so that z = 1.96 and s = 450 and B = 15 as before gives us:

$$n = \frac{(1.96)^2(450)^2}{15^2} = 3,456$$

If no estimate for variance exists, but it is estimated that 90 per cent of holiday-makers are satisfied, and no other information exists, then given this paucity of information it is still possible to calculate the required sample from the formula:

$$n = \frac{z^2 P q}{B^2}$$

where n = sample size
    P = population proportion or estimate
    $q = 1 - P$
    B = allowable error
    z = z score based on desired confidence level

So, using the conventions of a 95 per cent confidence level where $z = 1.96$, and an error rate of plus or minus 3 per cent, and the assumption of 90 per cent of holiday-makers being satisfied, then:

$$n = \frac{(1.96)^2 (0.9)(0.1)}{(0.03)^2}$$

Having calculated the size of the sample, some assessment has to be made for non-response. Non-response is also important because it can become a source of bias within the sample, as previously noted on p. 139. The calculation of the non-response rate is simply undertaken, and is given by the formula:

$$R = 1 - \frac{(n - r)}{n}$$

where
    R = response rate
    n = the original sample size and
    r = the number of respondents.

Thus, if 3,000 questionnaires were sent out and 1,100 were returned, the response rate is $1 - (3,000 - 1,100)/3,000 = 0.37)$ and the non-response rate 0.63 or 63 per cent. The seriousness of the non-response bias depends upon the extent to which the population mean of the non-response stratum differs from that of the response stratum. Moser and Kalton (1989) propose that the bias due to non-response is the difference between the average of estimates of a mean derived from an infinite number of samples ($u1$) and the mean of a simple random sample (u), and arises from the ratios of response to non-response within each stratum. They note that:

its (non-response) biasing effects will be the greater, the greater is ... the non-response proportion. Secondly, ... that the seriousness of the non-response bias depends on the extent to which the population mean of the non-response stratum differs from that of the response stratum (Moser and Kalton 1989:167–8).

They give the example of a survey of cinemagoers. If 800 respond from 1,000 in a simple random survey, then the non-respondents account for 20 per cent of the total. We might find from the sample that cinemagoers make an average of one visit per week. But, what if the non-respondents were non-respondents because they were more frequent cinemagoers, and hence were not at home for the field researchers. If the 200 non-respondents visited the cinema twice a week, then the real average number of cinema visits were 800 multiplied by 1 plus 200 multiplied by 2 (i.e. 1,200 visits), and hence the average number of visits to the cinema is not once per week, but 1.2 times per week. The sample is thus biased by 0.2 in its finding. They conclude their discussion by reinforcing the need to obtain information about non-respondents.

NON-RESPONSE AND RECALLING

It has been noted that it is important for researchers to have detailed instructions about how to obtain their sample. In the case of stratified samples interviewers might be given specific quotas. What of research that involves visiting households? An example of the type of instruction as to when attempts to contact a respondent would be ceased are as follows:

(a) When a successful interview with an eligible person aged 16 or over is obtained.
(b) The address was abandoned because it was an ineligible address (e.g. it turns out to be a business premises).
(c) The address was abandoned because it could not be found.
(d) No one was contacted at the address after at least four calls; interviewers are instructed that at least two of these calls should be in an evening or on Saturday or Sunday.
(e) A refusal by an eligible person was recorded.

These instructions are taken from the Welsh Inter Censal Survey of 1986, but are quite common and have been used by the author in research into resident attitudes towards tourism. The interviewer must then be instructed as to what to do when a respondent is not contactable. In the case of samples based on geo-demographic databases, the interviewer can be instructed to interview the neighbour, and this can maintain the validity of the sample. This process raises a series of potential issues. One such question is whether there is a best time for undertaking interviews? In their study Swires-Hennessy and Drake found definite patterns in data collection that reflected field interviewer working practices, and, after an analysis of results where interviewers recorded the date and time of interview, concluded that the 'highest probability of a successful outcome occurs between 17.00 hours and 22.00 hours' (1992:72).

One question that has received little attention in the market research literature or indeed in the literature relating to tourism research, contains what is the effect of re-interviewing respondents? But why should respondents be subjected to a second interview? In some cases (as discussed on pages 30–4) it might be because the nature of a longitudinal study requires repeat visits to the respondent. Within a short time frame, it might also be a means of assessing reliability of the data. Such research abounds with problems. If, within a short period of time, some difference in response is found, how is this to be interpreted? Is it in part due to a learning curve on the part of the respondent? Does the discrepancy arise because of a lack of recall – in which case at what time did the memory fault occur – at the first or second interview? Is there a difference between questions with a factual as distinct from an evaluative basis? On the other hand, to be able to compare responses from a known set of respondents with those from a fresh group of respondents might generate some advantages, especially, for example, if researchers were attempting quickly to find respondents from specific niches. One area of growing interest to commercial operators within the UK is that of the markets composed of the ethnic minorities. On the whole there has apparently been little academic research done into the holiday patterns of such groupings. Yet, at a common-sense level, there are significant travel patterns associated with such groups. Access to these groups might be one problem associated with such research, and there might be a need for researchers to use specific sets of respondents. One study that does report findings into these types of related issues is by Hahlo (1992). His study relates to a range of consumer durables and groceries, but also included questions about activities on Christmas Day. He notes that:

> there are no major significant differences on factual or behavioural questions. This difference on awareness questions would seem to stem from a greater willingness to be helpful in the re-interview sample. They are more positive, they try harder and so generate more responses on average.
>
> In my opinion, this is a positive contribution to the research process. Respondents who try harder to answer the questions put to them, should provide more valuable and more sensitive research findings, especially from open-ended questions (Hahlo 1992:108–9).

His opinion again raises the question of the nature of the research design and the purposes and functions of the research. Is a sample that 'tries harder' representative? What is more important, quality of response in terms of richness of data, or quality in terms of a strict adherence (if this is possible) to some concept of a sample being representative?

Techniques and questionnaire design – the question of predictions

In Chapters 2 and 3, a discussion was undertaken as to what underlying conceptual framework is to be adopted in analysing data. As an introduction to the following chapters, and as a linkage between the previous points and those yet to be made, it might be worth concluding this chapter with a general discussion of the implications that various statistical techniques might have for questionnaire design. This is not to argue that the statistical technique should determine the nature and pattern of the questions – far from it – but if the way of putting the question is recognised as being important in terms of obtaining data, then equally the form of analysis to be selected must also be a consideration.

For example, the design of the questionnaire appears very different as to whether multi-attribute analysis, conjoint measurement or other methods such as multi-dimensional scaling are to be used. Failure to consider this at an early stage in the questionnaire can create a proclivity towards a series of questions that are unrelated, thus leading to a loss of richness and diversity in the analysis.

A number of these issues have already been discussed in Chapter 5, where reference is made to the problems of part-worths within regression analysis. A further question that the researcher must consider when designing a question-naire is whether or not the researchers are seeking, from their hypotheses, to be able to make predictions of, for example, holiday satisfaction. One thing the researcher would be able to do is to assess the degree to which elements within the research design correlate with each other. Although this is an issue that is further discussed in more detail in the chapter relating to regression analysis, it is pertinent to comment on the matter here, because it has implications for sampling and research implementation. Indeed, it will be argued that the use of a coefficient of correlation matrix should be part of an initial screening in assessing whether or not the data were able to support the emergence of underlying factors or clusters. The same correlation coefficient can be used as an assessment of the closeness of prediction with recorded outcome in the case of a linearly related dependent and independent variable. Regression analysis simply takes the procedure further in that it predicts a dependent variable (e.g. holiday satisfaction) on the basis of values attached to independent variables (such as age, expectation, travel career or other variables thought to determine satisfaction). Indeed, the outcome, satisfaction, can be measured with reference to the scores derived from clusters ascertained from factor analysis.

* In a linear relationship, the formula between the dependent variable, y, and the independent variable, x, is $y = bx + a$. Assuming that a least squares line of best fit through a scatter plot of x and y is used, the slope of the line as given by b, is calculated as $b = r_{xy}(s_y/s_x)$ where s_y and s_x are the standard deviation of y and x respectively, and r_{xy} is the correlation between the two variables. The value a is the intercept (i.e. the value of y when x equals zero), and is the value of the mean of y minus the mean of x multiplied by the value of b as defined above.

Utilising this approach, it becomes possible either to predict the value of the dependent variable, or to utilise the difference between the predicted and actual value as a measure of the validity of the proposed set of relationships. However, if the regression model is being used for either purpose, the researcher must be aware of some of the sources of prediction errors, and the means of measuring them. Least squares estimation uses squared errors (because errors are squared to eliminate the sign, i.e. whether the error is positive or negative). But because it is normal to be interested in errors in the dependent (predicted) variable, it is the standard deviation of errors in the y variable that is calculated. This is given by the formulation se $= s_y \sqrt{(1 - r^2_{xy})}$. However, because error standard deviation is an average error across all the data, it is not always a good estimate of a particular score group. For example, a sample might have been divided between high, medium and low scorers of satisfaction, and hence the average standard error might not be appropriate. The assumption of equal variability across all groups is known as the homoskedacity assumption. Errors can also be measured by use of standardised scores rather than raw scores.

The errors that can arise are normally associated with three types of problem. These are, bias in sampling, sampling error and error of measurement. Sampling error is the departure of sample statistics from population statistics that derive from chance differences between the sample and the population. Errors of measurement occur when there is a discrepancy between a measurement observed and the intended measurement, and may arise through faulty research or, in this instance, questionnaire design. If the measurements are systematically wrong, then they lack validity. If the measurements are erratically at fault, then they are said to be unreliable.

The impact of error of measurement on the correlation is straightforward; the correlation is reduced in direct proportion to the amount of error in the dependent and independent variable. For example, suppose a large sample was used, the variables were perfectly measured, and the resultant correlation was found to be 0.60. Under these circumstances the error of measurement would approach zero, and the correlation could be used for predictive purposes with high degrees of confidence. On the other hand, suppose an attitude was measured by the use of a single item. Levine and Hunter (1983) note that under these circumstances, 'studies of the error of measurement usually have a reliability of 0.50 or less' (1983:338). Under these circumstances the correlation of 0.60 would be cut by half, that is, it becomes 0.30. Levine and Hunter further note that if the effect of sample error is superimposed upon reductions of correlation due to an error of measurement, then 'the results could be disastrous' (1983:339). Improvement of results can be obtained by increasing the size of the sample and improving measurement.

Reliability might be measured by the correlation between the observed and the perfect measurement, and is usually defined as the square of the correlation between true and observed scores. One obvious problem in much of social science research is a lack of knowledge about the 'true' score. Accordingly tests of reliability can often be more correctly described as scores of internal consistency. Various techniques can be used, and these will be described later when considering the statistical tests associated with these problems. One such test is the Cronbach Alpha Coefficient.

CONCLUSIONS

Although it appears that quantitative research possesses an inherent 'objectivity', this review of issues and concepts has shown that the reality is far more complex. While the nature of the sample is an important consideration, the validity and reliability of the results would appear to be far more dependent upon the wording that is actually used. It is worth restating that the paradox of the validity of statistical inferences is based not simply upon the scientifically proven relationships of probability, but also upon the art of question formulation.

Indeed, many aspects of questionnaire design, formulation and implementation are a question of an art that is honed through experience. The researcher is forever making judgements not only about the questionnaire design, the wording, the layout, the use of open versus closed questions, or the use of prompts to aid recall or not, as the case may be. Judgements are also made about what to do with non-respondents, the need for follow ups – in fact, as seen, a set of related and complex issues. The judgement can only be made with reference to the overriding aim of the research, and the information which is needed to support that research and the hypotheses upon which it is based. Yet, while this seems to call for clarity of purpose, such clarity becomes a hindrance if it implies an inflexibility of approach that denotes an inability to respond to what the respondents are saying.

It is worth reiterating that although the problems of sample design are dealt with in detail in many textbooks of statistics, there is a school of thought which argues that more error emerges from poor questionnaire design than from poor sample composition. Yet this is no argument for a lack of attention to the nature of the sample. The sampling method to be used is important and, wherever possible, the researcher should pay specific attention to the nature of the population from which the sample is to be derived.

APPENDIX 7.1

Stratified sampling – calculation of the sample

In outline the process involves:

where N = population size
n = sample size
L = number of strata
N_i = population size in stratum i
n_i = sample size allocation in stratum i
σ_i = population standard deviation of stratum i
W_i = allocation weight for stratum i

(a) Define the number of strata, L.
(b) Estimate the number of sampling units in each stratum, N_i, as the number of stratum number from 1 to L.
(c) Determine the number of sampling units in the population N where

$$N = \sum_{i=1}^{L} N_i$$

(d) Estimate the variance of the characteristic measure of interest within each stratum. A rule of thumb such as Tchebysheff's theorem might be used.

(e) Denote allocation weight w_i for strata where

$$\sum_{i=1}^{L} w_i = 1.00$$

The allocation of weights can be proportionate to a stratum's size, disproportionate for some analytical or convenience reason (e.g. to establish sufficient size for testing) or optimum where the weight selected is proportionate to the variability as well as the size of the strata.

(f) Determine the appropriate confidence level desired by choosing the appropriate z (level of confidence) score for the normal distribution.

(g) Determine the degree of allowable level.

(h) Determine an estimate for the variance for the population estimator using the value B in the following equation:

Mean	Proportion
$Z\sqrt{\sigma_x^2} = B$	$Z\sqrt{\sigma_p^2} = B$
$\sigma_x = \dfrac{B^2}{z^2} = D$	$\sigma_p = \dfrac{B^2}{z^2} = D$

(i) Calculate n, the sample size, needed to estimate the population estimator within the tolerable levels prespecified by B.

For mean

$$n = \frac{\displaystyle\sum_{i=1}^{L} \frac{N_i^2 \sigma_i^2}{w_i}}{N^2 D + \displaystyle\sum_{i=1}^{L} N_i \sigma_i^2}$$

For proportion

$$n = \frac{\displaystyle\sum_{i=1}^{L} \frac{N_i 2 p_i q_i}{w_i}}{N^2 D + \displaystyle\sum_{i=1}^{L} N_i p_i q_i}$$

(j) Calculate $n_1, n_2, \ldots n_L$ based on allocation procedures.

Tchebysheff's theorem

Tchebysheff's theorem states that for any set of sample measurements with mean

x and standard deviation s, the proportions of the total number of observations in the sample falling within the intervals $x \pm 2s$ and $x \pm 3s$ are as follows:

$x \pm 2s$: at least 75 per cent
$x \pm 3s$: at least 89 per cent

The approximate value of a standard deviation in the population can be estimated by the formula:

standard deviation = range/4.

So, if the level of expenditures of holiday-makers at a destination ranges from £4.00 to £34, the standard deviation can be estimated as (£34 − £4)/4; equals £7.50.

Chapter 8

Coding data and obtaining descriptive statistics

INTRODUCTION

In this chapter and in subsequent chapters examples of deriving statistics and their interpretation will be undertaken with reference to commonly used statistical packages. These are described as follows.

SPSS/PC+™

(Statistical Package for the Social Sciences) is a large and versatile package that has been long used by researchers in the social sciences. In this book the PC version will be referred to. There is another version SPSS-X, which is the version used on mainframe computers. For the purposes of the statistical tests described in this book, the commands between the two are identical, and in many cases a student or researcher might actually be using SPSS-X because they are using a terminal to a mainframe system such as a VAX computer. If that is the case, then, as below in the case of the other packages, there may be means of entry specific to the package. Today, most log-on systems give rise to a menu system whereby the available statistical packages are listed.

MINITAB

MINITAB is widely used in universities because when compared to earlier versions of SPSS it was a much more user-friendly system. The typing of the word HELP brings immediate recourse to any user of MINITAB. MINITAB was originally developed at the University of Pennsylvania as an aid to the teaching of statistics, and, like the other packages, is continually being developed and updated. Again like some other packages, it is also supported by an active bulletin board where suggestions as to macros, uses and suggested improvements can be found.

NCSS

NCSS (Number Cruncher Statistical System) is popular among students in North

America for its ease of use, because it is primarily menu-driven in its tests. It also possesses a number of advanced capabilities, and is available at reasonable prices from its originator Jerry Hintze. Dr Hintze was a professor of statistics and wished to be able to teach statistics and its uses via a program that was easily accessible both in terms of cost and ease of use.

These packages are continually being monitored, reviewed and updated. For example, the latest edition of NCSS has significantly added to its curve-plotting facilities relating to various forms of trend analysis. MINITAB in 1993 was up to release version 9, which meant not only (when compared to, say, version 5) the possession of a spreadsheet format for data entry, but also new graphic facilities, more powerful functions for linear modelling, the introduction of pull-down menus and support for mouse functions for point and click operation.

In the following text it is recognised that not everyone has access to the latest version of the software, and hence reference is made to the instructions in text format, that is the researcher keys in the relevant instructions. It must also be noted that opinions vary as to the usefulness of features such as drop-down menus. Some older researchers prefer to key in instructions; they feel more in control, and can more easily access the data and past commands if an error has been made. For example in the case of SPSS, West notes that 'almost no-one I know uses the menu system because it is very cumbersome' (1991:204). It is, however, a question of taste and need. There are occasions, such as doing a quick scan, when the menus are of use; at other times, when perhaps transforming data and undertaking more serious analysis, the researcher may wish to be able to revisit the process adopted. Then a 'text' entry which can either be printed or filed may be felt to be advantageous. On the basis that it is easy to adapt from text to menu functions, the rubric followed below when discussing SPSS or MINITAB is to give the text instructions.

There are, of course, numerous other programs. Statgraphics, SAS and MYSTAT (to mention but three) possess their own advantages. As is the case with many computer packages, it is for the users to determine what their needs (and finances) are. In many cases, familiarity with a program brings increased efficiency of use, and indeed, even a sense of affection for its quirks. Many users take advantage of such quirks to speed up their use of the program and to avoid longer, more correct ways of doing things.

Statistical functions are also being provided with an increasing number of spreadsheets. For many years these have possessed the ability to produce simple descriptive statistics such as averages, standard deviations, and frequencies, but increasingly more tests are being added. Also, the use of macros enables the user to build up the formulas for sophisticated calculations, although a high degree of knowledge would be required for many non-parametric tests and for multiple discriminate analysis. There is a process of continuous evolution of computer software. Statistical packages are taking on the spreadsheet formats of data entry and are being allied to databases, while spreadsheets assume more statistical functions, as do databases.

COLLATING AND INPUTTING DATA

The basic preparation

Once the research questionnaire has been designed and implemented, and having received possibly several hundreds if not thousands of responses, the problem becomes one of preparing data for the computer. There is perhaps no single right way to do this, for each project creates its own peculiarities, but there are some ways which are better than others. Also, some of the problems can be avoided by reference to careful design of the layout of the questionnaire, and the nature of the questions asked. What most computer programs will require is the completion of a matrix of data with the columns representing the coded answers to the questions, and the rows representing the replies to those questions by each respondent in turn. So, for the beginner, what are the basics of data entry, and how do these affect questionnaire design? To start at basics, it is probably wise to take the following steps.

Check each response as it comes in to ensure that the questionnaire has been fully completed

In some cases respondents might have failed to realise that a page was printed on both sides, and perhaps they have answered questions only on alternate pages. Some respondents will not have wanted to complete the personal details concerning age, income and similar other factors. Some respondents may have omitted the questions that they felt unable to answer.

Some of these problems can be minimised in a number of ways. For example, numbering the pages of the questionnaire can help, especially if supported by a rubric at the end of the questionnaire or within the accompanying letter, which asks the respondent to be sure they have filled in all eight pages of the questionnaire (if eight pages is the actual length). Similarly, give assurances of confidentiality. If the actual name or address is not required (e.g. for any follow-up procedures), it might help in the accompanying letter to point out that confidentiality is assured and that the respondent's name or address is not sought. If this is done, ask yourself carefully how you are going to ensure the representativeness of the usable sample. Making commitments as to confidentiality, and then coding the questionnaire or reply envelope in a way that permits identification of the respondent is generally unethical at worst, and at best assumes that respondents will not recognise that this is occurring; in many instances it is an invalid assumption, and one that can affect the return rate or the nature of the responses.

Depending on the number of responses, and the level of completion of the questionnaire, the researcher will have to make decisions about:

(a) policy towards incomplete questionnaires (i.e. to retain or discard a return);
(b) if retained, how to treat incomplete data.

The answer will depend upon the character of the research and the nature of the omissions. If substantial parts of a questionnaire have been omitted, it is probably better to omit the questionnaire, but if the informant has only withheld personal data, it can generally be retained for subsequent analysis.

Number the questionnaires that are being retained in chronological order or some other sequence that makes sense to the researcher

It is probably advisable that the first code to be entered into the computer is the number of the respondent. This means that any subsequent checking will enable you to identify quickly the original questionnaire, allowing the researcher to go back and to correct the data entry from the original form. Do not try to guess the value of coded data without reference to the original form at the checking stage. This also implies that the questionnaires are kept in some ordered fashion which enables ease of access to the forms. Piles of forms on the floor have a nasty habit of falling over and getting out of sequence. Keep them in boxes, or box files. In any case, keep the original questionnaires – do not discard them upon entry of data into the computer. Apart from not being able to recorrect wrongful data entry, there is the question of being able to access precise wording of qualitative replies, and being able, if necessary, to prove that the research was properly carried out. Depending upon the nature of the privacy legislation and any data protection legislation that is operating within the researcher's country, there may be a legal requirement to hold such records for a minimum time period to permit informants to question any data held on a computer.

Determine your policy towards the coding of missing data

Many computer programs only permit the use of numeric data within cells subjected to statistical analysis. Hence it is important to take care that you are able to identify the presence of missing values. This is one of the reasons for undertaking frequency counts to ensure that findings are based on a sufficient number of replies. In attitudinal research it is also important for the researcher to consider how the missing value is going to be treated – is the fact of non-reply to an item itself an important piece of information? For example, consider the question in Table 8.1.

Table 8.1 Non-reply – allowed for

How would you rate the services provided by the courier?					
Very poor				Very good	No reply
1	2	3	4	5	0

In the case in Table 8.1, if a respondent circles the zero, it could be omitted from the calculation because the respondent, arguably, felt unable to make a judgement. Perhaps they had not used the courier's services. But now consider the 'other half' of a Fishbein approach to questioning as shown in Table 8.2.

Table 8.2 Non-reply – not allowed for

How important to you are the services provided by the courier?				
Of no importance				Very important
1	2	3	4	5

In this instance perhaps the respondent has not replied. The question is a perceptual one. Does non-reply imply a lack of importance? If coded zero, is that zero now to be incorporated into the calculation of a mean score? In general it is 'safer' if such non-replies are not included in the data on the premise that it is dangerous for the researcher to make any imputation as to what is in the state of mind of the respondent at the time of the response; but it is a question that each researcher must consider in the light of patterns of response, need for the data, method of treatment (e.g. is a paired comparison being made) and any other information being present.

Consistency of response checking

When keying in the data the researcher might become aware of inconsistencies in a respondent's pattern of answers. For example, they might at one stage rate highly social needs from a holiday, but then respond negatively to a question about how important was time spent with friends. In many cases such inconsistencies can arise due to questions being mixed as to the use of positively or negatively phrased questions, or, if the questionnaire has been poorly designed in layout, where the meaning of a scale has been reversed (e.g. in one section the figure 5 represented the highest positive score and in another, the figure 5 represented the highest negative opinion). Some of these issues were discussed in Chapter 6. However, it is generally best to follow the rule of consistency in order to avoid these types of problems. Consistency has the advantage of not causing undue difficulties for informants. Ways of achieving consistency and aiding the respondent include the following points.

(a) Ensure scales are of equal length – (i.e. use consistently 5-, 7-, 9- or 11-point scales where a range is being offered to the respondent).
(b) Ensure the scale is consistent in direction. If, for example, 7 is the highest number in the sense of being the most positive reaction, ensure that this is so throughout the questionnaire.

Table 8.3 Basic data – the need for coding

Could you please tick the boxes that describe you:

Gender	Male	☐
	Female	☐
Age	Less than 16	☐
	16 to 25	☐
	26 to 35	☐
	36 to 45	☐
	46 to 65	☐
	66 to 75	☐
	76 and over	☐

(c) If a series of questions are preceded by a rubric indicating the nature of the scale, but the series of questions is continued over a page, it is helpful to repeat the scale's instructions at the top of the page.

(d) Keep the layout of the page clean and simple – avoid a cluttered appearance.

The checking of questionnaires for such problems can be done either prior to coding and inputting data, or in batches, or sequentially while actually keying in data, dependent upon the number and complexity of the questionnaire; but whenever it is done, consistency of policy is required. The next stage to be considered is the actual coding of the questions. This is where the advantage of Likert-type or semantic differential scales is obvious. In a sense, the respondent has actually done the coding for the researcher by circling or ticking the appropriate number. Where a series of options are given, it is best simply to code these sequentially from one to the maximum number (see Table 8.3).

Gender can therefore be coded 1 for males, and 2 for females. The ages are coded from 1 to 7. In the design of the questionnaire it is useful if spaces are left for codes to be entered in either the left- or right-hand margin. It is even more helpful if these spaces are numbered according to the sequence in which the data are keyed into the computer. Two advantages accrue. First, the search for information is easier if there is a need to check a specific item on any questionnaire. Second, if the researcher has decided not to use variable labels (see page 198) it becomes easy to identify any item with a particular question by simply looking at any questionnaire. If this is done, note that variable one is the number of the questionnaire, and hence question one is actually column two in any input. Also, if new variables are created by combining data, then these are numbered in an appropriate order. For example, suppose there were 40 variables associated with a questionnaire, and the items relating to gender and age were numbered 36 and 37. The researcher might want to do a comparison between young men and young women, and thus create new variables by combining the gender and age data. So, for example, males under the age of 25 now become variable 41, and females under the age of 25 become variable 42.

Items such as age and income can pose some difficulty in selecting the actual age or income bands to be used, for example if retired individuals are to be identified. If, as in the UK, females retire at 60, and males retire at 65, the above combination of ages and gender information would not correctly identify retired females because they fall into the 46 to 65 category. There are at least five possible approaches to such problems. First, simply ask respondents to record their age and gender. This produces more correct data, but also runs the risk of respondents refusing to reply. A second approach is to use different coloured forms for, in this case, males and females, so that if field researchers are being used, they use the appropriate colour form with an amended age bracketing printed on the form for each gender. Third, if the research is going to produce findings that are going to be compared with any other research, it is necessary to use the age groupings of the comparable research report. Fourth, apply the age categories used in official sets of data (e.g. demographic reports in series such as, in the UK, the Monthly Digest of Statistics). Fifth, if any other alternative is used, know why it is being selected.

The main problem will be coding open-ended replies. Various approaches might be adopted:

(a) Either as the result of a pilot study or researcher experience, draw up lists of expected answers and allocate numbers to these.
(b) Build up a pattern of responses in a sequential fashion from the actual questionnaire and simply number these in order starting with the first.

This second approach can only be carried out if a single researcher is undertaking the whole process of data coding and entering the data into a computer. In academic circles this is quite common for both staff and students, even with quite sizeable samples of, say, two thousand. Although time consuming, this method does possess the advantage of avoiding questions of inconsistency between coders; it also means that the researcher is very close to the quality and nature of the data – a very real benefit when interpreting and writing up results. The former method is essential where more than one person is concerned with data entry, as there is the problem of ensuring consistency of response between coders. The researcher (or research team) need to create a series of examples for each code number, so as to clarify what is and what is not to be included in any specific code.

One common problem with open-ended questions is that respondents will often make more than one comment about the issue. For example, suppose there was the question: Please briefly indicate what for YOU, was the highlight of the holiday? The respondent could reply: Being able to share the beauty of the Alps with my wife. This answer contains two features:

(a) an appreciation of natural beauty; and
(b) the importance of reaffirming family ties and bonding.

Both of these might have been anticipated responses to the question, but if the coding design only permits one code, how is the response to be coded? Or is a third category created, which combines the two previously identified responses? If so, how is it treated in any frequency count of 'holiday highlights'? One method is to allocate more than one code space to the actual item. So, if the question above was item 32 on the questionnaire, in the coding framework it might be allocated two columns to code such double answers. With open-ended questions the researcher has to decide how much space will be allocated, but there will inevitably be lost information. On the other hand, it is easy enough to retrieve such information from the original questionnaires simply by identifying informants from the code indicating respondent number, and the fact that they have responded fully to the open-ended question because all code spaces allocated to that item have been used.

Entering the data

Having coded the questions, the next stage is actually to enter the information into the computer. Most statistical software packages permit entry from three different sources: (a) the use of a spreadsheet; (b) from within the package itself; and (c) from an ASCII file. The ways in which packages permit data entry from within the package itself can vary. For example, MINITAB (from version 7) permits data entry via a spreadsheet format. Alternatively the data may be keyed directly into MINITAB. Suppose there were four columns of information, the first being the number of the respondent, the second their gender (where 1 is male and 2 is female) and the third and fourth columns were responses to questions. The data could be entered as shown in Figure 8.1.

In Figure 8.1 c1–c4 means enter into columns 1, 2, 3 and 4. If more than four columns were required, then the second 'c' would simply be c6, c50 or as required. Type end (or END) when the final item of data has been entered.

The Number Cruncher Statistical System (NCSS) also possesses a file editor

```
MTB >   READ c1–c4
DATA> 1 2 4 3
DATA> 2 2 3 4
DATA> 3 1 2 4
DATA> 4 1 3 4 etc

DATA> END
```

Figure 8.1 Entering data with MINITAB

```
DATA LIST /respond sex item1 item2.
BEGIN DATA.
1 2 4 3
2 2 3 4
3 1 2 4
4 1 3 4 etc

END DATA.
```

Figure 8.2 Entering data with SPSS

that takes the form of a spreadsheet and can be used to enter data, although it is not recommended for this purpose as it is slow and somewhat cumbersome. Statistical Package for the Social Sciences (SPSS) also has a data command. This is used in conjunction with a DATA LIST command, which defines the variable names and could take the form shown in Figure 8.2. However, one of the easiest ways to prepare data is to use the DOS editor to be found in MS-DOS (or PC-DOS), or to use a word processing package such as WordPerfect, which can save the data as an ASCII file. A number of advantages accrue from this:

(a) The resultant file can be used with any of the above packages. This can be fairly useful if you have a preference for one of the packages for a particular function. In many cases it is simply a matter of personal preference, but this method keeps open the option.

(b) Although the editing functions on software packages are improving, the use of the DOS editor or a word processing package arguably retain some advantages. For example, the search function or the ability to cut and paste can be of real advantage in saving time and effort.

(c) It allows preparation of the data on a computer other than the one where the package is located. For example, a student may be using SPSS at their university, but does not have SPSS on a computer at home. The data file can be prepared at home, and simply taken to university on a disk. The preparation of data as an ASCII file therefore possesses the significant advantage of convenience, thus saving time.

(d) Having the data in an ASCII file may also permit the option of being able to use a spreadsheet or graphics package, which permits the preparation of graphs to a higher standard than might be possible under the statistics software. Although software graphics facilities are fast improving (in the case of SPSS, being increasingly tied into software such as Geographical Information Systems), at present it is perhaps true that specialist graphics programs, and indeed some spreadsheets, possess advantages in the area of preparing graphs.

(e) Space is saved on the computer memory. For example, if the SPSS data editor is used to save data it will assume that each item has eight significant digits unless specifically told otherwise, and hence will take up considerably more space. It can be compressed, but data then take longer to retrieve.

If the DOS Editor is being used, it becomes a simple matter to type at the DOS prompt the word EDIT followed by the name of the file (e.g. Edit a:myfile where the file to be edited is on disk drive a. This calls the editor, and the information is simply typed in:

1 2 4 3
2 2 3 4
3 1 2 4
4 1 3 4

Spaces are placed between the numbers and the return key is used at the end of each line. The data are then saved by simply clicking the mouse on the 'file' menu at the top of screen to call the drop-down menu; then click save or save as as required. This file can then be imported into the statistical package that is being used after the data have been checked.

Checking the data

Checking the data is a time-consuming but all important matter. The first thing that can be done is to use some of the facilities available within the statistical package. In the case of SPSS this is done by loading the file and using the LIST command for column one. SPSS-PC operates a menu system, which can be turned off by typing ALT-M (i.e. by depressing the ALT key and the M key simultaneously). Users become familiar with using a combination of menu commands, which they type in directly; each person should develop a pattern of work with which they are happy. Basically, the method to obtain a list of input data is shown in Figure 8.3.

The result of the action shown in Figure 8.3 will be, assuming that variable 1 is the number of the respondents, a series of numbers, namely: 1, 2, 3, 4, etc. If this sequence is broken it will be because the line of data for a given respondent carried the wrong number of items within the line. It is now possible to go back to the original line of data in the DOS Editor accessible from within SPSS by using the DOS option on the SPSS menu); look up the original questionnaire, re-enter the line or otherwise correct it. Where the questionnaire has a large number of questions, it can be quite difficult to find the omitted response. It is worthwhile, if the omission is not immediately obvious, to begin to re-enter the row next to the original row. When the error is found, correct the original row, and delete the new row using either the 'cut' function of the editor or the delete key.

In the case of MINITAB the command PRINT c1 will produce the same list. In NCSS simply use the menus to list data. While this process immediately

Command	Commentary
DATA LIST File 'a:myfile' FREE/ var1 to var4.	If you have prepared the data on another computer you are here directing the program to the data held on a disk in the 'a' disk drive. Myfile is simply the name of the file. The term var1 to var4 simply identifies that there are 4 variables carrying the names var1, var2, var3 and var4. Note that each line in SPSS ends with a full stop.
LIST var1.	This command will list variable 1.
FINISH.	

Figure 8.3 Listing variable values with SPSS

identifies problems caused by incorrect field sizes in a free-form format, it is not in itself a guarantor of correctly entered data. Nor in fact is the situation met if fixed format is used where each variable is defined in terms of its size, that is the number of digits required. Great care must be taken when entering data. One way is to:

(a) Ask a friend to read the codes from the questionnaires aloud to you as you enter the items.
(b) Print out the list of data.
(c) Read out the list to a friend who checks them against the codes on the original questionnaire.

This is painstaking, takes time, but will generally catch any errors of data entry. Another way is to use some of the software now available that can do data entry checks, usually by assessing whether or not an item exceeds limits. For example, if the item gender is coded as either 0 (missing data), 1 (male) or 2 (female), then if the software finds the value 4, this is obviously an error. A similar process can be obtained from within the statistics packages by doing a frequency check. On the item relating to gender, if 4 appears, it is obviously wrong, but the advantage of specialist software is that it will identify where the error has occurred, which is not the case in the simple frequency count. If the data file is extremely large, and the error cannot be found, it could be recoded as missing data to avoid producing any false estimates.

HANDLING MISSING DATA

Once the decision has been made that an item has to be regarded as missing data, it is important to ensure that the computer program identifies the value as representing information that is not to be processed. This is simply done by storing the value within the commands. In MINITAB the default missing code is an asterisk (*). Therefore, when keying in the data simply enter an * and the program will automatically identify it as a missing item and not undertake any calculations.

A similar default mechanism exists within NCSS. When entering data enter the missing value as a full stop (.) or simply press the return key and a full stop is automatically inserted in the cell. Again this will be ignored when calculations are undertaken.

In the case of SPSS the process is slightly different. The researchers can decide for themselves what value to use as missing data (by convention a zero is used). Then, when setting up the data, use the instruction MISSING VALUE followed by a list of variables; the code is thus inserted before calculations begin. So, for example, if two variables are to be examined and the mean score calculated, the rubric would read as shown in Figure 8.4.

NAMING VARIABLES

In the figures demonstrating the listing of data no name (other than var1 var2 etc.) was given. Different researchers differ in their attitudes to the naming of variables. If you are working alone it is surprising how quickly you become accustomed to the data and know exactly what is the difference between var1 and var15. However, if the printouts are going to be used by more than one person, it can help to attribute a more descriptive name to the variable as an aid to understanding.

Ascribing a name is quite simple for each of the packages being discussed (see Figures 8.5 and 8.6). Suppose we wish to give the names 'respdt', 'sex', and

Command	*Commentary*
DATA LIST File = 'a:myfile'	Obtains file.
FREE/var1 to var4.	
MISSING VALUE var1 to var4 (0).	Inserts missing value code
DESC var1 to var4 /sta=all.	Calculates means etc. of remaining respondents.
FINISH.	Finishes calculation and exits SPSS.

Figure 8.4 Coding missing data in SPSS

'attitude' to the first three scores on our questionnaire to denote the respondent number, gender and a score. This is done as follows.

In MINITAB

After retrieving the data, simply enter the instruction NAME after each prompt as indicated.

MTB > Name C1 = 'Respdt'   (and return)
MTB > Name C2 = 'sex'   (and return)
MTB > Name C3 = 'attitude'   (and return)

Figure 8.5 Naming variables in MINITAB

In NCSS

From the menu, simply:

Open or create a database.
Edit the database.
Enter a label as directed.

NCSS permits you to label both columns and rows, so that the respondent number could be the name of the actual respondent, or an identifying number on each of the rows.

In SPSS

Both the variable name and variable values can be labelled using SPSS. So that if, for example, the variable 'attitude' consisted of responses to a 5-point scale, and you wished to list respondents by sex on any output, this is done as shown in Figure 8.6.

Generally speaking software limits variable names to eight characters, and some might not be acceptable. In earlier editions of MINITAB one problem is that the program does not retain the name given to a variable when the file is saved, so you might find that you need to repeat the name command each time you use the program.

Having entered your data and variable names and, in the case of SPSS, variable labels and values, you will want to be able to save these for future use, and be able to retrieve them. In the case of MINITAB and NCSS this is very simple, and is done as follows.

Command	Commentary
DATA LIST FILE = 'A:myfile' FREE/ Respdt sex attitude.	Gets file and attributes labels.
VARIABLE LABELS Respdt 'Respondent number' / sex 'gender' / attitude 'attitude score'.	Gives in greater detail what will now be printed out on the actual screen or printout.
VALUE LABELS sex 1 'male' 2 'female' / attitude 1 'very good' 2 'good 3 'fair' 4 'poor' 5 'very poor'.	Gives labels to each value within the label. Note carefully the location of the '/' and full stop marks.

Figure 8.6 Naming variables in SPSS

In MINITAB   to save a file on a given disk drive:

MTB > SAVE 'a:myfile' where a is the disk drive and myfile is the file name
to retrieve a file simply type
MTB > Retrieve 'a:myfile.mtw'

Any MINITAB file saved will have the letters MTW allocated after the file name if no extension is given.

In NCSS   simply save the file as directed by the menus.

SPSS   presents a slightly more difficult procedure. There are different ways of going about this, and hence a careful reading of the manual is certainly advantageous. One way is to take advantage of the fact that when finishing a session with SPSS the program automatically creates two files – SPSS.LOG and SPSS.LIS. SPSS.LIS is the output of the results, and these can be directly imported into a word processing package such as WordPerfect. All one does, in the case of WordPerfect, is to use the F5 function to retrieve the file. This has the great advantage of being able to incorporate results directly from SPSS into any write up of the report, although there is a need to note the absence of tabulation spaces in the imported file.

The SPSS.LOG file contains a copy of all the commands that SPSS has executed during the current session in the order in which processed. Therefore, once the variable names and labels have been set up, they can be saved and subsequently retrieved for future use. If you set up a file with variable names you will want to access it many times, so it is probably worth copying the SPSS.LOG file and then use the retrieval function within SPSS. To do this either type FINISH. or use the FINISH command from the SPSS menu and go back into DOS. Then:

C: > Copy spss.log names.log

This creates a copy of the original spss.log file (which is overwritten by SPSS on future occasions) and the copy is now called names.log. To retrieve this again, once you have logged into SPSS, press ALT-M as before and simply press F3. This sets up a small menu at the bottom of the screen. Move to the menu item to insert a file and press Enter. Type in the name of the file c:names.log, press Enter; and it reappears for use in the SPSS Scratch pad for you to add your instructions.

OBTAINING SIMPLE DESCRIPTIVE STATISTICS

Any batch of numerical data contains three major properties for it to be described fully. These are:

(a) its central tendency;
(b) its dispersion;
(c) its shape.

The central tendency is commonly measured by the mean because that indicates the central 'location' of the data. The dispersion is measured by the variance and standard deviation because these indicate the degree of difference from the mean that exists within a sample or population. The shape is measured by frequencies of values arranged in order and by measures such as skewness and kurtosis. So, having entered and checked the data, and set up any names which are required, the next stage is to obtain some results that explain the property of the data along

---

The following factors relate to why people go on holiday, and what they find there. If you had an entirely free choice as to destination and type of holiday, could you please indicate how important the factors are to YOU, personally, by circling the appropriate number.

The scale is	Very important	7
		6
	Important	5
		4
	Of some importance	3
		2
	Of no importance	1
	No opinion	0

Motivations – while on holiday I like to

| Increase my knowledge | 1 | 2 | 3 | 4 | 5 | 6 | 7 | | 0 |
| Avoid the hustle and bustle of daily life | 1 | 2 | 3 | 4 | 5 | 6 | 7 | | 0 |

Figure 8.7 Data for analysis

these dimensions. Let us assume that we have series of scores on a Likert-type scale relating to attitudes towards holiday-taking motivations, and that one of the questions asked was as shown in Figure 8.7.

The first thing we might wish to do is to assess how many people have responded, and what is the pattern of response. Thus the frequency of replies to each of the scales might be required. This is simply done as shown in Figures 8.8 and 8.9.

In MINITAB

Command	Commentary
MTB > retrieve 'a:myfile.mtw' MTB > name c2 = 'know' MTB > name c3 = 'avoid' MTB > tally c2 c3; SUBC > PERCENTS.	Note the use of the semi-colon and full stop at the end of the final two lines.

Figure 8.8 Frequency of response in MINITAB

If additional data such as the percentages as well as the absolute numbers are required, sub-commands exist, as shown in Figure 8.9. These sub-commands will give the count, percentages, and accumulated count and percentages for each of the scores for each of the questions and the number who have not responded to the questions.

Command	Commentary
MTB > retrieve 'a:myfile.mtw' MTB > name c2 = 'know' MTB > name c3 = 'avoid' MTB > tally c2 c3; SUBC > all.	Note the use of the semi-colon and full stop at the end of the final two lines. Gives percentages.

Figure 8.9 Frequency of response in SPSS

In NCSS

Simply use the menus for retrieving a file, undertaking statistical analysis for descriptive statistics of univariate data.

Command	Commentary
FREQ VARIABLES=KNOW AVOID	FREQ is short for FREQUENCY. SPSS will operate on the first 3 letters of a command.

Figure 8.10 Frequency of response for named variables in SPSS

In SPSS

Once you have logged into SPSS the data can be retrieved by the use of the editor as described above. The additional commands are shown in Figure 8.10. This

KNOW   increase knowledge

Value Label	Value	Frequency	Percent	Valid Percent	Cum. Percent
	.00	6	3.8	3.8	3.8
no importance	1.00	1	.6	.6	4.5
	2.00	9	5.7	5.7	10.2
	3.00	24	15.3	15.3	25.5
	4.00	20	12.7	12.7	38.2
	5.00	61	38.9	38.9	77.1
	6.00	12	7.6	7.6	84.7
very important	7.00	24	15.3	15.3	100.0
Total		157	100.0	100.0	

Valid cases   157   Missing cases   0

AVOID   avoid daily hustle

Value Label	Value	Frequency	Percent	Valid Percent	Cum. Percent
	.00	3	1.9	1.9	1.9
no importance	1.00	6	3.8	3.8	5.7
	2.00	3	1.9	1.9	7.6
	3.00	14	8.9	8.9	16.6
	4.00	12	7.6	7.6	24.2
	5.00	35	22.3	22.3	46.5
	6.00	23	14.6	14.6	61.1
very important	7.00	61	38.9	38.9	100.0
Total		157	100.0	100.0	

Figure 8.11 Output of frequency for named variables in SPSS

produces the output as shown in Figure 8.11. From the result shown in Figure 8.11, the question of what to do with the non-respondents can be decided. It can be noted that since they are few in number, then they will simply be treated as missing data.

Calculating the mean score

As noted in Chapter 4, one of the first analyses that will be undertaken is to estimate the mean and standard deviation because this, along with the frequency count, will indicate the nature of the distribution, and whether or not assumptions of a normal distribution can be made. Again, this is quite simple. As before, retrieve the files. The commands are therefore as follows.

In MINITAB   use the commands MTB> DESCRIBE C1. This will produce the values for the mean, median, tmean, standard deviation, standard error mean, maximum and minimum values, the values of the third and first quartile, and the numbers of respondents and missing data. The tmean (trimmed mean) figure is the mean score of the sample less the extreme ranges possessed by 5 per cent of the sample. In the case of a Likert-type scale no extremes are going to exist, but if the data being analysed was, for example, a range of incomes, the existence of those on unemployment benefits on the one hand, and some millionaires on the other, could result in the calculation of a mean that was not at all representative of the major part of the sample.

In NCSS   the process will be one of selecting from the menus the following options:

    select statistical and data analysis;
    then select descriptive statistics;
    then select univariate statistics;
    then select the column to be analysed.

The resulting statistics include the mean, standard deviation, variance, standard error of the mean, coefficient of variation, number of observations, number of missing values, coefficient of skewness, coefficient of kurtosis and a t-value testing against a mean of zero.

In SPSS   the process is broadly similar, but various options exist. These are:

Command	*Commentary*
DESC KNOW AVOID.	Produces the mean, standard deviation, minimum and maximum scores.

A range of sub-commands exists that produces additional statistics, but the use of the sub-command ALL will produce additional data:

Number of Valid Observations (Listwise) =   157.00

Variable	Mean	Std Dev	Minimum	Maximum	N	Label
KNOW	4.56	1.68	.00	7.00	157	increase knowledge
AVOID	5.36	1.81	.00	7.00	157	avoid daily hustle

desc know avoid /sta=all.

PAGE TOO NARROW TO PRINT COLUMNAR STYLE DESCRIPTIVE STATISTICS – Too many statistics are requested to print them in columns. Serial format is used.

Number of Valid Observations (Listwise) =   157.00

Variable   KNOW   increase knowledge

Mean	4.561	S.E. Mean	.134
Std Dev	1.681	Variance	2.825
Kurtosis	.440	S.E. Kurt	.385
Skewness	−.644	S.E. Skew	.194
Range	7.000	Minimum	.00
Maximum	7.000	Sum	716.000

Valid Observations –	157	Missing Observations –	0

Figure 8.12 Descriptive statistics for named variables in SPSS

Command	*Commentary*
DESC KNOW AVOID / STA = ALL.	Produces all of the above data plus kurtosis, skewness, the standard error of the mean and the range of the data.

A third approach is to combine all of these data with the frequencies command thus:

Command	*Commentary*
FREQ VAR=KNOW AVOID /STA=ALL.	Produces all of the above plus the frequencies.

Some of the output that is produced by the first two commands is shown in Figure 8.12.

IMPLICATIONS OF THE DATA

What are the implications of the data. The terms mean, variance and standard deviation have been explained on p. 170, but can be summarised as follows.

The mean score   is the average calculated by dividing the total value by the number of respondents.

The variance   is the sum of the squared differences from the mean of each of the observations, and is a measure of dispersion.

The squared deviation   is the square root of the variance.

The standard error of mean   is the standard deviation of a sample mean.

The coefficient of variation   is a measure of variation within the sample and is measured by the variance divided by the mean and multiplied by 100. The higher score, the greater the variance, and the coefficient can be used to compare the variance between two samples with different means and variances.

The first quartile   when the values of respondents are ordered from the lowest to the highest value, this value is that of the item which falls one quarter of the way between the lowest and highest value.

The third quartile   when the values of respondents are ordered from the lowest to the highest value, this value is that of the item which falls three quarters of the way between the lowest and highest value.

Skewness   measures the departure from symmetry implied by a normal distribution. There are in fact three measures of the average:
(a) the mean as described above;
(b) the mode, the value of the most frequently mentioned value which is derived from the frequency count;
(c) the median, which is 'half-way' quartile (i.e. when the values of respondents are ordered from the lowest to the highest value, this value is that of the item which falls half way between the lowest and highest value).

In a normal distribution, all three coincide. If however, that does not occur, the sample is said to be skewed. Therefore, measures of skew are derived from:

(mean−mode)/standard deviation   or
(mean−median)/standard deviation

The range of values exist from −3 to +3, the greater the difference from 0, the more the skew, while the sign denotes whether the skew is to the left or right. As a rule of thumb, a moderate degree of skew has a value of −1 to +1.

Kurtosis is a measure of the 'peakedness' of the distribution. A curve can be described as being:

if $K = 1$ the curve is normal;
if $K < 3$ the curve is flat and is platykurtic;
if $K > 3$ the curve is 'peaked' and is leptokurtic.

The results from the questionnaire as to the variables acquiring knowledge and avoiding daily hustle and bustle are given as above. One way of displaying information so that it is more meaningful to the reader is to give the average scores in a descending order of importance. This helps to clarify immediately from the questionnaire which are the more or less important items.

TRANSFORMING DATA

Having calculated some mean scores, the researcher might wish to create new variables, and calculate the means of such new variables. For example, suppose the questions as shown in Figure 8.13 were included on the questionnaire. The researcher might wish to create a 'satisfaction' score by summing the values of these three questions. This would mean creating a new variable, which might be labelled TOTSAT standing for total satisfaction. One factor to watch would be to ensure that the summation process referred only to those respondents who had replied to all three questions, and hence it is important first to sort out the missing data. As noted above, in MINITAB and NCSS this poses no problem, but in SPSS it is essential to use the MISSING VALUE command. Suppose the three questions above were variables 41, 42 and 43. In the case of summation, the process is as outlined below.

By the end of the holiday,

| To what extent were you satisfied with your accommodation? | 1 | 2 | 3 | 4 | 5 | 6 | 7 | 0 |

| To what extent could you say you really enjoyed the holiday? | 1 | 2 | 3 | 4 | 5 | 6 | 7 | 0 |

| To what extent would you recommend this holiday to a close friend who shares your interests? | 1 | 2 | 3 | 4 | 5 | 6 | 7 | 0 |

Figure 8.13 Data for transformation

In MINITAB

MTB > LET c50 = (c41 + c42 + c43)/3
MTB > name c50 = 'TOTSAT'
MTB > DESC 'TOTSAT'

In NCSS   the use of menus is again the technique. Simply select the DATA TRANSFORMATIONS menu and identify the columns to be summed and the column where the result is to be placed. To calculate a mean, simply select the descriptive statistics options as previously described.

In SPSS   the process is similar to that of MINITAB, except there is the need to allow for the presence of missing values. The process, once the data has been retrieved is thus:

MISSING VALUES var41 var42 var43 (0).
COMPUTE TOTSAT = (var41 + var42 + var43)/3.
DESC TOTSAT.

In both MINITAB and SPSS the computation of the TOTSAT score is shown as being divided by 3 in order to retain a seven-point scale for the score. In NCSS one method is simply to divide the scores in the new column by 3. Both MINITAB and NCSS will save the additional column simply by saving the new file. SPSS offers a range of options, but if the data are being worked from a DOS file and there is a need to reuse the TOTSAT score again at some future time, probably the easiest method is to retain the new list of commands by copying the SPSS.LOG file as noted before.

In most cases data can be transformed in any number of ways – scores can be added, subtracted, multiplied, divided, categorised, squared, the logs calculated – practically anything can be done. The important thing is that the researcher is aware that these options exist, and can thus access the manual to find out the specific instructions for the required task. The RECODE command in SPSS is fairly typical if a researcher wanted to undertake, for example, an analysis on only high and low scorers on any given scale. For example, it might be thought important to assess any differences between highly satisfied and highly dissatisfied holiday-makers. So using the TOTSAT score, one might be interested in comparing the attitudes of those scoring 1 and 2 on the satisfaction score (the dissatisfied), with those scoring 7 (the satisfied). TOTSAT could then be recoded as follows (remember the need to delete codes 3 to 6 from the analysis if required):

RECODE TOTSAT (1,2 = 1) (7 = 2).

This creates two categories, and the mean scores of these two groups can now be compared on the required variables. This is undertaken on p. 218, when comparing the means and assessing the significance of any difference is discussed.

PRESENTING RESULTS

Having calculated the mean and standard deviations of scores, how should these results be presented. The simplest, and in many ways the best format, is to simply present the results as a table. However, some guidelines are worth adhering to.

(a) Only reproduce a table in the main text if it is illustrating something of substance.
(b) If a table is reproduced, refer to it in the text.
(c) If the table contains only one or two items of interest, report these directly within the text and produce the table as an appendix.

Tables have the advantage of reproducing the actual results. There is a tendency to take advantage of graphics software and produce histograms of mean scores, but such diagrams have disadvantages. An emphasis on the mean drawn in figures such as a histogram often means that the writer omits the standard deviation, which is valuable if the results are to be understood. Additionally, data is often withheld from the reader by the scales used on the histogram. If for example, a 5-point scale is used and the scale simply denotes the integer, the reader is left to guess whether the actual score was, say, 3.6, 3.7 or 3.8. If scores are clustered together, the differences in means, allied with their standard deviations, might be of importance, but this is not conveyed by a histogram. If,

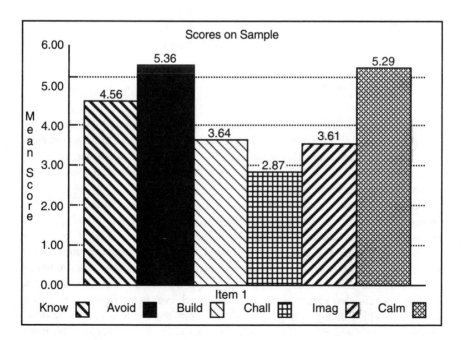

Figure 8.14 Scores on sample

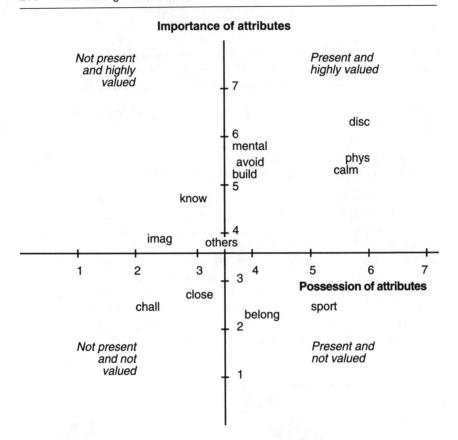

Figure 8.15 Importance of attributes

therefore, the researcher wishes to use something other than a table to convey the results to the reader, then care must be taken to ensure that real information is in fact conveyed. One way of overcoming this objection is to combine both the diagram and the data as indicated in Figure 8.14 if the researcher specifically wants to use diagrams rather than tables.

One such example might be where the research has utilised a specific approach in its measurement of attitude. In Chapter 2 it was noted that the Fishbein method of attitude measurement presents some real advantages in its distinction between the attributes possessed by a place, and the importance attributed to those attitudes. It will be noted that the sample questionnaire consists of two components – what did people think was important about a holiday, and to what extent were they able to achieve the particular behaviours associated with holiday-taking. The results from these two sets of questions permit a simple matrix to be set out (as shown in Figure 8.15). The most important parts of a holiday, in the sense that both attributes were thought to be

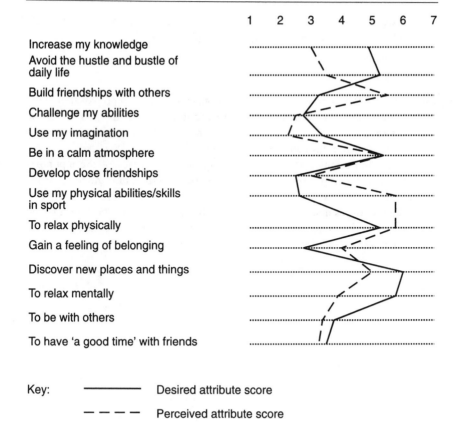

Key: ——————   Desired attribute score

              — — — —   Perceived attribute score

Figure 8.16 Line diagram of the sample data

important and were indeed present in the holiday, are to be found in the top right-hand corner of the matrix. In this case, arguably, Figure 8.15 is reinforcing the results in a way that might otherwise be lost in a simple table of results.

The questionnaire also permits the use of a gap analysis as possibly a measure of satisfaction, as discussed in Chapter 2. If satisfaction is a congruence between perceived attributes of a desired holiday, and the actual attributes of a holiday, then where the actual experience falls short of the desired experience, a level of dissatisfaction might be said to have occurred. Again a simple diagram can express that idea possibly better than a table to identify the difference in mean scores. This is shown in Figure 8.16, where the mean score is simply drawn on a 5-point scale for each item.

It is argued that diagrams of this nature are much more helpful in conveying the nature of the analysis than simple descriptive diagrams such as histograms or similar figures. While it is true that a picture is better than a 'thousand words' the researcher still has a duty to ensure that the picture chosen actually advances a fuller understanding of the concepts rather than, as sometimes unfortunately happens, inhibiting understanding by over-simplifying results.

SUMMARY

It was noted that an important part of the process is the careful preparation of the data for input into the computer. This preparation begins with considering the very questions and design of the questionnaire – as this can make subsequent stages easier or more difficult as the case may be.

The next important stage is the checking of the accuracy of the input – a painstaking and at times boring task, it must be admitted, but nonetheless one that is essential. Failure to do this will invalidate all the careful preparation, and the writing up of results. The next stage is to begin checking for both results and accuracy by undertaking some initial checks. These include frequency checks, after which some descriptive statistics can be calculated.

Chapter 9

The significance of mean scores

INTRODUCTION

A series of situations can be envisaged where a mean has been calculated and the researcher wishes to analyze its significance. These include:

(a) the calculation of mean scores on questionnaire items where no comparative average exists;
(b) where a comparison between means by the same respondents is required, for example, the difference between scores relating to expected and actual experiences of a holiday;
(c) where a comparison between the scores on items by different groups of respondents is required, for example, the difference between males or females, or between different age groups.

The nature of the problem is therefore easily illustrated. Suppose it was found that males scored 2.8 on a questionnaire item such as 'to use my physical abilities/skills in sport', while females scored 2.4. How significant is the difference? Assuming that a normal distribution exists, essentially the comparison involves two main forms of tests. These are the *t-test* and *analysis of variance.*
One of the features of sampling is that even when the population tends not to have a normal distribution, any pattern of means derived from samples will often possess the characteristic of being normally distributed. The t-test is essentially a comparison between the two means of the two samples and their associated standard errors.

Statistical software will undertake the calculations and provide the significance of the resultant t-test. These tests are based on the t-distribution, which arises from the known behaviour of distributions taken from samples of population. The F-ratio is a means of comparing the mean scores of subgroups and is used where more than two groups are involved in the comparison. Possibly the best way for a non-statistician to begin to appreciate the meaning of the tests is to examine where they might be used, and what the results derived from the software actually mean.

INTERPRETING THE RESULTS

In the tests given below, the key figure in many senses is the probability that is associated with the test statistic. It indicates the likelihood of the result arising by chance, and the convention is that the researcher will be looking for any probability that is less than 0.05. This means that the result would have occurred only five times out of a hundred by chance. Since this is most unlikely, the result is therefore deemed to be significant. To put it another way, the researcher can be 95 per cent confident that they have discovered something of significance. A crude assessment of the levels of probability can be stated as being:

$p < 0.1$ in the predicted direction, but not significant
$p < 0.05$ significant
$p < 0.01$ more significant (occurs by chance less than once in a hundred times)
$p < 0.001$ very significant (occurs by chance less than once in a thousand times).

Of course, just as people do win the lottery or football pools – the one in a thousand chance does occur!

THE SIGNIFICANCE OF A MEAN SCORE WHERE NO COMPARATIVE DATA EXIST

It is quite common for a questionnaire to contain a series of items where mean scores can be calculated, but where no comparative data exist. Consider, for example, the questions illustrated in Table 9.1. With such a listing the researcher might want to give some indication of the significance of the resultant mean scores. How might these be done?

Whichever method is used, an assumed mean will have to be selected for the purpose of comparison. One way is to argue that the assumed mean is the mid-point of the seven-point scale, and thus the test of significance for, say, a mean score of 4.36 for the item, 'to increase my knowledge' is to compare this with 3.5. Again the software permits this type of comparison quite easily. In the case of MINITAB the command is:

TTEST of MU = 3.5, ON KNOW

where KNOW is the name given to the variable.

NCSS automatically gives a t-test where any mean is compared with an assumed mean of zero in its normal reporting, and when the menus for descriptive statistics and univariate tests are selected, gives the lower and upper limits of confidence automatically. For undertaking a t-test however, a different set of menus exist, and the researcher simply selects analysis of variance/t-test menu from the statistical and data analysis set. However, earlier editions of NCSS

Table 9.1 Sample questionnaire

The following factors relate to why people go on holiday, and what they find there. If you had an entirely free choice as to destination and type of holiday, could you please indicate how important the factors are to YOU, personally, by circling the appropriate number.

The scale is	Very important	7
		6
	Important	5
		4
	Of some importance	3
		2
	Of no importance	1
	No opinion	0

Motivations – while on holiday I like to

Increase my knowledge	1	2	3	4	5	6	7	0
Avoid the hustle and bustle of daily life	1	2	3	4	5	6	7	0
Build friendships with others	1	2	3	4	5	6	7	0
Challenge my abilities	1	2	3	4	5	6	7	0
Use my imagination	1	2	3	4	5	6	7	0
Be in a calm atmosphere	1	2	3	4	5	6	7	0
Develop close friendships	1	2	3	4	5	6	7	0
Use my physical abilities/skills in sport	1	2	3	4	5	6	7	0
To relax physically	1	2	3	4	5	6	7	0
Gain a feeling of belonging	1	2	3	4	5	6	7	0
Discover new places and things	1	2	3	4	5	6	7	0
To relax mentally	1	2	3	4	5	6	7	0
To be with others	1	2	3	4	5	6	7	0
To have 'a good time' with friends	1	2	3	4	5	6	7	0

require any t-test to compare two columns; thus if an assumed mean is being used, this will have to be set up within a dummy column using the data editor.

Within SPSS the procedure is similar to that of MINITAB. As the t-test is essentially a two sample procedure, a dummy mean is set up by use of the COMPUTE command. This is:

```
COMPUTE MEAN = 3.5.
T-TEST PAIRS = KNOW MEAN.
```

However, the comparison between the item mean and the assumed mean of the half-way point on any scale lacks any real rationale, and this is a problem with any comparison between actual and assumed means. Some researchers have argued that if the questions are all postulated the same way (e.g. positively), then assuming that possibly some level of acquiescence might be working consistently, there might be some validity in taking the mean of the sum of the items for the purpose of comparison of single item scores. This therefore requires summing the scores, and, to retain the same point scale, dividing the sum by the number of questions. So, if there are 14 items, this takes the form of, in the case of SPSS, for the sample questionnaire in the appendix: COMPUTE MEAN = (Know+avoid+...+time)/14 and then use the t-test command as before.

These procedures are tentative in their attempt to measure significance, and little reliance can really be placed upon them since the assumptions behind the assumed mean in these cases have, at best, a tenuous logic. Where, however, an assumed mean is derived from another piece of relevant research, the process begins to develop a greater degree of validity.

THE COMPARISON OF SCORES BY THE SAME RESPONDENTS

This is a common requirement of comparison in attitudinal research where a multi-attribute or gap analysis approach has been adopted. For example, a respondent will have answered a question as to the perception of an event happening, and then subsequently an assessment of the actual event. Suppose a respondent has been asked to comment on the importance of avoiding the daily hustle and bustle while on holiday, and then subsequently asked to assess how successful they were in doing that. In the case of the sample data provided in the Appendix, respondents scored a mean score of 5.36 as to their requirement avoiding hustle, and 3.59 as to their success on achieving it. How significant is the difference? In this case a paired t-test may be required, that is the observations are in pairs, one drawn from each group, and the sizes of the two samples must be the same.

The commands for a paired t-test are as follows. For MINITAB:

TWOSAMPLE 'AVOID' 'AVOID2'

where AVOID and AVOID2 are the names previously allocated by the command 'NAME' to the appropriate columns. One point to note in the case of MINITAB is that it assumes by default that the test is to be carried out at the 95 per cent confidence level. Second, by default, it assumes that the two populations do not have the same variance. As will be noted below, this is important, and if the variances are equal then the pooled sub-command is used. In NCSS the menus are used as noted above. In SPSS the command is equally straightforward:

T-TEST PAIRS=AVOID AVOID2.

The output from SPSS is again quite typical of the type of response gained from such commands, and is illustrated in Figure 9.1.

```
Paired samples t-test:  AVOID    avoid daily hustle
                        AVOID2   actual avoid

Variable            Number                           Standard      Standard
                    of Cases          Mean           Deviation     Error

AVOID               157               5.3631         1.812         .145
AVOID2              157               3.5860         2.091         .167

(Difference)  Standard Standard  I    2-Tail    I    t      Degrees of  2-Tail
   Mean       Deviation Error    I  Corr.  Prob. I  Value   Freedom     Prob.
   1.7771     2.721    .217      I  .033   .680  I  8.18    156         .000
```

Figure 9.1 Output for F-test (SPSS)

What do these results mean. Figure 9.1 indicates that there were 157 who answered the two questions. The average score for the first was 5.36; for the second, 3.58. The standard deviation and the standard error, as previously described in Chapter 5, are both given. The difference between the two mean scores is 1.7771, and the dispersion of the differences is given by the standard deviation (2.72) and the standard error (0.217). The correlation between the two questions is 0.033, which is not significant ($p = 0.68$). The Coefficient of Correlation is a measure of the level of association between the two questions. The values range from $+1$ to -1. A value of $+1$ means that the two series are positively, highly correlated. A value of -1 indicates a high correlation, but an inverse relationship – that is as the one value increases, the second declines in some proportionate relationship. Hence, values of near to zero indicate little correlation between the two, implying that, for this sample, there was little relationship between the motivation for an escape from the daily hustle and bustle and the actual experience of the holiday. The t statistic is the test of difference as previously described, and the higher it is the more likely it is that the differences are going to be significant. However, the actual significance is calculated and given to the researcher by the probability, in this case 0.000 – indicating that the difference is significant. The degrees of freedom, in the case of a t-test, is simply the size of the sample minus 1. The way in which this would be reported by the researcher would probably be along the lines of 'the difference between mean scores as to motivation (5.36) and experience (3.58) was significant ($t = 8.18$, $p = 0.000$, $df = 156$)'. This gives all the relevant information to the reader.

It should be noted that in this example the pairing was obtained by omitting missing cases. Statistical software, when directed to undertake a paired t-test, will usually seek to make comparisons only where paired data exist. If in any doubt, use the command for missing values and this will usually be sufficient to overcome the problem. In the case of SPSS the default situation is that it automatically deletes pairs where missing items exist.

COMPARISONS BETWEEN TWO GROUPS

In cases where the comparison is between mean scores of different groups a grouped t-test is undertaken. In MINITAB the same commands are used, but differences exist for NCSS and SPSS. The main problem with MINITAB is that the data may first have to be sorted into new columns before the tests can be carried out, and this must be done through the use of the transformation commands. For the sake of illustration, suppose that the scores on responses to the knowledge motivation on holidays is in a column named as KNOW, and sex is in a column duly called SEX, and that there are a total of 37 coded variables. The logic of MINITAB dictates that the male scores are abstracted from the KNOW column and placed in a new column, the same is done with the female scores, and the subsequent t-test then undertaken. The procedure is therefore as shown in Figure 9.2:

Command	Commentary
COPY 'KNOW'INTO C38; USE 'SEX' = 1.	Sorts out the males' scores into column c38.
COPY 'KNOW'INTO C39; USE 'SEX' = 2.	Sorts out the female scores into column c39.
TWOSAMPLE C38 C39.	Undertakes the t-test for males and females on the item 'KNOW'

Figure 9.2 Generating sub-samples in MINITAB

In the case of NCSS the menu system is again used, but in this instance the unpaired t-test option is selected. SPSS permits a number of alternatives depending on how the researcher wishes to select the groups. The most thorough approach is illustrated in Figure 9.3. For this case let us assume that the difference between males and females is sought on the item relating to the importance of wanting to use abilities for sporting pursuits on holiday, and the importance of building friendships. In the preparation of the data, males were coded as 1 and females as 2. Respondents' gender was placed under the variable name sex. Hence, the two groups are defined by the group name sex (1,2). Automatically, this will exclude missing data (coded 0) from the calculation. The command thus becomes:

Independent samples of SEX

Group 1: SEX EQ   1.00   Group 2: SEX EQ   2.00

t-test for: SPORT   use abilities in sport

	Number of Cases	Mean	Standard Deviation	Standard Error
Group 1	40	2.8250	1.920	.304
Group 2	63	2.3651	2.002	.252

		Pooled Variance Estimate				Separate Variance Estimate		
F Value	2-Tail Prob.	t Value	Degrees of Freedom	2-Tail Prob.		t Value	Degrees of Freedom	2-Tail Prob.
1.09	.790	1.15	101	.251		1.17	85.74	.247

Figure 9.3 T-test results for relationship between sex and sport (SPSS)

T-TEST GROUPS = SEX(1,2)/VARIABLES = SPORT BUILD.

The results for the relationship between sex and sport is shown in Figure 9.3. The results are as discussed before. Many statistical packages, including the ones discussed here, permit various options with reference to whether pooled data are being used or not, but regardless of the options being used, any researcher must be aware that the t-test is based upon some important assumptions. These are:

(a) The populations from which the samples are selected both have approximately normal relative frequency distributions.
(b) The variances of the two populations are equal.
(c) The random samples are selected in an independent manner from the two populations.

However, it should be noted that Berenson and Levine write:

> With respect to the assumption of normality, the *t* test is 'robust' in that it is not sensitive to modest departures from normality. As long as the sample sizes are not extremely small, the assumption of normality can be violated without serious effect on the power of the test (1992:415).

Where the assumption of normal distributions cannot be made, and where the sampled populations are decidedly non-normal (especially if small), then any inferences drawn from the t-test are suspect, and an alternative non-parametric test such as the Wilcoxon rank sum test should be used. As will be noted below, most software packages include this. To determine whether this is necessary, the results from tests of distribution, skew and kurtosis should be examined. One possible effect of failing to do this is that differences may be held not to be significant due to the strict assumptions of the t-test, when in fact a Wilcoxon test may show them to be results of other than chance.

Where the variances are not equal then, as has already been noted in the case of MINITAB, the software may permit testing to be undertaken. In many instances this is based upon solutions to what has been termed the Behrens–Fisher problem. The usual solution is posed through the use of the separate variances t-test devised by Cochran. SPSS permits testing for homogeneity of variance, but this is a subset of the ONEWAY command. Where there are two groups such as gender, it is quite possible to use the ONEWAY command as if it is a t-test, and the use of the sub-command selecting the option STATISTICS = 3 will call forth the tests for homogeneity of variance. The command under SPSS is thus:

ONEWAY KNOW BY SEX (1,2) / STA = 3.

This produces in addition to the results of the t-test, three further tests for homogeneity of variance, the Cochran C test, the Bartlett–Box and the Maximum/minimum variance ratio. The final test should have a value of approximately 1 for the assumption of equality of variance not to be violated, while the other two tests are calculated with associated probability levels. Providing these values are not at levels of $p < 0.05$, the assumption of equality of variance can still be maintained. However, of these tests, it is worth noting that:

> many of them are not very useful since they are influenced by characteristics of the data other than the variance ... even if the variances appeared to be different, but the sample sizes in all groups were similar, there would be no cause for alarm since the ANOVA (Analysis of Variance) test is not particularly sensitive to violations of equality of variance under such conditions (Norusis 1990a:B-29).

If the assumptions listed on page 219 cannot be met then non-parametric tests must be used.

COMPARISONS BETWEEN MORE THAN TWO GROUPS

The possibility that such tests have to be used is more probable when comparing the mean scores of a number of sub-samples from within the population. It should, incidentally, be noted that the same assumptions underlie the F-ratio as for the t-test. Consider, from the questionnaire in the Appendix, the different age groups. The researcher might want to look at differences by age as against the items relating to motivation for holidays. How is this to be done? In this case there are six age groups. Here the researcher is looking for tests of analysis of variance, usually shortened to ANOVA. Again, the tests are quite simple to run on the computer. In the case of MINITAB the command is:

```
- - - - - - - - - - O N E W A Y - - - - - - - - - -

    Variable  KNOW        increase knowledge
    By Variable  AGE

                        Analysis of Variance

                        Sum of        Mean       F       F
    Source          D.F.  Squares      Squares   Ratio   Prob.

    Between Groups    5    73189.3935  14637.8787  3.8124  .0021
    Within Groups   646  2480339.373   3839.5346
    Total           651  2553528.767
```

Figure 9.4 Output of analysis of variance (SPSS)

ONEWAY 'KNOW' 'AGE'

NCSS possesses a number of tests, and again a menu is used to select the tests, but this time the menu item ANOVA is selected. As might be expected SPSS permits a series of tests to be used, and a distinction exists with SPSS between assessing the variance of means when considering (a) the mean scores of sub-groups; or (b) a matrix of two or more variables that might include frequencies. The former is obviously the simpler arrangement, and in many cases will more than satisfactorily meet the needs of the researcher. The process is as described above in the case of the more complicated t-test command. Given the six age groups and the need to compare the mean scores on the KNOW variable, the command is simply:

ONEWAY KNOW BY AGE(1,6).

To derive some potentially useful sub-tests, a fuller statement would be:

ONEWAY KNOW BY AGE(1,6)/RANGES = SCHEFFE/STA = 3.

An example of the type of output from this command is illustrated in Figure 9.4. The key data that are given here are the F-ratio and the F-probability. The F-ratio is akin to the t-test in that it is a measure of the differences of the means of the sub-groups. The higher the score, the more likely it is that the differences are significant, and this is given by the probability. So, the results indicate that the differences are significant between different age groups as $F = 3.81$, $p = 0.002$. It will be noted that the figure of 3.8124 has been derived from the Between Groups Mean Square (14637.8787) being divided by the Within Groups Mean Square figure (3839.5346). As the data are presented from the responses, there are two possible sets of variance that occur – variability *within* each age group, and variability *between* the groups.

Tests for Homogeneity of Variances

Cochrans C = Max. Variance/Sum(Variances) =   .8320, P = .000 (Approx.)
Bartlett-Box F =   401.666, P = .000
Maximum Variance / Minimum Variance   1201.708

- - - - - - - - - - O N E W A Y - - - - - - - - - -

    Variable KNOW   increase knowledge
By Variable AGE

Multiple Range Test

Scheffe Procedure
Ranges for the .050 level -

(*) Denotes pairs of groups significantly different at the .050 level

    Variable KNOW   increase knowledge
    (Continued)

                    G G G G G G
                    r r r r r r
                    p p p p p p

Mean   Group   6 5 4 3 2 1

4.6270   Grp 6
5.1942   Grp 5
5.2157   Grp 4
5.4348   Grp 3
5.8205   Grp 2   * *
6.3091   Grp 1   * *

Figure 9.5 Scheffé test

The Within Groups Sum of Squares is a measure of the former and is simply the sum of the variances multiplied by the number of respondents in each age group. This sum is the 2480339.373 given by the results, and the mean is this figure divided by the sample size as measured by the DF figure. Similarly the Between Groups Sum of the Squares is the sum square of the difference between the

age group mean and the total sample mean, multiplied by the number in that age group. So, the figure of 14637.8787 is the result of the sum of those squares being divided by the degrees of freedom (DF). The DF is the number of groups considered, and is akin to sample size if such size is considered not as the number of respondents but number of groups of comparison.

The second part of the results (see Figure 9.5) is in response to the sub-commands 'ranges = scheffe/sta = all.' The purpose of the Scheffé test is to highlight where the differences between the groups are actually occurring. So the results now give us the actual mean scores for each age group, and a diagram which indicates that the differences are at their greatest between age groups one and two, and groups five and six; indicating therefore a real difference between the older and younger groups within the sample. It is therefore worth utilising the Scheffé test because it does serve this purpose of specifically highlighting where differences might be occurring.

The statistics sub-command also provides the researcher with the tests for assessing the homogeneity of variance as described before. It will be noted that the ratio as shown by the maximum/minimum variance differs considerably from one, and that the other two tests give a probability of 0.000. This indicates that one of the assumptions for the F-ratio is *perhaps* being violated. It is a warning to the researcher that the differences between the means as calculated might not be total proof of any hypothesis about age being a factor determining attitude in this case. The researcher would have to look at the numbers within each group to assess if this is a cause of the problem, and come to their own conclusions as to how to treat the results. If, as in this case, the age groups are very unequal in size, then caution would need to be exercised before coming to any firm conclusion about the role of age as a determining variable of attitude.

Finally, it should be noted that checks on ANOVA assumptions can be performed by examining the residuals from a regression procedure, and this will be covered in Chapter 11.

TESTS TO BE USED WHEN ASSUMPTIONS OF NORMAL DISTRIBUTION ARE NOT VALID

It has been commented that the above tests strictly assume random examples and patterns of normal distribution, and where the assumption of homogeneity of variance is relaxed, it is assumed that the samples are approximately the same size. What happens when these assumptions are invalid? Under these circumstances the researcher has to use non-parametric tests, which are based upon the median as the measurement of the average rather than the mean. In testing the significance of differences of the average (as measured by the median) between the samples, the Wilcoxon or Mann–Whitney test also possesses other advantages. The form of the distribution does not have to be specified, and, unlike the above tests, the assumption of interval data does not have to be present. It is therefore quite valid to use these tests on an ordinal scale. The main assumption for these tests to be used is that the data have been taken from a random sample.

It must again be emphasised that the t-test and ANOVA are notably more rigorous in their examination of the data because they utilise much more of the information contained within the data, utilising as they do more information about the dispersion of the distribution. However, in addition to being able to analyse ranked data the non-parametric tests also permit examination of data where distributions markedly differ from normal, or where problems might arise due to unequal sample sizes. They are therefore an important part of the arsenal of any researcher.

Again, let us assume that the researcher wishes to compare, on the one hand, two median scores produced by the same set of respondents, and on the other, medians between two or more sub-groups or populations.

MINITAB, in its commands, makes a distinction between the Mann–Whitney test and the Wilcoxon test simply to differentiate between different sets of circumstances. The Wilcoxon test is generated by the command WTEST which can take one of two main formats, namely:

> WTEST C3.   or
> WTEST 3.5 C3.

where c3 is the column to be analysed. In the former case the test is for a sample median against an assumed median of zero, which is the default set of circumstances. In the latter case it will test for a comparison between sample median and an assumed average (median) of 3.5. The output will give the Wilcoxon statistic and its associated probability.

NCSS is again menu driven, but in this case the researcher will select the menu 'nonparametric tests' from the options associated with statistical and data analysis. The researcher will then be asked to select either a Wilcoxon matched pairs or a Mann–Whitney two sample test. The latter is an unpaired t-test. Further, in the case of the Mann–Whitney test, the two samples do not have to be of equal size.

SPSS permits many tests under the command NPAR TESTS and they take the form:

```
- - - - - Mann-Whitney U - Wilcoxon Rank Sum W Test

    SPORT       use abilities in sport
by SEX

   Mean Rank  Cases

      56.54      40  SEX = 1.00 male
      49.12      63  SEX = 2.00 female
                 ---

               103  Total

                    Corrected for Ties
      U          W          Z       2-tailed P
   1078.5     2261.5     −1.2651       .2058
```

Figure 9.6 Output for Mann–Whitney Test (SPSS)

NPAR TESTS *testname* = *varlist*

So, if the researcher wants to use a Mann–Whitney test, the rubric is:

NPAR TESTS M-W = SPORT BY SEX(1,2).

This would undertake a test to assess the significance of the average (median) scores of males and females on their attitude to the variable, SPORT, defined from the questionnaire in the Appendix as being the importance of being able to use their abilities in sport while on holiday. The output of such a command would appear as shown in Figure 9.6. How is the output interpreted? Figure 9.6 shows that there were 103 cases. The mean rank is the total score on the question divided by the number of respondents of each sex. The W score is 56.54 multiplied by the number of males (40) – and is hence the sum of rank for the smaller group. The U score is the number of times in which the larger group has a score preceding the smaller group in a series of rotations where each case is compared with all the other cases. The Z score is the standard normal deviate. The actual calculation of this score in fact varies depending on the size of the sample (Sincich 1992). The value of $p = 0.206$ indicates that the hypothesis that males and females have the same distribution of scores on the item 'sport' cannot be rejected. This confirms the result derived from the conventional t-test.

Just as in Chapter 8 a series of statistics were defined, it is worth categorising the non-parametric tests available, each being accompanied by a brief description. The purpose of this is to enable the researcher to be aware of the test and its purpose should the nature of their data make the customary parametric tests unfeasible. They are the analogies of the parametric tests discussed above, and hence are operable where the assumptions required for those tests have been violated. Thus, they can be used where the data are not of a normal distribution, or where the data is not derived from scales. They are therefore particularly important where respondents have been asked to rank a sequence in any order of importance. Additionally, the samples do not have to be of equal size. Some of the more important of these tests are as follows.

Wald–Wolfowitz Runs Test

This test is used to test the randomness of a sequence of numbers made up of only two numbers. If, for example, a questionnaire consisted of respondents making choices between two alternatives, this test would be a measure of the consistency of response by rejecting a null hypothesis that the selection is random.

The Kolmogorov–Smirnov Test

This tests how random a sequence of numbers is by comparing the sequence with that expected from a given type of distribution (i.e. a normal, uniform or Poisson distribution).

The Friedman Test

This is an important test when working with ranked data, and comparing two or more samples. Mean ranks are calculated and compared. If, therefore, respondents are asked to rank cities in order of attraction, this test would produce a test statistic with an associated probability to indicate whether the rankings were significant.

Kendall's Tau Coefficient

The above parametric tests have indicated that it is possible to calculate a coefficient of correlation between two series of responses. Kendall's Tau Coefficient undertakes a similar process where the series are non-parametric. Spearman's rank correlation undertakes a similar process, and as indicated, both can be used where the data is ranked rather than a (interval) rating.

Kruskal–Wallis

Another important test for non-parametric data is the non-parametric analog of parametric one-way analysis of variance. All the cases are ranked by their respective groups, and, as described in the above example of analysis of variance, sums are derived from the rankings. As a null hypothesis it is assumed that the groups possess the same distribution, and the deviations from this are measured to produce the Kruskal-Wallis statistic (H). Incidentally, while MINITAB and NCSS produce the H statistic, SPSS labels it as a chi-square statistic in its output (at least in versions up to version 4 of the program). In spite of the label – it is the H statistic.

SUMMARY

This chapter has discussed the means by which an average score can be assessed for its significance under the conditions of comparing it with assumed means, comparing scores by the same respondents, and comparing scores by different groups. It was noted that these comparisons are based upon sets of quite specific conditions, but that where these assumptions are shown to be invalid, a series of alternative tests, known as non-parametric tests, can be used.

It was also shown that the non-parametric tests have additional advantages, most notably their ability to cope with responses derived from ranking procedures within questionnaires. This implies that researchers need not restrict themselves to questions based on ratings if statements of preference are considered to be of more importance. Such rankings can be subjected to tests of significance just as ratings can be.

Chapter 10

Analysing categorical data

INTRODUCTION

In Chapter 9 data derived from rating scales were reviewed. Here techniques that can be applied to categorical data are examined. Such data can be derived from ratings or rankings, but equally can be based on classifications where various categories are being cross-tabulated on the basis of frequency occurrence. These might, for example, include a count of clients who booked with X and Y tour operators, and with x and y hotels. No rating on scales has been undertaken, but a distribution across cells has been created as shown in Table 10.1. Not that tests like the chi-square test, which are used for analysing this type of data are restricted to information of this kind. Another common example is where categories have been created where respondents have responded to questions requiring a yes or no answer. Or, as will be demonstrated, the researcher might want to examine the responses of 'extreme' groupings which are 'isolated' from the remaining part of the sample, so as to examine more carefully the relationship between proposed dependent and independent variables.

ONE- AND TWO-WAY TABLES

The nature of the problem being considered here can be easily illustrated. Suppose we had access to the reports of a tour operator that showed from their studies that 30 per cent of their clients were very satisfied, 50 per cent of clients

Table 10.1 A categorisation of holiday-makers by tour operator and hotel

Tour operator		Hotel		Total
		x	y	
	X	125	115	240
	Y	87	212	299
Total		212	327	

Table 10.2 One-way table of category counts of holiday-makers

| Number in category | | | |
Very satisfied	Satisfied	Dissatisfied	Total
25	50	25	100

were satisfied, and 20 per cent were dissatisfied. Now suppose that from a sample of 100 who responded to another questionnaire, the results indicated a distribution of 25 per cent being very satisfied, 50 per cent satisfied and 25 per cent, dissatisfied. This latter data can be shown in what is termed a one-way table, as illustrated in Table 10.2. The question thus arises, do these data disagree with the results of the tour operators' survey?

Now consider another situation. Suppose a further sample of 100 respondents known to have booked with two different tour operators, but holidaying in the same location, had been asked to rate the attractiveness of their accommodation. A two-way table might now be constructed that presents the results shown in Table 10.3.

This type of table is also known as a contingency table, in that the people falling into the cells of accommodation satisfaction depend on (or are contingent upon) their patronage of a given tour operator. Or, to put it another way, the table has been constructed on the premise of sample categorisation, that is, respondents have been allocated to a cell on the basis of their tour company and the degree of satisfaction with the accommodation. The data are analogous to a correlation analysis. The question to be answered is also similar – does the distribution indicate a relationship between the two sets of variables? The null hypothesis to be tested is that there is no relationship between tour operator patronage and the degree of satisfaction with the accommodation. The two variables are deemed to be independent.

Table 10.3 Two-way table of category counts of holiday-makers

| Level of satisfaction with accommodation | Tour operators used | | Total |
	Sunshine Tours	Med-Tours	
Satisfied	35	30	65
Dissatisfied	5	30	35
Total	40	60	100

THE χ^2 (CHI-SQUARE) TEST

The same question is true of Table 10.2. Is the distribution of the sample independent from that of the tour operator's return? To answer the question the approach undertaken is to compare the actual, observed distribution with an expected distribution, and to compare the result. So, in Table 10.2, a comparison is to be made between the observed distribution of 25:50:25 with an expected distribution of 30:50:20. But the obvious question is, 'how is the expected distribution calculated?'. This is done on the basis of the ratios inherent in the row and column totals. In Table 10.3, if there was no relationship between the tour operator and the level of satisfaction with the hotels, then we would expect the ratio of satisfied holiday-makers to split 40:60 between the two companies, and equally, the two companies' sets of holiday-makers to split 65:35 between satisfied and dissatisfied holiday-makers. The expected observations are calculated from the formula:

$$\frac{\text{Product of row and column totals}}{\text{Grand total}}$$

So, (65 multiplied by 40)/100 = 26.0
   (65 multiplied by 60)/100 = 39.0
   (35 multiplied by 40)/100 = 14.0
   (35 multiplied by 60)/100 = 21.0

The expected frequencies are shown in Table 10.4.

The process that is now undertaken is similar to establishing the deviation from the average when calculating the variance in a normal distribution, in that the difference between the actual and observed frequency in the cell is squared, and it is then divided by the expected cell count. These results are summed together to produce what is known as the chi-square statistic.

So, for the example given, chi-square is $(35-26)^2/26+(39-30)^2/39+(14-5)^2/14+(30-21)^2/21$; equalling 14.833. The next thing to consider is the size of the sample as represented by the degrees of freedom. As in the case of ANOVA, what is being considered is the number of groupings. In fact, the

Table 10.4 Expected frequencies of holiday-taker distribution

Level of satisfaction with accommodation	Sunshine Tours	Med-Tours	Total
Satisfied	26	39	65
Dissatisfied	14	21	35
Total	40	60	100

concept of degrees of freedom is a complex one, and is based upon the number of options that need to be known before the final value can be calculated. In the general case of a contingency table, the number of such degrees of freedom is calculated by the number of rows less one multiplied by the number of columns less one, i.e. $(R - 1)(C - 1)$. In this instance there are 2 rows and 2 columns; thus the degrees of freedom are 1, namely, $(2-1)(2-1)$. This method is based on the notion that, given the outcome of 65 satisfied customers, and knowing that the sample is divided between the two companies on a ratio of 40:60, this in itself contains sufficient knowledge to complete the expected number of satisfied clients.

Given a chi-square statistic (commonly written as χ^2) of 14.83 with one degree of freedom, consulting a table of probabilities based on the known properties of such distributions, yields the answer that this is significant at less than the 0.001 level – indicating that the null hypothesis has to be rejected, and that there is a significant relationship between the tour company selected and the level of satisfaction expressed with holiday accommodation.

THE CALCULATION OF χ^2 (CHI-SQUARE)

Statistical software packages permit rapid calculation of the chi-square test and (generally) its significance. MINITAB simply requires the command:

> MTB > TABLE C23 BY C24;
> SUB > COLPERCENTS;
> SUB > CHISQ.

This will give not only the observed frequencies in cells and the chi-square statistic, but also the columns with percentages calculated. Row percentages are calculated with the sub-command ROWPERCENTS. With earlier versions of MINITAB, the one drawback is that although the chi-square statistic is given with the associated degrees of freedom, the actual significance is not, and there is a need to refer to a set of tables. Furthermore, this approach does not show the expected observations and the residuals. To obtain this the command CHISQ C23 C24 is used. This will produce the table, the chi-square statistic and its component parts. What is also useful is that it produces the number of cells and will show those with a frequency count of less than 5. The implication of this is considered below. Therefore, if the researcher is using earlier versions of MINITAB both sets of commands (plus a set of tables) are required.

NCSS, after the use of the menus, requires simply an identification of the column numbers, and then presents a full analysis of the data, which includes not only the chi-square statistic, but also the degrees of freedom, its significance, and measures of association such as Phi, Cramer's V, Pearson's Contingency Coefficient, Kendall's tau-B and tau-C and much else. Finally, before proceeding to the use of SPSS commands, it should also be noted that for both MINITAB and NCSS it may be necessary to transform data to set up new columns if, for example, differences between sub-groups within a sample need to be considered – e.g. sex categories or age groupings.

To calculate chi-square by using SPSS the command CROSSTABS is used. Referring to the data obtained from the Appendix, let it be assumed that a researcher is wanting to explore the relationship between gender and degrees of satisfaction with a holiday. A new variable TOTSAT has been calculated as in Chapter 8, that is by summing the scores on questions relating to satisfaction with accommodation, enjoyment, and the ability to recommend the holiday to a friend. A simple two-way table can be constructed by counting only those who are highly satisfied (scoring over 18 on the TOTSAT scale) and those who are highly dissatisfied (scoring less than 12 on the TOTSAT measure). (In this case the total is not divided by 3 to retain the 7-point scale because this creates answers that are not integers, which although not an insurmountable problem is a nuisance.) One of the common features of satisfaction ratings of holidays is that they tend to be high, and hence a problem associated with creating groups of dissatisfied holiday-makers is that using criteria such as the bottom two points on a seven-point scale often means sample sizes are too small for meaningful comparison. An alternative approach is to look at the standard deviation of the distribution and define high scorers as having a score greater than the mean plus one standard deviation, and the low scorers as having a score less than the mean minus one standard deviation. The problem about this approach is that it assumes a normal distribution. If the distribution is skewed to the higher end of the range, it again means a small sample of low scorers. Thus, amongst the other

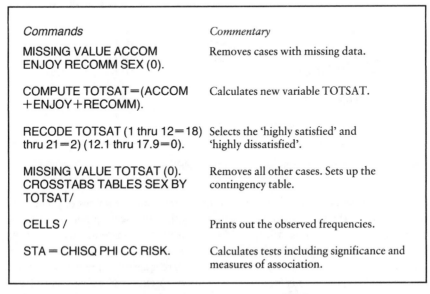

Commands	Commentary
MISSING VALUE ACCOM ENJOY RECOMM SEX (0).	Removes cases with missing data.
COMPUTE TOTSAT=(ACCOM +ENJOY+RECOMM).	Calculates new variable TOTSAT.
RECODE TOTSAT (1 thru 12=18) thru 21=2) (12.1 thru 17.9=0).	Selects the 'highly satisfied' and 'highly dissatisfied'.
MISSING VALUE TOTSAT (0). CROSSTABS TABLES SEX BY TOTSAT/	Removes all other cases. Sets up the contingency table.
CELLS /	Prints out the observed frequencies.
STA = CHISQ PHI CC RISK.	Calculates tests including significance and measures of association.

Figure 10.1 Creating contingency tables and tests in SPSS

```
SEX by TOTSAT
                    TOTSAT            Page 1 of 1
            Count      |
            Row Pct    |
            Col Pct    |                  Row
            Tot Pct    |   1.00  |  2.00 |  Total
SEX         ----------+----------+-------+
            1.00       |   6     |  14   |   20
    male               |  30.0   |  70.0 |  29.9
                       |  25.0   |  32.6 |
                       |   9.0   |  20.9 |
                     +----------+-------+
            2.00       |   18    |  29   |   47
    female             |  38.3   |  61.7 |  70.1
                       |  75.0   |  67.4 |
                       |  26.9   |  43.3 |
                     +----------+-------+
            Column         24       43        67
            Total         35.8     64.2      100.0
```

Chi-Square	Value	DF	Significance
Pearson	.42020	1	.51684
Continuity Correction	.13677	1	.71151
Likelihood Ratio	.42711	1	.51341
Mantel–Haenszel test for linear association	.41393	1	.51998

Statistic	Value	ASE1	T-value	Approximate Significance
Phi	.07919		.51684	*1
Cramer's V	.07919		.51684	*1
Contingency Coefficient	.07895		.51684	*1

*1 Pearson chi-square probability

Number of Missing Observations: 90

Figure 10.2 Contingency tables and output in SPSS

approaches that can be used is one of simply comparing the values of those that score less than the value of the first quartile with those scoring above the third quartile. By definition this will give 25 per cent of the sample in each category, but it too suffers from the disadvantage that the cut off point is somewhat arbitrary. There may be many clustering on these quartile markers, and if the value of those quartiles are used for calculation, in excess of 50 per cent of the sample end up being counted.

One further pragmatic approach is to accept that the cut-off line will be arbitrary, and simply to assess the implications of different values in terms of resultant sub-group sizes, so long as those values have, at the very least, a plausible logic for indicating high and low scorers. For the purpose of the exercise in Figure 10.1 the criteria selected are quite arbitrary and are chosen solely for showing the steps undertaken and the type of results which computer packages such as SPSS and NCSS produce. The procedure under SPSS is therefore shown in Figure 10.1.

A MEASURE OF RELATIONSHIP

As can be seen, the results produce a contingency table that shows not only the observed frequencies, but also the percentages of the row, column and total sample that each cell accounts for. If the expected frequencies are required, these can be derived by the use of the sub-command EXPECTED within the CELLS command (i.e. CELLS = EXPECTED). Following the contingency table a number of results are shown, beginning with the chi-square test result. Generally speaking, when reference is made to the chi-square test, the actual test referred to is the Pearson Chi-Square. It was this test that was described above. Essentially the test is simply a measure of the degree of independence that exists between the variables of the cross tabulation. In the specific result shown in Figure 10.2 it is indicated that χ^2 has a significance of 0.516, and hence the null hypothesis that there is no difference between the sexes in their rating of satisfactory holiday experiences cannot be rejected. But, what if p had been less than 0.05 – what then? What the result would specifically mean is that there is a lack of independence, but, rather like the Pearson Coefficient of Correlation, no automatic conclusion as to the direction of causality can be assumed. In this instance, it is unlikely that a measure of holiday satisfaction is a determinant of sex, but in other cases the direction of causality may be more difficult to assess. For example, suppose that the two variables were categories based on social activity and courier assessment where it was shown that low social activity seem to be related to higher ratings of courier performance. Does this mean that the less active use couriers more than their more socially active counterparts, or do couriers find it easier to cope with (possibly) a less demanding group of holiday-makers. It is quite possible that other hypotheses could be advanced. In short, in this instance the test would have rejected a null hypothesis of a lack of independence between the variables, but it does not assess the nature of the relationship.

The next statistic is the *continuity correction*. This result will be produced only in the case of a two by two contingency table, and it involves subtracting 0.5 from the positive differences between the expected and observed frequencies, and adding 0.5 to the negative differences prior to squaring. A similar process is undertaken for the normal approximation to the binomial probability. A contingency table possesses the properties of a multinomial experiment, and belongs to the same family of tests as a binomial probability. Hence, arguably, (Mantel 1974), the Yates correction can be applied.

It will be noted that the likelihood ratio is close to the Pearson Chi-square, and indeed for large samples the two give very similar results. The likelihood ratio is applicable where small samples exist, for it can be regarded as a χ^2 adjusted for small sample size. It will also be pertinent to use this measure when a cell possesses fewer than five respondents.

MEASURES OF ASSOCIATION

It has been noted that the chi-square test measures the degree of relationship, but not the level of causality. Indeed, such levels must depend upon the theoretical constructs being proposed by the researcher, but there are additional tests that might help in the interpretation of the results. These are known as measures of association (again, note, not measures of dependence). They are however, of use as an aid in understanding the data contained in the cells of the cross-tabulation. But, in looking at these tests it is important to consider not one in isolation, as they measure different things, and hence a low score means that the data are not related in the way in which the test is examining the data – the data may still possess relationships in other ways. In short, no single measure is the best for all situations. Such tests include the Mantel–Haenszel Statistic.

The Mantel–Haenszel Statistic

This is akin to the Pearson correlation coefficient, and indeed is derived from it in that it is the square of that correlation multiplied by the number of cases minus one. It therefore assumes other than nominal data, and hence should not be used where such data exists within the cells. In the example therefore where M—U = 0.41, p = 0.52, it can be seen that the association is weak.

Also, from the table of results, it will be noted that three test results are given with values of approximately 0.079 – these being the Phi-coefficient, Cramer's V and the coefficient of contingency. All of these tests produce results from 0 to 1 in value, and attempt to show the strength of association on a scale where scores near to zero imply no relationship. Scores approaching one possess a strong degree of association. It will be noted that in the example these scores are supporting the low, insignificant chi-square statistic as meaning that gender is not a determining variable in the level of satisfaction being gained from the holiday. The underlying premise of each of these figures is that they seek to clarify the chi-square value by minimising the influence of sample size and the number of cells within the matrix. Each of the tests is in fact based on the Pearson chi-square, but represents successive levels of sophistication:

The Phi Coefficient

The Phi Coefficient divides the Pearson Chi-square by the sample size and takes the square root of the result. However, under certain circumstances, a misleading value of one can be obtained, and so Pearson suggested the Coefficient of Contingency.

Coefficient of Contingency

This divides the Pearson Chi-square by the sum of the Chi-square plus the sample size, and again the square root of the result is taken. This will, by definition, produce a number between zero and one, but it had been noted that the upper limit is almost unattainable. Therefore, Cramer's V was suggested.

Cramer's V

Again the Pearson Chi-square is divided, but this time by the product of the sample size multiplied by the number of rows or columns (whichever is the smaller) less one. As before, the square root of the result is calculated. The Cramer's V does permit values of one to be attained.

A series of alternative measures also exists, which is based upon the proportional reduction in error. Of these one of the better known is Goodman and Kruskal's lambda. Essentially this is a ratio of the degree of error that exists in predicting the values of one variable based on the knowledge of that variable alone, and the same measure of error applied to predictions when another variable is added. Consider the data in Table 10.5. This shows the ranking of hotels by visitors booked with different tour operators, where the cell numbers indicate the number of times a hotel has been selected as the 'best' hotel. Within this matrix the largest outcome category is the selection of 'The Mansion' hotel,

Table 10.5 Number of times hotels ranked 'best' by tour operator clients

Tour operators	The Grand	Number Tot Percent The Royal	The Mansion	Total
Sun Tours	18	13	20	51
	12.86	9.29	14.28	36.43
Med Hols	17	14	25	56
	12.14	10.00	17.86	40.00
Pacific Group	12	6	15	33
	8.57	4.28	10.71	23.56
Total	47	33	60	140
	33.57	23.57	42.86	

with 42.86 per cent of the selections. The estimate of an incorrect classification is hence $p(1) = 1-0.428 = 0.572$.

The next stage is to take, for each tour operator client group, the outcome category that occurs most frequently for that variable. The probability of error thus becomes the sum of the remaining cells (i.e. $p(2) = 0.1286+0.0929 +0.1214+0.1000+0.0857+0.0428 = 0.5714$). Goodman and Kruskal's lambda is calculated as:

$$\frac{p(1)-p(2)}{p(1)} = \frac{0.572-0.5714}{0.572} = -0.0008$$

This implies that the introduction of the variable 'tour operator client' reduces error by only 0.0008 (i.e by little at all). Thus it can be concluded that no relationship exists between the ranking of the hotels and the tour operator who is sending the clients to the hotel. Lambda always has a value between 0 to 1, and a value of 0 means the independent variable is of no help in predicting the dependent variable. A value of 1 means the independent variable perfectly predicts the categories of the dependent variable. However, it is worth noting that other measures of association can produce a relationship even where lambda possesses a value of zero – the Goodman and Kruskal lambda only measures association in this one particular manner of error reduction.

The chi-square statistic and its derivations such as Cramer's V are obviously important tests. It is therefore pertinent to observe the warning issued by Sincich, namely:

> Because it is widely used, the chi-square test is also one of the most abused statistical procedures. The user should always be certain that the experiment satisfies the properties of a multinomial experiment before proceeding with the test. **In addition, the chi-square test should be avoided when the estimated probability distribution gives a poor approximation to the sampling distribution of the chi-square statistic.** As a rule of thumb, an estimated expected cell count of at least 5 will mean that the chi-square distribution can be used to determine an approximate critical value to specify the rejection region (Sincich 1992:1003) [Original author's emphasis retained].

That warning retains significant validity, even when contingency tests designed to overcome the problem of containing less than five in a cell are used. The requirements for a chi-square test are defined by Sincich as being:

(a) there should be n identical trials;
(b) there are k possible outcomes to each trial;
(c) the probabilities of the k outcomes remain the same from trial to trial, where the total of such probabilities equal one;
(d) the trials are independent.

This last point is vitally important, and implies that no one representative of an independent variable influences any other respondent. Thus, in the above example of the clients rating the hotels, no one holiday-maker is deemed to have influenced the ranking of hotels by any other holiday-maker. It is for the researcher within the confines of the research design to determine the degree to which this condition has been met.

HIERARCHICAL LOG LINEAR MODELS

The following comments are designed simply as a means of making the researcher aware of what further analysis can be undertaken. As such, the text is designed to introduce some issues and permit an initial analysis to be undertaken utilising hierarchical log-linear models, but while permitting some results to be obtained, the reader should be aware that many more features are available. Additionally, if the researcher has little or no training in the more advanced statistical techniques, it is recommended that advice is sought before using these tests.

The matrices so far examined were comparatively straight forward, but it is possible to construct quite complex patterns. Suppose, for example, some categorisation of tourists had been undertaken on the basis of their motivation. Following, as an example, the work of Yiannakis and Gibson (1992) referred to in Chapter 4, tourists might be categorised as being sun-lovers, action seekers, thrill seekers or mass tourists. They might be asked to state their degree of satisfaction with a series of given tourist attractions. Say, to retain simplicity, they were asked to state their views about sea, mountains and cities. Even a simple representation of the data can become comparatively complex, as demonstrated in Table 10.6. How then can this type of matrix be examined to identify the possible contribution to satisfaction that is derived from personality categorisation and the nature of the tourist attraction? Different approaches can be adopted. Hintze comments in the manual to NCSS that where rating data is used, research at Utah State University suggests F-tests derived from factorial models can give results as accurate as those derived from a general linear model approach. Indeed, the problem is similar to that analysed by regression analysis, except that in the example shown in Table 10.6 the variable, 'satisfaction', is dichotomous (i.e. it has two states, satisfied or not satisfied). One means of analysis that is possible is to utilise hierarchical log linear models. Under these the dependent variable is deemed to be the actual number of frequencies that exist in the cells – the other variables are independent, determining variables. However, the student or researcher should not shy away from the analysis of such multi-way matrices if they have access to statistical software that permits them to analyse the problem, although, again, it is recommended that they take advice, if required, to ensure that the problem is being correctly defined, and the results being properly interpreted. The researcher may, however, take some degree of comfort from the fact that the results include the chi-square and lambda statistics already examined above.

In Table 10.6 the number of cases in each cell can be seen as the function of

Table 10.6 Numbers satisfied with attractions by tourist type

	Satisfied	Not satisfied
Sun lovers		
Sea	42	8
Mountains	38	12
Cities	10	15
Action seekers		
Sea	22	10
Mountains	9	18
Cities	35	5
Thrill seekers		
Sea	15	6
Mountains	20	4
Cities	8	15
Mass tourists		
Sea	15	3
Mountains	12	4
Cities	8	2

tourist type, scenery, degree of satisfaction, and the interaction between each of these variables, that is, as stated, the dependent variable is deemed to be the number in the cell. To obtain a linear model, the natural logs of the cell counts rather than the actual counts are used. To simplify, the first cell has a value of 42 (log = 62325) and the log linear model for the first cell is

$$\log(42) = \mu + \text{type/sun-lover} + \text{scenery/sea} + \text{satisfied/yes}$$
$$+ \text{sun-lover/sea/satisfied}$$

where μ is the average of the logs of the frequencies in all table cells, and the lambda parameters represent the increments or decrements from the base value (μ) for the particular combinations of values of the row and column variables. So type/sun-lover is the effect of being a sun-lover and not a member of the other groups; scenery/sea the effect of being a seascape; satisfied/yes the effect of being satisfied; and sun-lover/sea/satisfied the effect of the interaction between the variables. In this manner the model is akin to the more conventional chi-square test in that a comparison between observed and expected frequencies can subsequently be undertaken. In SPSS the command:

HILOGLINEAR SATIS(1,2) TYPE(1,4) SCENE(1,3)
/DESIGN = SATIS TYPE SCENE.

will print a list of expected and observed frequencies, and the value of the residuals (that is the difference between them for an unsaturated model (i.e.

where no interaction is assumed), while the fully saturated model (where interactions are assumed) by the command:

HILOGLINEAR SATIS(1,2) TYPE(1,4) SCENE(1,3)
/DESIGN = SATIS*TYPE*SCENE.

The use of the sub-command PRINT = ESTIM will produce the chi-square statistic with the associated probabilities. Additionally, it is possible to refine the analysis by more carefully delineating the contribution of each variable to the model. To this end partial chi-square values and their observed significance levels can be calculated, and additionally, it is possible to undertake a 'stepped' model whereby the effects of removing variables from the equation upon the chi-square statistic can be observed. Thus this forms a means of measuring the importance of individual terms. If such steps are adopted it is also useful to be able to analyse the residuals, and many statistical packages permit making plots of these. As will be discussed in Chapter 11, the residuals should form a normal distribution.

SUMMARY

This chapter is concerned with categorical data that are located within cells indicating the numbers who have selected various choices. The questions that are examined are akin to those previously discussed, namely, what is the nature of the relationship between the variables, and what level of dependency might exist? The statistic normally selected for this is the chi-square test, but it has been noted that, like many other tests, it is valid only when sets of conditions have been met. It has also been noted that the test can be further developed not only to examine whether a relationship exists, but also to test the contribution each variable might make to the model in terms of being able to identify the most important factors that may be operating.

Chapter 11

Correlations and multiple regression analysis

INTRODUCTION

In Chapter 6 reference was made to the coefficient of correlation. In this chapter the purpose of the coefficient of correlation will be restated, and alternative correlations will be briefly reviewed. After this has been completed, the purpose of multiple regression will be examined.

COEFFICIENTS OF CORRELATION

Measures of correlation yield values between -1 and $+1$. A value of $+1$ means a perfect association whereby two variables go up and down together. A value of zero means there is no relationship between the two, and a result of -1 means that there is a perfect inverse relationship. Under this latter circumstance, as one variable increases in value the other proportionately falls. The most commonly used coefficient is the Pearson Coefficient of Correlation, and this tests for a linear relationship between the variables. The assumption of linearity is often quite sufficient for testing data, but any researcher would be wise to check that it does exist. Fortunately, this is quite simply done by plotting the two variables against each other. It has been previously noted that, at least historically, statistical software has been relatively poor in drawing diagrams when compared to specialist graphics packages or spreadsheets. It must be noted that increasingly this criticism has less validity, but the researcher who has only access to earlier versions of the software will find that sufficient facilities exist to indicate whether the assumption of linearity can apply. The importance of drawing the scatter diagram is confirmed by Norusis, who notes:

> It is important to examine correlation coefficients together with scatter plots since the same coefficient can result from very different underlying relationships ... the correlation coefficient should be used only to summarise the strength of linear association (1990a:B-17).

Thus, variables that possess a U-shaped relationship would have a correlation coefficient approaching zero, even though there would obviously be a close relationship between x and y. It is also important to draw the plot because correlation calculations can be sensitive to outliers, and the scatter diagram will quickly identify if these exist.

CALCULATING THE COEFFICIENT OF CORRELATION

The commands between the three illustrative pieces of software are very similar in this case. In MINITAB the command is simply:

> MTB> CORR 'KNOW' 'KNOW2'
> MTB> PLOT 'KNOW' vs 'KNOW2'

to calculate the Pearson Coefficient of Correlation and to draw a scatter diagram for the two variables 'KNOW' and 'KNOW2'.

In NCSS the correlation/regression menu is selected, and then bivariate statistics. The columns containing the data are then identified, and the results contain not only the coefficient of correlation but also the linear equation with both intercept and slope being given, plus other details. Alternatively, the researcher can select the correlation option when several variables are being examined. The scatter diagram is drawn by selecting the plots option within the statistical and data analysis menu, and simply identifying the appropriate columns.

SPSS requires a similar approach. The commands would be:

> CORR VAR = KNOW KNOW2.
> PLOT PLOT = KNOW WITH KNOW2.

The results are shown in Figure 11.1. The result is set out in a matrix because, with SPSS, it is possible to test for pair-wise correlations across a large number of variables simultaneously. As will be shown in Chapter 12, this can be quite advantageous when considering larger sets of data. The correlation between the two variables of 0.268 is quite low, and this is further indicated by the scatter diagram which does not show any clear pattern. Incidentally, the numbers and letters show the number of observations grouping at that spot. With large sample sizes letters are used to indicate groupings of above 10 in number.

ONE- OR TWO-TAIL TESTS

It is to be noted that unlike the significance testing previously carried out, the probability value given in this case is a one-tail test. The two-tail test used before is based on the normal distribution and the convention that testing is carried out at the 95 per cent confidence level. The remaining 5 per cent of cases are thus divided at each extreme of the normal distribution, that is, 2.5 per cent of cases have values of less than the mean minus 1.96 standard deviation, and the other 2.5 per cent have values above the mean plus 1.96 standard deviation. The adoption of the two-tail test therefore implies a testing where the alternative

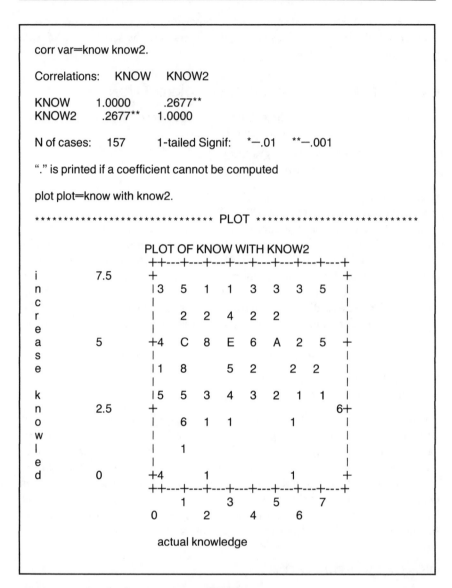

Figure 11.1 Testing for correlations (SPSS)

hypothesis does not specify departure from the null hypothesis in any particular direction. In the case of a linear relationship the direction of the association can generally be applied in advance, and hence a one-tail test is acceptable. If, however, nothing is known, a two-tail probability can be used.

A NOTE ON MISSING DATA

The researcher may have to make allowance for the possibility of missing data, and hence a missing data command might be required, depending on the conventions of the software being used. In previous chapters one concern has been the need to check the nature of the data to ensure whether parametric tests are appropriate. The same concerns arise in the case of the Pearson Coefficient of Correlation, and alternatives do exist if the assumptions of bivariate normality appear to be violated. In other words, for the test to be used, both x and y need to possess a normal distribution. As previously noted, this can be checked for by examining the frequency distribution of the data. Also, as mentioned, missing values can be a potential problem, and the researcher will need to be certain that these have a random distribution. If a missing value is in part a function of the other variable, this might also invalidate the use of the test. An example where this might occur is where a researcher examines a relationship between holiday expenditure and income. Respondents might withhold information on either one or both of these variables, and it is possible that low income groups might be the more likely to do so. This requires care in the interpretation of the remaining data, as the coefficient (r) might be either over- or under-estimating the nature of the relationship. SPSS permits the researcher to use option commands that permit either the inclusion or exclusion of cases with missing values. It is advisable to use both as a first step in examining the random nature of the missing values.

NON-PARAMETRIC TESTS

West (1991) suggests two other tests to be used under certain conditions. The first is where there is a relationship where higher values are associated with higher scores on a second variable, but the relationship is not linear (i.e. it is said to be monotonic). Here Spearman's rho (r) or Rank Correlation Coefficient should be used. This is accessible within NCSS within the menus for non-parametric tests, sub-item, correlation statistics. With SPSS, it may depend upon the version that you are using. Thus, under SPSS-X the command:

NONPAR CORR VAR1 VAR2 / PRINT
= TWOTAIL /MISSING = PAIRWISE.

will produce the required results for variables named VAR1 and VAR2. With SPSS-PC and MINITAB, the Spearman r more clearly betrays its origin as a non-parametric test based on the ranking of the scores. Before the test is used there is a need to rank the scores. Both pieces of software possess a RANK command that will do this for the researcher. In MINITAB, RANK C1 C4 will take the data from column one, rank it, and then place it into column 4. Undertaking a second, similar procedure will then produce the second column for the correlation, and the conventional CORR command is then used for the new columns. SPSS also uses a similar RANK command, after which the CORR VAR command illustrated above is applied. One further point to note if SPSS-PC is being used, and that is if the sample is less than approximately 30, the researcher will need to refer to tables of Spearman's *r* to assess the statistical significance. If the sample is above this in number, then the probability value given in the output can be used. An alternative approach is to set the data up within a crosstabs table and use the STA=CORR sub-command within CROSSTABS.

The second non-parametric test that can be considered is Kendall's tau *b*. This will be used where a monotonic relationship exists, but where at least one of the variables being considered can take on only a limited number of values. Suppose, for example, one was seeking to assess whether more satisfied holiday-makers undertook more expenditure at a given attraction. The levels of daily expenditure could range from, say, £5 to £100, whereas the visitors might have been categorised as simply dissatisfied, satisfied and very satisfied. The NCSS procedure described above produces Kendall's tau as well as Spearman's rho. With SPSS there is again a difference between SPSS-X and SPSS-PC. Under SPSS-X the command is:

> NONPAR CORR VAR1 VAR2/PRINT
> = TWOTAIL/KENDALL/MISSING = PAIRWISE.

Under SPSS-PC, the format is:

> CROSSTABS TABLES=VAR1 by VAR2 /STA=BTAU.

COEFFICIENT OF DETERMINATION

The Coefficient of Correlation measures the strength of a linear (straight line) relationship between the two variables x and y. An inference about the slope β_1 of the linear model leads to a determination as to whether the independent variable x contributes information for the prediction of the dependent variable y. This measure is known as the Coefficient of Determination. The basic approach is again based upon deviation from the mean. Suppose that one wanted to predict tourist expenditure from tourist income. If no data existed about income, then, with no information about the relative frequency distribution of expenditure, the only prediction one could make about expenditure (y) is that it would equal the average (mean) expenditure $(\bar{y})$. The sum of squared prediction errors (SS_{yy}) would be:

$$\Sigma(\text{Actual } y - \text{Predicted } y)^2 = \Sigma(y - \bar{y})^2$$

This magnitude, the sum of the squares, is an indicator of how well the mean expenditure behaves as a predictor of the actual expenditure. If the income data was now used to predict the tourist spending, the sum of the squares about the predicted values will be the total of the differences between the actual and predicted spending (the sum of squared errors, SSE). The coefficient of determination is thus calculated as:

$$r^2 = \frac{SS_{yy} - SSE}{SS_{yy}}$$

The Coefficient of Determination measures the proportion of variation that is explained by the independent variable. If r^2 for the relationship between tourist income and tourist spending was 0.61, what this would mean is that 61 per cent of the variation in spending amongst tourists could be attributed to their income, and 39 per cent was due to other factors not considered in the model.

MULTIPLE REGRESSION ANALYSIS – THE ASSUMPTIONS

Regression analysis seeks to take this explanation of the relationship between dependent and independent variables further by including more than one variable as an explanatory factor. For example, from the data available from the Appendix, the researcher might want to explore a hypothesis that holiday satisfaction is a function of experience. The proxies for experience might be age and the number of past visits undertaken. The relationship to be examined takes the form of:

Satisfaction = f(age, times) [using the variable names]

which is rewritten as:

Satisfaction = $\beta_0 + \beta_1 \text{Age} + \beta_2 \text{Times} + e_i$

where the β (regression coefficients) terms are unknown and the e_i term is representative of independent random variables that are normally distributed with a mean 0. The assumptions of a multiple regression model are as follows:

(a) There is a *normal distribution* of the dependent variable for every combination of the values of the independent variables in the model.

(b) The variation around the line of regression be constant for all values of x. This means that y varies the same amount for any given value of x, whether x is high or low in value. This is technically known as *homoscedasticity*. If this is not the case, then weighted least squares methods or data transformation will be required.

(c) That *independence of error* exists, that is the residuals (the differences between observed and predicted values of y) should be independent for each value of x. This gives rise to the test whereby the researcher looks for the residuals to be normally distributed.

Statistical software packages present many powerful tools of analysis for any researcher within the portfolio of commands that apply to regression analysis, and if a sophisticated analysis is required then a study of the appropriate manual will be well rewarded. Amongst the most common features provided are some form of step-wise analysis whereby the independent variables are either introduced, or deducted from the equation, one at a time. This permits the researcher to note the impact of each independent variable upon the Coefficient of Determination; thereby indicating the relative importance of the independent variable. Additionally packages may offer means of analysing curvi-linear regression. Also, many tests exist to test for the validity of data in terms of ensuring the true independence of the determining variables.

OBTAINING AND INTERPRETING RESULTS

To begin with basics. The commands under MINITAB for the example shown above would be:

REGRESS 'TOTSAT' on 2 PREDICTOR 'AGE' 'TIMES'

where TOTSAT has been created as before. This will produce not only the regression equation and R^2 score but also list the actual and predicted dependent variable (TOTSAT) with the residuals.

With NCSS the multiple regression option within the correlation regression menu is selected. Again, identify the columns to be used and their role as dependent or independent variables. A full list of reports is available within the menus, including residual analysis and diagnostics output.

Within SPSS one way of laying out the commands is shown in Figure 11.2.

Commands	Commentary
REGRESS VAR = TOTSAT AGE TIMES /	Identify variables for regression.
DEPENDENT = TOTSAT /	Identifies dependent variable.
METHOD = ENTER AGE TIMES/	Identifies sequence and forces solution.
CASEWISE=ALL DEPEND PRED RESID/	Prints out value of predicted TOTSAT as dependent variable and residual.
RESID = HIST.	Creates histogram of residuals.

Figure 11.2 Commands for regression analysis (SPSS)

The results can be looked at one by another (see Figure 11.3). The first result from the first row of the METHOD command, and give the key values of the regression. These show that the Coefficient of Determination is extremely low ($R^2 = 0.0119$), indicating that total satisfaction is not dependent upon age or past experience as measured by the number of times a holiday-maker has visited the attraction. The actual equation for the regression equation is:

TOTSAT = 15.12+0.241AGE−0.102TIMES

The high value of the constant compared to the potential value of the TOTSAT variable (a maximum value of 21) is itself indicative of the low predictive ability

```
                **** MULTIPLE REGRESSION ****
Equation Number 1    Dependent Variable..   TOTSAT

Variable(s) Entered on Step Number
   1..   TIMES    no. of times to destination
   2..   AGE

Multiple R              .10917
R Square                .01192
Adjusted R Square      −.00389
Standard Error         3.67169

Analysis of Variance
                 DF   Sum of Squares   Mean Square
Regression        2      20.32525       10.16262
Residual        125    1685.16694       13.48134
F =     .75383      Signif F =   .4727
------------------------------------------------------------

                **** MULTIPLE REGRESSION ****

Equation Number 1    Dependent Variable..   TOTSAT

--------------- Variables in the Equation -----------------

Variable        B        SE B       Beta        T Sig T

TIMES       −.102290   .292387    −.031107    −.350   .7270
AGE          .241768   .204671     .105031    1.181   .2397
(Constant) 15.118967   .961954               15.717   .0000

        End Block Number   1    All requested variables entered.
```

Figure 11.3 Output for multiple regression (SPSS)

of this relationship. The interpretation of the individual components of the equation is:

15.12 is the value of the intercept, β_0 (where the straight line crosses the vertical axis on a graph), and it represents the level of satisfaction when the other two variables have a zero value.

0.241AGE is that for every increase in age by one unit (the age grouping) the total satisfaction will increase by 0.241 units for any given level of experience.

−0.102TIMES means that for any given age grouping, the level of total satisfaction will decrease by 0.102 units for every unit of additional visits made to the attraction.

It is a mistake to regard the value of the regression coefficients as indicators of the relative importance of the variables. The actual value is very much dependent upon the absolute measurements of the factor being considered. To make the regression coefficients somewhat more comparable the Beta weights are calculated, and these can be regarded as standardised beta coefficients. They are better indicators of relative importance, but are still nonetheless affected by the correlations of the independent variables. It is for this reason that researchers will adopt step-wise procedures that assess the impact of any one factor on the Coefficient of Determination. SPSS also calculates the analysis of variance. The F-test is a test of the null hypothesis as to whether there is a linear relationship between the dependent variable (TOTSAT) and the set of other independent variables. It is to be noted that the value and significance of F indicates that this is not necessarily the case in this specific example.

RESIDUAL ANALYSIS – ITS PURPOSE

The next set of commands seek to establish the value of the residual, and Figure 11.4 shows an extraction from the results produced by SPSS. It can be seen that a case-by-case result is given showing the actual value of TOTSAT, the predicted value, and the residual, with a simple chart indicating location of a standardised residual. In Figure 11.4 it can be noted that in some cases due to missing data within the calculation of the TOTSAT score, no actual score is given, but an imputed predicted score is allocated to the case. In analysing the validity of a

```
Casewise Plot of Standardized Residual

*: Selected    M: Missing

         −3.0        0.0        3.0
Case #      O:.............:............:O              *PRED      *RESID
  1           .     *    .          .       12.00     15.2584    −3.2584
  2           .         .*          .       16.00     15.2956     .7044
  3           . *       .           .        7.00     16.0581    −9.0581
  4           .         .           .                 15.1562      .
  5           .        *.           .       13.00     15.5002    −2.5002
  6           .         .           .                 15.5002      .
  7           . *       .           .        8.00     15.2584    −7.2584
  8           .         .           .                 15.5002      .
  9           .        .*           .       17.00     15.5002     1.4998
 10           .         .           .                 15.1933      .
Case #      O:.............:............:O              *PRED      *RESID
         −3.0        0.0        3.0
```

Figure 11.4 Plotting residuals (SPSS)

```
Histogram – Standardised Residual

N EXP N       (* = 1 Cases,    .: = Normal Curve)

 0   .50   2.67 .
 0  1.14   2.33 .
 0  2.34   2.00 .
 1  4.28   1.67 * .
14  7.02   1.33 ******.*******
 8 10.32   1.00 ********  .
21 13.59    .67 *************.*******
15 16.04    .33 ***************.
22 16.94    .00 ****************.*****
12 16.04   −.33 ***********   .
10 13.59   −.67 **********   .
10 10.32  −1.00 ********.:
 5  7.02  −1.33 *****.
 3  4.28  −1.67 ***.
 3  2.34  −2.00 *:*
 1  1.14  −2.33 :
 1   .50  −2.67 :
 1   .20  −3.00 *
 1   .10   Out *
```

Figure 11.5 Histogram of residuals – SPSS output

multiple regression solution to a problem the role of the residuals are quite important. SPSS makes it possible to plot these as shown, and provides information which shows the number of observed residuals in each interval (N), and the number expected (Exp N). It also indicates the existence of outliers that deserve closer examination. The consistency of the data in Figure 11.4 are shown, in that as expected from the F-test, the distribution of residuals does not form a normal (bell-shaped) distribution. It therefore appears that not only are the results poor in terms of the actual values, but the model is itself poorly specified and a linear relationship cannot be assumed.

The researcher must carefully define the nature of the residuals being examined. If standardised residuals are being assessed, then if it appears that the standardised residuals vary for different levels of the predicted y variable, then this provides evidence of a possible curvilinear effect and/or the need to transform data. See Figure 11.5.

MULTI-COLLINEARITY

It has been noted that one of the important assumptions of multiple regression is the assumption that the variables are independent. Multi-collinearity is the term given to the situation where this does not exist, and variables are closely related to, and affect, each other. Thus the researcher will need to carefully consider the nature of these relationships. For example, in an attempt to model tourist flows with reference to economic data, the use of variables such as income, savings, the rate of inflation, prices of holidays, exchange rates and similar data are often used. Yet, the variables are linked together. If holiday expenditure is an activity funded from discretionary income – so too are savings. Substitution effects occur within the constraint of income. But the researcher may seek to utilise multiple regression as a means of examining the relationship! Hence, there is a need to be able to assess the nature of interaction within the variables being built into the model. A first useful check as to whether multi-collinearity is going to be a problem is to develop a matrix showing the Coefficient of Correlation between the independent variables. If there are high degrees of correlation, the researcher may well have to reconsider their approach. It will mean the independent variables are influencing each other, and hence it becomes difficult to assess their subsequent influence upon the determined or dependent factor.

TESTS FOR MULTI-COLLINEARITY AND OUTLIER'S INFLUENCE

A common method for examining the regression equation for multi-collinearity is to calculate what is known as the *Variance Inflationary Factor* (VIF). In MINITAB the sub-command VIF will print this. VIF is one of the results automatically produced by NCSS in the process described above, while in SPSS, the sub-command TOL (short for tolerance) is appended in the form STA = TOL. This produces a figure and Marquandt (1980) suggests the following interpretation:

   VIF = 1 set of explanatory variables are un-correlated
   VIF > 10 too high a level of VIF suggesting too much correlation.

However, earlier, Snee (1973), argued that a VIF of 5 was in fact too high, and implied high levels of multicollinearity.

   Problems with multiple regression can occur not only through multi-collinearity, but also through individual observations having too great an effect upon the pattern of response. Most pieces of software permit the identification of outliers, which may require removal in order to obtain a better fit between the actual and predicted observations. Most of these are based on the distance from a mean value, and hence packages will produce outputs such as Mahalanobis' Distance or Cook's Distance Statistic. Generally speaking, the higher the value of the statistic, the more likely it is that the case to which it is referring ought to be removed. If the researcher is unsure of the processes involved in such procedures, it must again be emphasised that scatter plots of the original data are an appropriate initial means of identifying some of the potential problem cases. It should further be emphasised that removal of any observation in order better to devise a fit between predicted and actual observation necessitates a careful examination of the problem case. If it arises because of matters such as inconsistency of response, or values that appear wildly inconsistent with others so as to represent very much a special case, then the researcher might safely remove it. Nonetheless, almost by definition, the exceptional requires, where possible, additional investigation.

STEPWISE PROCEDURES

It has been noted earlier that much of theory construction is concerned with seeking parsimonious explanations, that is reducing complexity to an abstract whereby much of the variance in outcomes can be explained by a few key factors. Computer software aids that in the case of multiple regression by permitting stepwise procedures. These either add one variable at a time, or delete it from the overall model. The researcher then looks at the result upon the Coefficient of Determination. If the addition or removal of any one variable creates a significant change in the coefficient, it might be said to be an influential factor – if it does not, it might be worth removing the variable from the model. Thus, for example, with MINITAB the command:

STEPWISE REGRESS Y IN C1, PREDICTORS IN C2-C7

will produce an output showing, amongst other statistics the R^2 (Coefficient of Determination) at each stage. Again, NCSS provides this information within the standard commands in the Multiple Regression Report Output. It produces a statistic that the package calls the Sequential R-squared, and this shows the increment in R^2 as each variable is introduced into the calculation. SPSS offers a very useful sub-command, namely:

/METHOD = STEPWISE.

and useful in the sense that the output indicates not only the included, but also the excluded variables, and shows the changing regression coefficients for each included item.

SUMMARY

The Pearson Coefficient of Correlation is potentially an extremely useful statistic for any researcher, both for the information that it provides in itself, and second as a check as to the need or desirability of further statistical testing. The Coefficient shows the degree to which a relationship exists between two variables. That calculation might be important if the researcher is considering examining relationships between three or more variables. It has been noted that one of the requirements of multiple regression is that the variables are independent, and hence a correlation matrix showing the degree of independence through low *r* scores is a useful first step.

Another useful first step prior to undertaking multiple regression is simply to plot the frequency distribution of the variables, in that a normal distribution is being sought. Further, the researcher could benefit from undertaking scatter diagrams between the variables to indicate whether linear relationships existed. If they did not, then possibly the data might have to be transformed, perhaps by taking the log of the value.

Assuming that the requirements for multiple regression have been met, it is a powerful technique that permits predictions to be made subject to the important proviso that it is valid to extrapolate past trends into the future. Once again, the issue of the means by which qualitative and quantitative research entwine can be illustrated. The existence of a past trend cannot be interpreted as meaning that the social forces that gave rise to that trend will be maintained in the future. Nowhere is this perhaps more evident than in holiday-taking.

For example, in the UK market in the past patterns of cruise shipping patronage have been linked to numbers and income of those over the age of 55 (Ryan 1989–90). Yet, given the changing past experiences and expectations of succeeding generations, a product that has been successful with those over 55 in the 1980s has no guarantee of success with those that will be over 55 in the new century. Past experience of travel, and expectations from travel between the two cohorts of those over 55, but separated by two decades, could well imply changing tastes. Yet the question is a difficult one for shipping companies, in that the current investment decisions as to the design and features of cruise ships taken now in response to present demand will nonetheless determine the basic asset that is still being used in the next decade. Hence the qualitative data obtained from research could determine the future consistency of relationship between variables identified as being important in the past through statistical testing.

In short, even the more powerful of statistical techniques such as multiple regression require processes of checking – processes derived not only from simpler descriptive statistics as noted above, but also a monitoring of attitudes that should, perhaps, also incorporate some qualitative study.

Chapter 12

Factors and clusters

INTRODUCTION

Before commencing with this chapter, the warning contained in the Introduction needs to be restated. The data contained in the Appendix is not, strictly speaking, sufficient to support the tests being considered here. Therefore, this chapter must be read with this in mind, and hence the emphasis is upon the nature of the tests rather than the specific outcomes. Nonetheless, it is thought that the purpose of the tests is evident from the samples given. The chapter reviews three related tests, principal components analysis, factor analysis and cluster analysis. The concern of all three tests is to enable the researcher to identify whether an underlying grouping exists within a series of responses, and in that way to reduce the number of explanatory variables. The nature of the task is illustrated in Figure 12.1. Let us assume that a series of questions relating to attitudes towards holidays has been posed. The top row indicates the individual items. The process consists of grouping those items that correlate with each other to form another variable, one that itself possesses high levels of correlation with each of the individual items.

Such calculations require large numbers of repetitive procedures, and until the emergence of computers were not generally possible for large data sets. The emergence of the more powerful desktop computer with a maths processor chip

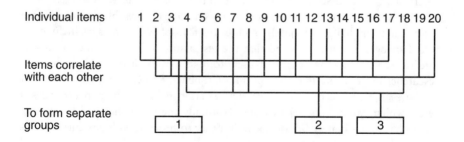

Figure 12.1 The derivation of clusters or underlying groups

at prices of below £1,500 since about 1988 has led to an increased number of reported studies using these techniques in the journals of tourism and marketing. Additionally, increased low-cost computing power has led to the development of major commercial clusters of names and addresses in market research. For example, in the UK, CCN Systems of Nottingham has developed a lifestyle grouping known as Persona which is derived from over 3 million responses to CMT's National Shoppers' Survey. National tourist boards have also taken advantage of these technological breakthroughs to help target their limited promotional funds to ensure a higher rate of return per pound or dollar of advertising expenditure. For example, the United States Tourism Administration and Tourism Canada have undertaken studies that build up psychographic profiles of client groups in tourist generating countries for North America, and, as indicated in Chapter 4, so too has the New Zealand Tourism Board.

The techniques are powerful and significant in their aid towards understanding and developing tourism groupings. One such example derived from the literature was the work of Yiannakis and Gibson (1992) referred to in Chapter 4, but it should be emphasised that this is but one of many such studies. Given the accessibility of such techniques, it is pertinent to ask what are the steps involved, the requirements of data for such processes, and how are the results to be interpreted?

FIRST STEPS

There are at least two important first stages to be undertaken before using these tests. The first is for the researcher to test that the scale being used is reliable, the second is to test whether correlations between items exist.

Cronbach's Alpha Coefficient

Reliability is a question of the internal consistency of the scale that has been devised. One way is to split the sample into half and to correlate the scores between each group. Normally this requires a random division of respondents between the two halves. A second approach is to use the Cronbach Alpha Coefficient. This possesses the advantage in that it is a measure of the reliability of a test by measuring the correlations that exist for each possible way of splitting a set of items in half. Fortunately many statistical software packages include the test. However, it must be noted that the test assumes that the data consists of interval scales. In other cases of dichotomous or nominally scaled data the researcher must ensure that the option – Cronbach KR-20 is available. The test measures the degree of covariance that exists between items and produces a result which varies from zero to one. Normally the researcher will be seeking values of approximately 0.7 or above in order to proceed with any further tests such as those described here.

SPSS produces the alpha coefficient as an option within the RELIABILITY

```
RELIABILITY ANALYSIS - SCALE (ALL)


RELIABILITY COEFFICIENTS

N OF CASES =    157.0      N OF ITEMS = 14

ALPHA =   .7382


-----------------------------------------------------------
```

Figure 12.2 RELIABILITY command (SPSS)

command. Applying it to the first set of attitudinal statements in the illustrative data set contained in Appendix I, the procedure is:

RELIABILITY /VAR = KNOW TO TIME /MODEL = ALPHA

which produces the result shown in Figure 12.2.

One of the problems with the Cronbach Alpha Coefficient is that it can produce quite high results if the number of items on the scale is large, even if the average inter-item correlation between the variables is quite small. Thus, even where the alpha coefficient is satisfactory, it is still important to examine the correlations between the items. Arguably, to do so also possesses other advantages in that the researcher becomes more aware of the quality and the nature of the data set by doing so, rather than, as it were, being aware of it at arm's length.

Testing correlations

The commands for the Coefficient for Correlation were discussed in Chapter 11. SPSS additionally possesses a number of tests for the correlation matrix that are of help in determining whether a more sophisticated analysis is appropriate and these are accessed through sub-commands such as KMO in Figure 12.3. These tests include the following.

Bartlett's Test for Sphericity

This tests for the possibility that the correlation matrix forms an identity, that is the diagonal values are all one, and all off-diagonal values are zero. In practice, no correlation matrix will consist of off-diagonal values of zero, but the test will measure the degree of difference from zero. SPSS provides a significance figure. The researcher is looking for a large test statistic for sphericity and a small associated significance level to reject the hypothesis that the correlation matrix is an identity. If the results are otherwise, factor analysis should not be undertaken.

The Kaiser–Meyer–Olkin model

This tests for the adequacy of the sample. It produces values from zero to one, and Kaiser (1974) suggests that:

> KMO > 0.9 are 'marvellous'
> KMO in the 0.8s are 'meritorious'
> KMO in the 0.7s are 'middling'
> KMO in the 0.6s are 'mediocre'
> KMO in the 0.5s are 'miserable'
> KMO < 0.5 is 'unacceptable'

To obtain these figures the command:

FACTOR VAR = KNOW TO TIME / PRINT CORR KMO

will produce both the correlation matrix and the test statistics. Examination of the data shows that the correlations would appear to form groupings, and the two tests are in the appropriate range for further testing. For example, the items 'Close' and 'Build' which relate to friendships correlate at 0.58. The Bartlett Test for Sphericity yields a significant result, but the Kaiser–Meyer–Olkin test is 'mediocre', albeit towards the higher end of the range. It should also be noted that in examining a correlation matrix researchers should not only seek the items with high positive correlations, but also examine the data for the low correlations and to reassure themselves that these are as expected.

Once the researcher has determined that the data possess sufficient reliability and validity to continue, the next stage is to decide what tests are actually required. West (1991) suggests a number of rules which include:

> If your purpose is no more than to 'reduce the data' to manageable proportions, you should use a principal components analysis.... It does not matter whether factors produced have any theoretical validity.

> Conversely, if you are trying to discover psychologically meaningful underlying dimensions you should try a maximum likelihood factor analysis (1991:140).

DATA REQUIREMENTS

Before undertaking any of the following tests there are some rules of thumb to be followed. These include:

(a) If there is little correlation between the variables, the tests are pointless. In the case of principal components analysis it will simply lead to components that are almost identical with the original variables. Factor analysis will have factor var = know to time /print corr kmo.

---- F A C T O R   A N A L Y S I S ----

Correlation Matrix:

	KNOW	AVOID	BUILD	CHALL	IMAG	CALM	CLOSE
KNOW	1.00000						
AVOID	−.11656	1.00000					
BUILD	.34371	−.01201	1.00000				
CHALL	.29914	−.02788	.38112	1.00000			
IMAG	.48414	−.00202	.36236	.50222	1.00000		
CALM	.07510	.55517	.08745	−.10401	.08277	1.00000	
CLOSE	.18973	.14663	.58649	.36233	.28327	.10093	1.00000
SPORT	.09161	.16490	.24207	.51416	.17935	.00162	.38761
PHYS	−.14168	.37713	−.01496	−.15131	−.04079	.40444	.03553
BELONG	.06953	.03996	.30919	.28989	.14158	.15326	.39042
DISC	.41456	.03533	.14397	.20040	.28991	.09392	.09864
MENTAL	−.16953	.41410	−.09026	.03647	−.10466	.33165	.07415
OTHERS	.04562	−.05217	.42962	.14665	.11478	−.06398	.35963
TIME	−.00541	.16244	.32518	.09044	.15629	.04234	.38442

	SPORT	PHYS	BELONG	DISC	MENTAL	OTHERS	TIME
SPORT	1.00000						
PHYS	−.14667	1.00000					
BELONG	.20139	.08304	1.00000				
DISC	−.04739	.00414	.05851	1.00000			
MENTAL	.05763	.51780	.09967	−.00114	1.00000		
OTHERS	.24468	.04394	.23507	.13329	−.00090	1.00000	
TIME	.30810	.04906	.00242	.15464	.07408	.64417	1.00000

Kaiser–Meyer–Olkin Measure of Sampling Adequacy = .66969
Bartlett Test of Sphericity = 679.93279, Significance = .00000

Figure 12.3 Correlation matrix

nothing to explain, and cluster analysis will produce large numbers of loosely connected clusters even after many iterations.

Figure 12.3 indicates how statistical software can be used to lay out a correlation matrix. (The example is derived from the sub-command 'corr' as part of the factor command in SPSS.) The researcher is thus looking for groups of correlations that 'make sense'. For example, avoiding crowds (labelled AVOID) and seeking a calm atmosphere (labelled CALM) correlate to 0.55, while, on the other hand, AVOID and OTHERS (being in the company of others) has little correlation (−0.05). Patterns of clusters of correlation indicate the possibility of underlying factors existing in the responses to the questionnaire, and hence the researcher might now wish to continue.

(b) Factor analysis requires a normal distribution on the variables. If this is not the case, then principle components analysis (PCA) can be used. Indeed, PCA can be used in the case of dichotomous data, that is, data that requires a 'yes-no' or 'either-or' response.

(c) The size of the sample must be large. This is like saying how long is a piece of string? How long – how large? Generally speaking the procedures will incorporate large and indeterminate margins of error if they are less than several hundred. If the sample is less than 200 it is unlikely that the results will give much validity as if there are more than 10 variables being examined.

Figure 12.3 also indicates that tests for the adequacy of the sample are also available, as shown by the Kaiser–Meyer–Olkin test which is provided by the sub-command KMO of the factor command in SPSS.

(d) The number of variables must be correspondingly large. Again – how large is large? The larger the number of items relating to a hypothesis, the greater is the opportunity for correlations to exist which possess some form of theoretical as well as statistical validity. As the theories are concerned with the development of parsimonious model building, then a requirement for 'fat' exists in order for any shedding process to take place. In other situations, the pre-selection of variables may have taken place. This is not to say that such a pre-selection is not without some advantages in given circumstances, but as a rule pre-judgement is to be avoided. In many instances of significant research such as the development of the SERVQUAL model, or the Ragheb and Beard Leisure Motivation Scale, the researchers have developed scales of approximately 35 items as a result of pruning from an original number of over 120.

(e) Generally speaking, there should not be less than 10 variables. Further, the rule of thumb to be adopted is that there should be 10 or more respondents per item subject to a constraint of an absolute minimum of 150 respondents. If there are over approximately 500 respondents, the number of items per respondent can be relaxed, but should be never less than 5 respondents per variable. In this context variable, item and question on a questionnaire are interchangeable terms.

TESTING FOR GROUPS – THE NATURE OF THE TESTS

There are a number of tests of group frequency and identity. As variants of discriminant analysis some are applicable where *a priori* knowledge exists about the group identity. Others refer to specific types or data, or are operable only under fairly strict constraints. One such example is correspondence analysis, which operates on categorical data in the form of contingency tables. Generally speaking this technique applies to two-dimensional tables and produces a graphical representation of the residuals from the independence model, but, as with other techniques, it is being explored in order to apply it to other situations involving multiple variables (see Greenacre 1983 and, for a marketing application, Fox 1993). A software package such as SPSS will present the researcher with the option of using either one of three common techniques, namely principal components analysis, factor analysis and cluster analysis. Although they appear alike, some differences exist. They also possess parallels with the regression analysis referred to in Chapter 11.

Principal components analysis

Reference has been made to the process of model building where the researcher seeks to develop a parsimonious model where as few variables as possible explain as much of the variance as possible. Principal components analysis is such a method. It looks for a few linear combinations of the original variables that can be used to summarise a data set, losing as little information as is possible. It consists of transforming a set of generally correlated variables to a new, smaller set which are uncorrelated. Of this new set, the first is the combination that explains the largest amount of variance, the second explains the next largest amount, and so on. The total potential number of components is the same number as the number of variables, which, of course, will explain all of the variance. This therefore raises the question – at what point does the researcher stop seeking new components? This is discussed below for the same considerations apply to factor analysis.

Factor analysis

Factor analysis is essentially the same as multiple regression, except that the observed variables are regressed on unobservable factors. For example, suppose the researcher is wishing to measure holiday-maker satisfaction. This could be regarded as an unobservable measure, but indicators of the level of satisfaction might be held to exist. Some may be directly observable, and the researcher might create an index based on the number of smiles, the number of jokes, the number of activities undertaken, the number of repeat trips – in short a series of actions reveal the indirect substance termed satisfaction. Equally, the researcher might create a series of items on a questionnaire relating to measures of satisfaction, and seek to assess which are the more important proxies of satisfaction.

Factor analysis begins with the calculation of the principal components in order to define the number of factors that are required. As will be demonstrated, this initial calculation produces a series of factor loadings, which can be regarded as the standardised regression coefficients in the multiple regression equation – they are the correlations between the factors and the variable. But at this stage most factors are correlated with many variables, and hence the process, rotation, is introduced. This is where the axes are rotated, which changes the values of the items, but retains their distance or relative position from each other. If the axes are maintained at 90 degrees from each other, the rotation is said to be orthogonal. Otherwise an oblique rotation is carried out. The implication of this is noted below. The result is that the observed variables fall into mutually exclusive groups with loadings being high on single factors, and small on the remaining factors. This will be easier to understand when examining the example in Figure 12.5.

So, what is the difference between the two techniques? Principal components analysis makes no assumptions about the correlational structure of the variates. It is simply a transformation of data. A parallel might be drawn with the transformation of data whereby the log is taken to obtain a linear relationship. Factor analysis on the other hand does assume that a relationship exists whereby a set of latent variables exists that are sufficient to count for the interrelationships of the variates, though not for their full variances. The literature reveals the debate about the technique. Everitt and Dunn state:

> Because the factor loadings are not determined uniquely by the basic factor model many statisticians have complained that investigators can choose to rotate factors in such a way as to get the answer they are looking for. Indeed, Blackith and Reyment (1971) suggest that the method has persisted precisely because it allows the experimenter to impose his preconceived ideas on the raw data (1991:254).

They go on to note:

> Factor analysis should be regarded as simply an additional tool for investigating the structure of multivariate observations. The main danger in its use is taking the model too seriously, since it is likely to be only a very idealised approximation to the truth in the situations in which it is generally applied. Such an approximation may, however, prove a valuable starting point for further investigations (1991:255).

In the area of tourist attitude and behaviour research this last point is important. As noted, many writers have created typologies of tourists based on motivational characteristics identified from responses to sets of questionnaires. Thus the mass tourist, the eco-tourist, the jet-setter and the action seeker have graced the pages of the journals and books. Yet our own daily experience informs us that our behaviour is changeable, dependent in part upon the roles we feel we want to play, or feel obliged to play. In a sense, the tourist does not cease to be a social chameleon when on holiday, and the typologies discovered by researchers do not represent fixed categorisations, but rather a series of potential roles. Of these roles, the holiday-maker or holiday-taker (is our language more revealing here than is normally noted?) may play a few or many, and in one sequence or another throughout the period of the holiday. The typologies are hence one approximation of a truth, not the entire truth.

Cluster analysis

Cluster analysis is a related, but different technique. The groups are created from a fusing of an individual with the closest next individual. At the next stage, another fusing is created. At some stage, the fused group may be joined with another. After a number of stages all of the sample is joined together as one large group. A hierarchical process based on similarities is thus developed. This is illustrated graphically by the dendogram, as it is known, and is demonstrated when discussing the computer commands below. It also follows that different approaches to measurement may be undertaken. On the one hand measures of similarity can be used – the inverse is to use measures of dissimilarity. This description of the process also highlights another potential problem with cluster analysis, and that is the phenomenon of chaining. This term is used to describe the tendency of the method to incorporate an intermediate point into an existing cluster rather than commence a new grouping. Hence sophisticated computer packages present a series of alternative approaches, and, as in many cases, the researcher has to utilise the options available, while clearly understanding the bases of such options.

Cluster analysis is used where not only the membership of groups is unknown, but also the actual number of groups. It is therefore perhaps the most susceptible of the three techniques to imposition of a solution upon the data by the researcher because at some stage a group is either going to be formed or broken down into a cluster, which may support the hypothesis the researcher is hoping to find. An additional difficulty is that as the groups break down into smaller groupings, inequalities of group size inevitably emerge. The need to produce a finer distinction by splitting the larger groups tends to produce, at the other extreme, smaller clusters which have yet to fuse into larger groups. Thus researchers have to appreciate the nuances in their data – one of the arguments for them to key in their own data rather than let another do it for them is that this is one way in which they develop that intuitive feel. This has to be combined with a number of tests for determining the optimum number of clusters. Everitt and Dunn (1991) strongly argue that scatter plots should be used in this process. Others such as Cohen *et al.* (1977) also suggest plotting squared distances from cluster centroids to entities near the centroid as a means of examining the cohesiveness of the grouping. Again, many computer packages include diagram construction features. Having outlined some of the features of the tests, the next stage is to look at each in turn in relation to the results that can be obtained, and how to interpret them.

PRINCIPAL COMPONENTS ANALYSIS

In MINITAB the command is simply PCA followed by the columns which are to be examined. In NCSS the item 'Principal Component Analysis' is selected from within the Statistical and Data Analysis option. The columns to be examined are chosen, and the researcher can then select from a number of reports. For SPSS the command is within the portfolio of commands relating to Factor Analysis, and is, for the data in the Appendix:

FACTOR VAR = KNOW TO TIME.

The result derived from this is shown in Figure 12.4. The first table of results show that Principal Components Analysis produces the same number of components as there are variables, but has grouped them in such a way as to indicate that 5 components 'explain' 70.2 per cent of the variance. How one selects the number of factors with which to work is discussed below. One way of interpreting the components is to think of the first factor as representing a regression line which best fits all the data points. This factor accounts for 24.7 per cent of the variance. Having drawn this first line, a second regression calculation is undertaken on the differences between the variable scores and the line (i.e. on the residuals), and this forms the second factor. This second factor 'explains' 17.3 per cent of the variance; and so on. The table also includes the heading labelled 'eigenvalue'. This can be viewed as an index of how much variance in the original set of variables a factor or principal component accounts

factor var = know to time.

---- FACTOR ANALYSIS ----

Extraction 1 for Analysis 1, Principal-Components Analysis (PC)

Initial Statistics:

Variable	Communality	*	Factor	Eigenvalue	Pct of Var	Cum Pct
KNOW	1.00000	*	1	3.46388	24.7	24.7
AVOID	1.00000	*	2	2.42423	17.3	42.1
BUILD	1.00000	*	3	1.58926	11.4	53.4
CHALL	1.00000	*	4	1.33578	9.5	63.0
IMAG	1.00000	*	5	1.01335	7.2	70.2
CALM	1.00000	*	6	.73995	5.3	75.5
CLOSE	1.00000	*	7	.72335	5.2	80.6
SPORT	1.00000	*	8	.55781	4.0	84.6
PHYS	1.00000	*	9	.51578	3.7	88.3
BELONG	1.00000	*	10	.44681	3.2	91.5
DISC	1.00000	*	11	.34635	2.5	94.0
MENTAL	1.00000	*	12	.34457	2.5	96.4
OTHERS	1.00000	*	13	.25615	1.8	98.3
TIME	1.00000	*	14	.24272	1.7	100.0

    PC Extracted   5 factors.

Figure 12.4 Deriving eigenvalues for factor analysis

```
            ---- FACTOR ANALYSIS ----

  Factor Matrix:

            FACTOR 1 FACTOR 2 FACTOR 3 FACTOR 4 FACTOR 5

  KNOW      .46870   -.31124   .59412    .14189    .02302
  AVOID     .14124    .75889   .11834    .00841    .35290
  BUILD     .75621   -.09734  -.05534    .09666   -.26340
  CHALL     .65708   -.23284   .16346   -.44016    .16481
  IMAG      .61136   -.18825   .44463    .00910    .11152
  CALM      .15339    .69411   .36224    .13442    .01063
  CLOSE     .75328    .12138  -.17563   -.11210   -.15230
  SPORT     .52906    .03735  -.25786   -.50509    .45989
  PHYS      .02187    .72897   .09886    .21301   -.21537
  BELONG    .48220    .15832  -.00961   -.30854   -.61971
  DISC      .33856   -.15396   .46077    .49315    .11755
  MENTAL    .11645    .74941   .03673   -.24362    .00621
  OTHERS    .58648   -.03467  -.53118    .39205   -.10368
  TIME      .52046    .10688  -.51046    .47941    .29912
```

Figure 12.5 Factor analysis

for. As the researcher is seeking to find a component that explains more of the variance than the original variable accounted for, then the convention is that one selects as being important the number of factors that possess an eigenvalue of greater than one.

The next table of statistics produced by SPSS is a table of correlations between the variables and the factors. This is shown in Figure 12.5. It indicates that while a series of correlations appear to exist they are not without some difficulty in interpretation. Factor one seems, for example, to correlate quite highly with some social factors such as 'building friendships' (0.76), but also with some intellectual components such as the 'use of imagination' (0.61). However, inasmuch as this factor is accounting for the single most important contribution to total variance, some such pattern of correlation is to be expected.

FACTOR ANALYSIS

As described above, factor analysis takes the process further, based on an assumption that linear relationships apply between the variables and unobserved latent factors. Under NCSS the factor analysis panel is selected, and this presents the researcher with the option of defining the criteria to be used in selecting factors. Thus, the number of factors to be used may be defined, or criteria relating to the minimum eigenvalue can be selected. The report will present the results, and also offer the plots of the factors against each other so the researcher can check their cohesiveness. The command under SPSS for basic factor analysis using a varimax rotation is as above.

This raises the question – what criteria are to be used for determining the number of principal components or factors to be used? Generally speaking the following criteria apply.

(a) Include just enough components or factors to explain some relatively large percentage of the total variation. At least two-thirds of the variation should be explained, preferably over 70 per cent, by the major four to eight factors depending upon the number of variables.
(b) Exclude those factors or principal components whose eigenvalues are less than one. Variants of this rule exist. Joliffe (1972, 1973) has proposed in the case of principal components analysis that values of above 0.7 be used.
(c) Cattell (1965) suggested a test that has been widely adopted, known as the scree test. This involves making a plot of the eigenvalues and choosing the number of factors at the point where the eigenvalues begin to level off to form a horizontal line – it is a turning point on the curve. SPSS permits the plotting of the scree test with the command:

FACTOR VAR = KNOW TO TIME / PLOT EIGEN.

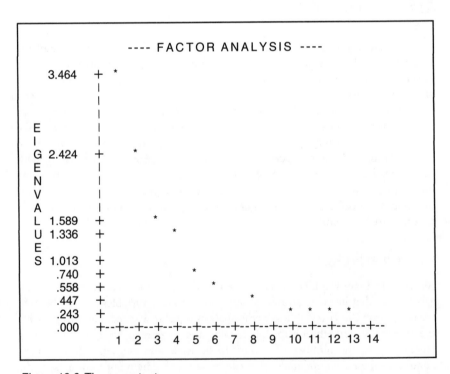

Figure 12.6 The scree test

The resultant scree plot in this instance (see Figure 12.6) is again quite interesting in that the curve appears to begin to bend after the fourth factor, but seems to 're-adjust' itself around the fifth factor.

This lends itself to a fourth rule:

(d) Carefully examine the data, observing the contents of the factor loadings, and the results of running with more or less factors. There is, of course, a significant problem with such advice, and that is that there is the danger that the researcher selects that result which best suits the sought for explanation.

With respect to this the comments of Babbie are pertinent:

> If you are unable to specify the conditions under which your hypothesis would be disproved, your hypothesis is in reality either a tautology or useless. In a sense, factor analysis suffers this defect. No matter what data input, factor analysis produces a solution in the form of factors. Thus if you were asking, 'Are there any patterns among these variables?' the answer always would be 'yes'... The generation of factors by no means insures meaning (1979:508).

Factor analysis is a technique for the exploration of data. Not to explore the data in order to better understand the information it conveys would represent a failing on the part of the researcher. Equally, it is for the researcher to appreciate the purpose of the technique, the means that exist for further testing the information, and to report the findings in as full a manner as is possible. Such reporting includes the necessity of indicating that the chosen interpretation might have been considered the most 'optimal' solution, and the criteria for so believing this must be stated.

The next stage is now actually to rotate and examine the nature of the results. These will have been fully generated by the commands indicated above. Hence the need now is to assess and explain the resultant tables (see Figure 12.7). The first of the final statistics tables reproduces the eigenvalues, and lists the communality for each variable. The communality is the proportion of variance explained by the common factors, that is it represents the extent to which the item can be 'explained' by some combination of the five factors. This again relates back to the parsimonious nature of developing theory. Here the researcher will be looking for values of 0.6 or above, dependent on the size of the sample. The next stage of the table represents the actual factor loadings after the rotation has been completed. What is being sought here? Ideally, each item should be heavily loaded on one factor (that is 0.6 and above), and lightly loaded on the remaining factors (that is have scores of 0.2 or less).

In this particular case it would seem that factor one consists of items relating to relaxation 'avoid hustle and bustle' (0.81); 'be in a calm atmosphere' (0.77); 'physically' and 'mentally relax' (0.71 and 0.71 respectively). Factor two has an intellectual component whereby 'improve knowledge' (0.81), 'develop imagination' (0.70) and 'discover new places' (0.73) correlate closely. Factor three has two items 'be with others' (0.83) and 'have a good time' (0.91) – implying

```
                ---- FACTOR ANALYSIS ----

Final Statistics:

Variable    Communality  *  Factor  Eigenvalue  Pct of Var  Cum Pct

KNOW          .69018     *    1      3.46388       24.7       24.7
AVOID         .73448     *    2      2.42423       17.3       42.1
BUILD         .66312     *    3      1.58926       11.4       53.4
CHALL         .73359     *    4      1.33578        9.5       63.0
IMAG          .61942     *    5      1.01335        7.2       70.2
CALM          .65472     *
CLOSE         .64877     *
SPORT         .81441     *
PHYS          .63341     *
BELONG        .73691     *
DISC          .60765     *
MENTAL        .63591     *
OTHERS        .79177     *
TIME          .86218     *


Rotated Factor Matrix:

             FACTOR 1 FACTOR 2 FACTOR 3 FACTOR 4 FACTOR 5

KNOW         −.08808   .80899  −.05972   .08568   .13058
AVOID         .81136  −.01032   .08769   .19805  −.17074
BUILD        −.04227   .36449   .43287   .15415   .56333
CHALL        −.10822   .38105  −.00922   .68987   .31728
IMAG          .01366   .70061   .04702   .30130   .18809
CALM          .77646   .19503  −.03617  −.09725   .05495
CLOSE         .13937   .15476   .41115   .35599   .55643
SPORT         .06381  −.05475   .20393   .87208   .07226
PHYS          .70825  −.07412   .07561  −.30897   .15848
BELONG        .11805   .00707  −.00766   .07749   .84667
DISC          .04345   .73445   .18046  −.15176  −.10362
MENTAL        .72636  −.20880  −.06932   .17176   .17438
OTHERS       −.08375   .03384   .83826   .01834   .28388
TIME          .09995   .05536   .90575   .14321  −.09076
```

Figure 12.7 Factor analysis of leisure motivation scale

perhaps a social factor at operation. Factor four contains physical components relating to sport (0.87) and 'challenging physical abilities' (0.69). Lastly factor 5 is heavily loaded on developing a sense of belonging (0.84). It is also to be noted that the items 'building' and 'developing friendships' are divided between the social group and this factor. The researcher might conclude that there is evidence for the Ragheb and Beard Leisure Motivation Scale discussed in Chapter 2, but

```
                    ---- FACTOR ANALYSIS ----

Factor Correlation Matrix:

              FACTOR 1 FACTOR 2 FACTOR 3 FACTOR 4 FACTOR 5

FACTOR 1       1.00000
FACTOR 2        .05465  1.00000
FACTOR 3        .14818  -.05279  1.00000
FACTOR 4       -.14568   .00480  -.12198  1.00000
FACTOR 5       -.17103  -.07711  -.16530   .21771  1.00000
```

Figure 12.8 Correlation between factors

will also have to consider in more detail how these two items might be treated. For example, perhaps the fit can be improved if 'a sense of belonging' is dropped? Would the other two factors now merge into the 'social' factor? But what would this signify? One of the advantages of the computer is that it permits the researcher to develop a series of alternative scenarios to be easily structured and considered.

Earlier reference was made to forms of rotation – orthogonal and oblique. Orthogonal rotation seeks to maximise the lack of correlation between the resultant factors – to produce uncorrelated factors. Various algorithms are used, of which the most common is the varimax.

The differences that are obtained from these various techniques are generally small. That being the case it is worthwhile for the researcher to undertake an oblique rotation. Although this will change the factor loadings to a degree, it should not change the composition of the factor. What is now permitted, at least under SPSS, is the calculation of the factor correlation matrix. The command for doing this is:

FACTOR VAR = KNOW TO TIME/ROTATION = OBLIMIN.

The resultant factor correlation matrix is shown in Figure 12.8. The reason for the test now becomes obvious. Orthogonal rotation creates an 'identity' in the correlation matrix. This is not true of oblique rotation where it is now possible to examine the degree of inter-action between the factors. It would appear to be comparatively small, and hence the independence of the factors is confirmed.

A NOTE ON PRESENTATION

As might have already been discovered, trying to follow the tables while the variables retain the order of listing as it originates in the questionnaire is not particularly easy. It becomes even harder when the questionnaire might contain

Rotated Factor Matrix:

	FACTOR 1	FACTOR 2	FACTOR 3	FACTOR 4	FACTOR 5
AVOID	.81136	−.01032	.08769	.19805	−.17074
CALM	.77646	.19503	−.03617	−.09725	.05495
MENTAL	.72636	−.20880	−.06932	.17176	.17438
PHYS	.70825	−.07412	.07561	−.30897	.15848
KNOW	−.08808	.80899	−.05972	.08568	.13058
DISC	.04345	.73445	.18046	−.15176	−.10362
IMAG	.01366	.70061	.04702	.30130	.18809
TIME	.09995	.05536	.90575	.14321	−.09076
OTHERS	−.08375	.03384	.83826	.01834	.28388
SPORT	.06381	−.05475	.20393	.87208	.07226
CHALL	−.10822	.38105	−.00922	.68987	.31728
BELONG	.11805	.00707	−.00766	.07749	.84667
BUILD	−.04227	.36449	.43287	.15415	.56333
CLOSE	.13937	.15476	.41115	.35599	.55643

Figure 12.9 Presenting factors

as many as over one hundred items. A good discipline to develop is to present the items in the amended order of the clusters as demonstrated in Figure 12.9. This is much clearer to follow. Fortunately SPSS permits this to be done from within the software by the use of the sub-command FORMAT = SORT. The command takes the form of:

FACTOR VAR = KNOW TO TIME / FORMAT = SORT.

One advantage of this format is that not only is it much easier to read, but also, of course, it can be incorporated directly into a document being prepared with the use of a word-processing package such as WordPerfect by simply importing the resultant SPSS.LIS file. Of more importance is for the researcher now to begin interpreting the context in terms of the grouping of the variables, and to attribute to each factor a name that encapsulates the context.

CLUSTER ANALYSIS

It may be recalled that cluster analysis was described as a technique where the researcher seeks to identify the underlying, latent groups, where neither the number or composition of the groups are known. It is a furtherance of knowledge of the data because, unlike factor analysis, which has been used simply to develop a number of groups, cluster analysis will actually permit the researcher to allocate respondents to specific categories. Suppose that cluster analysis confirmed the finding that motivations could be grouped into five. The researcher would now be able to allocate the respondents to each group, and subsequently examine the differences within each either by scores on items contained in the questionnaire, or by socio-economic variables. Cluster analysis thus represents a very powerful tool for the researcher. Unfortunately, it is also one of the more complex and requires considerable checking of results. Unlike many of the statistical techniques so far discussed, it might require a series of qualitative judgements on the part of the researcher. Again, the best way to demonstrate this is to work through an example using the data derived from the Appendix.

The number of clusters will almost certainly not be the same as the number of factors identified by using factor analysis. The reason for this is obvious. Suppose that the factor, relaxation was discovered as a motivation for taking holidays. Almost certainly, holiday-makers could be categorised as having either high, medium or low relaxation needs. The one factor thus develops into three clusters. Now, in considering a five-factor solution, and attributing a threefold categorisation of high, medium or low to each immediately creates a matrix of fifteen potential different clusters of holiday-makers. In practice there will not be that many, but the problem is just how many? Indeed, dependent on what are seen as the key axes, the researcher may end up with a smaller number of clusters. To add to the difficulty, there is no one definite way of answering the question of how many clusters there are. A common starting point is to use what is known as an icicle plot or dendogram. Cohen *et al.* (1977), as noted above, suggests the plot of squared distances from cluster centroids. Everitt and Dunn (1991) suggest canonical plots. The user of statistical software possesses the advantage of being able to rerun the analysis using a number of different clusters and examine the outcome of each run to identify which solution appears to be the most optimum. Hence, again, the process possesses a tautology in the sense that a solution will be derived. It can only be stressed that solutions to a degree possess some validity only in terms of the original theory being proposed, and the methodology being used to test the theory. In many instances of tourism research, this places a heavy emphasis upon questionnaire design. The danger of this category of techniques is that however badly phrased the questions are, or however dubious is the questionnaire content the computer produces answers.

While SPSS permits the drawing of an icicle plot or dendogram, in the author's experience these are of comparatively limited use when the sample size consists of several thousands. The first problem for the researcher is that the desktop PC may not possess sufficient computing power. Indeed, the minimum specification for dealing with a sample size of over a thousand respondents with a hundred variables per respondent of which, say, 25 are to be incorporated into the analysis, is a 386DX with a maths processor, with 4 MB memory. The second problem is that having printed out several reams of paper, it is difficult visually to scan the result in any meaningful manner.

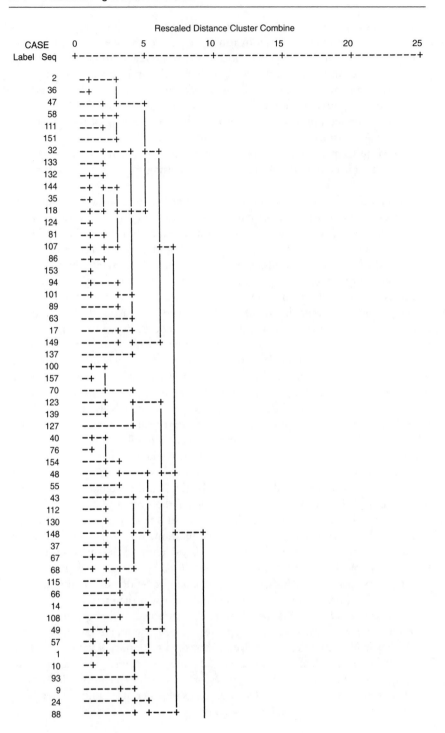

Rescaled Distance Cluster Combine

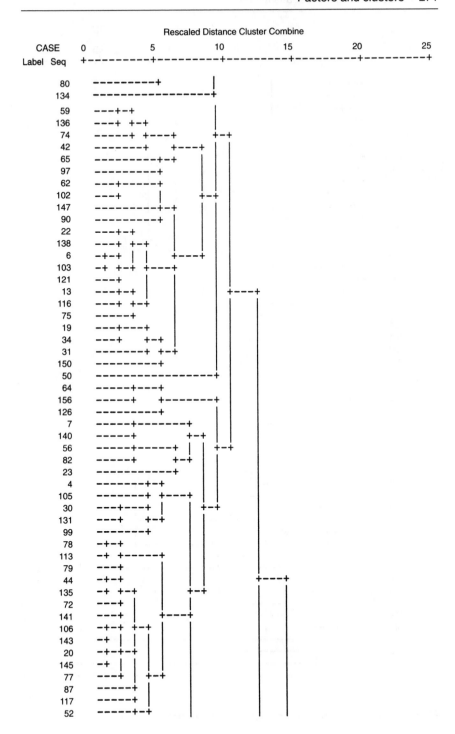

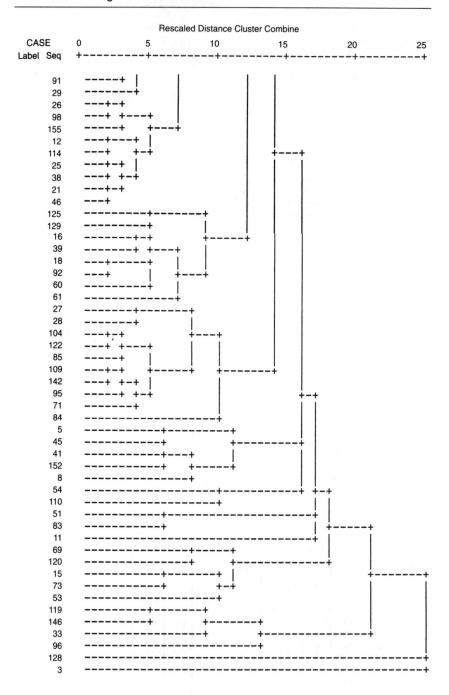

Figure 12.10 Dendogram using average linkage (between groups)

With small samples, the problems are not so great, and this can be illustrated with a dendogram derived from the data in the Appendix. The dendogram (Figure 12.10) seems to show that respondents 2, 36, 47, 58, 111 and 151 form one close group, but these are subsequently linked to another close group consisting of respondents 32, 133, 132, 144, 35, 118, 124, 81, 107, 86, 153 and 94. But equally it can be seen that others are near to this unit. The visual interpretation of the dendogram quite quickly becomes difficult to sort out, other than it can be seen that groups are clustered together, while at the other extreme, towards the end of the dendogram, it can be seen that there are outliers such as respondents 128 and 3. At this point it is worth checking back to the original data in order to see if the existence of a larger number of non-responses might account for these outliers.

A more fruitful approach is probably to undertake a series of runs to produce clusters and in particular to assess the value of the cluster centres. Here, one is using the capability of the software to produce cluster centre values under different scenarios to identify the number where clusters have large distances between them, thereby indicating the existence of independent groupings. Generally speaking the software will permit the researcher to define the number of clusters. This can be supported by an analysis of variance. Therefore, after an initial examination of the data the researcher might want to try to narrow down the optimal number of groups by (under, for example, SPSS) typing in a series of commands that produce output for subsequent decision taking. This would take the form:

QUICK CLUSTER KNOW TO TIME/CRITERIA = CLUST(4)
/PRINT DISTANCE ANOVA.

This shows the number of clusters being examined being increased from 3 to 15. The type of output that results from such commands is examined in Figure 12.11. It should be noted that the original data derived from the 7-point scale are being used because in this case all the variables possess the same scale. Where this is not the case the researcher may wish to use the variables in a standardised form. At this stage it must be noted that the following table does not purport to be an optimal solution – it is designed to show the stages involved in the procedures.

The first set of results is derived from the calculation of the final cluster centres. It can be seen that cluster 1 seems to be differentiated in the sense that it is scoring more highly on the relaxation items, while cluster 2 tends to score more highly on the social components. Cluster 4 appear to be moderates, while cluster 3 would appear to be a 'strange' grouping.

The distance between the clusters appears to be 'good', and this is confirmed by the Analysis of Variance (ANOVA). This is shown in Figure 12.12.

The results also indicate the number in each group, and from this it can be seen that cluster 3 simply consists of two in number. It is also to be noted that all respondents were included, and hence the 2 that form cluster 3 were probably quick cluster know to time /criteria=clust(4) /print=distance anova

Final Cluster Centers.

Cluster	KNOW	AVOID	BUILD	CHALL
1	3.6346	5.5385	2.5192	1.5000
2	5.0366	5.6829	4.5244	3.8293
3	6.0000	7.0000	6.0000	4.0000
4	4.8571	3.5238	2.7143	2.4286

Cluster	IMAG	CALM	CLOSE	SPORT
1	1.9808	5.5192	1.5385	1.5385
2	4.4634	5.5244	3.4634	3.4878
3	6.0000	7.0000	5.0000	4.0000
4	4.0476	3.6667	1.2381	1.4286

Cluster	PHYS	BELONG	DISC	MENTAL
1	5.9615	2.0769	5.5962	6.4231
2	5.4268	3.2561	6.3293	5.8171
3	5.0000	6.0000	3.0000	5.0000
4	3.3333	1.6190	6.0952	3.4762

Cluster	OTHERS	TIME
1	2.7308	2.4615
2	4.5488	4.7561
3	3.5000	1.0000
4	3.4762	3.0000

Distances between Final Cluster centers.

Cluster	1	2	3	4
1	.0000			
2	6.0210	.0000		
3	10.0530	7.9707	.0000	
4	5.5817	6.2913	11.8513	.0000

Figure 12.11 Final cluster centres

outliers, perhaps due to missing data. This can easily be checked in that the composition of the different clusters can now be viewed from the subset of the SPSS command:

Analysis of Variance.

Variable	Cluster MS	DF	Error MS	DF	F	Prob
KNOW	23.0519	3	2.4282	153.0	9.4933	.000
AVOID	28.7962	3	2.7838	153.0	10.3443	.000
BUILD	52.8627	3	2.2073	153.0	23.9490	.000
CHALL	59.8999	3	3.0441	153.0	19.6771	.000
IMAG	71.0642	3	2.7211	153.0	26.1163	.000
CALM	22.8079	3	2.4320	153.0	9.3782	.000
CLOSE	56.5896	3	2.1773	153.0	25.9911	.000
SPORT	51.9513	3	3.1017	153.0	16.7495	.000
PHYS	35.1419	3	2.3703	153.0	14.8261	.000
BELONG	30.6033	3	3.9233	153.0	7.8004	.000
DISC	11.8453	3	1.3623	153.0	8.6948	.000
MENTAL	56.2053	3	2.0927	153.0	26.8575	.000
OTHERS	35.9300	3	2.4462	153.0	14.6879	.000
TIME	65.3523	3	3.7258	153.0	17.5405	.000

Number of Cases in each Cluster.

Cluster	unweighted cases	weighted cases
1	52.0	52.0
2	82.0	82.0
3	2.0	2.0
4	21.0	21.0
Missing	0	
Total	157.0	157.0

Figure 12.12 Analysis of variance

QUICK CLUSTER KNOW TO TIME /CRITERIA =
CLUST(4) /PRINT = ID(NUMBER).

From Figure 12.13 it can be seen that respondent 3 has a very low distance score, and is in fact one of the outliers that was also identified from the dendogram. Those forming group 3 might now be omitted from any further examination.

The next stage is to examine the different clusters more carefully to note the differences between them. Their scores on the respective variables, including the ANOVA and associated probabilities is known, and at this point the researcher departs entirely from the 'science' of statistics into the purely verbal if not 'artistic' by identifying the three groups by a descriptive name. Cluster 1 might be called the 'relaxers', cluster 2 the 'marginally more socially minded' and cluster 3 the 'moderates'. How can one obtain more information about each of the groups.

quick cluster know to time /criteria=clust(4) /print=id(number)
QUICK CLUSTER requires 1336 BYTES of workspace for execution.

NUMBER	Cluster	Distance
1.00	1	7.016
2.00	1	6.877
3.00	3	.455
4.00	2	7.710
5.00	2	10.478
6.00	2	7.409
7.00	2	8.053
8.00	2	10.245
9.00	1	7.361
10.00	1	7.902
11.00	1	11.212
12.00	2	7.137
13.00	4	8.793
14.00	1	9.158
15.00	2	6.431
16.00	1	10.401
17.00	1	8.796
⋮		
161.00	2	8.123
162.00	2	8.432
163.00	2	7.944
164.00	1	9.525

Figure 12.13 Clusters – analysing variance

Command	Commentary
QUICK CLUSTER KNOW TO TIME/CRIT=CLUST(4) /SAVE=CLUSTER(MEMBER).	Sets up the four clusters and saves the allocation of respondents to a variable entitled 'MEMBER'.
RECODE MEMBER (3,0)	Prepares data for excluding cluster three.
MISSING VALUE MEMBER SEX (0).	Deletes missing values for sex and the recoded cluster three.
ONEWAY KNOW BY MEMBER(1,4) /STA=1,3. CROSSTABS TABLES= MEMBER BY SEX /STAT=CHISQ.	Does analysis of variance. Does test for gender composition of clusters.

Figure 12.14 Using clusters for further analysis

---- O N E W A Y ----

Variable KNOW   increase knowledge

By Variable MEMBER

Analysis of Variance

Source	D.F.	Sum of Squares	Mean Squares	F Ratio	F Prob.
Between Groups	2	64.9581	32.4790	13.3601	.0000
Within Groups	152	369.5194	2.4310		
Total	154	434.4774			

Group	Count	Mean	Standard Deviation	Standard Error	95 Pct	Conf	Int for Mean
Grp 1	52	3.6346	1.8044	.2502	3.1323	To	4.1370
Grp 2	82	5.0366	1.3828	.1527	4.7327	To	5.3404
Grp 4	21	4.8571	1.5584	.3401	4.1478	To	5.5665
Total	155	4.5419	1.6797	.1349	4.2754	To	4.8085

Tests for Homogeneity of Variances

Cochrans C = Max. Variance/Sum(Variances) = .4286, P = .126 (Approx.)
Bartlett-Box F = 2.254, P = .105
Maximum Variance / Minimum Variance   1.703

Figure 12.15 Testing for analysis of variance between clusters

Generally speaking the software will permit the user to create a new variable or new column in which the information is taken from the last set of results, and an 'identifier' is allocated to each respondent indicating their membership of a particular cluster. In the case of SPSS the sub-command /SAVE = CLUSTER(MEMBER) will allocate a new column to a new variable. In the casee of earlier versions of MINITAB and NCSS the researcher might have to do this by actually keying in the data into new columns. This now permits an examination of the groups by using the commands previously discussed. For example, the researcher might wish to check, say, the scores on the variable KNOW in more detail, and to find whether the clusters are marked by any significant differences in composition by gender.

The way in which this can be set up is illustrated in Figure 12.14. Note that the commands have taken advantage of the recode function in order to allocate to cluster 3 a missing value code, which therefore means that it is now excluded from the following tests. The commands that are used are those of ONEWAY and CROSSTABS as already described.

The results (see Figure 12.15) confirm those noted above in the cluster centres and ANOVA test. It will be seen that the mean score for the first cluster is 3.63, with a standard deviation of 1.8, and for the other two clusters the scores are respectively, 5.03 and 1.3 for cluster 2, and 4.85 and 1.5 for cluster 4.

It is also to be noted in Figure 12.15 that the exclusion of cluster 3 has actu-

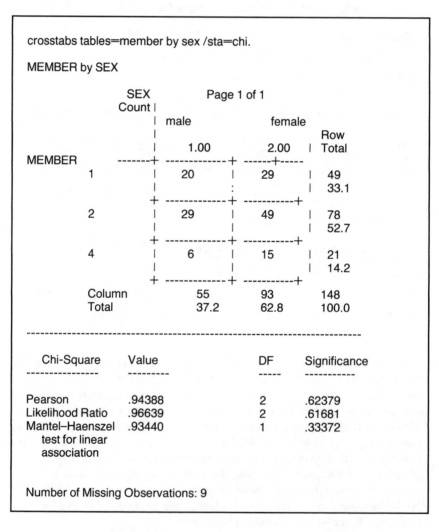

```
crosstabs tables=member by sex /sta=chi.

MEMBER by SEX

                    SEX          Page 1 of 1
                  Count I
                      I  male           female
                      I                            Row
                      I     1.00          2.00  I  Total
MEMBER        -------+ -------------+ ------+-----
          1           I    20       I    29    I    49
                      I             :           I    33.1
                      + -------------+ -----------+
          2           I    29       I    49    I    78
                      I             I           I    52.7
                      + -------------+ -----------+
          4           I     6       I    15    I    21
                      I             I           I    14.2
                      + -------------+ -----------+
          Column              55         93        148
          Total               37.2       62.8      100.0

----------------------------------------------------------------

     Chi-Square      Value              DF     Significance
  ----------------   ---------          -----  -----------

Pearson            .94388               2      .62379
Likelihood Ratio   .96639               2      .61681
Mantel–Haenszel    .93440               1      .33372
   test for linear
   association

Number of Missing Observations: 9
```

Figure 12.16 Testing frequencies between clusters

ally improved the F-Ratio from 9.49 to 13.36. Note too the degrees of freedom have been reduced from 3 to 2, reflecting the changed composition of the sample in terms of number of groupings. The other scores also referred to earlier with regard to the homogeneity of variance are also present.

The final set of commands permitted the testing of the clusters as to one aspect of their socio-economic structure – namely gender composition. This again used a test previously discussed, namely crosstabs with a request for the chi-square statistic. The result of this is shown in Figure 12.16. It can be seen that there is no significant difference in the sexual make up of the three clusters.

SUMMARY

This chapter has reviewed the use of three powerful statistical techniques. It has also been argued that the tests require prior to their use a number of tests to ensure that the data are sufficient for these techniques. The final series of commands illustrate that to understand best the results of these classification techniques, they need to be used in harness with the simpler ones described in previous chapters.

It was also noted that in using these techniques the researcher is not dependent upon the computer or the technique to produce 'the' answer. Rather, there is an art in statistics, in that the final clustering that is produced is a question of judgement, aided by statistics it is true, but still nonetheless a matter of judgement. That judgement can only be made by reference to the underlying model that the researcher has proposed, and by an intimate knowledge of the quality and nature of the data they are handling. This is probably true of many of what are deemed to be the more sophisticated statistical techniques, and hence there is a responsibility upon the researcher to ensure that they are familiar with the raw data they have obtained.

It has been a theme of the chapters that the relationship between hypothesis creation, research design, questionnaire design, evaluative techniques being used and the interpretation of outcomes are not sequential stages in a process, but are all part of a holistic procedure, where the failure of any one stage, or the failure to consider properly any one point, can invalidate the whole. This is probably at its most evident in the tests that have been considered in this chapter.

Chapter 13

Final words

There are some natural extensions of the tests described in the preceding chapters. The researcher may wish to test for the differences between clusters using discriminate analysis once the number of clusters have been identified. Nonetheless, the tests described in the earlier chapters will permit the researcher into tourist attitudes to undertake a significant degree of thorough testing of statistical data. What will also be clear is that the simpler tests are of importance and that any researcher should not immediately seek to apply more sophisticated constructs without a proper appraisal of the nature of their data. In short, it does pay to examine carefully the frequencies and distribution of data, to test the correlations and the cross-tabulations before moving to more complex tests.

In the review of the literature, the importance of the nature of the question, its wording, its meaning and the setting of its voicing were all found to be very important. The failure to properly consider the question, whether in question-naire design, focus groups or conversation can only lead to results of lesser value than might otherwise have been the case. Time spent in asking simple questions such as:

Why do I want this information?
Why is it important?
If important, how do I ask it?
If important, when do I ask it?

are all as important as what do I ask? In spite of all the words spoken and written about research, and regardless of the advances in research design, and computer analysis, the four words, what, why, when and how are still the basic questions to be asked by any researcher. It is to be noted that they refer not only to the grand scheme of the research and the hypotheses and contentions being examined, but also to the detail of the actual research process.

Given that this is the case, and given the main concern of research into tourist satisfaction, the researcher must always be aware of the interaction between the supposed objective and the experienced – between the rational and the individualistic interpretation of events called the subjective. As noted, this raises questions of the methodology to be adopted in the research, and hence the concern with means of attitude measurement outlined in Chapters 3 and 4. This concern is not simply one of identifying the nature and content of attitudes, but of seeking to ensure that the researcher obtains the richest possible data from the time spent with the respondent. The situation rarely occurs where the researcher can return to the respondent and ask for amplification of a viewpoint. Hence, in the one-shot situation that is characteristic of much of student research, it is important to adopt some of the practices suggested in the earlier chapters. The use of gap analysis between expectation and perception is better than a simple frequency count of activities. The use of scales either to rank or score responses permits a range of techniques to be used that are superior to simply requiring a yes or no response.

Perhaps in many ways the researcher into tourism satisfaction is a naïve and optimistic animal, feeling capable of reducing complex human emotions into a series of definable terms that might permit future understanding of future experiences by other tourists in new places. The task is daunting. Consider how MacCannell describes his reaction to a visit to the Vietnam Memorial in Washington, DC.

> In the back streets of the universe where the literal and the figurative converge, in the unconscious, black is also the colour which permits reflection. When you approach the Vietnam Memorial, you see yourself clearly reflected in the polished surface. It involves you.... First you see your feet only. It is not really you. It is just your feet. Then you descend the gentle slope, and the monument ascends above you, and the names of the dead.... Suddenly, at the moment you no longer notice the reflection of your own feet, you see your own face in the monument with the name of a dead soldier written across it, one across your forehead, another across your eyes, cheeks, mouth. This is the moment, often remarked, where many of the visitors to the Vietnam Memorial ... break down and cry (MacCannell 1992:281).

In this piece of powerful text MacCannell writes from the soul of his experience of a visit in a way which is not going to be caught by a questionnaire. It catches a truth that he expresses for many. It is all the more powerful being based on an informed and imaginative insight born of an experience of research and an ability to empathise with fellow visitors.

The subjective in researching tourism satisfaction must always be borne in mind. Tourism possesses the potential, at least momentarily, to calm the troubled mind as the tourist seeks relaxation. It possesses the capacity for catharsis. In his play *Shirley Valentine* Willy Russell illustrates how the fortnight escape changed the life of his heroine, and her husband, as in a new environment she discovered her own self beneath the layers of (self) imposed senses of duty. This phenomenon is not a work of fiction, but of a novelist again observing the reality of some people's lives. In research in Majorca in 1993, the author talked to a lady in a bar at Puerto de Andraitx. She described herself as the 'original Shirley Valentine'. She had arrived for a holiday over a decade earlier, found in herself the strength to divorce her husband and returned to live, without regrets, in Majorca.

The implications of such experiences for researchers into tourism satisfaction are many. They must capture the tedium and the excitement of the tourist experience, identify what accounts for it without loss of the emotion, while remaining true to the wider picture of movements of people, and the implications of such movements for hosts, environments and economic results. The researchers must also both trust and distrust their own emotion. Trust it because they too are tourists and can identify with the actions and feelings of their peers – distrust it because their background, reading and past research experience are not typical of those tourists. There is the temptation to project feelings, motives and interpretations on to others, who may be far less (or perhaps even more) critical of either self or situation than the researcher.

Thus, from the complex tests of the last few chapters, the circle begins to complete itself. In undertaking research the researcher exposes not only the events, the feelings and the assessments of their respondents, but also themselves. The choice of what was thought to be important, the means of examining it, the interpretations imposed upon the data, are not simply statements arising from the implementation of some research method, but are also the expression of how the researcher has chosen to approach the subject and respondents. Researchers are faced with choices – to use qualitative methods, or quantitative; to ignore or discuss the minority viewpoint; even to publish or not to publish; to honour or not to honour the confidentiality of the data – and, in the final analysis, to lie or be truthful, and not to engage in the semantics that do not fully reveal the findings that did not support the hypothesis. In short, just as the first chapter dealt with the ethics of research, so it is pertinent to finish with the same topic.

For research to illustrate some truth about tourist behaviour, to seek to understand the implications of this complex part of human interaction with environment and others within a context of relaxation – a type of relaxation that is possibly a characteristic of contemporary human society and one not experienced by the majority in past societies, it requires the researcher to be thorough, exhaustive, methodical, imaginative, emphatic, informed, decisive, and communicative. But all of these virtues are naught if integrity is omitted. The use of the word integrity is perhaps in itself indicative. Why not the word truth? Perhaps it is the curse of the modern researcher that, denied the certainties of Victorian forebears, there is doubt as to what is truth. What can be reported is the truth as perceived by the researcher – and this requires an explicit statement about the assumptions, the methods chosen, the nature of the sample – all the things discussed in previous chapters.

Thus the task is difficult and its requirements are onerous. Is the task of value? From one perspective the answer is that for any tour operator or attraction owner to provide a satisfactory experience for visitors they need to know what is effective. They need to know what works in order to attract repeat visitation, and to spread recommendation by word of mouth to attract new visitors. This is no mundane matter or simply a question of profits. There are employees and their families dependent upon the income that such attractions provide. From a wider perspective, one needs to return to part of the debate contained within Chapter 1. If Western society is moving into a post-industrial age that increasingly values individualistic experience, then the findings from tourist research may have very wide implications. Tourism is part of an educative-entertainment dimension that is beginning to play larger roles in increasing numbers of people's lives. The importance of the authentic in the tourist experience can have implications for the emergent lifestyles based around the network and interaction of computers, mass media, home entertainment and travel. Faced with technologies that promise virtual reality, the pseudo realities inherent in many tourist attractions and the way in which visitors respond to them can perhaps give some indication of the future patterns of society. The need for research into tourist satisfaction can be evidenced by the needs for better visitor management to protect environments, to maintain jobs, and possibly, to understand better future society as technology makes us tourists in our own home as well as outside of it. Tourists are visitors to a different place – perhaps the future will make our homes part of that different place. If so, it is all the more important to be able to understand our motivations and needs.

Appendix I

The following is a sample questionnaire that contains the items used in the text for the sample calculations.

The following questionnaire has been designed to be easily completed. If you feel a question is not appropriate to you, *score the item as a zero*.

The following factors relate to why people go on holiday, and what they find there. If you had an entirely free choice as to destination and type of holiday, could you please indicate how important the factors are to YOU, personally, by circling the appropriate number.

The scale is	Very important	7
		6
	Important	5
		4
	Of some importance	3
		2
	Of no importance	1
	No opinion	0

Motivations – while on holiday I like to

Increase my knowledge	1	2	3	4	5	6	7	0
Avoid the hustle and bustle of daily life	1	2	3	4	5	6	7	0
Build friendships with others	1	2	3	4	5	6	7	0
Challenge my abilities	1	2	3	4	5	6	7	0
Use my imagination	1	2	3	4	5	6	7	0
Be in a calm atmosphere	1	2	3	4	5	6	7	0
Develop close friendships	1	2	3	4	5	6	7	0
Use my physical abilities/skills in sport	1	2	3	4	5	6	7	0
Relax physically	1	2	3	4	5	6	7	0
Gain a feeling of belonging	1	2	3	4	5	6	7	0
Discover new places and things	1	2	3	4	5	6	7	0

To relax mentally	1	2	3	4	5	6	7	0
To be with others	1	2	3	4	5	6	7	0
To have 'a good time' with friends	1	2	3	4	5	6	7	0

How long was this holiday (in terms of days away from home) . . . .

How many times have you been to that destination before (please tick)

never before	. . . .	three to five times before	. . . .
once or twice before	. . . .	six or more times	. . . .

Try to remember the holiday. Again we have a list of factors that people say are important. Remembering the holiday, to what extent were you able to achieve the following activities?

The scale is	To a very large extent	7
		6
	To some extent	5
		4
	To a small extent	3
		2
	Not at all	1
	No opinion	0

During the holiday I was able to

Increase my knowledge	1	2	3	4	5	6	7	0
Avoid the hustle and bustle of daily life	1	2	3	4	5	6	7	0
Build friendships with others	1	2	3	4	5	6	7	0
Challenge my abilities	1	2	3	4	5	6	7	0
Use my imagination	1	2	3	4	5	6	7	0
Be in a calm atmosphere	1	2	3	4	5	6	7	0
Develop close friendships	1	2	3	4	5	6	7	0
Use my physical abilities	1	2	3	4	5	6	7	0
Relax physically	1	2	3	4	5	6	7	0
Gain a feeling of belonging	1	2	3	4	5	6	7	0
Discover new places and things	1	2	3	4	5	6	7	0
To relax mentally	1	2	3	4	5	6	7	0
To be with others	1	2	3	4	5	6	7	0
To have 'a good time' with friends	1	2	3	4	5	6	7	0

I would like you to think about the pattern of your activities during the length of the holiday. Please answer the following questions on the following scale:

The scale is	To a very large extent	7
		6
	To some extent	5
		4
	To a small extent	3
		2
	Not at all	1
	No opinion	0

By the end of the holiday

To what extent were you satisfied with your accommodation?	1	2	3	4	5	6	7		0
To what extent could you say you really enjoyed the holiday?	1	2	3	4	5	6	7		0
To what extent would you recommend this holiday to a close friend who shares your interests?	1	2	3	4	5	6	7		0

Last, for purposes of classification, I would be grateful if you could complete the following questions about yourself.

Are you –   married   ....
                   single   ....

Are you –   male   ....
                   female   ....

What is your age group?
          0 – 15   ....
          16 – 24   ....
          25 – 35   ....
          36 – 65   ....
          66 – 75   ....
          over 76   ....

Appendix II

1	1	6	1	2	1	2	2	1	2	2	1	2	2	2	4	1	2	2	2	4	1	6	2	2	6	2	6	7	0
1	1	1	2	2	2	2	1	1	1	1	2	2	2	2	2	2	2	2	1	2	2	2	1	2	2	6	2	0	2
0	1	2	2	1	1	0	1	2	1	1	2	1	1	2	1	1	2	1	1	2	0	2	1	1	2	4	5	0	5
6	4	3	0	1	0	2	0	6	0	0	5	3	6	7	0	5	1	6	0	0	0	0	1	5	4	0	2	6	0
4	6	2	7	6	5	3	5	5	4	7	6	6	6	7	6	5	7	5	6	5	7	7	5	5	7	1	4	0	3
2	6	0	1	0	1	1	5	4	5	0	4	3	5	1	0	0	1	1	3	4	3	0	7	1	1	1	0	1	0
1	1	7	1	0	1	1	0	4	5	0	4	3	5	2	4	0	1	4	5	6	5	3	5	5	7	0	1	1	0
6	1	6	0	6	3	2	8	4	3	0	2	2	6	2	5	3	6	6	6	6	6	1	5	7	0	1	7	7	2
5	1	1	1	7	5	3	5	6	9	5	6	5	0	6	5	7	5	5	5	5	7	4	6	5	6	7	4	5	7
5	6	1	6	5	3	5	2	0	1	3	0	0	2	6	5	4	0	7	4	6	6	7	4	5	7	6	2	1	6
6	2	7	7	6	5	5	3	6	6	7	4	5	3	7	5	5	7	4	7	6	6	5	7	6	6	6	5	1	7
5	6	7	7	3	5	5	6	3	2	6	4	7	3	6	7	2	3	7	3	5	7	6	6	6	7	3	5	1	7
1	6	1	3	5	1	3	7	1	3	3	4	2	5	3	0	5	4	4	3	3	7	1	1	4	1	5	6	5	
4	6	7	6	5	4	4	4	7	3	5	7	5	4	7	4	7	5	5	1	5	7	4	5	5	7	6	7		
1	5	5	2	0	2	2	1	4	1	7	6	1	2	1	1	2	1	4	7	0	1	7	6	2	1	0	4		
3	3	5	0	4	2	2	0	1	1	0	2	6	1	1	2	1	4	7	0	1	7	6	2	1	0	4			
3	2	7	6	4	4	5	7	4	6	6	5	3	1	2	4	4	5	4	5	7	4	1	3	7					
0	5	1	3	7	2	2	3	1	2	4	6	1	7	3	2	4	6	4	5	3	3	3	3	4					
1	5	1	3	2	3	1	7	6	2	1	6	3	0	2	4	4	7	1	5	3	3	3	3	5					
1	3	5	2	1	1	4	2	1	1	3	1	1	1	2	1	1	2	4	1	1	2	3	2	4					
14	10	1	5	14	17	10	3	10	14	21	14	15	19	7	7	14	14	8	10	15	5	14	14	7	7	7	7	16	
6	2	1	3	7	3	2	7	4	5	0	6	6	5	1	3	0	7	4	0	3	7	5	3	2	3	7	4	6	
6	2	13	7	3	6	6	3	5	2	7	0	4	4	2	7	6	5	5	6	2	5	4	3	7	5	4	4	4	
4	6	3	7	6	6	5	6	6	4	4	7	7	6	7	6	7	6	7	6	3	1	7	7	7	7	7			
6	1	5	7	2	6	5	6	2	4	1	3	7	3	7	0	4	7	1	5	1	1	5	1	1	6	1	1	0	
6	6	5	7	7	0	7	6	2	1	4	6	7	3	5	5	5	6	4	7	5	2	4	2	3	1	1	5	6	7
0	2	7	0	3	6	5	1	1	0	5	1	1	5	0	4	4	4	6	1	1	5	3	5	3	3	5			
1	1	7	2	4	3	4	5	3	1	5	1	1	7	0	2	4	4	3	3	1	1	4	5	3	7	3			
5	1	3	7	7	3	3	5	5	2	1	7	5	0	7	5	5	3	6	1	5	4	3	6	7	3				
1	3	7	7	3	4	4	7	2	1	1	2	0	3	6	3	4	5	5	3	5	2	4	0	1	3	5			
0	1	5	3	6	4	4	4	3	6	7	1	1	5	5	6	6	5	6	3	1	1	4	0	3	4	3	5		
3	1	5	2	4	4	4	3	5	5	1	6	3	2	6	1	1	3	6	1	1	4	5	2	6	3	3	3		
5	4	7	7	1	7	5	5	4	4	7	7	7	3	7	5	3	3	7	7	5	4	7	5	5	7	7	7	7	7
1	3	7	7	3	5	6	3	5	2	7	3	6	2	7	4	3	6	5	3	4	7	5	5	7	5	4	4	3	5

33 34 35 36 37 38 39 41 42 43 44 45 46 47 48 49 50 51 52 53 54 55 56 57 58 59 60 61 62 63 64 65

66	67	68	69	70	71	72	73	74	75	76	77	78	79	80	81	82	85	86	87	88	89	90	91	92	93	94	95	96	97	98	99
4	4	2	3	5	2	0	2	3	4	3	4	4	4	4	4	1	4	5	3	3	2	2	4	1	4	6	1	2	4	0	3
2	2	2	2	0	0	1	2	2	1	1	2	2	1	1	1	2	2	2	2	2	2	2	1	1	2	1	2	2	1	0	2
1	2	2	2	1	2	0	0	2	1	1	1	1	2	2	1	1	1	1	2	1	1	1	3	1	1	0	2	1	2	2	1
1	2	2	1	2	0	0	1	7	5	4	1	1	0	4	0	2	0	7	0	3	1	1	3	2	3	4	1	1	2	3	6
6	7	1	7	7	6	7	5	1	5	4	4	6	1	3	7	7	7	3	7	5	7	5	5	1	6	5	7	6	7	6	6
6	7	0	7	7	6	7	5	6	6	7	4	7	6	7	7	7	4	5	7	7	3	7	7	5	6	1	7	6	6	6	6
0	1	6	2	7	6	0	0	1	3	6	3	6	3	5	1	3	3	5	1	3	4	5	1	6	1	1	2	5	0	0	1
1	3	6	5	6	6	0	0	1	3	6	3	5	5	1	6	3	6	1	5	4	5	1	6	1	7	1	5	0	0	1	
3	5	1	5	5	5	0	7	1	7	7	2	6	6	1	7	6	3	1	3	2	0	4	2	1	3	2	0	5	0	5	2
5	7	7	7	7	7	4	5	1	7	7	6	6	6	7	6	7	5	2	7	2	7	4	5	7	7	0	6	6	7	5	6
4	5	1	3	3	4	0	6	1	7	7	0	3	5	7	6	7	5	3	1	3	5	0	3	2	5	3	3	5	4	4	5
7	7	1	5	6	6	3	6	6	6	5	5	5	7	7	5	5	7	7	5	7	6	6	7	7	3	7	6	7	6		
5	7	7	7	6	4	7	6	6	7	7	7	7	5	7	5	6	5	5	5	6	7	1	4	5	5	7	7	6	4	6	5
3	5	1	1	2	3	0	4	3	5	7	2	4	4	7	7	5	2	7	6	0	7	0	3	2	3	5	1	5	4	3	6
5	7	1	1	5	7	5	2	4	4	6	1	5	4	7	6	7	4	7	7	5	7	6	6	7	7	4	7	6	6	6	
3	1	1	1	0	3	0	0	4	4	1	1	2	5	1	7	6	1	1	0	7	0	1	1	3	1	1	1	7	0	3	4
3	1	1	1	2	3	6	0	1	7	7	1	3	5	1	7	6	2	1	1	5	0	2	1	3	2	2	0	5	4	6	2
7	7	5	5	6	6	3	6	5	5	1	5	5	5	6	7	7	5	4	7	6	7	4	6	6	3	7	4	6	6	6	7
2	2	5	7	1	5	3	6	4	1	6	7	5	7	4	7	6	3	0	1	4	7	0	1	2	6	1	1	4	4	3	2
2	2	7	1	2	3	6	0	1	5	7	5	5	4	1	3	5	1	1	4	0	0	1	1	2	1	1	1	6	0	0	2
2	2	1	1	2	3	2	1	1	2	2	2	1	2	3	1	4	1	1	3	4	1	1	1	3	1	1	1	3	0	3	3
10	14	15	8	11	14	18	8	7		17	22	15	8	14	9	14	7	5		15	14	28	14	10	16	22	21	14	14	10	17
3	3	1	5	6	5	0	7	0	7	0	3	0	2	4	6	7	5	3	3	2	7	0	1	4	6	3	1	3	7	1	3
4	3	1	5	5	5	0	4	0	6	3	0	5	4	6	6	5	4	3	4	2	7	0	2	4	5	2	2	3	6	4	3
7	7	5	5	6	2	6	6	6	7	3	5	3	7	7	7	4	7	7	7	5	7	7	7	2	7	4	7	7			
5	7	7	7	6	7	6	7	6	7	7	7	4	7	6	7	4	7	5	4	0	4	6	6	7	7	5	5	7	5	6	6
6	1	1	0	1	1	0	3	0	4	7	0	3	3	5	6	5	1	3	5	7	0	0	4	3	1	5	0	5	4	2	6
6	6	7	5	6	7	3	6	4	6	3	5	5	7	7	4	6	5	7	7	7	4	7	7	7	4	7	4	7	7		
3	0	1	1	1	3	5	0	4	3	1	0	2	5	4	5	5	1	5	4	0	1	1	1	0	1	6	6	6	1	0	1
3	6	1	3	6	3	5	2	0	6	7	0	3	6	6	6	2	1	1	7	0	2	3	1	6	0	3	3	5	1		
7	7	6	7	6	6	5	5	5	5	3	4	5	5	7	6	6	6	6	7	5	5	6	7	6	7	4	6	7	5	7	
2	7	7	3	3	5	7	4	0	4	7	4	7	5	7	6	6	4	4	0	0	2	4	7	1	3	4	4	4	2	1	
3	2	6	5	1	3	3	7	0	0	4	7	5	5	2	5	3	6	6	0	1	5	0	0	2	3	1	2	3	5	0	1
3	6	1	6	3	3	6	4	0	5	7	2	5	4	5	7	7	3	3	7	0	2	4	5	4	2	2	3	7	5	1	
7	6	3	5	5	5	3	6	5	7	3	3	5	7	7	7	5	2	5	7	7	6	6	7	3	7	5	6	4	5	7	
0	5	7	5	5	7	7	5	5	7	5	5	7	5	5	5	4	7	0	2	5	5	7	3	7	3	5	4	7	3	2	7
6	7	8	9	0	1	2	3	4	5	6	7	8	9	0	1	2	5	6	7	8	9	0	1	2	3	4	5	6	7	8	9
6	6	6	6	7	7	7	7	7	7	7	7	7	7	8	8	8	8	8	8	8	8	9	9	9	9	9	9	9	9	9	9

```
4 4 2 3 4 2 1 1 1 4 0 4 3 5 2 1 3 4 6 4 4 3 2 2 4 5 5 3 5 4
2 2 2 1 1 1 1 1 1 2 1 1 1 2 2 2 1 1 2 1 2 2 2 2 2 1 1 1 2 1 2
1 2 1 1 1 2 1 1 1 1 1 1 0 1 1 2 2 2 1 1 1 2 2 1 2 2 2 1 1 1 2 1
2 1 1 1 4 4 6 1 6 3 5 0 7 7 1 6 2 1 1 1 7 1 2 7 7 5 6 2 6 6 7 5 7 7
2 7 7 5 7 4 7 6 6 5 5 2 7 7 5 6 7 6 7 6 5 1 7 7 1 4 5 6 5 7 1 7 7
6 7 5 7 6 6 4 5 3 5 6 7 7 3 6 7 3 5 7 7 1 5 7 5 5 0 6 6 7 6 7 6
0 0 0 3 3 1 1 7 1 1 4 5 2 7 1 3 2 1 4 3 2 1 1 5 2 5 5 3 1 1 4 1 2 1
0 7 0 4 5 1 1 7 1 2 5 1 2 6 1 3 1 1 2 6 7 1 3 1 5 2 7 3 1 1 7 1 3 1
0 7 0 6 7 6 1 3 1 3 1 1 7 4 3 1 1 3 2 4 7 7 1 1 5 2 6 7 1 1 0 4 3 0
6 4 7 7 7 3 7 6 6 3 1 6 7 1 6 7 7 7 7 6 2 1 7 7 3 7 5 7 7 1 7 7
0 7 3 4 3 3 1 3 3 1 7 3 5 1 1 3 3 4 6 7 7 1 5 2 3 7 5 1 0 7 3 7
6 0 7 7 5 6 6 6 3 3 7 7 7 6 3 7 7 7 5 5 5 7 7 1 5 4 5 7 5 2 7
6 7 6 7 7 6 5 6 6 2 6 7 7 7 4 5 5 7 7 7 7 6 7 7 1 7 6 5 7 4 6 4
6 5 0 3 0 1 1 4 2 2 6 3 4 1 3 0 3 4 6 2 1 0 5 4 1 7 5 1 0 6 6 0
6 7 7 5 6 5 6 2 4 5 1 5 7 7 6 0 7 6 6 2 5 5 5 7 3 5 3 7 6 2 7
0 0 0 5 3 0 1 2 3 1 6 4 1 1 1 0 2 3 6 6 1 1 3 2 1 7 1 1 0 1 0 4
5 0 0 5 1 0 1 1 2 1 2 3 1 1 1 0 1 3 6 6 1 1 3 2 5 5 3 1 0 6 2 4
6 7 6 7 3 3 6 6 5 2 2 7 7 5 7 6 6 7 4 1 7 7 1 1 5 7 6 4 7
0 0 7 5 4 2 1 4 4 0 9 3 2 7 1 7 2 0 7 2 2 5 6 2 1 5 4 3 7 0 4 4 4
0 0 5 7 3 1 1 3 4 0 4 2 1 3 1 0 3 0 7 7 1 4 6 2 1 7 3 3 0 2 2 4
4 4 3 2 1 3 1 4 1 4 1 4 2 1 1 1 3 1 1 1 1 1 2 4 3 1 2 4 1 2 2
11 5 14 24 12 7 7 7 7 5 15 14 6 15 10 14 7 8 37 7 7 8 7 7 16 18 7 21 8 7 16
0 7 0 5 5 6 1 4 3 2 1 6 3 4 1 7 2 5 7 5 5 1 6 2 7 4 3 1 7 2 0 3
0 7 0 3 5 5 3 3 3 4 2 5 3 4 1 5 3 3 6 4 3 4 6 4 7 4 5 1 4 5 5 7
6 0 7 7 7 6 7 6 4 4 7 7 7 7 6 5 7 7 7 6 5 3 7 7 0 2 4 4 7 6 5 5

6 7 6 5 7 7 7 6 6 3 7 7 6 7 5 7 7 6 7 7 5 6 7 7 5 5 7 5 7 6 7 7
0 0 0 4 1 1 6 0 4 1 1 3 1 1 6 3 1 1 0 6 2 1 3 6 6 0 0 3 1 0 5 6 0
6 0 4 3 6 7 7 2 5 2 7 7 6 7 6 3 7 6 6 6 3 7 6 7 7 3 2 6 3 7 5 4 7
0 0 0 5 4 1 1 2 3 1 5 4 1 5 1 1 3 3 6 7 1 2 3 2 1 5 1 1 0 3 0 1
0 0 0 3 0 1 2 2 4 4 2 1 3 1 1 0 3 4 6 3 1 3 2 0 2 3 1 0 4 0 4
6 7 6 7 4 5 7 4 4 5 7 7 5 5 5 7 4 7 7 6 5 7 7 1 4 3 4 7 7 4 7
0 0 7 5 4 4 2 4 4 0 4 6 2 2 1 7 3 0 7 2 5 5 6 3 4 4 2 7 4 7 7
0 0 5 5 3 1 1 3 4 0 4 4 2 2 1 0 3 0 7 4 3 4 6 3 1 7 3 1 0 3 4 4
0 5 5 3 4 3 3 3 5 0 4 5 3 1 1 0 3 4 6 2 3 7 3 5 7 5 1 4 3 7 4
5 3 7 6 7 7 6 5 5 3 7 5 5 6 7 6 6 7 6 7 6 7 7 1 4 5 3 7 7 0 7
0 7 5 5 6 5 2 5 5 3 7 5 4 3 5 5 7 4 7 6 5 5 1 5 5 2 4 5 7 7
100 101 102 103 104 105 108 109 110 111 112 113 114 115 116 117 118 119 120 121 122 123 124 125 126 127 128 129 130 131 132 133
```

```
                    134 135 136 137 138 139 140 141 142 143 144 145 146 147 148 149 150 151 152 153 154 155 156 157 158 159 160 161 162 163 164
                      4   1   4   5   4   4   4   3   5   4   4   4   4   4   4   4   3   4   2   0   4   3   4   4   3   2   0   3   4   4   4
                      2   1   1   2   2   1   1   2   1   2   1   1   2   1   1   1   1   2   1   2   2   1   2   2   2   2   1   1   2   0   0
                      2   1   3   2   1   1   2   1   1   1   1   1   1   1   1   1   1   1   1   1   2   1   1   1   1   2   1   1   1   1   1
                      7   2   3   7   7   7   6   7   7   4   7   5   6   7   6   4   7   7   7   1   7   7   6   1   1   2   7   7   5   7   7
                      7   7   0   6   3   7   6   3   6   6   6   6   6   7   5   4   1   7   6   5   7   4   7   6   7   5   7   6   3   7   7
                      7   7   0   0   5   7   7   6   7   7   6   6   6   5   6   0   7   7   6   6   0   7   7   6   7   7   5   5   6   5   7
                      1   0   0   3   3   5   1   1   0   1   1   2   0   3   2   1   6   2   1   0   1   1   7   7   5   5   3   5   2   2   4
                      3   4   0   3   7   3   1   1   3   1   3   4   5   3   4   1   6   2   1   0   1   1   7   7   5   5   3   0   2   4
                      7   1   0   6   6   7   5   1   1   6   1   1   3   6   5   5   1   5   2   0   5   7   5   2   1   1   7   1   7   5   0   6   7
                      7   0   6   5   7   7   3   6   4   7   6   6   3   7   5   7   7   7   7   4   6   4   7   6   7   7   6   7   7   5   3   7   7
                      7   7   4   7   7   7   3   1   5   1   3   4   3   7   6   1   5   3   0   7   7   3   1   5   1   7   3   6   3   5   7
                      7   4   4   5   7   7   5   1   5   4   6   6   7   7   7   7   6   3   4   3   7   3   7   6   7   7   6   3   6   7
                      7   0   6   7   7   7   4   5   5   6   4   4   7   7   6   4   7   5   7   7   4   6   5   7   5   2   6   5   3   3   7   7
                      1   3   5   5   0   3   2   6   4   3   2   6   0   7   4   1   5   3   5   3   5   4   4   5   3   1   1   3   3   3   4   5
                      5   7   5   5   5   5   6   5   5   5   1   7   5   7   5   6   6   5   4   4   6   5   5   5   2   7   5   3   5   7
                      1   0   0   0   1   1   1   5   3   1   3   2   5   5   1   5   4   1   5   2   4   3   4   1   5   4   1   5   3   3   1   0
                      5   0   2   4   5   2   1   1   5   2   6   3   1   5   1   5   2   3   4   2   1   1   5   1   5   3   5   5   4   5
                      6   7   6   6   7   7   6   6   6   5   5   7   7   6   7   7   7   7   5   2   7   1   5   5   3   6   6   5   4   6
                      1   4   5   4   7   3   1   6   3   6   3   2   4   7   4   5   4   2   5   5   2   1   5   3   2   2   5   6   7
                      1   6   4   1   5   1   3   6   3   1   3   4   7   4   4   1   5   2   4   5   2   4   7   6   2   2   5   6   0
                      1   1   2   2   1   2   1   1   4   1   3   1   3   1   2   1   1   1   1   4   3   2   1   4   4   1   2   4   3   1
                     30   7  10  10  14   9   8  14  14  14  23  14  13   7  16   8  16  28  14  14  14   7  10  14
                      3   0   2   4   7   2   1   3   6   1   2   3   5   3   5   1   6   2   6   5   6   4   2   1   7   5   5   5   3   6
                      7   3   7   4   4   7   7   2   3   5   1   4   3   2   3   6   1   4   7   6   3   6   6   2   3   1   6   2   5   5   4
                      7   7   3   6   7   7   3   1   6   5   7   5   7   7   7   7   7   6   7   2   5   7   6   5   7   7   7   5   5   7   7

                      7   2   7   6   7   7   5   7   5   7   5   5   6   5   7   7   5   7   6   7   6   7   6   4   7   5   5   6   3   7   7
                      1   6   3   1   0   3   1   4   2   3   2   3   0   6   4   1   4   3   4   1   2   4   1   1   3   4   1   5   3   0
                      7   4   3   1   5   7   3   7   5   7   6   6   3   5   7   3   7   7   6   5   1   7   3   3   5   4   5   1   7   6
                      1   5   5   2   1   3   1   1   3   1   1   5   4   2   4   2   4   1   5   4   4   3   1   7   1   5   5   1   0
                      1   0   0   3   3   1   2   1   4   1   2   4   5   3   1   2   5   1   4   3   3   2   4   0   3   1   7   3   3   5   6   0
                      5   0   5   6   7   7   5   7   7   6   6   5   5   6   7   7   6   7   7   7   7   1   3   7   7   1   5   2   5   5   6
                      5   0   5   3   5   3   1   4   4   2   5   5   7   4   1   4   2   6   5   6   2   1   5   3   3   4   5   5   5   4
                      0   4   3   3   5   3   5   2   1   1   3   6   2   2   3   1   5   1   1   4   1   2   4   4   5   3   6   1   5   5   0
                      6   3   5   4   5   2   1   3   6   1   2   4   3   5   3   1   5   5   3   3   2   4   2   5   5   6   4   5   5   3
                      7   0   7   7   7   7   6   5   3   6   4   7   7   5   7   7   7   1   4   7   1   5   5   5   6   5   7   5   5   6
                      7   0   7   4   7   5   3   5   4   4   5   5   5   6   5   5   2   3   6   5   7   5   5   6
```

Appendix III

SET UP FOR SPSS FILE USED FOR CALCULATIONS IN THE TEXT

DATA LIST FILE 'c:\wp51\research\book.dat' FREE/ number know avoid build chall imag calm close sport phys belong disc mental others time length times know2 avoid2 build2 chall2 imag2 calm2 close2 sport2 phys2 belong2 disc2 mental2 others2 climate accom enjoy recomm marital sex age.

Variable labels number 'respondent number'/
           know 'increase knowledge'/
           avoid 'avoid daily hustle'/
           build 'build friendships'/
           chall 'challenge abilities'/
           imag 'use my imagination'/
           calm 'be in calm atmosphere'/
           close 'develop close friendships'/
           sport 'use abilities in sport'/
           phys 'relax physically'/
           belong 'gain sense of belonging'/
           disc 'discover places'/
           mental 'relax mentally'/
           others 'to be with others'/
           time 'have a good time'/
           length 'length of holiday'/
           times 'no. of times to destination'/
           know2 'actual knowledge'/
           avoid2 'actual avoid'/
           build2 'actual build'/
           chall2 'actual challenge'/
           imag2 'actual imagination'/
           calm2 'actual calm'/
           close2 'actual close friends'/
           sport2 'actual phy abil'/
           phys2 'actual phys relax'/
           disc2 'actual discovery'/
           mental2 'actual mental relaxation'/
           others2 'actuall with others'/
           climate 'actual climate'/
           accom 'satis with accomm'/

enjoy 'enjoyed holiday'/
recomm 'recommend to friend'.

Value labels know 1 'no importance' 7 'very important'/
avoid 1 'no importance' 7 'very important'/
build 1 'no importance' 7 'very important'/
chall 1 'no importance' 7 'very important'/
imag 1 'no importance' 7 'very important'/
calm 1 'no importance' 7 'very important'/
close 1 'no importance' 7 'very important'/
sport 1 'no importance' 7 'very important'/
phys 1 'no importance' 7 'very important'/
belong 1 'no importance' 7 'very important'/
disc 1 'no importance' 7 'very important'/
mental 1 'no importance' 7 'very important'/
others 1 'no importance' 7 'very important'/
time 1 'no importance' 7 'very important'/
times 1 'never before' 2 'once or twice'
3 '3 to 5 times' 4 'six or more'/
avoid2 1 'no importance' 7 'very important'/
build2 1 'no importance' 7 'very important'/
chall2 1 'no importance' 7 'very important'/
imag2 1 'no importance' 7 'very important'/
calm2 1 'no importance' 7 'very important'/
close2 1 'no importance' 7 'very important'/
sport2 1 'no importance' 7 'very important'/
phys2 1 'no importance' 7 'very important'/
belong2 1 'no importance' 7 'very important'/
disc2 1 'no importance' 7 'very important'/
mental2 1 'no importance' 7 'very important'/
others2 1 'no importance' 7 'very important'/
climate 1 'no importance' 7 'very important'/
accom 1 'no importance' 7 'very important'/
enjoy 1 'no importance' 7 'very important'/
recomm 1 'no importance' 7 'very important'/
marital 1 'married' 2 'single'/
sex 1 'male' 2 'female'/
age 1 '0-15' 2 '16-24' 3 '25-35' 4 '36-65'
5 '66-75' 5 'over 76'.

Notes

3 TOURIST SATISFACTION – CONCEPTS AND RESEARCH ISSUES

1 There are two aspects to this. The destination may be 'new' to the tourist industry, or 'new' to the traveller. In either case it may be argued that the tourist may experience some feelings of psychological risk.

5 QUALITATIVE RESEARCH

1 'The Club' is a UK tour operator selling holidays to the 18–30 age group. Originally '18 to 30', a subsidiary of the now dissolved International Leisure Group, in its original guise, the company had an image of being a holiday characterised by discos and parties as an opportunity for meeting other young people for casual sex. As such, from time to time, it provided copy for the UK tabloid press. 'The Club' has been seeking to change this image by moving a little upmarket, but it is difficult to shake off its past heritage. It would be a pertinent research topic to see how much this past still shapes the perceptions of those booking holidays with the company!

References

Adorno, T., Frenkel-Brunswick, E., Levinson, D.J. and Sanford, R.N. 1950, *The Authoritarian Personality*, Harper, New York

Ajzen, I., 1988, *Attitudes, Personality and Behaviour*, Open University, Milton Keynes

Alexander, M. and Valentine, V., 1989, *Cultural class – researching the parts that social class cannot reach*; Market Research Society Annual Conference, London

Alhadeff, D.A., 1982, *Microeconomics and Human Behaviour: toward a new synthesis of economics and psychology*, University of California Press, Berkeley, California

Allport, G.W., 1953, The trend in motivational theory, *American Journal of Orthopsychiatry*, vol. 23, pp. 107–119

Allport, G.W., 1961, *Pattern and Growth in Personality*, Holt, Rinehart and Winston, New York

Argyle, M., Furnham, A. and Graham, J.A., 1981, *Social Situation*, Cambridge University Press, Cambridge

Babakus, E. and Boller, G.W., 1992, An empirical assessment of the SERVQUAL scale, *Journal of Business Research*, vol. 24, pp. 253–268

Babbie, E.R., 1979, *The Practice of Social Research*, 2nd edition, Wadsworth Publishing, Belmont, California

Bacon, A.W., 1975, Leisure and the alienated worker: a critical reassessment of three radical theories of work and leisure, *Journal of Leisure Research*, vol. 7, pp. 179–190

Bagozzi, R.P., 1988, The rebirth of attitude research in marketing, *Journal of the Market Research Society*, vol. 30, no. 2, April, pp. 163–196

Bagozzi, R.P. and Warshaw, P.R., 1988, *Broadening the Theory of Reasoned Action to Encompass Goals and Outcomes: an empirical comparison of two models and extensions*, unpublished working paper, The University of Michigan

Baker, K., 1989, Using demographics in market research surveys, *Journal of the Market Research Society*, vol. 31, no. 1, January, pp. 37–44

Baker, K. and Fletcher, P., 1987, Outlook – TGI's new lifestyle system, *Admap*, March, no. 261, pp. 218–222

Baker, K., Harris, P. and O'Brien, J., 1989, Data fusion: an appraisal and experimental evaluation, *Journal of the Market Research Society*, vol. 31, no. 2, April, pp. 153–212

Baldwin, K.S. and Tinsley, H.E.A., 1988, An investigation of the theory of Tinsley and Tinsley's (1986) theory of leisure experience, *Journal of Counselling Psychology*, vol. 35, no. 3, pp. 263–267

BARB Bulletin, 1987a, March

BARB Bulletin 1987b, August

Barker, E., 1967, *Greek Political Theory*, London, Methuen

Bateson, J.E.G., 1989, *Managing Services Marketing*, Dryden Press, Orlando

Beard, J.G. and Ragheb, M.G., 1980, Measuring leisure satisfaction, *Journal of Leisure Research*, vol. 12, no. 1, pp. 20–33

Beard, J.G. and Ragheb, M.G., 1983, Measuring leisure motivation, *Journal of Leisure Research*, vol. 15, no. 3, pp. 219–228

Belson, W.A., 1964, Readership in Britain, *Business Review*, vol. 6, pp. 416–420

Berenson, M.L. and Levine, D.M., 1992, *Basic Business Statistics, Concepts and Applications*, Prentice Hall Inc., Englewood Cliffs, NY

Berg, I.A., 1967, *Acquiescence and Context in Response Set in Personality Assessment*, Aldine Publishing Co.

Bitner, M.J., Booms, B.H. and Tetreault, M.S., 1990, The service encounter: diagnosing favorable and unfavorable incidents, *Journal of Marketing*, vol. 54, January, pp. 71–84

Boden, A., 1990, *Requirements of Quality Service*, seminar paper, Centre for Urban and Rural Studies, University of Birmingham, 26 November

Bojanic, D., 1992, A look at a modernised family life cycle and overseas travel, *Journal of Travel and Tourism Marketing*, vol. 1, no. 1, pp. 61–80

Bojanic, D. and Calatone, R., 1990, Price bundling in public recreation, *Leisure Sciences*, vol. 12, no. 1, pp. 67–78

Booms, B.H. and Nyquist, J., 1981, Analysing the customer/firm communication component of the service marketing mix, in *Marketing of Services*, Donnelly, J.H. and George, W.R. (eds), Chicago, American Marketing, pp. 172–177

Bowler, I. and Warburton, P., 1986, *An Experiment in the Analysis of Cognitive Images of the Environment: the case of water resources in Leicestershire*, Leicester University, Department of Geography, Occasional Paper no. 14

Brown, T.J., Churchill, G.A. and Peter, J.P., 1993, Research note: improving the measurement of service quality, *Journal of Retailing*, vol. 69, no. 1, Spring, pp. 127–139

Bryant, B.E. and Morrison, A.J., 1980, Travel market segmentation and the implementation of market strategies, *Journal of Travel Research*, vol. 18, no. 3, pp. 2–6

Buckley, P.J. and Klemm, M., 1993, The decline of tourism in Northern Ireland: the causes, *Tourism Management*, vol. 14, no. 3, pp. 184–194

Burckhart, A. and Medlik, R., 1990, *Tourism, past and present*, Heinemann, Oxford

Burgess, R.G., 1984, *In the Field – an introduction to field research*, George Allen and Unwin, London

Butler, R., 1980, The concept of a tourism area cycle of evolution, *Canadian Geographer*, vol. 24, no. 1, pp. 5–12

Cadotte, E.R. and Turgeon, N., 1988, Key factors in guest satisfaction, *The Cornell Hotel and Restaurant Administration Quarterly*, vol. 28, no. 4, February, pp. 44–51

Calantone, R.J. and Mazanec, J.A., 1991, Marketing management and tourism, *Annals of Tourism Research*, vol. 18, no. 1, pp. 101–119

Carman, J.M., 1990, Consumer perceptions of service quality: an assessment of Servqual dimensions, *Journal of Retailing*, vol. 66, no. 1, Spring, pp. 33–55

Carmichael, B., 1992, Using conjoint modelling to measure tourist image and analyse ski resort choice, in *Choice and Demand in Tourism*, Johnson, P. and Thomas, B. (eds), Mansell, London, pp. 93–106

Cattell, R.B., 1965, Factor analysis: an introduction to essentials, *Biometrics*, vol. 21, pp. 190–215

Chatfield, C. and Collins, A.J., 1980, *Introduction to Multivariate Analysis*, Chapman and Hall, London

Chick, C. and Roberts, J.M., 1990, *Harmful and Benign Conflict in the Monday Night Pool League*, Proceedings of the 6th Canadian Congress on Leisure Research, University of Waterloo, pp. 363–366

Christie, R., Havel, J. and Seidenberg, B., 1956, Is the F Scale irreversible? *Journal of Abnormal Social Psychology*, vol. 56, pp. 143–159

Cliff, A., 1994, *The Application of Servqual to New Zealand Travel Agencies*, unpublished paper, Department of Management Systems, Massey University, New Zealand

Cohen, A., Gnanadesikan, R., Kettenring, J.R. and Landwehr, J.M., 1977, Methodological developments in some applications of clustering, in *Proceedings of Symposium on Applications of Statistics*, Krishnaiah, P.R. (ed.), North Holland, Amsterdam

Cohen, E., 1974, Who is a tourist? A conceptual clarification, *The Sociological Review*, vol. 22, pp. 527–555

Cohen, E., 1979, Rethinking the sociology of tourism, *Annals of Tourism Research*, vol. 6, pp. 18–35

Cohen, E., 1982, Thai girls and *Farang* men: the edge of ambiguity, *Annals of Tourism Research*, vol. 9, pp. 403–428

Cohen, E., 1983, Hill tribe tourism, in *Highlanders of Thailand*, McKinnon, J. and Bhruksasri, W. (eds), Oxford University Press, Kuala Lumpur

Cohen, E., 1986, Lovelorn Farangs: the correspondence between foreign men and Thai girls, *Anthropological Quarterly*, vol. 59, no. 3, pp. 115–127

Cohen E., 1992, Who are the *chao khao*? 'Hill tribe' postcards from Northern Thailand, *International Journal of Soc. Lang.*, vol. 98, pp. 101–125

Cohen, E., 1993, Mitigating the stereotype of a stereotype, in *Tourism Research: critiques and challenges*, Pearce, D.G. and Butler, R.W. (eds), Routledge, London and New York

Cohen, K., 1968, Multiple regression as a general data-analytic system, *Psychological Bulletin*, vol. 70, no. 6, pp. 426–443

Converse, J.M. and Presser, S., 1986, *Survey Questions: handcrafting the standardised questionnaire*, Sage Publications, New Delhi

Cornish, P., 1989, Geodemograhic sampling in readership surveys, *Journal of the Market Research Society*, vol. 31, no. 1, January, pp. 45–52

Cornish, P. and Denny, M., 1989, Demographics are dead – long live demographics, *Journal of Market Research Society*, vol. 31, no. 3, pp. 363–374

Costa, P.T. and MacCrae, R.R., 1988, Personality in adulthood: a six year longtitudinal study of self reports and spouse ratings on the NEO personality inventory, *Journal of Personality and Social Psychology*, vol. 54, pp. 853–863

Couch, A. and Heniston, C., 1960, Yeasayers and naysayers; agreeing response set as a personality variable, *Journal of Abnormal Social Psychology*, vol. 60, pp. 151–174

Crask, M.R., 1981, Segmenting the vacationer market: identifying the vacation preferences, demographics and magazine readership of each group, *Journal of Travel Research*, vol. 20, no. 2, pp. 29–33

Crompton, J.L., 1979, Motivations for pleasure vacations, *Annals of Tourism Research*, vol. 6, no. 1, October/December, pp. 408–424

Cronbach, I.J., 1951, Coefficient alpha and the internal structure of tests, *Psychometrika*, vol. 16, September, pp. 297–334

Csikszentimihalyi, M., 1975, *Beyond Boredom and Anxiety*, Jossey-Bass, San Francisco

Csikszentimihalyi, M. and Csikszentimihalyi, I., 1988, Introduction to Part IV, in *Optimal Experience: psychological studies in flow consciousness*, Csikszentimihalyi, M. and Csikszentimihalyi, I. (eds), Cambridge University Press, Cambridge, pp. 251–265

Davis, D. and Cosenza, R.M., 1988, *Business Research for Decision Making*, PWS-Kent Publishing, Boston

Denis, D.H., 1989, *Attitudes towards Holiday Destinations*, unpublished paper, College of Commerce, University of Saskatchewan

di Benedetto, C.A. and Bojanic, D.C., 1993, Tourism area life cycle extensions, *Annals of Tourism Research*, vol. 20, no. 3, pp. 557–570

Diener, E., 1992, *Assessing Subjective Well-being: progress and opportunities*, unpublished paper, University of Illinois

Diener, E. and Larsen, R.J., 1984, Temporal stability and cross-situational consistency of affect, behavioral and cognitive responses, *Journal of Personality and Social Psychology*, vol. 47, pp. 871–883

Diener, E., Colvin, C.R., Pavot, W. and Allman, A., 1991, The psychic costs of intense positive emotions, *Journal of Personality and Social Psychology*, vol. 61, pp. 492–503

Dimanche, F., Havitz, M.E. and Howard, D.R., 1991, Testing the involvement profile (IP) scale in the context of selected recreational and touristic activities, *Journal of Leisure Research*, vol. 23, no. 1, pp. 51–66

Dommeyer, C.J., 1985, Does response to an offer of mail survey results interact with questionnaire interest? *Journal of the Market Research Society*, vol. 27, no. 1, pp. 27–38

Dommeyer, C.J., 1988, How form of the monetary incentive affects mail survey response, *Journal of the Market Research Society*, vol. 30, no. 3, July, pp. 379–386

Dommeyer, C.J., 1989, Offering mail survey results in a lift letter, *Journal of the Market Research Society*, vol. 31, no. 3, July, pp. 399–408

Doxey, G.V., 1975, *A Causation Theory of Visitor-Resident Irritants: Methodology and Research Inference*, Paper given at San Diego, California, The Travel Research Association Conference, no. 6, TTRA, pp. 195–198

Elliott, L. and Ryan, C., 1993, The impact of terrorism on Corsica – a descriptive assessment, *World Travel and Tourism Review*, Wallingford, CAB International Publications, vol. 3, pp. 287–293

Everitt, B.S. and Dunn, G., 1991, *Applied Multivariate Data Analysis*, Edward Arnold, London, Melbourne and Auckland

Fenton, M. and Pearce, P., 1988, Multidimensional scaling and tourism research, *Annals of Tourism Research*, vol. 15, no. 2, pp. 236–254

Fern, E., Monroe, K.B. and Avila, R.A., 1986, Effectiveness of multiple request strategies: a synthesis of research results, *Journal of Marketing Research*, vol. 23, May, pp. 144–152

Fishbein, M., 1967, *Readings in Attitude Theory and Measurement*, John Wiley and Sons, New York

Fox, J. and Crotts, J., 1990, A longitudinal investigation into script development and the evaluation of a service, *Proceedings of the 21st Annual Decision Science Institute*, San Diego, California, 15 June

Fox, M.F., 1983, A multi-dimensional exploration of the decision process using correspondence analysis, *Marketing Bulletin*, vol. 4, May, pp. 30–42

Foxall, G., 1990, *Consumer Psychology in Behavioural Perspective*, Routledge, London and New York

Friedman, H.H., Friedman, L.W. and Gluck, B., 1988, The effects of scale checking styles on responses to a semantic differential scale, *Journal of the Market Research Society*, vol. 30, no. 4, October, pp. 477–481

Funkhouser, A., 1983, A note on the reliability of certain clustering algorithms, *Journal of Marketing Research*, vol. 20, February, pp. 99–102

Gallup, G., 1947, The quinamensional plan of question design, *Public Opinion Quarterly*, vol. 3, pp. 385–393

Garland, R., 1990, A comparison of three forms of the semantic differential, *Marketing Bulletin*, vol. 1, May, pp. 19–24

Gendall, P. and Hoek, J., 1990, A question of wording, *Marketing Bulletin*, vol. 1, May, pp. 25–36

Glaser, B. and Strauss, A.L., 1967, *The Discovery of Grounded Theory: strategies for qualitative research*, Aldine Publishing Co., New York

Gold, R.L., 1969, Roles in sociological field observation, in *Issues in Participant Observation*, McCall, G.J. and Simmons, J.L. (eds), Addison-Wesley, Reading, Massachusetts, pp. 30–39

Gowers, E.A., 1954, *The Complete Plain Words*, HMSO, London, Penguin (Pelican Books), Harmondsworth

Grafton, C. and Taylor, P., 1990, *Sport and Recreation – an economic analysis*, E and F N Spon, London

Gray, J.A., 1987, *The Psychology of Fear*, Cambridge University Press, New York

Green, P.E., 1984, Hybrid models for conjoint analysis: an expository review, *Journal of Marketing Research*, vol. 21, May, pp. 155–169

Green, P.E. and Rao, V.R., 1971, Conjoint measurement for quantifying judgemental data, *Journal of Marketing Research*, vol. 8, August, pp. 355–363

Greenacre, M., 1983, *Theory and Applications of Correspondence Analysis*, Academic Press, New York

Grey, A., 1983, *Saigon*, Pan Books, London

Gronroos, C., 1978, A service-oriented approach to the marketing of services, *European Journal of Marketing*, vol. 12, no. 8, pp. 588–601

Groves, J., Moore, B. and Ryan, C., 1987, *Staunton Harold Hall – a study of traffic flows and visitor activities*, report for the Ryder Cheshire Foundation and North West Leicestershire District Council, Tourism and Recreation Studies Unit, The Nottingham Trent University

Gunn, C., 1988, *Tourism Planning*, Taylor and Francis, New York, Philadelphia and London

Gyte, D., 1988, *Repertory Grid Analysis of Images of Destinations: British tourists in Mallorca*, Trent Working Papers in Geography, Department of Geography, The Nottingham Trent University

Gyte, D., 1989, Patterns of destination repeat business; British tourists in Mallorca, *Journal of Travel Research*, vol. 28, no. 1, Summer, pp. 24–28

Hagerty, M.R., 1985, Improving the predictive power of conjoint analysis: the use of factor and cluster analysis, *Journal of Marketing Research*, vol. 22, May, pp. 168–184

Hahlo, G., 1992, Examining the validity of re-interviewing respondents for quantitative surveys, *Journal of the Market Research Society*, vol. 34, no. 2, April, pp. 99–118

Hair, J.F., Anderson, R.E. and Tatham, R.L., 1987, *Multivariate Data Analysis – with readings*, Collier Publishing Co., London, American Publishing Co., New York

Hall, E.T., 1984, *The Dance of Life: the other dimensions of time*, Doubleday and Co. Inc., New York

Hampden, T.C., 1971, *Radical Man*, Duckworth, London

Harrison, J. and Saare, P., 1975, Personal construct theory in the measurement of environmental images, *Environment and Behaviour*, vol. 7, no. 1, pp. 3–58

Headey, B. and Wearing, A., 1989, Personality, life events, and subjective well being: toward a dynamic equilibrium model, *Journal of Personality and Social Psychology*, vol. 57, pp. 731–739

Hebditch, N., 1994, The effect of TV programmes on tourism and tourists, work in progress, unpublished MA thesis, Nottingham Business School, Nottingham Trent University

Henderson, K.A., Stalnaker, D. and Taylor, G., 1988, The relationship between barriers to recreation and gender-role personality traits for women, *Journal of Leisure Research*, vol. 20, pp. 69–80

Heron, R.P., 1991a, The institutionalization of leisure: cultural conflict and hegemony, *Loisir et Société*, vol. 14, no. 1, pp. 171–190

Heron, R.P., 1991b, Tourism as institutionalized leisure and interpretation, *Proceedings of the Heritage Interpretation International Third Global Congress*, 3–8 November, Honolulu, University of Hawaii, Sea Grant College, pp. 182–184

Hill, A.B. and Perkins, R.E., 1985, Towards a model of boredom, *British Journal of Psychology*, vol. 76, pp. 235–240

Hintze, J.L., 1990, *Number Cruncher Statistical System*, Kaysville, USA

Hirschman, E.C., 1984, Leisure motives and sex roles, *Journal of Leisure Research*, vol. 16, no. 3, pp. 209–223

Holloway, J.C., 1990, *The Business of Tourism*, Pitman, London

Holmes, C., 1974, A statistical evaluation of rating scales, *Journal of the Market Research Society*, vol. 9, no. 4, October, pp. 444–446

Howard, J.A. and Sheth, J.N., 1969, *Theory of Buyer Behaviour*, John Wiley and Sons, New York

Hughes, E.C., 1937, Institutional office and the person, *American Journal of Sociology*, vol. 43, pp. 404–413

Humby, C.R., 1989, New developments in demographic targeting – the implications of 1991, *Journal of the Market Research Society*, vol. 31, no. 1, January, pp. 53–74

Iso-Ahola, S. and Weissenger, E., 1990, Perceptions of boredom in leisure: conceptualisation, reliability and validity in the leisure boredom scale, *Journal of Leisure Research*, vol. 22, no. 1, pp. 1–17

Iso-Ahola, S.E., 1982, Towards a social psychology of tourism motivation – a rejoinder, *Annals of Tourism Research*, vol. 9, pp. 256–261

Jaccard, J., Brinberg, D. and Ackerman, L.J., 1986, Assessing attribute importance: a comparison of six methods, *Journal of Consumer Research*, vol. 12, March, pp. 463–468

Jackson, E., 1983, Activity specific barriers to recreation participation, *Leisure Sciences*, vol. 6, pp. 47–60

Jackson, E., 1988, Leisure constraints: a survey of past research, *Leisure Sciences*, vol. 10, pp. 203–215

Jackson, E., 1990a, Variations in the desire to begin a leisure activity: evidence of antecedent constraints?, *Journal of Leisure Research*, vol. 22, pp. 55–70

Jackson, E., 1990b, Trends in leisure preferences: alternative constraints – related explanations, *Journal of Applied Recreation Research*, vol. 15, no. 3, pp. 129–145

Jackson, E. and Dunn, E., 1988, Integrating ceasing participation with other aspects of leisure behaviour, *Journal of Leisure Research*, vol. 20, pp. 310–45

Jackson, E. and Searle, M.S., 1983, Recreation non-participation: variables related to the desire for new recreational activities, *Recreation Research Review*, vol. 10, no. 2, pp. 5–12

Johnson, R., 1974, Trade off analysis of consumer values, *Journal of Marketing Research*, vol. 11, May, pp. 251–263

Joliffe, I.T., 1972, Describing variables in principal components analysis (1) Artificial data, *Applied Statistics*, vol. 21, pp. 160–173

Joliffe, I.T., 1973, Describing variables in principal components analysis (2) Real statistics, *Applied Statistics*, vol. 22, pp. 21–31

Jordan, J.W., 1980, The summer people and the natives: some effects of tourism in a Vermont Vacation Village, *Annals of Tourism Research*, vol. 7, no. 1, pp. 34–55

June, L.P. and Smith, S.L.J., 1987, Service attributes and situational effects on customer preferences for restaurant dining, *Journal of Travel Research*, vol. 26, no. 2, pp. 20–27

Kamins, M.A., 1989, The enhancement of response rates to a mail survey through a labelled probe foot-in-the-door approach, *Journal of the Market Research Society*, vol. 31, no. 2, April, pp. 273–284

Kay, T. and Jackson, G., 1990, *The Operation of Leisure Constraints*, Proceedings of the Sixth Canadian Congress on Lesiure Research, pp. 352–355

Kelly, G.A., 1955, *The Psychology of Personal Constructs*, Norton, New York

Kerlinger, F.N., 1986, *Foundations of Behavior Research*, 3rd edition, Holt, Rinehart and Winston, New York

Kermath, B.M. and Thomas, R.N., 1992, Spatial dynamics of resorts: Sousa, Dominican Republic, *Annals of Tourism Research*, vol. 19, no. 2, pp. 173–190

Kim, J.O. and Mueller, C.W., 1978, *Introduction to Factor Analysis: what it is and how to do it*, Sage University Paper Series on Quantitative Applications in the Social Sciences, series no. 07-013, Sage Publications, Beverley Hills

Kish, L., 1965, *Survey sampling*, Wiley, New York

Kohli, R., 1988, Assessing attribute significance in conjoint analysis: nonparametric tests and empirical validation, *Journal of Marketing Research*, vol. 25, May 1988, pp. 123–133

Labaw, P.J., 1980, *Advanced Questionnaire Design*, Art Books, Cambridge, Massachusetts

Laing, A., 1987, *The Package Holiday Participant, Choice and Behaviour*, unpublished Ph.D. thesis, Hull University

Langer, E.J. and Newman, H., 1979, The role of mindlessness in a typical social psychology experiment, *Personality and Social Psychology Bulletin*, vol. 5, pp. 295–299

Langer, E.J. and Piper, A.T., 1987, The prevention of mindlessness, *Journal of Personality and Social Psychology*, vol. 52, pp. 269–278

Laurent, G. and Kapferer, J.N., 1985, Measuring consumer involvement profiles, *Journal of Marketing Research*, vol. 22, February, pp. 41–53

Lawler, E.E., 1973, *Motivation in Work Organisations*, Brooks/Cole, Monterey, California

Laws, E., 1986, Identifying and managing the consumerist gap, *Service Industries Journal*, pp. 131–143

Laws, E., 1990, Effectiveness of airline responses to passengers during service interruptions – a consumerist gap analysis, in *Proceedings of Tourism Research into the 1990s*, Johnson, P. and Thomas, B. (eds), Durham University

Laws, E. and Ryan, C., 1992, Service on flights – issues and analysis by the use of diaries, *Journal of Travel and Tourism Marketing*, vol. 1, no. 3, pp. 61–72

Lawson, R., 1991, Patterns of tourist expenditure and types of vacation across the family life cycle, *Journal of Travel Research*, Spring, pp. 12–18

Lazarsfeld, P., 1955, Foreword in *Survey Design and Analysis*, Hyman, Herbert, Free Press, New York

Lego, R. and Shaw, R.N., 1992, Convergent validity in tourism research: an empirical analysis, *Tourism Management*, vol. 13, no. 4, December, pp. 387–393

Lehtinen, U. and Lehtinen, J.R., 1982a, Service quality: a study of quality dimensions, unpublished working paper, Service Management Institute, Helsinki, quoted by Swartz, T.A. and Brown, S.W., 1989, Consumer and provider expectations and experiences in evaluating professional service quality, *Journal of the Academy of Marketing Science*, vol. 17, no. 2, pp. 189–195

Lehtinen, U. and Lehtinen, J.R., 1982b, *Service quality: a study of quality dimensions*, unpublished paper, Service Management Institute, Helsinki

Lever, A., 1987, Spanish tourist migrants – the case of Lloret de Mar, *Annals of Tourism Research*, vol. 14, no. 4, pp. 449–470

Levine, L.L. and Hunter, J.E., 1983, Regression methodology: correlation, meta analysis, confidence intervals and reliability, *Journal of Leisure Research*, vol. 4, pp. 323–343

Lewis, R.C., 1983a, When guests complain, *The Cornell Hotel and Restaurant Administration Quarterly*, vol. 24, no. 2, August, pp. 23–32

Lewis, R.C., 1983b, Getting the most from marketing research, *The Cornell Hotel and Restaurant Administration Quarterly*, vol. 24, no. 3, November, pp. 81–85

Lewis, R.C. and Klein, D.M., 1987, The measurement of gaps in service quality in *The Services Challenge, Integrating For Competitive Advantage*, Czepiel, J.A., Congram, C.A. and Shanahan, J. (eds), American Marketing Association, Chicago, pp. 33–38

Lewis, R.C. and Pizam, A., 1981, Guest surveys – a missing opportunity, *The Cornell Hotel and Restaurant Administration Quarterly*, vol. 22, no. 3, November, pp. 37–44

Lodge, D., 1992, *Paradise News*, Penguin Books, London

Lofland, J., 1966, *Doomsday Cult; A Study of Conversion, Proselytization and Maintenance of Faith*, Prentice Hall, Englewood Cliffs, N.J.

Lofland, J., 1971, *Analyzing Social Settings*, Wadsworth Publishing, Belmont, California

Loundsbury, J.W. and Franz, C.P., 1990, Vacation discrepancy – a leisure motivation approach, *Psychological Reports*, vol. 66, no. 2, pp. 699–702

Loundsbury, J.W. and Hoopes, L., 1988, Five year stability of leisure activity and motivation factors, *Journal of Leisure Research*, vol. 20, no. 2, pp. 118–134

Lutz, J. and Ryan, C., 1993, Hotels and the businesswoman: an analysis of business-women's perceptions of hotel services, *Tourism Management*, vol. 14, no. 5, October, pp. 349–356

Lyon, A., 1982, *Timeshare – the decline*, unpublished thesis, Nottingham Business School, The Nottingham Trent University, England

MacCannell, D., 1976, *The Tourist: a new theory of the leisure class*, Macmillan, London

MacCannell, D, 1992, *Empty Meeting Grounds*, Routledge, London

McDaniel, Jr, C.D. and Gates, R., 1993, *Contemporary Marketing Research*, 2nd edition, West Publishing Co., Minneapolis St Paul

McIntosh, R.W. and Goeldner, C.R., 1986, *Tourism, Principles, Practices and Philosophies*, Wiley, New York

McNeil, J.K., Stones, M.J. and Kozma, A.A., 1986, Subjective well being in later life, issues concerning measurement and prediction, *Social Indicators Research*, vol. 18, pp. 35–70

Mandelbrot, B., 1989, 'Fractals in geophysics' in *Fractals in Geophysics*, Scholtz, C.H. and Mandelbrot, B.B., Birkhauser Verleg, Basel

Mannell, R., Zuzanek, J. and Larson, R., 1988, Leisure states and 'flow' experiences: testing perceived freedom and intrinsic motivation hypotheses, *Journal of Leisure Studies*, vol. 20, no. 4, pp. 289–304

Mantel, N., 1974, Comment and a suggestion on the Yates Continuity Correction, *Journal of the American Statistical Association*, vol. 69, pp. 378–380

Marquandt, D.W., 1980, You should standardize the predictor variable in your regression models, discussion of 'A Critique of Some Ridge Regression Methods', by Smith, G. and Campbell, F., *Journal of the American Statistical Association*, vol. 75, pp. 87–91

Marsh, C. and Scarborough, E., 1990, Testing nine hypotheses about quota sampling, *Journal of the Market Research Society*, vol. 32, no. 4, October, pp. 485–506

Maslow, A.H., 1943, A theory of human motivation, *Psychological Review*, vol. 50, no. 4, pp. 370–396

Maslow, A. H., 1970, *Personality and Motivation*, Harper and Row, New York

Matthieson, A. and Wall, G., 1982, *Tourism, its economic, social, and environmental impacts*, Longman, Harlow

Mayhew, M., 1851, *London, Labour and the London Poor*, Griffin Bohn, London

Mayo, E.J. and Jarvis, L.P., 1981, *The Psychology of Leisure Travel*, CBI Publishing Co., Boston, Massachusetts

Mazanec, J., 1981, *The Tourism/Leisure Ratio: anticipating the limits to growth*, paper presented to AIEST Conference, Cardiff, Wales

Middleton, V.T.C., 1992, *Effective Management of European Tourism Demands Upon Adequate Measurement*, Proceedings of the Tourism in Europe Conference, 8–10 July, The Centre for Travel and Tourism, University of Northumbria and New College, Durham

Milligan, J., 1989, *Migrant Workers in the Guernsey Hotel Industry*, unpublished thesis, Nottingham Business School, The Nottingham Trent University

Mills, A.S., 1985, Participation motivations for outdoor recreation: a test of Maslow's theory, *Journal of Leisure Research*, vol. 17, pp. 184–199

Minitab Inc., 1988, *Minitab Reference Manual*, Penn. State, Pennsylvania

Montgomery, D. and Ryan, C., 1994, The attitudes of Bakewell Residents to Tourism and issues in community responsive tourism, vol. 15, no. 4, in press

Moser, C.A. and Kalton, G., 1989, *Survey Methods in Social Investigation*, Gower Publishing, Aldershot

Mosher, D.L., 1968, Measurement of guilt in females by self-report inventories, *Journal of Consulting and Clinical Psychology*, vol. 32, no. 6, pp. 690–695

Mosher, D.L., 1979, The meaning and measurement of guilt, in *Emotions in Personality and Psychopathology*, Izard, C.E (ed.), Plenum, New York

Moutinho, L., 1987, Consumer behaviour in tourism, *European Journal of Marketing*, vol. 21, no. 10, pp. 1–44

Moutinho, L., 1989, Tourism marketing research, in *Tourism Marketing and Management Handbook*, Witt, S.F. and Mountinho, L. (eds), Prentice Hall, London

Murphy, P., 1985, *Tourism – a community approach*, Methuen, London

Murphy, P.R., Daley, J.M. and Dalenberg, D.R., 1991, Exploring the effects of postcard prenotification on industrial firms' response to mail surveys, *Journal of the Market Research Society*, vol. 33, no. 4, October, pp. 335–342

Murray, H.A., 1943, *Manual of Thematic Apperception Test*, Harvard University Press, Cambridge, Massachusetts

Murray, H.A., Barrett, W. and Homburger, E., 1938, *Explorations in Personality*, New York, Oxford University Press

Myers, J.H. and Alpert, M.I., 1977, Semantic confusion in attitude research: salience vs importance,' in *Advances in Consumer Research*, Perrault, W.D. (ed.), vol. 4, Association for Consumer Research, Atlanta, Georgia, pp. 106–110

Myrdal, G., 1970, *Objectivity in Social Research*, Duckworth, London

Nachimias, D. and Nachimias, C., 1981, *Research Methods in the Social Sciences*, 2nd edition, St. Martin' Press, New York

Norton, G., 1987, Tourism and international terrorism, *The World Today*, February, pp. 29–33

Norusis, M.J. and SPSS Inc., 1990a, *SPSS/PC+^{TM} 4.0 Statistics for the IMB/XT/AT and PS/2*, SPSS Inc., Chicago

Norusis, M.J. and SPSS Inc., 1990b, *SPSS/PC+^{TM} 4.0 Advanced Statistics for the IMB/XT/AT and PS/2*, SPSS Inc., Chicago

Norusis, M.J. and SPSS Inc., 1990c, *SPSS/PC+^{TM} 4.0 Base Manual for the IMB/XT/AT and PS/2*, SPSS Inc., Chicago

Nunnally, J.C., 1967, *Psychometric Theory*, McGraw-Hill, New York

O'Brien, S. and Ford, R., 1988, Can we at last say goodbye to social class?, *Journal of the Market Research Society*, vol. 30, no. 3, July, pp. 289–332

Oppenheim, A.N., 1966, *Questionnaire Design and Attitude Measurement*, Heinemann, London

Osgood, C. E., Suci, G. J. and Tannenbaum, P.H., 1957, *The Measurement of Meaning*, The University of Illinois Press, Urbana

Parasuraman, A., Zeithaml, V.A. and Berry, L., 1985, A conceptual model of service quality and its implications for future research, *Journal of Marketing*, vol. 49, no. 4, Autumn, pp. 41–50

Parasuraman, A., Zeithaml, V.A. and Berry, L., 1988, SERVQUAL: a multiple-item scale for measuring consumer perceptions of service quality, *Journal of Retailing*, vol. 64, no. 1, Spring, pp. 12–37

Parasuraman, A., Zeithaml, V.A. and Berry, L., 1991, Refinement and reassessment of the SERVQUAL scale, *Journal of Retailing*, vol. 67, no. 4, Winter, pp. 421–450

Parasuraman, A., Zeithaml, V.A. and Berry, L., 1993, Research note: more on improving service quality measurement, *Journal of Retailing*, vol. 69, no. 1, Autumn, pp. 140–147

Parrinello, G.L., 1993, Motivation and anticipation in post-industrial tourism, *Annals of Tourism Research*, vol. 20, no. 2, pp. 233–249

Parsons, T., 1951, *The Social System*, New Press, New York

Parsons, T., 1952, *Towards a General Theory of Action*, Harvard University Press, Cambridge, Massachusetts

Patrick, A., 1982, Clinical treatment of boredom, *Therapeutic Recreation Journal*, vol. 16, pp. 7–12

Pearce, D.G., 1993, Comparative studies in tourism research, in *Tourism Research, Critiques and Challenges*, Pearce, D.G. and Butler, R.W. (eds), Routledge, London and New York, pp. 20–35

Pearce, P.L., 1982, *The Social Psychology of Tourist Behaviour*, Pergamon Press, Oxford

Pearce, P.L., 1988, *The Ulysses Factor: evaluating visitors in tourist settings*, Springer Verlag, New York

Peterson, R.A., Albaum, G. and Kerin, R.A., 1989, A note on alternative contact strategies in mail surveys, *Journal of Market Research Society*, vol. 31, no. 3, July, pp. 409–418

Pizam, A. and Catalone, R.J., 1987, Beyond psychographics – values as determinants of tourist behaviour, *International Journal of Hospitality Management*, vol. 6, no. 3, pp. 177–181

Plog, S.C., 1977, Why destinations rise and fall in popularity, in *Domestic and International Tourism*, Kelly, E.M. (ed.), Institute of Certified Travel Agents, Wellesley, Massachusetts, pp. 26–28

Plog, S.C., 1990, A carpenter's tools: an answer to Stephen L.J. Smith's review of psychocentricism/allocentrism, *Journal of Travel Research*, vol. 28, no. 4, Spring, pp. 43–44

Podilchak, W., 1991, Distinctions of fun, enjoyment and leisure, *Leisure Studies*, vol. 10, no. 2, May, pp. 133–148

Prentice, R., 1993, Community-driven tourism planning and residents' perceptions, *Tourism Management*, vol. 14, no. 3, June, pp. 218–227

Przeclawski, K., 1993, Tourism as the subject of interdisciplinary research, in *Tourism Research, Critiques and Challenges*, Pearce, Douglas G. and Butler, Richard W. (eds), Routledge, London and New York, pp. 9–19

Quelch, J.A. and Ash, S.B., 1981, Consumer satisfaction with professional services in *Marketing of Services*, Donnelly, J.H. and George, W.R. (eds), American Marketing Association, Chicago

Ragheb, M.G. and Beard, J.G., 1982, Measuring leisure attitudes, *Journal of Leisure Research*, vol. 14, pp. 155–162

Reid, L.J. and Andereck, K.L., 1989, Statistical uses in tourism research, *Journal of Travel Research*, vol. 28, no. 4, pp. 45–49

Riley, S. and Palmer, J., 1975, Of attitudes and latitudes: a repertory grid study of perceptions of seaside resorts, *Journal of the Market Research Society*, vol. 17, no. 2, pp. 74–89

Rinschede, G., 1992, Forms of religious tourism, *Annals of Tourism Research*, vol. 19, no. 1, pp. 51–67

Robinson, D. and Stephens, D., 1989–90, Stress in adventure recreation: types of stressors and their influences during an extended adventure-based expedition, *Journal of Applied Recreation Research*, vol. 15, no. 4, pp. 218–238

Robson, S. and Wardle, J., 1988, Who's watching whom? A study of the effects of observers on group discussions, *Journal of the Market Research Society*, vol. 30, no. 3, July, pp. 333–360

Rojek, C., 1993, *Leisure Studies, Post-modernism, and Social Theory*, Proceedings of 3rd Leisure Studies Conference, Loughborough University, ed. S. Glyplis

Russell, C., 1993, *Academic Freedom*, Routledge, London

Ryan, C., 1976, *A Personality for Business*, unpublished M.Ed. dissertation, University of Nottingham

Ryan, C., 1989–90, New directions for cruise line holidays: an assessment of British attitudes, *Journal of Applied Recreation Research*, vol. 15, no. 4, pp. 201–217

Ryan, C., 1991a, The effect of a conservation program on schoolchildren's attitudes toward the environment, *The Journal of Environmental Education*, vol. 22, no. 4, pp. 30–35

Ryan, C., 1991b, *Recreational Tourism, A social science perspective*, Routledge, London

Ryan, C., 1991c, Tourism research into the 1990s, *Tourism Management*, vol. 12, no. 2, July, pp. 157–158

Ryan, C., 1991d, *Tourism, Terrorism and Violence*, Research Institute for Studies into Conflict and Terrorism, London

Ryan, C., 1991e, Geo-demographics and psychographics in tourism marketing, Conference on local authority tourism marketing, Centre for Urban and Regional Studies, University of Birmingham, June

Ryan, C., 1993, Crime, violence, terrorism and tourism: an accidental or intrinsic relationship? *Tourism Management*, vol. 14, no. 3, June, pp. 173–183

Ryan, C., 1994a, Islands and life stage marketing, in *Issues in Island Tourism*, Conlin, M. and Hawkins, D. (eds) John Wiley, London, in press

Ryan, C., 1994b, The tourist experience and motivation – a review, a theory and some findings, in *Tourism, the State of the Art*, Seaton, A. (ed.), John Wiley, London

Ryan, C. and Groves, J., 1987, High income holiday takers – some attitudes, *Working Papers, New Series*, no. 2, Trent Business School, Trent Polytechnic

Saaty, T.L., 1980, *The Analytical Hierarchy Process: Planning, Priority Setting*, McGraw-Hill, International Book Co. New York

Saleh, F. and Ryan, C., 1991a, Analysing service quality in the hospitality industry using the Servqual model, *Service Industries Journal*, vol. 11, no. 3, July, pp. 324–345

Saleh, F. and Ryan, C., 1991b, *Client Choice of Hotels – a multi-attribute model*, Proceedings of New Horizons in Tourism and Hospitality Education, Training and Research Conference, Calgary, July, pp. 2–5

Saleh, F. and Ryan, C., 1992, Client perception of hotels – a multi-attribute approach, *Tourism Management*, vol. 13, no. 2, pp. 163–168

Schlegelmich, B.B. and Diamantopoulos, A., 1991, Prenotification and mail survey response rates: a quantitative integration of the literature, *Journal of the Market Research Society*, vol. 33, no. 3, July, pp. 243–254

Scholz, C. and Mandelbrot, B.B. (eds), 1989, *Fractals in GeoPhysics*, Birkhauser Verlag, Basel, Boston

Scott, D.R., Schewe, C.D. and Frederick, D.G., 1978, A multi-brand attribute model of tourist state choice, *Journal of Travel Research*, vol. 17, no. 1, Summer, pp. 23–29

Sefton, J.M., 1989, *Examining the Factor Invariance of Ragheb and Beard's Leisure Satisfaction and Leisure Attitude Scales*, unpublished paper, Office of Research Services, University of Saskatchewan, June

Sefton, J.M. and Burton, T.L., 1990, The measurement of leisure motivations and satisfactions: a replication and extension, *Leisure Studies Division – The 5th Canadian Congress on Leisure Research*, p. 29, Dalhousie University, Halifax

Selin, S.W. and Howard, D.R., 1988, Ego involvement and leisure behaviour: a conceptual specification, *Journal of Leisure Research*, vol. 20, no. 3, pp. 237–244

Shaw, S.M., 1990, *Where has all the leisure gone? The Distribution and Redistribution of Leisure*, Keynote paper, Sixth Canadian Congress on Leisure Research, University of Waterloo, May, pp. 9–12

Sincich, T., 1992, *Business Statistics By Example*, 4th edition, Macmillan, New York

Skinner, B.F., 1972, A lecture on 'having' a poem, *Cumulative Record*, 3rd edition, Appleton-Century-Crofts, New York

Skinner, B.F., 1977, Why I am not a cognitive psychologist, *Behaviorism*, vol. 5, no. 1, pp. 1–10

Sleight, P. and Leventhal, B., 1989, Applications of geodemographics to research and marketing, *Journal of the Market Research Society*, vol. 31, no. 1, January, pp. 75–102

Smith, R.B. (ed.), 1982, *A Handbook of Social Science Methods – Quantitative Methods: Focused Survey Research and Causal Modelling*, vol. 3, Praeger, New York

Smith, S.L.J., 1990, A test of Plog's allocentric/psychocentric model: evidence from seven nations, *Journal of Travel Research*, vol. 28, no. 4, Spring, pp. 40–42

Smith, S.L.J. and Godbey, G.C., 1991, Leisure, recreation and tourism, *Annals of Tourism Research*, vol. 18, no. 1, pp. 85–100

Snee, R.D., 1973, Some aspects of non-orthogonal data analysis, part one, Developing prediction equations, *Journal of Quality Technology*, vol. 5, pp. 67–79

Stephenson, J.B. and Greer, L.S., 1981, Ethnographers in their own cultures: two Appalachian cases, *Human Organization*, vol. 40, no. 2, pp. 123–130

Stewart, D.W., 1981, The application and misapplication of factor analysis in Marketing Research, *Journal of Marketing Research*, vol. 18, February, pp. 51–62

Swartz, T.A. and Brown, S.W., 1989, Consumer and provider expectations and experiences in evaluating professional service quality, *Journal of the Academy of Marketing Science*, vol. 17, no. 2, 189–195

Swires-Hennessy, E. and Drake, M., 1992, The optimum time at which to conduct survey interviews, *Journal of the Market Research Society*, vol. 34, no. 1, January, pp. 61–72

Thompson, E.P., 1967, Time, work-disciple and industrial capitalism, past and present, *A Journal of Historical Studies*, vol. 38, pp. 56–77

Tiechk, G. and Ryan, C.A., 1990, *The Attitude of Japanese Tourists to Canada*, unpublished paper, College of Commerce, University of Saskatchewan

Timmermans, H., 1984, Decompositional multi-attribute preference models in spatial choice analysis: a review of some recent developments, *Progress in Human Geography*, vol. 8, no. 2, pp. 189–221

Tinsley, H.E.A., 1986, Motivations to participate in recreation: their identification and measurement, in *President's Commission on America's Outdoors: a literature review*, US Goverment Printing Office, Washington DC

Tinsley, H.E.A. and Tinsley, D.J., 1986, A theory of the attributes, benefits, and causes of leisure experience, *Leisure Sciences*, vol. 8, no. 1, 1–45

Tourism Canada, 1988, *Pleasure Travel Markets to North America: Switzerland, Hong Kong, Singapore – Highlights Report*, Tourism Canada

Toy, D., Rager, R. and Guadagnolo, F., 1989, Strategic marketing for recreational facilities: a hybrid conjoint analysis approach, *Journal of Leisure Research*, vol. 21, no. 4, pp. 276–296

Uhl, K.P. and Upah, G.D., 1983, The marketing of services: why and how is it different, *Research in Marketing*, vol. 6, pp. 231–257

Urry, J., 1991, *The Tourist Gaze*, Sage Publications, Beverley Hills

Ursic, M.L. and Helgeson, J.G., 1989, Variability in survey questionnaire completion strategies: a protocol analysis, *Journal of the Market Research Society*, vol. 31, no. 2, April, pp. 225–240

Utrecht, K.M. and Aldag, R., 1989, Vacation discrepancy: correlates of individual differences and outcomes, *Psychological Reports*, vol. 65, pp. 867–882

Veal, A.J., 1989, Leisure, lifestyle and status: a pluralist framework for analysis, *Leisure Studies*, vol. 8, no. 2, May, pp. 141–153

Voelkl, J.E. and Ellis, G.D., 1990, *Use of Criterion Scaling in the Analysis of Experience Sampling Data*, Proceedings of the 6th Canadian Congress of Leisure Research, pp. 216–220

Wells, S., 1991, Wet towels and whetted appetites or a wet blanket. The role of analysis in qualitative research, *Journal of the Market Research Society*, vol. 33, no. 1, January, pp. 39–44

West, R., 1991, *Computing for Psychologists – statistical analysis using SPSS and Minitab*,

Harwood Academic Publishers, Chur

Wheeller, B., 1990, *Is Responsible Tourism Appropriate*, Proceedings of Tourism Research into the 1990s, University College, University of Durham, pp. 297–298

White, R., 1951, *Value-analysis: the nature and use of the method*, Society for the Psychological Study of Social Issues, New York

Witt, C. and Wright, P., 1990, Tourist motivation: life after Maslow, in *Proceedings of Tourism Research into the 1990s*, Johnson, P. and Thomas, B. (eds), Conference proceedings, 10–12 December, Durham University, pp. 1–16

Witt, S., 1980, An econometric comparison of UK and German foreign holiday behaviour, *Managerial and Decision Economics*, vol. 1, no. 3, pp. 123–131

Witt, S. and Martin, C., 1987, Deriving a relative price index for inclusion in international demand estimation models, *Journal of Travel Research*, vol. 25, no. 3, pp. 38–40

Woodside and Carr, 1988, Consumer decision taking and competitive marketing strategies: applications for tourism planning, *Journal of Travel Research*, vol. 26, no. 3, pp. 2–7

WTO, 1991, *Resolutions of the 1991 Ottawa Conference on International Travel and Tourism Statistics*, WTO, Madrid

Yerkes, R.N. and Dodson, J.D., 1908, The relation of strength of stimulus to rapidity of habit formation, *Journal of Comparative Neurological Psychology*, vol. 18, pp. 459–482

Yiannakis, A. and Gibson, H., 1992, Roles tourists play, *Annals of Tourism Research*, vol. 19, no. 2, pp. 287–303

Young, B., 1983, Touristization of traditional Maltese fishing-farming villages, *Tourism Management*, vol. 4, no. 1, March, pp. 35–41

Young, M. and Willmott, P., 1960, *Family and Class in a London Suburb*, Routledge and Kegan Paul, London

Young, S., Ott, L. and Feigen B., 1978, Some practical considerations in market segmentation, *Journal of Marketing Research*, vol. 15, August, p. 408

Zeithaml, V.A., Berry, L.L. and Parasuraman, A., 1993, The nature and determinants of customer expectations of service, *Journal of the Academy of Marketing Science*, vol. 21, no. 1, Winter, pp. 1–12

Zeithaml, V.A., Parasuraman, A. and Berry, L., 1985, Problems and strategies in services marketing, *Journal of Marketing*, vol. 49, no. 1, Spring, pp. 33–46

Zuzanek, J. and Mannell, R., 1983, Work leisure relationships from a sociological and social psychological perspective, *Leisure Studies*, vol. 2, September, pp. 327–337

Zweig, F., 1948, *Labour, Life and Poverty*, Gollancz, London

The following references might also be of interest as an introduction to the discussion relating to scientific concepts of 'chaos theory' being applied to social structures

Bloor, D., 1976, *Knowledge and Social Imagery*, Routledge and Kegan Paul, London, Boston

Latour, B., 1987, *Science in Action: how to follow engineers and scientists through society*, Harvard University Press, Cambridge, Massachusetts

Latour, B. and Woolgar, S., 1979, *Laboratory Life, The Construction of Scientific Facts*, Sage Publications, Beverley Hills

Law, J., 1994, *Organizing Modernity*, Blackwell, Oxford, UK, Cambridge, Massachusetts

Woolgar, S., *Science, the Very Idea*, Ellis Homwood, Chichester

Woolgar, S. (ed.), 1989, *Knowledge and Reflexity: New Frontiers in the Sociology of Knowledge*, Sage, London

Index